Norms and Nannies

The New International Relations of Europe
Series Editor: Ronald H. Linden

Norms and Nannies

The Impact of International Organizations on the Central and East European States

Edited by
Ronald H. Linden

ROWMAN & LITTLEFIELD PUBLISHERS, INC.
Lanham • Boulder • New York • Oxford

ROWMAN & LITTLEFIELD PUBLISHERS, INC.

Published in the United States of America
by Rowman & Littlefield Publishers, Inc.
A Member of the Rowman & Littlefield Publishing Group
4720 Boston Way, Lanham, Maryland 20706
www.rowmanlittlefield.com

P.O. Box 317, Oxford OX2 9RU, United Kingdom

British Library Cataloguing in Publication Information Available

Library of Congress Cataloging-in-Publication Data

Norms and nannies : the impact of international organizations on the central and
east European states / edited by Ronald H. Linden
        p. cm. — (New international relations of Europe)
    Includes bibliographical references and index.
    ISBN 0-7425-1602-4 (alk. paper) — ISBN 0-7425-1603-2 (pbk. : alk. paper)
        1. Europe, Eastern—Politics and government—1989– 2. Democratization—
Europe, Eastern. 3. Non-governmental organizations—Europe, Eastern. 4.
International agencies—Europe, Eastern. 5. Political socialization—Europe, Eastern.
I. Linden, Ronald Haly. II. Series.

JN96 .A58 N67 2002
320.943—dc21   2002017604

Printed in the United States of America

∞™ The paper used in this publication meets the minimum requirements of
American National Standard for Information Sciences—Permanence of Paper
for Printed Library Materials, ANSI/NISO Z39.48-1992.

To All Those Working for a Europe Whole and Free

Contents

Illustrations

TABLES

FIGURES

Abbreviations

ADACS	activities for the development and consolidation of democratic stability (Council of Europe)
AVNOJ	Antifascist Council of the National Liberation of Yugoslavia (Antifašističko Veče Narodnog Oslobođenja Jugoslavije)
AWS	Solidarity Electoral Action (Akcja Wyborcza "Solidarno") (Poland)
BCE	Romanian Commercial Bank
BSP	Bulgarian Socialist Party
CAP	Common Agricultural Policy
CAS	country assistance strategy
CBA	currency board arrangement
CDF	comprehensive development framework
CDR	Convenţia Democrată România (Democratic Convention of Romania)
CEEC	Central and East European country
CEFRES	Centre Français de recherche en sciences sociales (French Center for Research in the Social Sciences)
CEFTA	Central European Free Trade Area
CES	Economic and Social Council
CICD	Centre for International Cooperation and Development
CISAC	International Confederation of Societies of Authors and Composers (Confédération Internationale des Sociétés d'Auteurs et Compositeurs)
CITUB	Confederation of Independent Trade Unions in Bulgaria
COSAC	Conference of Standing Committees

CSCE	Conference on Security and Cooperation in Europe
CSFR	Czech and Slovak Federal Republic
ČSSD	Czech Social Democratic Party (Ceska Strana Socialne Demokraticka) (Czech Republic)
DIT	inflation targeting
EBRD	European Bank for Reconstruction and Development
ECJ	European Court of Justice
ECSC	European Coal and Steel Community
EMU	Economic and Monetary Union
EPC	European Patent Convention
EPO	European Patent Organization
EPU	European political union
ERM	exchange rate mechanism
ESF	European Social Fund
ETUC	European Trade Union Confederation
FDI	foreign direct investment
FKgP	Independent Smallholders Party (Független Kisgazdápart)
FNI	National Investment Fund (Romania)
FOI	freedom of information
GEF	global environmental facility
IBRD	International Bank for Reconstruction and Development
IEG	International Center for Economic Growth
IFC	International Finance Corporation
IGC	intergovernmental conference
ILO	International Labor Organization
IMF	International Monetary Fund
IO	international organization
ISPA	Instrument for Structured Policies for Preaccession
JPC	joint parliamentary committee
KDNP	Christian Democratic People's Party (Kereszténydemokrata Néppárt) (Hungary)
LLR	lender of last resort
MBI	Music Business International
MDF	Hungarian Democratic Forum (Magyar Demokrata Fórum)
MDNP	Hungarian Democratic People's Party
MEP	member of European Parliament
MLSA	Ministry of Labor and Social Affairs (Czech Republic)
MMNSZ/CEHIC	Confederation of Hungarian Employer Organizations for International Cooperation
MNB	Magyar Nemzeti Bank (National Bank of Hungary)
MRD	Ministry for Regional Development (Czech Republic)
MSzP	Hungarian Socialist Party (Magyar Szocialista Párt)
NBH	National Bank of Hungary

NCTC	National Council for Tripartite Cooperation (Bulgaria)
NTF	National Training Fund
NUEM	National Union of Economic Managers (Bulgaria)
NUTS	Nomenclature des Unités Territoriales Statistiques
ODS	Civic Democratic Party (Obcanská Democratická Strana) (Czech Republic)
OECD	Organization for Economic Cooperation and Development
OPZZ	All-Poland Alliance of Trade Unions (Ogólnopolskie Porozumienie Zwiazków Zawodowych)
OSA	Society for the Protection of Authors (Czechoslovakia)
OSCE	Organization for Security and Cooperation in Europe
PDSR	Partidul Democraţiei Sociale din România
PEP	Preaccession Economic Program
PfP	Partnership for Peace
PHARE	Poland and Hungary Assistance for Restructuring the Economy
PRM	Partidul România Mare (Greater Romania Party)
PSAL	private sector adjustment loan
PSD	Partidul Social Democrat (Romania)
PSDR	Partidul Social Democrat Român
RCC	Regional Coordination Committees
RICOP	Enterprise Restructuring and Employment Conversion Program
RIPP	Regional Industrial Property Program
SAL	structural adjustment loan
SAPARD	Special Accession Program for Agriculture and Rural Development
SDR	special drawing rights
SFRY	Socialist Federal Republic of Yugoslavia
SGP	Stability and Growth Pact
SLD	Democratic Left Alliance (Sojusz Lewicy Demokratycznej) (Poland)
SME	small and medium enterprise
SOF	State Ownership Fund (Romania)
SPC	supplementary protection certificate
SPP	special preparatory program for structural policy
STANAG	standardization agreement
SzDSz	Alliance of Free Democrats (Szabad Demokraták Szövetsége) (Hungary)
TACIS	Technical Assistance for the Commonwealth of Independent States
TEU	Treaty on European Union

TRIPS	trade-related aspects of intellectual property rights
UDF	Union of Democratic Forces (Bulgaria)
UDMR	Hungarian Democratic Union of Romania (Uniunea Democratica Maghiara din România)
VAT	value-added tax
WIPO	World Intellectual Property Organization

Preface and Acknowledgments

The studies in this volume focus on what Frank Schimmelfennig (in the introduction) calls "the other side of enlargement." The chapters offer us one of the first looks at what has actually been happening in the countries of Central and East Europe as a result of their pursuit of their often expressed desire to "rejoin Europe." Asserted by leaders and the public throughout the region, this goal has been pursued by governments on both the right and the left, though not always with the same effectiveness or ardor.

In practical terms this has taken the form of applying and negotiating for membership in the European Union and NATO. These international organizations have responded by putting forth certain norms of behavior for the states to follow and acting as nannies to see that they are applied. While studies of the effect of proposed enlargement on the international organizations are multiplying, there are few works exploring the social, political, or economic impact on the possible (or actual) new members themselves. The authors in this volume present such studies. Some have done so synoptically, looking at the impact on certain countries overall; some have concentrated on certain policy areas such as social and labor policy; minority rights; economic, information, or regional policy; or intellectual property rights; while others look at security structure or foreign policy.

All are original studies, written for this volume. As the editor of the volume, my first thanks, therefore, must go to the authors themselves. Four of us (Iankova, Michta, Williams, and myself) presented our work at the 2000 Annual Meeting of the International Studies Association in Los Angeles on a panel chaired by Geoff Harris. Others were then identified who were looking at the process from the perspective of the affected countries, leading to invitations to Grigorescu; Šabič; Freyberg-Inan; Ram; Sissenich; Jacoby and

Cernoch; and Hallerberg, de Souza, and Clark to join the project. Frank Schimmelfennig then graciously agreed to provide an introduction which synthesizes the contributions and links them to broad theoretical questions raised by the "norms and nannies" dynamic. All of these authors reacted creatively, effectively, and—equally importantly—promptly, to my intrusive and annoying comments on their original drafts and to comments provided by an anonymous external reviewer secured by Rowman & Littlefield. Each of the authors revised his or her manuscript several times and updated them in light of more recent events. I am grateful for their conscientiousness, professionalism, and good humor, as well as for the merits of their contributions.

I must also thank Susan McEachern, executive editor at Rowman & Littlefield, who supported the idea of this volume from my earliest pitch to her and helped us keep it moving despite the bumps on the road that inevitably accompany publication, especially of a multiauthored work. April Leo and an anonymous copyeditor provided careful and attentive control to the production of the final manuscript. Andrew Konitzer-Smirnov developed the index, a task deserving of fulsome credit because of the special difficulties involved in indexing an edited volume. I was able to hire Andy for this task because of the generous support provided by the Center for Russian and East European Studies, the Center for West European Studies/European Union Center, and the Department of Political Science of the University of Pittsburgh—support for which I am genuinely grateful.

On a more personal note I would like to express my continued appreciation of and love for my wife, Nancy Israel, who patiently and skillfully kept my eyes on the goal as I tried to make the volume work and to my children who were very gracious about letting Dad use the computer.

Pittsburgh, Pa.

May 2002

1

Introduction: The Impact of International Organizations on the Central and Eastern European States— Conceptual and Theoretical Issues

Frank Schimmelfennig

This book is about the impact of international organizations (IOs) on the Central and Eastern European countries (CEECs). It explores the channels and mechanisms through which international, mostly European, organizations— the "nannies"—disseminate their norms in the states and societies of Central and Eastern Europe. It also analyzes the conditions and scope of influence these norms have on the political systems, processes, and policies of the CEECs. The book thus belongs to the growing field of studies on "international socialization," which I propose to define as the process directed toward a state's adoption of the (constitutive) norms of an international community.[1]

Moreover, the book is about the most massive international socialization process currently under way in the international system. In the aftermath of the Central and Eastern European revolutions and the breakdown of communism, the CEECs have turned to international organizations for guidance and assistance in their political and economic transformation, and international organizations have become strongly involved in the domestic politics of the CEECs, the restructuring of domestic institutions, and the entire spectrum of material policies. In addition, this process takes place in an international environment that is arguably the most highly and densely institutionalized region of the international system. In Europe, international organizations regulate virtually every issue of domestic politics and foreign policy and, in the European Union, the transfer and pooling of national sovereignty has attained an unprecedented quality. Yet the international socialization of Central and Eastern Europe has rarely been analyzed in a systematic, theory-oriented, and comparative way.[2]

The contributions to this book do not follow a common framework of analysis and are not set up as comparative case studies. They analyze different

1

international organizations, norms, and CEECs, and they draw on different theories. In this introduction, I will address some general conceptual and theoretical issues in the analysis of international socialization and establish some general conditions regarding the impact of international organizations in Central and Eastern Europe. First, I will briefly discuss three literatures to which this book, and the study of the international socialization of Central and Eastern Europe in general, can make a contribution: enlargement, transition, and Europeanization. In the second part, I will address conceptual issues that concern the central items listed in the book title: Who are the "nannies" in Central and Eastern Europe? What are the "norms" they disseminate, teach, or enforce? And how do we conceptualize and measure their domestic "impact"? In the third part of the introduction I will bring up some theoretical issues: What are the main factors and mechanisms of international socialization proposed in the literature? What are the prevalent international and domestic conditions in the international socialization of Central and Eastern Europe, and how do they affect the impact of international organizations in this region? Finally, I will contrast the "model story" of international socialization, according to which the states to be socialized learn and institutionalize the international norms taught by the international organization, with several unintended or counterproductive effects that international socialization may have and for which ample evidence can be found in the studies assembled in this volume. I conclude the introduction with brief methodological suggestions for further research.

LITERATURE: THE CONTRIBUTION OF THE STUDY OF INTERNATIONAL SOCIALIZATION IN THE CEECs

The analysis of the impact of international organizations on the Central and Eastern European states potentially contributes to and links three different literatures—the enlargement literature, the transition or transformation literature, and the emerging literature on Europeanization. Moreover, it addresses, and promises to fill, systematic gaps in all three of them.

Enlargement

The literature on the eastern enlargement of Western European organizations, mainly NATO and the European Union, is growing fast, reflecting that enlargement constitutes a major and long-term policy project in the post–Cold War development of these organizations that will have lasting and far-reaching consequences for both the organizations themselves and the structure of the European regional system. However, the enlargement literature generally focuses on the Western organizations and their enlargement decisions[3] and on the enlargement interests and policies of the member states.[4] In addition, a considerable number of studies explain the interest of Central and Eastern European governments in NATO and EU membership and analyze public opinion in the CEECs on this issue.[5]

Sociological analyses of eastern enlargement seek to show that norms, particularly the constitutive liberal norms of the Western international community and the membership norms of the Western organizations, play an indispensable role in the explanation of why the EU and NATO decided to expand east. Moreover, the divergent CEEC record of compliance with and adoption of these norms accounts fairly well for the Western organizations' differentiation among the CEECs and their selection of candidates for membership.[6]

Thus, in various respects, international socialization constitutes the other side of enlargement: socialization prepares the CEECs for membership in international organizations, and membership is conditional on successful socialization (to the degree required by the organization). The prospect of membership creates a major incentive for the adoption of organizational norms, and the adoption of organizational norms by the candidates increases the pressure on the member states to admit them to the organizations. The same international norms that are the content of socialization also define the conditions of enlargement. However, this other side of enlargement and the linkages between the two sides are seriously understudied in the enlargement literature.[7] In order to study the effects of enlargement conditionality, of the progressive strengthening of institutional relations between the organization and the candidates for membership, and of the norm transfer that accompanies enlargement, it is necessary to look beyond the boundaries of the CEECs into their domestic systems and politics—something that the IR (international relations) scholars or Europeanists who make up the majority of enlargement researchers are rarely prepared or equipped to do.

Transition

The literature on the transformation of the former communist systems of the CEECs and their more or less successful transition to democracy looks at the adoption and institutionalization of liberal norms and the consolidation of democratic systems from the other angle—that of national political systems and domestic politics. It compares the CEECs with one another and sometimes with transition regimes in other regions such as Latin America and Southern Europe. And it tries to explain why some CEECs have made great progress in democratic consolidation whereas others stagnate or have even embarked on a path of autocratic consolidation. By contrast, the international environment and the impact of international organizations have traditionally been regarded as secondary in the literature on transitions[8] and are usually not systematically integrated into these comparisons and explanations.

To be sure, no account of Eastern European transition fails to emphasize the international factors that have contributed to and accelerated the breakdown of communist systems. International demonstration, domino, and snowballing effects as well as the "Gorbachev factor" (caused to a great extent by international factors such as the growing costs of the arms race and hegemony in the East) are an indispensable part of the standard account of the Central and Eastern European revolutions.[9] Moreover, the obvious international influences on Eastern European transitions have spurred comparativists to begin looking at the "international dimensions of democratization" in a systematic way.[10] Finally, it is generally recognized that external and internal developments must be analyzed in close connection and that the international environment continues to exert a considerable, although ambivalently evaluated, influence on the CEECs. Whereas some authors highlight the conduciveness of international conditions to the consolidation of democracy in the CEECs,[11] others deplore the not always helpful imposition of Western standards on the CEECs, the lack of Western support for democratization, or both.[12]

According to Schmitter, "external intervention will have a greater and more lasting effect upon the consolidation of democracy than upon the transition to it."[13] However, when it comes to explaining the divergent paths of development in the CEECs and their different degrees of success in liberal democratic consolidation, the transition literature generally reverts to domestic factors like political culture and traditions or initial transition conditions. Summary evaluations stress the continuity of elites and mass political culture,[14] the different, newly created political institutions and systems of government,[15] or the institutional structure of the communist systems or the strategic constellations that shaped the starting points and pathways of transition.[16] What is missing in these accounts is a systematic integration of international factors into the comparisons, tests, and explanations. While this is certainly a deficit of the transition literature, it also presents a major challenge to the perspective of international socialization: Does the neglect of international factors indicate that the impact of international organizations on the CEECs is only marginally important for their political development? Could it be that international socialization simply does not matter after all?

Europeanization

The literature on "Europeanization," a comparatively new field in European integration studies, links the systemic perspective of enlargement studies with the subsystemic perspective of transition studies. Europeanization studies are generally concerned with the impact of policy outcomes and institutions at the European level on domestic polities, politics, and policies.[17] The shared "second-image reversed" perspective[18] is not the only reason for which it would be useful to link the study of the impact of international organizations on the CEECs with the study of Europeanization. The Europeanization literature is beginning to leave the stage of exploratory and inductive case studies and to enter the stage of systematic comparison and theory building. There are discussions about the proper conceptualization of the dependent variable, the most important explanatory factors, and the causal mechanisms of impact.[19] To avoid theoretical insularity or reinventing the wheel, the study of the "Europeanization" of Central and Eastern Europe should take up and build on these discussions.

This would be all the more relevant as studies on the impact of European organizations on the CEECs could fill an empirical "blind spot" in the study of Europeanization. Up until now, Europeanization studies have been almost exclusively concerned with member states, and the few exceptions have dealt with West European nonmember states[20] but not with the CEECs. Adding the CEECs would not only make the empirical picture more complete but, above all, permit us to test some of the "established" variables in a new context and check some new variables. For instance, has the nonmember status of the CEECs facilitated the transformation of their domestic norms and policies (the reason being that, as states aspiring to membership, they are particularly eager to comply with European norms) or does it inhibit the domestic impact of European norms (assuming that states that have had a say in European decision making will also be more ready to comply)? Put more generally, do we see a covariation between the degree of integration into Western organizations and the degree of their impact on the CEECs? It is plausible to assume that the pressure for adaptation on nonmember countries is not only determined by the degree of "misfit" between international and domestic norms and institutions[21] but also by the density of their institutional ties with the international organizations. It even seems that the lower the "goodness of fit," the fewer the institutional ties and the lower the adaptation pressure (e.g., Belarus).

Moreover, it would be interesting to find out whether the specific features of CEECs that (still) distinguish them from Western member states have an influence on their Europeanization. For instance, does institutional inertia, the most important factor reducing the impact of European rules in the member states, play a lesser role in the CEECs because political institutions in these countries are in a process of transformation anyhow and have not taken root in the same way as in most West European democracies (cf. Sissenich, chapter 11 in this volume)? Finally, does the elite character of international and European politics further strengthen the Central and Eastern European states vis-à-vis societies that are already weak in comparison with Western democracies? Or does Europeanization empower substate, regional governments in the CEECs and societal actors such as interest groups and NGOs?[22]

CONCEPTS: NORMS, NANNIES, AND IMPACT

In this section, I discuss the main concepts involved in the study of international socialization: "norms"—the socialization contents, "nannies"—the international organizations that serve as socialization agencies, and "impact"— the socialization effects in the target countries. "Domestic impact" can also be considered the "dependent variable" in the study of international socialization.

Norms

Most generally, norms define a collective standard of the proper behavior of actors.[23] They have the form "Do X!" or "Don't Do Y!" Norms can be categorized in various ways, for instance, as formal and informal, legal and social, or explicit and implicit norms. For the purpose of studying international socialization, the most fundamental distinction is that between community or constitutive norms and specific or regulative norms.[24] *Community norms* are interrelated with the collective identity of an international community. They define the collective self by the way "we do things" and contain "behavioral prescriptions for the proper enactment of" the identity.[25]

By contrast, *specific norms* regulate behavior in individual issue areas. International socialization is mainly concerned with norms that are constitutive of the international community. By adopting and internalizing these constitutive norms, an outsider state becomes a member of the community. It is included in the collective identity of the community—regarded as "one of us" by the old community members. By contrast, specific norms are not decisive for community membership as such. On the one hand, compliance with the specific norms may be a prerequisite for formal membership in specific, functional organizations of the community but, on the other hand, it alone does not qualify outsider states for community membership if they do not also adopt the constitutive norms.

The Western international community is an interstate community with a postnational collective identity based on liberal norms of domestic and international conduct. *Liberal human rights*—individual freedoms, civil liberties, and political rights—are at the core of the Western community's identity. They are the "constitutive values that define legitimate statehood and rightful state action" in the domestic as well as in the international realm.[26] In the *domestic* realm, the *liberal principles of social and political order*—social pluralism, the rule of law, democratic political participation and representation, private property, and a market-based economy—are derived from, and justified by, these liberal human rights. Only a state that bases its domestic political system on these principles and reliably follows these values and norms in its domestic politics is regarded as fully legitimate by the Western international community.[27] In the *international* realm, liberal political culture is represented by the institutions of peaceful conflict management and multilateralist collaboration. In both cases, domestic liberal norms are transferred to the foreign policy of liberal states and to the international interactions between them: "Democracies externalize their internal norms when cooperating with each other."[28]

As a consequence of the end of the Cold War, the breakdown of the communist systems, and the liberalization and beginning transition to democracy, the constitutive norms of the Western international community became the "standard of legitimacy" for the entire European system of states. The symbolic turning point was the adoption of the Charter of Paris for a new Europe in 1990, in which the European governments declared that "we undertake to build, consolidate, and strengthen democracy as the only system of government for our nations" and that "full respect" for human rights "is the bedrock on which we will seek to construct the new Europe."[29] Although few (if any) of the CEECs qualified as democratic countries and community members at the time, the Charter of Paris and related CSCE (Conference on Security and Cooperation in Europe) documents established a declaratory consensus to which all European countries formally committed themselves. It could serve as a normative basis for international socialization and for evaluating the legitimacy and identity of the CEECs. At the same time, they ratified the "cultural hegemony" of the West in Europe.

These basic liberal norms are also constitutive for the international organizations of the Western community. They define the collective identity and the membership of these organizations. According to the preamble to the North Atlantic Treaty, the member states of NATO "are determined to safeguard the freedom, common heritage and civilization of their peoples, founded on the principles of democracy, individual liberty, and the rule of law." According to article 6 of the Treaty on European Union, the "Union is founded on the principles of liberty, democracy, respect for human rights and fundamental freedoms, and the rule of law, principles which are common to the Member States." And in the preamble to the Statute of the Council of Europe, the member states reaffirm "their devotion to the spiritual and moral values which are the common heritage of their peoples and the true source of individual freedom, political liberty, and the rule of law."

At the same time, each of the organizations developed and institutionalized specific norms that reflect its field of specialization, for instance, "market-making" and "market-shaping" norms in case of the EU, norms of international military coordination and standardization and norms of civil-military relations in the NATO case.[30] The chapters in this book reflect the great variety of norms defined, promoted, and enforced by the organizations of the Western international community. They deal with the impact of constitutive norms such as democracy, transparency, economic liberalization, minority rights, and multilateralist foreign policy as well as with specific norms such as the civil control of the military, intellectual property rights, monetary and regional policy norms, tripartism, and norms of social policy and employment legislation.

Nannies

The international organizations of the Western community not only act as "community representatives"[31] but also work as community-building agencies. As such, international socialization belongs to their fundamental tasks. It involves several "teaching" and "nursing" activities:[32] presentation of community norms to outside states, informational and technical support for the institutionalization of these norms in their domestic systems, monitoring and evaluation of institutionalization, and positive and negative sanctions to reward progress in institutionalization and punish the lack thereof.

The great variety of international organizations involved in Central and Eastern Europe can be classified according to the strategies they pursue. I propose two basic classifications. First, we can distinguish between inclusive and exclusive strategies. The *inclusive strategy* aims at socializing states from within. The organization first admits outsider countries and then teaches them the community rules. Together with accession, new members take on the obligation to learn and internalize the community norms. This is typical of the OSCE (Organization for Security and Cooperation in Europe). Its all-European membership had not only been a legacy of the CSCE, an East-West system of permanent conference diplomacy, but also of its policy to quickly admit all new states emerging from the multinational states of Central and Eastern Europe.[33] By contrast, the *exclusive strategy* of community building consists in socialization from the outside. The community organizations communicate their constitutive norms to outsider states and tell them which conditions they have to meet before being entitled to join. Accession to the community organizations as a full member then corresponds to a formal recognition that international socialization has been successful. The exclusive strategy is typical of NATO and the EU. Correspondingly, their membership is comparatively small and, at the time of writing, only three CEECs had been admitted to NATO (none to the EU). Finally, the Council of Europe pursues an intermediate strategy. It requires new members to fulfill some community norms (like democratic elections) before accession, requires them to commit themselves to other community norms at the time of admission, and monitors their compliance from within. Since 1996, all CEECs except Belarus, Bosnia, and Yugoslavia have been members of the Council of Europe.

Second, international organizations differ with regard to the *kind of norms* they focus on in their socialization efforts. Some concentrate on the community norms. This is most obviously the case for the Council of Europe with its strong emphasis on human rights promotion, protection, and enforcement. The OSCE also pursues many activities related to constitutive norms like the monitoring of elections or the promotion and monitoring of minority rights. Besides, however, it is concerned with pan-European security issues.

A second group of organizations focus on their functional tasks but link the teaching of specific norms to the fulfillment of the community norms. This is the case for the EU and NATO: They do not engage directly in activities of promoting and protecting democracy and human rights but outside states need to adhere to the community norms in order to benefit from the public goods (welfare and security) they provide for the community. Finally, some organizations like the International Monetary Fund (IMF) or the World Bank are not Western community organizations in the narrow sense. They focus on specific, technical norms and policies, and their membership and public good provision is not conditional on the fulfillment of the constitutive norms of the Western community. Table 1.1 combines both dimensions and gives examples of international organizations involved in the CEECs.

Impact

The dependent variable "domestic impact" is supposed to represent the effects that international norms and the socialization policies of international organizations have on the domestic political systems of the states to be socialized. I propose to conceptualize and measure these effects in two dimensions: the kind of normative effect and the degree of internalization.[34]

A *classification of normative effects* may usefully be based on the three different conceptions of norms discussed in the literature—the formal, the behavioral, and the communicative (or cognitive) conception.[35] According to the *formal* conception of norms, socialization effects will be seen in the transfer of international norms to national laws or in the establishment of formal institutions and procedures that correspond to and help to enforce an international norm. According to the *behavioral* conception, the effects of norms are measured by the extent to which the relevant behavior of the states to be socialized corresponds to the behavior stipulated by the norm in question. By contrast, according to the *communicative* conception of norms, socialization will primarily affect the communication or discourse among domestic actors.

Table 1.1. Socialization Foci and Strategies of International Organizations

	Inclusive	Intermediate	Exclusive
Community norms		Council of Europe	
Community and specific norms	OSCE, EBRD	OECD	EU, NATO
Specific norms	IMF, World Bank	WTO	

This conceptualization of the dependent variable gives rise to several theoretically interesting questions: Is there a *dominant kind* of normative impact of international organizations on the CEECs? Can we specify conditions under which we will see one kind of normative effect rather than another? Or can we detect a typical *sequence* of normative effects in these countries? The literature as well as some of the contributions to this volume suggest that internalization will usually start with communicative and then formal effects to be followed (but not inevitably) by behavioral effects. For instance, in their theoretical synthesis of various case studies on the socialization of authoritarian regimes to international human rights norms, Risse and Sikkink suggest a dynamic, "spiral model" of change according to which first socialization effects are observable when governments under international pressure "start 'talking the human rights talk'" (communicative effect). In the next phase, they begin institutionalizing international norms in the constitution and/or in domestic law (formal effect). Rule-consistent behavior is the final stage in the socialization process (behavioral effect).[36] In Central and Eastern Europe, a similar sequence seems to operate. Most CEE governments early on made the "return to Europe" their central foreign policy strategy, claimed to belong to the West and to share its values, and vowed to follow Western models and adopt its norms.[37] The intensification of institutional ties between the CEECs and the Western organizations then led to an increasing transfer of Western norms to the domestic institutions and laws of the CEECs. However, in many instances, this formal transposition—initially or permanently—led to mere "Potemkin harmonization"[38] or "facade democracies"[39] in which formal institutions were undermined by norm-violating factual behavior.[40]

The *degree or depth of internalization* measures the extent to which an international norm has been transposed into a state's domestic political institutions and culture. In the literature and in the contributions to this volume, this dimension of "impact" is categorized in various ways. For instance, we can distinguish deep, "constitutive" effects of norms, which change the identities and basic interests of the actors, from "regulative" effects, which merely affect their behavior but leave underlying identities and interests unchanged.[41] Or international norms may have an impact on political elites but not on the "masses," that is, society at large.[42] I propose a categorization that starts from a literal interpretation of the term and Coleman's definition of internalization as the development of an internal sanctioning system.[43] The highest level of internalization is reached when norm conformity is guaranteed by *intrapersonal* sanctioning, that is, "violating an established norm is psychologically painful"[44] or, more fundamentally still, norms are "taken for granted" and followed because other ways of doing things are simply inconceivable.[45] In this ideal-typical case, norms have constitutive effects indeed, and we will not observe (major) behavioral or communicative challenges to them. Formal institutions and rules are not necessary to ensure compliance. An intermediate level of internalization is indicated by effective *intrasocietal* sanctioning. In that case, we will see frequent challenges to an international norm in domestic politics because the state and other domestic actors do not follow this norm out of habit or conviction. However, domestic sanctioning mechanisms—such as formal sanctioning by domestic courts, behavioral sanctioning by voters in elections, or communicative sanctioning by the media—are sufficiently effective to prevent these challenges from turning into norm-violating governmental policy. Finally, the level of internalization is low in cases of *international* sanctioning, that is, if international actors must intervene (alone or together with norm-supporting but weak domestic actors) in order to ensure conformity and compliance.[46]

The analysis of international socialization, then, seeks to establish the conditions of different degrees of internalization. For instance, why are different international norms internalized to different degrees in a single state and why is the same norm differently internalized in various states to be socialized? In Central and Eastern Europe, internalization varies extremely. Even if we limit the analysis to fundamental community norms, there are countries in which internalization has hardly taken place at all (e.g., Belarus and, until recently, Serbia). In other countries, socialization is highly dependent on the use of international sanctioning (the most obvious case is Bosnia-Hercegovina). There are countries in which intrasocietal sanctioning is too weak to ensure compliance with basic Western community norms (such as Russia and Ukraine), whereas in the most consolidated democracies of the region, domestic sanctioning mechanisms appear to have taken root.

THEORETICAL ISSUES: MECHANISMS
AND CONDITIONS OF IMPACT

To explore and explain the domestic impact of international organizations, two questions must be asked and answered: First, *why* or *under what conditions* do international organizations have a domestic impact? Second, *how* or *through which causal mechanisms* do they influence domestic polities, politics, and policies? Both questions are often linked: different causal mechanisms may operate under different conditions and different conditions may matter depending on the causal mechanism of impact.[47] I begin by outlining two basic mechanisms of impact and then discuss conditions under which they are most likely to be effective.

Mechanisms

At a fundamental level, mechanisms of domestic impact can be differentiated according to the dominant logic of action they follow. The most widely used distinction is that between a "logic of appropriateness" and a "logic of consequentiality."[48] The logic of appropriateness mechanism can be further differentiated into cognitive and normative modes of action, the one based on a logic of consequentiality into rhetorical and bargaining modes. The central features of these mechanisms are listed in table 1.2.

According to the *logic of appropriateness*, actors follow norms for intrinsic reasons. Based on personal dispositions informed by social beliefs, they do what is deemed appropriate in a given situation and given their social role. In the *cognitive mode of action*, international organizations influence domestic actors "by providing the cognitive scripts, categories and models that are indispensable for action, not least because without them the world and the behaviour of others cannot be interpreted."[49] This activity can be subsumed under *teaching*. On the part of the domestic actors, the dominant activity is *imitation*. "For cognitive theorists, compliance occurs in many circumstances because other types of behavior are inconceivable; routines are followed because they are taken for granted as 'the way we do things.'"[50] As a result, international organizations will have a deep impact on domestic actors; compliance will be ensured by *intrapersonal*, cognitive mechanisms. Moreover, the discursive, formal, and behavioral impacts of international norms tend to be *convergent*.

In the *normative mode of action*, the domestic impact of international organizations has a more reflective and evaluative quality. International organizations seek to *convince* states of their norms. If their claims and arguments are convincing, domestic actors engage in (complex) *learning*, that is, they accept the norms as legitimate and comply with them out of moral commitment or a sense of *obligation*.[51] As in the cognitive mode, the domestic impact of international organizations will be deep: Once domestic actors have internalized the norms, sanctioning will be effective at an intrapersonal level. Moreover, personally internalized norms will generally result in convergence between discourse, formal institutions, and behavior.

Table 1.2.   Mechanisms of Domestic Impact

	Logic of Appropriateness		Logic of Consequentiality	
	Cognitive Mode	Normative Mode	Rhetorical Mode	Bargaining Mode
Activity of organization	teaching	convincing, arguing	social influence	material threats and promises
Activity of domestic actors	imitation	learning	acquiescence	adaptation
Role of norms	scripts	obligations	frames	constraints
Kinds of impact	convergent		divergent	
Depth of impact	international —> intrapersonal		international —> intrasocietal	

According to the *logic of consequentiality*, actors follow norms out of extrinsic motivations. Based on calculations of the costs and benefits of alternative courses of action, they choose the action that maximizes (or at least satisfies) their individual utility. Norms (or rather the negative and positive sanctions associated with them) increase the costs of norm-violating and the benefits of norm-conforming actions. Thereby they alter the incentive and opportunity structure for the actors and influence their choice of behavior.

In the *rhetorical mode of action*, international organizations use *social influence*, a "soft," social-psychological mechanism relying on *social* rewards (such as popularity and respect) for compliance and punishments (such as shaming and shunning) for noncompliance.[52] International organizations accord recognition, legitimacy, association, and membership to states (or withdraw it from them), thereby influencing the domestic and international image and standing of the state. To the extent that a change of the state's image and standing is costly or beneficial to this state, its behavior will be affected. In turn, the state strategically manipulates its image and the norms in question in order to increase social rewards and avoid punishment.[53] In this process, norms mainly function as *frames* of legitimate behavior that affect the image of the targeted state. If social influence is successful, the state and other domestic actors *acquiesce* to the norm. The impact of international norms, however, is expected to be *divergent*: For instance, states will "talk the talk" of international organizations or create new formal ("Potemkin") institutions required by them in order to gain the rewards associated with international legitimacy while, at the same time, continuing their old behavior and avoiding the costs of adaptation. Moreover, the impact of international norms is expected to lack depth: International norms will not be internalized at the intrapersonal level, that is, change the identity and interests of the actors. The best possible outcome is a shift from international social influence to effective domestic social influence as an *intrasocietal* sanctioning mechanism.

Finally, in the *bargaining mode*, it is *material*, not social, *threats and promises* that create the domestic impact of international organizations. International organizations use their material bargaining power directly to coerce a state to follow its norms or indirectly to alter the domestic balance of power in favor of actors that support its norms. If the costs of norm-violating behavior exceed the benefits, international norms work as effective *constraints* on domestic behavior and lead to domestic *adaptation*. As in the rhetorical mode, however, the impact of international organizations will likely be divergent and will not reach all the way down to the desires of domestic actors. At best, domestic institutions and power structures will be altered in such a way that they create a stable equilibrium in which actors have no incentive to deviate from the norms.

Conditions

The likelihood of the various mechanisms of impact to shape the process of the international socialization of the CEECs depends on several conditions at the international and the domestic level. At the *international level*, international socialization requires some sort of asymmetrical relationship between the international organization and the state to be socialized. For the cognitive, normative, and rhetorical mechanisms, the basic condition is the *normative power* stemming from the authority of the international organization and the legitimacy of the norms it propagates. According to Thomas Franck, the degree to which an international norm "will exert a strong pull on states to comply" depends on four properties: "determinacy"—the transparency or textual clarity of the norm, "symbolic validation"—the ritual and pedigree conferring legitimacy on the norm, "coherence"—"the degree to which a rule is applied coherently in practice," and "adherence" to a norm hierarchy.[54] I propose to add "consensus" to this list. Finnemore and Sikkink suggest that the number of countries in a region that adhere to a given norm determine its normative power.[55] Similarly, the degree to which a norm is contested indicates its capacity to represent an orthodox cognitive script, a strong obligation, or a dominant frame.

By contrast, the bargaining mechanism will only be effective if the international organization possesses *superior material bargaining power*. On the one hand, the international organization must be able to issue credible threats and promises as sanctions for norm-violating and norm-compliant behavior by the target state. On the other hand, the target state must be sufficiently sensitive or vulnerable to the actions of the international organization to react to sanctions in the desired way.

However, there is general agreement in the literature that international conditions alone are not able to explain the domestic impact of international norms and organizations. *Domestic conditions* must be included in the explanation as intervening variables. The two conditions that have received the greatest attention in the literature are domestic salience and domestic structure.[56] *Domestic salience* refers to the degree to which an international norm resonates with the culture of a society. The more an international norm matches with preexisting domestic values, norms, interests, and practices, the more easily it is diffused to the domestic sphere. The more salient a norm, the more likely it is accepted as a cognitive script or template (cognitive action), the more convincing arguments based on this norm will be (normative action), the more likely an international organization is able to shame a noncompliant state into compliance (rhetorical action), and the more likely it will find enough domestic allies to tilt the balance of power or interests in favor of compliance (bargaining). Conversely, if an international norm has only little domestic salience, the normative or bargaining power of the international organization will usually not be sufficient for a tangible domestic impact.

Domestic structure refers to the structure of the state and state-society relations. Although this variable is conceptualized and operationalized in very different ways in the literature, it essentially measures the degree to which the state is capable of controlling the domestic policy-making process. While domestic structure may not matter much if domestic salience is high throughout society, it determines whose interests prevail in situations of norm contestation. For instance, even if the normative or bargaining power of the international organization is high vis-à-vis the state, impact may be low if the state is fragmented and weak vis-à-vis society. On the other hand, if the state rejects international norms, the impact of international organizations may still be high if they are able to mobilize a strong domestic society against the state.

A third group of conditions that cannot be subsumed under international or domestic conditions are *issue- or norm-specific conditions* that may affect the way, the kind, and the depth of the domestic impact of international organizations. These conditions are still relatively little explored but have played some role in the theory of European integration[57] and in regime theory.[58] Recently, Knill and Lehmkuhl suggested that the mechanisms of Europeanization vary with policy issues and the type of integration they represent. They argue, for instance, that in cases of market-making or "negative" integration policies the dominant mechanism is based on the change of domestic opportunity structure and domestic impact will depend on the degree of power redistribution between domestic actors. By contrast, in cases of market-shaping or "positive" integration policies, states are directly confronted with an institutional model for compliance and domestic impact will depend on the degree of salience or "institutional compatibility."[59] In addition, it would be interesting to find out if there is a systematic variation with regard to process and domestic impact between "hard" and "soft" international norms or "political" norms (affecting the core of state authority and power) and more "technical" norms.

Conditions and Mechanisms of Domestic Impact in Central and Eastern Europe

There is widespread agreement among the contributors to this volume on the basic conditions and the dominant mechanism of the impact of international organizations on the CEECs. At the *international level*, the relationship between the international, mostly European, organizations and the CEECs has a clearly asymmetrical structure. First, it is characterized by *high normative power of the international organizations*. Generally, the norms advocated by the international organizations either belong to or follow from the constitutive liberal democratic community norms of the West that have been accepted as the pan-European standard of legitimacy by all CSCE/OSCE member states at the end of the Cold War and are institutionalized in international rules. Moreover, although not all OSCE member states comply with these norms, there is no competing standard of legitimacy in the European regional system that would openly challenge the Western norms. Therefore, with regard to basic consensus, symbolic validation, and adherence, these norms should exert a strong pull on states to comply. Moreover, as the standard setter for legitimate statehood in Europe, the Western community is in a position to provide authoritative interpretations of the norms, to accord or withdraw international recognition, and to confer international legitimacy upon states.

However, the *norms* analyzed in this volume *vary with regard to determinacy and coherence.* For instance, minority rights (understood as collective rights) have only recently been institutionalized at the international level as "soft law." They are unevenly implemented and sometimes contested in Western countries. This also applies to monetary policy. Tripartism may be generally accepted but is organized in different ways in EU member states. Moreover, as the Grigorescu chapter shows, even though there is a general consensus on the norm of freedom of information, specific laws have not been passed in all Western countries; and Sissenich points out in her chapter that EU social policy is weakened by comparatively strong noncompliance. In sum, those norms with comparatively less determinacy and coherence should exert a lower compliance pull than more determinate and coherently practiced norms because they represent a less orthodox script, a looser obligation, and a less persuasive frame.

Second, the *material bargaining power of the international organizations is clearly superior.* The international organizations analyzed in this book represent the most wealthy and powerful states of the world, whereas the examined CEECs are generally small states in the midst of political and economic transformation and are located in an insecure international environment with contested borders and unresolved nationality problems. In addition, whereas Western markets are critical to CEEC economies, the CEEC market is relatively unimportant for most Western countries. Under these conditions, the CEECs could use all the external support they could get, and the Western community was the only source of such support. It possessed the material resources to aid in economic transition, the knowledge about a functioning democracy and market economy, and the military power to stop large-scale ethnopolitical violence and to protect the smaller CEECs against the potential Russian threat they perceived. Finally, the configuration of relations is of a hub-and-spoke kind; each CEEC *individually* faces international organizations representing the *collective* power of its member states.[60]

At the *domestic level*, the case studies assembled here support the proposition that the domestic structure of the CEECs—to varying but generally high degrees—is characterized by *weak societies and strong states*. This is obvious in the presidential systems of government that prevail in the former Soviet republics but also applies to the advanced parliamentary democracies of Central Europe.[61] Even here, political parties have been organized top-down, are little rooted in society, rarely reflect social cleavages, and depend on the state for their resources. As cartel parties, they fail to fulfill the function of societal interest aggregation and bottom-up interest mediation. Moreover, industrial relations are generally characterized by a state-dominated corporatism (in many cases even patrimonial networks), and an active civil society has failed to emerge despite promising beginnings in the revolutions of 1989. As shown in the Harris chapter, this condition also applies to the Western organizations, for the time being. As a consequence, international socialization in Central and Eastern Europe is, to a high degree, an *elitist process* involving state agents (intergovernmental organizations, governments, and parliaments) and using *intergovernmental channels* of communication and influence. It is another consequence of this domestic structure that *norm salience with the state and the parties in government* will be the most important variable intervening between the international structure (generally conducive to successful international socialization) and the domestic impact of international organizations.[62]

Finally, there is general, although less explicit, agreement among the contributions to this volume that the dominant mechanisms of domestic impact follow a *logic of consequentiality*. On the one hand, there is ample evidence on how, in the context of international power asymmetry, the international organizations' policies of conditionality significantly increase the costs of noncompliance and the benefits of compliance with the international norms in question and thereby induce CEEC governments to cooperate with the international organizations and adopt their norms. For instance, the Grigorescu chapter shows how the informational demands of international organizations have increased the costs of secrecy for CEEC governments and have redistributed informational resources in favor of Central and Eastern European societies. In his chapter, Michta argues that the transformation of the Polish military and civil-military relations was a result of NATO conditionality and the price for Polish membership; the same applies to Williams's chapter about Hungary's bilateral treaties with the neighboring countries of Slovakia and Romania.

On the other hand, the studies generally point to the widespread use of rhetorical strategies by the CEEC governments. First, CEEC governments put great emphasis on self-presentation in their bid to join the Western organizations: They portray their countries as an indispensable part of

"Europe" and the European interstate community and as traditional adherents of Western or European values.[63] And they are highly aware of the need to be perceived as democratic, norm-abiding countries by the West in order to achieve their goal of EU and NATO membership.[64] Second, European and other international norms are strategically used in various ways in the domestic power struggle of the CEECs.[65] Parties in government refer to the need to comply with international norms in order to justify unpopular and costly policy measures in the face of domestic opposition.[66] Opposition parties invoke international norms in order to discredit government policies. And since membership in Western organizations is generally a high priority among the CEEC publics, all political forces tend to present their programs as conforming with Western norms and demands. Finally, as shown in the Šabič chapter, states hide their egoistic interests behind European norms in international negotiations.

The dominant logic of consequentiality is further corroborated by the observation of a *divergent impact* of international norms on domestic politics: The discrepancy between high impact on discourse and formal institutions and comparatively low impact on actual behavior can be attributed to CEEC rhetorical manipulation of international norms and the perceived need to create the impression of norm abidance. In addition, CEEC exploitation of information asymmetries allows them to behave in the old ways behind a norm-conforming facade. The case studies also provide ample evidence for the prevalence of international and intrasocietal sanctioning mechanisms in the current stage of the internalization process. In a cautious assessment, however, the lack of depth in the impact of international organizations and norms can also be explained by the relatively short duration of international socialization.

Intentions and Outcomes: Socialization Effects

Many of the case studies in this volume tell a simple *story of successful nannies, good pupils, and smooth socialization.*[67] International organizations propagate a norm and pursue a policy of conditionality—compliance and internalization are rewarded with material support, institutional association, and, ultimately, membership in the exclusive organizations of the West; noncompliance is punished by reduction or withdrawal of support and rejection of association and membership. To secure the material assistance they need and to achieve the membership in Western organizations that is their foremost foreign policy goal, Central and Eastern European governments accept and adopt the norm. Domestic costs are justified, and domestic protest is muffled, by reference to the demands of the international organizations and the prospects of EU and NATO membership. In sum, the combined effects of IO conditionality and the domestic salience of Western orientations result in an effective domestic impact of international organizations in the CEECs.

Besides this "model story" of intended, effective, and positive impact, many of the chapters in this book point to *unintended, and sometimes even counterproductive,* effects of Western policies toward the CEECs. Generally, these effects can be explained by the dominant logic of consequentiality and the elitist character of the socialization process. To order these diverse effects, I propose to distinguish "positive," norm-promoting and "negative," norm-inhibiting effects, on the one hand, and "intended," "unintended," and "coincidental" effects, on the other (see table 1.3). Whereas effects that do not match the intentions of, but were certainly brought about by, an international organization qualify as "unintended," "coincidental" effects cannot even be attributed to the international organization.

"Intended" Negative Effects

Egoistic interests on the part of the Western organizations and their member states often undermine their socialization efforts. Negative effects in the CEECs are at least accepted (if not intended) out of self-interest. In his chapter, Šabič shows how the socialization process can become hostage to the selfish governmental interests of individual member states (Italy in this case). Moreover, the association treaties of the EU with the CEECs generally prove the pervasiveness of short-term material interests. Although the association treaties provided for an asymmetrical liberalization of trade in industrial products in favor of the CEECs, the EU reserved protectionist "antidumping" and "safeguard" measures for itself and made an exception of exactly those sectors (agriculture, textiles, coal, iron, and steel) in which the Central and Eastern European economies were competitive and in which they could have earned the hard currency needed for financing economic transformation. Instead, the CEECs ran into a permanent trade deficit with the EU. The most dramatic example for this type of effect was the sustained reluctance of the West to intervene in a more than symbolic manner to end the war in

Table 1.3. Intentions and Outcomes

Effects	Positive	Negative
Intended	effective conditionality when high domestic salience	member-state self-interest undermines socialization
Unintended	norm-promoting indirect effects of IO-CEEC interaction	competition for membership and elitist process undermine socialization goals
Coincidental	enhanced compliance as a by-product of changes in government	ineffective conditionality when low domestic salience

Bosnia. Fear of high costs and lack of material interest were jointly responsible for this reluctance.

Unintended Negative Effects

This type of effect has received most attention among critical observers of the Europeanization process of the CEECs. For instance, in what he aptly terms the *divergence paradox* of enlargement, Jürgen Beyer describes how, in a context of competition for admission instigated by the EU and NATO policy of "self-differentiation," both international cooperation among the CEECs and harmonization of domestic norms and practices (in the field of privatization of state property) remained weak despite strong verbal encouragement by the Western organizations.[68]

In this volume, both the Iankova and Sissenich chapters show how EU demands for "transposition of the *acquis*" have led to the establishment of *inefficient duplicate structures and institutions without domestic functions* that mainly serve to satisfy the international organization and to demonstrate compliance.[69] The elitist character of the socialization process not only gives Central and Eastern European governments the opportunity to *exploit information asymmetries* vis-à-vis international organizations to their advantage—it is often difficult for international organizations to evaluate the extent to which a government follows international norms in practice or whether normative impact is merely declaratory or formal (see the Sissenich chapter). It also allows these governments to exploit information asymmetries vis-à-vis domestic societies that are little informed about the workings of the international organizations and the requirements for or the consequences of membership. In the final analysis, the elitist character of international socialization in the CEECs might further strengthen states that are already strong vis-à-vis society and thereby undermine the further democratization of the CEECs that international socialization is intended to support (see the Freyberg-Inan chapter). Finally, the chapter by Hallerberg and colleagues shows how the socialization process resulted in not only the intended transfer of Western monetary policy norms to the CEECs but also the unintended imitation of Western manipulations of these norms for election purposes.

Unintended Positive Effects

While most of the unintended effects of international socialization are of the negative variety, the Grigorescu chapter describes a case of unintended improvement. In his account, many CEECs introduced freedom of information legislation without the Western organizations having demanded its adoption. Rather, freedom of information was a by-product of the international organizations' high demand for (and subsequent public dissemination of) information on the CEECs.

Coincidental Positive Effects

In some cases in which the international organizations demanded the adoption of international norms and the CEECs eventually complied, domestic change had little to do with international socialization efforts. Rather, international organizations benefited from socialization by chance. For instance, Poland adopted the norm of parliamentary control of the military only after President Walesa had been defeated in presidential elections (see the Michta chapter); Bulgaria embarked on economic reforms and a pro-NATO foreign policy course only after the Union of Democratic Forces came to power in 1996–1997 (see the Linden chapter); in Hungary, the electoral victory of the Socialists in 1994 helped the rapprochement with Slovakia and Romania (see the Williams chapter); and in the Czech Republic, the resignation of the Klaus government over corruption charges opened the way for regional policy reform (see the Jacoby-Cernoch chapter). One could add the Slovak elections of 1998 and the Croatian and Yugoslav elections of 2000. In each case, international pressure on the incumbent government to comply with international norms was fruitless. Compliance improved only after elections resulting in a change in government. The incumbents, however, were not voted out of office because they violated the international norms in question or because the electorate heeded the calls of the international community. Rather, compliance was a by-product of electoral shifts caused by other concerns such as the deterioration of the economic situation.[70]

Ineffectiveness

Just as a combination of IO conditionality and domestic salience accounts for the success stories of domestic impact in the CEECs, the policy of conditionality loses its effectiveness, and the domestic impact of international organizations is severely reduced, if salience of Western orientations among the political elite is low or absent. Most obviously, this has been the case with openly autocratic and anti-Western regimes such as those of Lukashenka in Belarus and Milosevic in Yugoslavia but even in less extreme cases such as Bulgaria under the Socialist government (see the Linden chapter) and Slovakia under the Meciar government, the (threat of) exclusion from the shortlist of serious candidates for EU and NATO membership could do little to alter reform-adverse or norm-violating policies. It seems that Western socialization policies short of direct intervention and "internal reconstruction" do not directly matter under these conditions, indeed.[71]

CONCLUSION: METHODOLOGICAL SUGGESTIONS

Like many emerging fields of study, the study of the domestic impact of international organizations on the CEECs suffers from a number of "teething troubles": Key concepts and variables are ill-defined and used differently; theoretical approaches vary widely; and single-case studies dominate empirical research. While the contributions to this volume combine a common research question, a strong country or area expertise, and theoretical reflection—and thus mark an important advancement—work on this key process of contemporary European politics may further benefit from four interrelated methodological suggestions with which I will conclude this introduction: theoretical integration, comparative research designs, isolation of organizational effects, and feedback processes.

Generally, *theoretical integration* can take place at highly abstract (for instance, rational choice theory) or very concrete levels (such as specific propositions on the socialization of Central European countries). As I have indicated throughout this introduction, I think that integration with the *Europeanization* literature would be the most fruitful avenue for the near future. On the one hand, an emerging field itself, the Europeanization literature has made some progress in conceptual and theoretical consolidation on which studies on the CEECs could built. It integrates theoretical insights from both the IR (socialization and second image-reversed) literature and from comparative politics and policy analysis. On the other hand, the Europeanization literature is very close in substance to the study of international socialization in the CEECs. A combination of both fields could start from many constants (such as the international institutions and norms) but would also involve some interesting variables (such as the nonmember status of the CEECs and their domestic characteristics).

In order to test these variables, studies on the domestic impact of international organizations should move from the dominant single-issue, single-organization, and single-country format to *comparative studies* and from studies merely adding several countries, organizations, and issues to each other to studies in which *cases* are *carefully selected* on the variables to be analyzed. Although the chapters to this volume deal with a great variety of international norms and international organizations, issue and organizational characteristics have yet to be tested for their explanatory power.[72] Moreover, while the cases selected here involve a relatively small number of the more advanced CEECs, the study of domestic impact would benefit from both comparisons with West European nonmembers and members and comparisons with a larger group of CEECs.

One of the most difficult tasks involved in the study of the domestic impact of international organizations is the *distinction of organizational impact from other potential influences*. Only then will we be able to ascertain whether, to what extent, and how international organizations really matter in the domestic politics of the CEECs.[73] Since the involvement of international organizations is a constant in post–Cold War Central and Eastern European politics and the comparison of the Cold War and the post–Cold War era is of little use because both international and domestic factors changed dramatically, comparative case studies will generally not do. There are a couple of alternatives. First, and most basically, the contributions to this volume generally show that the norms they study had not been internalized in the CEECs before international organizations demanded their adoption. Second, some of them systematically take into account alternative explanations in order to strengthen or weaken the claim that domestic change has been an effect of IO policy (see, e.g., the Grigorescu and Linden chapters). In addition, this methodological problem may also be tackled by counterfactual thought experiments[74] or, alternatively, a process-tracing analysis that seeks to reconstruct the policy-making process in sufficient detail to establish the causal importance of IO influence.

Finally, one should not forget that the domestic impact of international organizations is part of a larger and dynamic process. Policy making within the international organizations both precedes and follows their attempts to disseminate their norms. Presumably, international organizations evaluate their domestic impact, learn from the unintended and counterproductive effects of their policies—or those that failed to materialize altogether—and change their policies accordingly. A full study of the domestic impact of international organizations in Central and Eastern Europe will therefore have to include *feedback loops* in the analysis.[75]

NOTES

1. International socialization is a major research focus of constructivism in international relations. See, e.g., Martha Finnemore, *National Interests in International Society* (Ithaca, N.Y.: Cornell University Press, 1996); Thomas Risse, Steve C. Ropp, and Kathryn Sikkink, eds., *The Power of Human Rights* (Cambridge: Cambridge University Press, 1999). For a recent account of the state of the art, see Martha Finnemore and Kathryn Sikkink, "International Norm Dynamics and Political Change," in *Exploration and Contestation in the Study of World Politics*, ed. Peter J. Katzenstein, Robert O. Keohane, and Stephen D. Krasner (Cambridge, Mass.: MIT Press, 1999), 247–77. For the definition, see Frank Schimmelfennig, "International Socialization in the New Europe: Rational Action in an Institutional Environment," *European Journal of International Relations*, March 2000, 112.

2. An early exception is Robert O. Keohane, Joseph S. Nye, and Stanley Hoffmann, eds., *After the Cold War: International Institutions and State Strategies in Europe, 1989–1991* (Cambridge, Mass.: Harvard University Press, 1993). See also the collection of case studies in Peter J. Katzenstein, ed., *Mitteleuropa: Between Europe and*

Germany (Providence, R.I.: Berghahn, 1997). For recent conceptual and theoretical approaches to the international socialization of Central and Eastern Europe, see, for instance, Wade Jacoby, "Priest and Penitent: The European Union as a Force in the Domestic Politics of Eastern Europe," *East European Constitutional Review* 8, no. 1–2 (1999): 62–67; Schimmelfennig, "International Socialization."

3. On NATO enlargement, see, for instance, Frank Schimmelfennig, "NATO Enlargement: A Constructivist Explanation," *Security Studies* 8, no. 2–3 (1998–1999): 198–234; Lars S. Skålnes, "From the Outside In, From the Inside Out: NATO Expansion and International Relations Theory," *Security Studies* 7, no. 4 (1998): 44–87. On EU enlargement, see Frank Schimmelfennig, "The Community Trap: Liberal Norms, Rhetorical Action, and the Eastern Enlargement of the European Union," *International Organization* 55, no. 1 (2001): 47–80; Ulrich Sedelmeier, "Eastern Enlargement: Risk, Rationality, and Role-Compliance," in *Risks, Reforms, Resistance, and Revival*, ed. Maria Green Cowles and Michael Smith (Oxford: Oxford University Press, 2001), 164–85. For a combined analysis, see Karen Fierke and Antje Wiener, "Constructing Institutional Interests: EU and NATO Enlargement," *Journal of European Public Policy* 6, no. 5 (1999): 721–42.

4. On U.S. NATO enlargement policy, see James M. Goldgeier, *Not Whether but When: The US Decision to Enlarge NATO* (Washington, D.C.: Brookings Institution, 1999). Collections of case studies can be found, for instance, in Karl Kaiser and Martin Brüning, eds., *East-Central Europe and the EU: Problems of Integration* (Bonn: Europa Union Verlag, 1996); David G. Haglund, ed., *Will NATO Go East? The Debate over Enlarging the Atlantic Alliance* (Kingston, Ont.: Centre for International Relations, Queen's University, 1996).

5. See, for instance, Andrew Cottey, *East-Central Europe after the Cold War: Poland, the Czech Republic, Slovakia, and Hungary in Search of Security* (Basingstoke, U.K.: Macmillan, 1995); Danica Fink Hafner, "Dilemmas in Managing the Expanding EU: The EU and Applicant States' Point of View," *Journal of European Public Policy* 6, no. 5 (1999): 783–801; George Kolankiewicz, "Consensus and Competition in the Eastern Enlargement of the European Union," *International Affairs* 70, no. 3 (1994): 477–95.

6. Schimmelfennig, "NATO Enlargement"; Schimmelfennig, "Community Trap."

7. For a promising conceptual approach, see Lykke Friis and Anna Murphy, "The European Union and Central and Eastern Europe: Governance and Boundaries," *Journal of Common Market Studies* 37, no. 2 (1999): 211–32.

8. See, above all, Guillermo O'Donnell, Philippe C. Schmitter, and Laurence Whitehead, eds., *Transitions from Authoritarian Rule* (Baltimore: Johns Hopkins University Press, 1986).

9. See, for instance, Attila Agh, *The Politics of Central Europe* (London: Sage, 1998); Klaus von Beyme, *Systemwechsel in Osteuropa* (Frankfurt: Suhrkamp, 1994); Samuel P. Huntington, *The Third Wave: Democratisation in the Late Twentieth Century* (Norman: University of Oklahoma Press, 1991).

10. See Geoffrey Pridham, "The International Dimension of Democratisation: Theory, Practice, and Inter-Regional Comparisons," in *Building Democracy? The International Dimension of Democratization in Eastern Europe*, ed. Geoffrey Pridham, Eric Herring, and George Sanford (New York: St. Martin's, 1994), 7–31; Philippe C. Schmitter, "The Influence of the International Context upon the Choice of National

Institutions and Policies and Neo-Democracies," in *The International Dimensions of Democratization: Europe and the Americas,* ed. Laurence Whitehead (Oxford: Oxford University Press, 1996), 26–54; Laurence Whitehead, "Three International Dimensions of Democratization," in *International Dimensions of Democratization,* 3–25.

11. See Huntington, *Third Wave,* 273; Adrian G.V. Hyde-Price, "Democratization in Eastern Europe: The External Dimension," in *Democratization in Eastern Europe: Domestic and International Perspectives,* ed. Geoffrey Pridham and Tatu Vanhanen (London: Routledge, 1994), 227.

12. See Agh, *Politics,* 33.

13. Schmitter, "Influence," 40.

14. Beyme, *Systemwechsel,* 355.

15. Wolfgang Merkel, *Systemtransformation: Eine Einführung in die Theorie und Empirie der Transformationsforschung* (Opladen: Leske & Budrich, 1999), 443.

16. Valerie Bunce, *Subversive Institutions: The Design and Destruction of Socialism and the State* (Cambridge: Cambridge University Press, 1999); David Stark and Laszlo Bruzst, *Postsocialist Pathways: Transforming Politics and Property in East-Central Europe* (Cambridge: Cambridge University Press, 1998).

17. For recent overviews of the literature, see Tanja Börzel and Thomas Risse, "When Europe Hits Home: Europeanization and Domestic Change," *European Integration Online Papers* 4, no. 15 (2000) <eiop.or.at/eiop/texte/2000-015a.htm> (July 27, 2001); Simon Hix and Klaus H. Goetz, "Introduction: European Integration and National Political Systems," *West European Politics* 23, no. 4 (2000): 1–26; Claudio M. Radaelli, "Whither Europeanization? Concept Stretching and Substantive Change," *European Integration Online Papers* 4, no. 8 (2000) <eiop.or.at/eiop/texte/2000-008a.htm> (July 27, 2001).

18. Peter Gourevitch, "The Second Image Reversed: The International Sources of Domestic Politics," *International Organization* 32, no. 4 (1978): 881–912.

19. For comparative case studies, see Maria Green Cowles, Thomas Risse, and James A. Caporaso, eds., *Transforming Europe: Europeanization and Domestic Political Change* (Ithaca, N.Y.: Cornell University Press, 2001); Adrienne Héritier, Dieter Kerwer, Christoph Knill, Dirk Lehmkuhl, and Michael Teutsch, *Differential Europe: New Opportunities and Restrictions for Policy Making in the Member States* (Lanham, Md.: Rowman & Littlefield, 2001). For attempts at theoretical synthesis, see Börzel and Risse, "Europe"; Christoph Knill and Dirk Lehmkuhl, "How Europe Matters: Different Mechanisms of Europeanization," *European Integration Online Papers* 3, no. 7 (1999) <eiop.or.at/eiop/texte/1999- 007a.htm> (July 27, 2001).

20. See, for instance, Stephan Kux, "Switzerland: Adjustment Despite Deadlock," in *Adapting to European Integration: Small States and the European Union,* ed. Kenneth Hanf and Ben Soetendorp (London: Longman, 1998), 167–85; Ulf Sverdrup, "Norway: An Adaptive Non-Member," in *Adapting to European Integration,* 149–66.

21. Börzel and Risse, "Europe," 5.

22. Note that recent studies on Europeanization reject any general propositions on the strengthening or the weakening of the state but regard these effects as dependent on domestic, institutional factors (see, e.g., Tanja A. Börzel, "Europäisierung und innerstaatlicher Wandel: Zentralisierung und Entparlamentarisierung?" *Politische Vierteljahresschrift* 41, no. 2 (2000): 225–50.

23. See Finnemore, *National Interests,* 22; Peter J. Katzenstein, "Introduction: Alternative Perspectives on National Security," in *The Culture of National Security: Norms and Identity in World Politics,* ed. Peter J. Katzenstein (New York: Columbia University Press, 1996), 5.

24. The distinction between "constitutive" and "regulative" norms follows a widespread classification of rules in social theory. See, e.g., David Dessler, "What's at Stake in the Agent-Structure Debate?" *International Organization* 43, no. 3 (1989): 454.

25. Paul Kowert and Jeffrey Legro, "Norms, Identity, and Their Limits: A Theoretical Reprise," in Katzenstein, *Culture of National Security,* 453.

26. Christian Reus-Smit, "The Constitutional Structure of International Society and the Nature of Fundamental Institutions," *International Organization* 51, no. 4 (1997): 558.

27. As long as these norms are observed in principle, domestic systems are allowed to vary, for example, with regard to presidential versus parliamentary democracy, to the amount of direct democratic elements, or the degree of state intervention in the economy.

28. Thomas Risse-Kappen, *Cooperation among Democracies: The European Influence on U.S. Foreign Policy* (Princeton, N.J.: Princeton University Press, 1995), 33.

29. Available at <www.osce.org/docs/english/1990-1999/summits/paris90e.htm> (February 16, 2001).

30. Both constitutive and specific norms were reiterated and further specified for the international socialization of Central and Eastern Europe. For NATO, see "Study on NATO Enlargement" <www.nato.int/docu/basictxt/enl-9501.htm> (July 27, 2001); for EU constitutive norms, see, e.g., the "Copenhagen criteria" in European Council, "Conclusions of the Presidency, Copenhagen, June 1993," *Bulletin of the European Communities* 26, no. 6 (1993); on its regulative norms, see, for instance, the white paper in European Commission, *Preparation of the Associated Countries of Central and Eastern Europe for Integration into the Internal Market of the Union,* COM (95) 163 final.

31. Kenneth W. Abbott and Duncan Snidal, "Why States Act through Formal International Organizations," *Journal of Conflict Resolution* 42, no. 1 (1998): 24.

32. On international organizations as "teachers of norms," see Finnemore, *National Interest.*

33. Only Yugoslavia's membership had been suspended until the fall of 2000.

34. In the "Europeanization" literature, the most common dimensions of the dependent variable are "domains of Europeanization" and "degree of change" (Börzel and Risse, "Europe"; Radaelli, "Whither Europeanization"). In my opinion, however, the distinction between the domains of "polity," "politics," and "policy" is unproductive for theory building, and "degree of change" (e.g., inertia, absorption, or transformation) does not exactly represent the focus of socialization studies, which are more concerned with the quality or depth of internalization than with the quantity of change. Depending on the level of prior domestic resonance or salience of the international norm in question, deep internalization might go together with little change and a high degree of change could still lead to little internalization.

35. See Andreas Hasenclever, Peter Mayer, and Volker Rittberger, *Theories of International Regimes* (Cambridge: Cambridge University Press, 1997), 14–21; Gregory

A. Raymond, "Problems and Prospects in the Study of International Norms," *Mershon International Studies Review* 41, no. 2 (1997): 217–18; and, referring to "norm salience," Andrew Cortell and James W. Davis Jr., "Understanding the Domestic Impact of International Norms: A Research Agenda," *International Studies Review* 2, no. 1 (2000): 70–71. Note that I do not refer to this discussion in search of the "best" conceptualization of norms but consider that each conception covers an important and different aspect of normative effects.

36. Thomas Risse and Kathryn Sikkink, "The Socialization of International Human Rights Norms into Domestic Practices: Introduction," in Risse, Ropp, and Sikkink, *Human Rights*, 27–31.

37. On the rhetorical use of Western norms by Central and Eastern European applicants to EU and NATO, see Iver B. Neumann, "European Identity, EU Expansion, and the Integration/Exclusion Nexus," *Alternatives* 23, no. 3 (1998): 397–416; Schimmelfennig, "International Socialization," 129–32.

38. Jacoby, "Priest."

39. Agh, *Politics.*

40. The discrepancy between formal and behavioral impact is emphasized by several contributions to this volume (see Grigorescu and Sissenich chapters).

41. See Šabič and Williams chapters. A similar distinction is that between "institutional" and "personal" internalization (see Freyberg-Inan chapter).

42. See Grigorescu chapter.

43. James S. Coleman, *Foundations of Social Theory* (London: Belknap, 1990), 293.

44. Robert Axelrod, "An Evolutionary Approach to Norms," *American Political Science Review* 80, no. 4 (1986): 1104.

45. Richard W. Scott, *Institutions and Organizations* (Thousand Oaks, Calif.: Sage, 1995), 44.

46. As indicated in this paragraph, the two classifications of the dependent variable can be combined. We can observe different kinds of normative effects (formal, behavioral, communicative) at different levels of internalization.

47. For combinations of conditions and mechanisms in research on international socialization and Europeanization, see, e.g., Börzel and Risse, "Europe"; Jeffrey T. Checkel, *Why Comply? Constructivism, Social Norms, and the Study of International Institutions,* ARENA Working Paper, no. 24 (Oslo: ARENA, 1999); Knill and Lehmkuhl, "Europe Matters."

48. James G. March and Johan P. Olsen, *Rediscovering Institutions: The Organizational Basis of Politics* (New York: Free Press, 1989), 160–61.

49. Peter A. Hall and Rosemary C. R. Taylor, "Political Science and the Three New Institutionalisms," *Political Studies* 44, no. 5 (1996): 947.

50. Scott, *Institutions,* 44.

51. Cf. the "logic of arguing" in Thomas Risse, "'Let's Argue!' Communicative Action in World Politics," *International Organization* 54, no. 1 (2000): 1–39.

52. Alastair Ian Johnston, "Treating International Institutions as Social Environments," *International Studies Quarterly* 45, no. 4 (2001): 487–515.

53. For a rhetorical perspective on the international socialization of Central and Eastern Europe and on the Eastern enlargement of Western organizations, see Schimmelfennig, "International Socialization"; Schimmelfennig, "Community Trap."

54. Thomas M. Franck, *The Power of Legitimacy among Nations* (New York: Oxford University Press, 1990), 49, 142.

55. Finnemore and Sikkink, "Norm Dynamics," 262–63.

56. Jeffrey Checkel, "International Norms and Domestic Politics: Bridging the Rationalist-Constructivist Divide," *European Journal of International Relations* 3, no. 4 (1997): 473–95; Jeffrey T. Checkel, "Norms, Institutions, and National Identity in Contemporary Europe," *International Studies Quarterly* 43, no. 1 (1999): 83–114; Andrew Cortell and James Davis, "How Do International Institutions Matter? The Domestic Impact of International Rules and Norms," *International Studies Quarterly* 40, no. 4 (1996): 451–78; Cortell and Davis, "Domestic Impact."

57. See the distinction between "low-politics" issues conducive to integration and "high-politics" issues that states seek to keep under national control, e.g., in Stanley Hoffmann, "Reflections on the Nation-State in Western Europe Today," *Journal of Common Market Studies* 21, no. 1–2 (1982): 29–30.

58. On the "problem-structural" approach to regime analysis, see, e.g., Volker Rittberger and Michael Zürn, "Towards Regulated Anarchy in East-West Relations," in *International Regimes in East-West Politics*, ed. Volker Rittberger (London: Pinter, 1990), 9–63.

59. Knill and Lehmkuhl, "Europe Matters."

60. As shown in the Šabič chapter, structural asymmetry also characterizes the relationship between individual member and nonmember states (such as Italy and Slovenia), and Sissenich argues in her chapter that the power of the European Commission vis-à-vis CEEC nonmember states is greater than vis-à-vis EU member states.

61. See Agh, *Politics*, 52, 106; Merkel, *Systemwechsel*, 494–532.

62. This is most clearly shown in the Linden chapter. See also the Iankova and Michta chapters.

63. See the Linden chapter on Bulgaria and the Williams chapter on Hungary. Cf. Schimmelfennig, "International Socialization," 131.

64. See Ronald H. Linden, "Putting on Their Sunday Best: Romania, Hungary, and the Puzzle of Peace," *International Studies Quarterly* 44, no. 1 (2000): 121–45. See also Williams and Ram chapters.

65. See Cortell and Davis, "International Institutions," 453. In this volume, this point is most explicitly made in the Freyberg-Inan chapter.

66. "Scapegoating" is also a common strategy of Western member states. See, e.g., Andrew Moravcsik, "Preferences and Power in the European Community: A Liberal Intergovernmental Approach," *Journal of Common Market Studies* 31, no. 4 (1993): 516.

67. See the Iankova, Jacoby/Cernoch, Michta, Ram, and Williams chapters.

68. Jürgen Beyer, "Integration und Transformation: Das Divergenz-Paradoxon des Beitrittswettbewerbs," *Politische Vierteljahresschrift* 40, no. 4 (1999): 537–64.

69. See also Wade Jacoby, "Talking the Talk: The Institutional Effects of the EU in Central and Eastern Europe" (paper prepared for the ISA Convention, Chicago, February 2001). For a general analysis of the ceremonial activities of organizations in an institutional environment, see John W. Meyer and Brian Rowan, "Institutional Organizations: Formal Structure as Myth and Ceremony," in *The New Institutionalism in Organizational Analysis*, ed. Walter W. Powell and Paul J. DiMaggio (Chicago: University of Chicago Press, 1991), 41–62.

70. For a similar analysis of regime-conducive foreign policies, see Michael Zürn, "Bringing the Second Image (Back) In: About the Domestic Sources of Regime Formation," in Rittberger, *Regime Theory and International Relations*, ed. Volker Rittberger (Oxford: Clarendon Press, 1993), 308.

71. G. John Ikenberry and Charles A. Kupchan, "Socialization and Hegemonic Power," *International Organization* 44, no. 3 (1990): 283–315.

72. Although it is not fully explored in their chapter, Jacoby and Cernoch give a useful example for a testable categorization of issue-area characteristics and their effect on the strength of EU norms.

73. On this problem in the Europeanization literature, see Hix and Goetz, "Introduction," 20–21.

74. Philip E. Tetlock and Aaron Belkin, *Counterfactual Thought Experiments in World Politics: Logical, Methodological, and Psychological Perspectives* (Princeton, N.J.: Princeton University Press, 1996).

75. See the Harris chapter for initial evidence.

I

EUROPEAN ORGANIZATIONS AND EAST EUROPEAN DEMOCRACY

2

The Democratic Dimension of EU Enlargement: The Role of Parliament and Public Opinion

Geoffrey Harris

EU ENLARGEMENT: DEMOCRACY AND EUROSKEPTICISM

Nineteen eighty-nine is remembered as the year democracy triumphed in Europe. A series of unexpected revolutions began in that year, and in the ensuing decade the international context of the European integration process was transformed. Since then a major enlargement of the EU has become the overriding priority for all institutions.

The leaders of countries seeking EU membership maintain that their democratic credentials should facilitate their chances of joining. Similarly, the EU institutions see the spread of democracy throughout Europe as a major contribution to the stability of the Continent. Yet democracy means that leaders have to carry their citizens with them. Thus the dimension of democracy provides the key to the success or failure of the project of European unification. At the beginning of the new century it is clear that the EU will be unable to achieve any of its immediate or long-term objectives without public acceptance. In September 2000 Denmark's citizens voted against joining the euro. Britain remains deeply divided on the issue, and the present Labour government has promised that people will have the last word on whether or not to keep the pound. At Nice in December 2000 the fifteen member states agreed on a new treaty intended to avoid future crises of legitimacy through the settlement of long-standing controversies over the size, content, and competency of EU institutions. The intergovernmental conference, which concluded in Nice, had as its principal objective making the EU ready for enlargement. On June 7, 2001, the treaty failed its first test with a rejection by the voters in the Republic of Ireland.

The EU is therefore committed to enlargement and to a revival of public confidence in the integration process, and yet the very changes needed to make it possible for the Union to enlarge could strengthen the forces of Euroskepticism.

Already in June 2000 the European Council meeting in Feira recognized the importance of securing continuing public support for enlargement through the provision of what was described somewhat defensively as "appropriate information." In September 2000, the commissioner responsible for enlargement sparked what quickly turned out to be a rather helpful controversy when he was widely misquoted as having called for a referendum on enlargement in his native country of Germany. As his misquote was then widely misinterpreted, commission president Romano Prodi and Commissioner Gunther Verheugen stood before the European Parliament in Strasbourg on September 6 and, to quote Prodi, committed themselves to gather the broadest possible consensus of citizens around the enlargement process, since, he feared, public opinion was not yet sufficiently convinced. As the dust has settled, it was clear that Verheugen had, not before time, stirred up a proper debate that had hitherto been sought only by those opposed to enlargement—particularly those on the populist or extreme right—or those representing views and interests potentially threatened by enlargement.

The *Financial Times* was among those defending the commissioner against EU government leaders who were irritated by his intervention. The *FT* identified them as the "real culprits."

> Today, Europe's leaders pay little more than lip service to enlargement. Their virtual silence is an invitation to demagogues on the right and left to whip up opposition. But it also suggests they have yet to make the case to themselves, let alone to the electorate.[1]

Whether or not the enlargement process proves successful will depend to a great extent on the ability of EU leaders to convince their citizens that they have been tough enough with the candidate countries in ensuring that they meet the criteria for membership.

It will also be necessary for the leaders of the countries trying to join the EU to ensure that their own citizens support this objective. Political leaders in Central Europe are already concerned that their countries' return to Europe is far too slow, and that EU imposition of costly conditions on their future membership will lead to a loss of public support. The leaders of the region are, perhaps, less used to the essential ambivalence and uncertainty that have come to characterize the process of European integration. This contrast between achievements and crises, ambitious projects and internal anxieties, confirms the obvious historical fact that the European Union is a young political structure, constantly evolving but with insufficient history to provide a sense of stability in times of crisis. The negative evolution of public opinion was confirmed in Eurobarometer surveys made inside the EU and the candidate countries in the course of 2001. If this trend continues and if the problems of ratifying the Nice treaty confirm that the Irish vote was not just an isolated hiccup, Frank Schimmelfennig's reference in chapter 1 of this volume to unintended negative effects of meeting the conditions for enlargement could prove prophetic.

On November 8, 2000, President Prodi and Commissioner Verheugen presented their proposals to bring a new momentum to the enlargement process. They specifically emphasized the importance of convincing the citizens of the EU and the candidate countries of the benefits of enlargement. Their strategy paper included, for the first time, a special section on this aspect, stating clearly that

> enlargement can only succeed if it is a social project involving all citizens and not just an elite. Only genuine participation can achieve this. Information is not enough. We have to set in motion a wide-ranging dialogue in our societies to make the risks and benefits clear to people and let them know their concerns are being taken seriously.[2]

BACKGROUND: THE EU REFORMS ITSELF

At the beginning of 1998 the EU opened accession negotiations with Cyprus, Hungary, Estonia, Slovenia, Poland, and the Czech Republic. In early 2000 Malta, Lithuania, Latvia, Bulgaria, Romania, and Slovakia also began accession negotiations.

In Helsinki at the end of 1999, Turkey was also given candidate status. Because the EU considers that country far from meeting the democratic criteria for membership, it will provide an excellent case study in the continuous tension between the EU trying to set norms of behavior for candidate countries' domestic and foreign policies and the candidates insisting that the demands of the "nanny" are sometimes unjustified or excessive or just an excuse to keep them from becoming full EU members.

At the end of 2000 the European Council in Nice adopted an idea first put forward by the European Parliament and then taken up by the Commission, namely, that the first new member states should join the Union in time for the 2004 European Parliament elections.

In spite of the pessimism and accusations of bad faith expressed by leaders from candidate countries, the fact is that ten years ago, such an advanced state of the fifth EU enlargement would have been unimaginable. The asymmetry of the whole process is confirmed when leaders in the candidate

countries explain the decline of public support for accession as a consequence of the slowness of the process and EU leaders face a disoriented
public opinion concerned at the rapidity of change involving enlargement,
institutional reform, and the introduction of the euro.

In March 1999 the EU executive body, the European Commission, as a
whole resigned, an event that symbolized dramatically the fact that the EU is
an emerging political and constitutional structure in which the European Parliament plays a role much stronger than many people (including, as it turned
out, even European commissioners) had hitherto realized. The entry into
force on May 1, 1999, of the Treaty of Amsterdam strengthened the role of
the European Parliament and provided the legal basis for the deepening of
the process of European integration in major policy areas. The treaty also
clarified in articles 6, 7, and 49 the fact that only democratic states could aspire to join or remain in the EU.

This is not the place to analyze whether the Treaty of Amsterdam should
have gone further in terms of the institutional reforms required to prepare for
the fifth enlargement. Indeed, the Treaty of Nice was agreed in December
2000 precisely in order (at least in theory) to complete the unfinished business of institutional reform. The concern originally expressed by the European Parliament, as well as some member states, that the Amsterdam treaty
did not make the Union's institutions ready for enlargement, had become the
received wisdom. Instead of these concerns leading to a slowdown of the
enlargement process, the advancement of that very process has profoundly
strengthened the need for institutional reform. The fact that the Union now
has the charter of fundamental rights confirms that it has advanced well beyond the frontiers of traditional intergovernmental cooperation based on the
inviolability of national sovereignty. Even if the text agreed and the lack of
enforceability disappointed those wishing to strengthen the extent of EU citizenship, it is clear that this distinctive new status exists for hundreds of mil-
lions of Europeans and that the charter is part of an ongoing constituent
process.

The agreement on some partial reforms of EU finances, structural funds,
and agricultural policy, which was reached in Berlin in March 1999, confirmed
how the enlargement process and the need for the Union to maintain its political credibility are keeping up the pressure for internal reform of the EU.
These reforms will not by themselves resolve all the problems that concern
enlargement, but the agreement by the European Council in Berlin in March
1999 on Agenda 2000 did remove the fear in the candidate countries that the
Union's internal problems would automatically slow down enlargement.[3.]

The modest institutional reforms agreed in the Nice treaty removed what
was, after Berlin, the last political obstacle to enlargement. Nice was, however, quickly reassessed as no more than part of the constituent process.
When it was signed on February 26, 2001, the presidents of the Council,

Commission, and Parliament all began focusing attention on a new round of reforms to be negotiated in 2004. European Council meetings in Ghent and Laeken in the latter months of 2001 confirmed that most member states wish to widen the agenda for constitutional reform and ensure that parliamentarians, NGOs, and public opinion are more involved in the process. In July 2001 the Commission published a white paper on European governance which recognized that people see the Union as both remote and intrusive and are losing confidence in the ability of a poorly understood, complex system to meet their expectations.

On February 28, 2002 a convention of government, Commission, and Parliament representatives started work on further reforms in a framework within which the thirteen candidate countries are fully involved.

PUBLIC VIEWS OF ENLARGEMENT: EAST AND WEST

In spite of some patchy successes in Austria, Great Britain, and France, the anti-integration movements are not particularly powerful. The low turnout in the 1999 euro elections and the Irish referendum did, however, confirm the inadequate level of active public involvement in the life of the EU. Such a worrying sign of the times could explain why Commissioner Verheugen felt it appropriate to make his point early on, well before the conclusion of any accession negotiations and at a time when public opinion in a number of EU countries is turning against enlargement, most notably in Germany and Austria as well as in Belgium and France. Eurobarometer findings published in April 2000 showed that only in Denmark (57 percent) and Greece (53 percent) does a majority of the population consider enlargement an appropriate priority for the Union. In this context it is hardly surprising that a survey confirmed public support for EU insistence that the candidate countries actually meet the membership criteria, whether it be in the field of human rights, social security, free competition, or environmental protection.

It is this interplay between EU leaders and their citizens that the leaders of the candidate countries must genuinely comprehend before they shoot from the hip with their challenges to the good faith of the EU commitment to enlargement. The Commission and the European Parliament will be stepping up public information campaigns in favor of EU enlargement, but it is the way the candidates approach the accession negotiations and their preparations for accession that will decide if and when they actually become members. In short, if they challenge the right of the EU to set certain norms, they will make it harder for EU leaders to gain public acceptance of their membership.

The dynamic situation inside the EU contrasts with first signs of disillusionment in the candidate countries. Poland, Hungary, and the Czech

Republic all hope to join the EU in the first five years of the new century, and their public opinion remains clearly pro-European. A study made in May 2000 by the Central European Opinion Research Group pointed out that support for the EU was actually higher in these countries than in existing member states such as Austria, Denmark, Finland, France, Sweden, and the United Kingdom.[4] The public in these countries was, however, less clear than their leaders on the urgency of accession. Fifty-eight percent of Poles saw domestic restructuring and modernization as more important than a rush to early membership; 49 percent of Hungarians and 38 percent of Czechs had similar views.

The leaders of the candidate countries appear, more and more, to feel that the EU has been too slow to bring them into the mainstream of Europe's political development. Their anguish has more to do with the need to show their voters some concrete political benefits flowing from the painful process of economic reform. Indeed, following the end of the Milošević regime in Yugoslavia the picture is remarkably positive.

Democracy has taken root. Elections are held regularly. Governments are voted in and out. Leaders of different parties come together in parliaments and sometimes divide among them key positions in the state. Problems with minority rights are being faced and resolved (e.g., Slovakia, Latvia). Hardly anybody votes for parties that would return to the communist system, and even the ultranationalist right has tended to fail the real test of the ballot box. The recent success of such a party in Romania is a worrying exception to a positive trend.

All countries concerned have had to subscribe to the basic values of democracy and human rights as set out in the Paris Charter and cooperate within the Organization for Security and Cooperation in Europe (OSCE). Democracy has thereby contributed hugely to continental stability. Professor Miroslawa Marody of the University of Warsaw has analyzed the potential threat of declining public support for accession in the candidate countries in terms of the "sociopolitical dimension of negotiations."[5] She argues that on specific issues that concern them directly social and political groups will try to slow down negotiations if they feel threatened. She sees insufficient knowledge of the accession process and the absence of institutionalized social dialogue as potential threats to the enlargement process. There is, therefore, a real danger that an attempt at quick accession, without adequate public information and involvement in the preparations and negotiations, could fail.

DEMOCRACY AS AN EU GOAL

In this context the decision by the European Council in Copenhagen in June 1993 to include democracy as the first, and nonnegotiable, criterion for EU membership, can be seen as both a contribution to and a reflection of the new situation in Europe where democracy and security are treated as two sides of the same coin. In Copenhagen the European Council included among the binding political criteria for future members the achievement of institutional stability as a guarantee of democratic order and the rule of law, and of ensuring respect for human rights, as well as the protection of the rights of minorities.[6]

This statement was strengthened by the new article F.I of the Treaty of Amsterdam, which stated, for the first time, that if there was a "serious and persistent breach" of basic democratic standards, a procedure could be set in motion to suspend the rights of a member state. The new wording of article O linked this procedure to the accession process, thereby establishing formally what was already the case informally: that countries not having established stable democratic institutions could not aspire to EU membership. This could be seen as adding a note of clarity. It could also, however, be seen as reflecting a doubt that in a rapidly enlarging Union the democratic transition so recently achieved in many countries could not automatically be considered as irreversible.

There can be little doubt that the decision of fourteen member states to arrange the diplomatic isolation of the Austrian coalition between March and September 2000 was intended to signal that the norm-setting process between the EU and its current and future members continues after accession. In September 2000 a special panel appointed by the governments of the member states of the EU to look at the human rights record of Austria concluded that the Christian Democrats' partner in the coalition (the Freedom Party) was a populist right-wing party with radical elements that had, on occasion, generated and played on xenophobia. The report was perhaps little more than an opportunity to get Austria's fourteen partner governments off the hook, but the "wise men's" call for further clarification of existing treaty provisions aimed at reinforcing common European values will certainly bring, in effect, a deepening of the integration process providing mechanisms for the surveillance of the behavior of the parties in government in EU member states. In a study of these events three academic observers referred to this as the "formation of social norms through enlargement practices." EU leaders defended their action as necessary to send a clear political signal that political integration had to be based on the irreversible acceptance of common values.[7] The Treaty of Nice provides in article 7 a formal basis for similar action in the future if the need arises. The Parliament, Commission, or member states will be able to take the initiative to issue warnings to any member state if the majority feels that common values are threatened.

While Mark Mazower[8] is quite correct in warning against any assumption that democracy is somehow naturally suited to Europe, it would be wrong, even in the light of recent events in Austria, to allow Europe's history to encourage a degree of pessimism about future prospects in a way that would undermine the common commitment so frequently made to enlargement of the EU as a contribution to the stability and well-being of all Europeans involved.

There is no doubt that for some, the end of the Cold War came at an "inconvenient" moment. The Cold War and the lack of democracy in Central and Eastern Europe initially provided the project of integration with what Attila Agh has characterized as "its cohesion, sense of purpose and stability."[9] It is, however, equally true that the end of the Cold War meant that democracy could develop as a major objective of evolving EU foreign policy. It was, moreover, the European Parliament that used its budgetary powers to force democracy into a high place on the list of objectives to be set for the assistance programs that were put in place to aid the first postcommunist governments of Central and Eastern Europe.

The advancement of the candidate countries' preparations for enlargement can also be seen as a process whereby democracy is extended, in an irreversible fashion, deep and wide across a region of Europe emerging from decades of dictatorship and/or foreign occupation. The possibility of EU membership has therefore become an extremely effective source of influence on the internal development of the candidate countries. This influence may, of course, be a source of irritation or, as in the case of the Meciar government in Slovakia, a source of open conflict with the government of a candidate country. But this does not detract from its existence as a political fact of life for all the countries involved in the enlargement process. The very fact that Croatia and Turkey were initially left out of this process confirms all the more clearly that a genuine commitment to democratic norms is a condition not just of accession but of arriving at the negotiation table in the first place. It is too early to say whether the end of the Milošević regime will bring stability and democracy to Serbia, Montenegro, and Kosovo. It is, however, clear to their leaders that EU and other Western assistance will depend on their willingness to start on the road to parliamentary democracy and the protection of human rights.

The deep EU involvement in the stability pact for the Balkans led, for the first time, to prospective Union membership for all parts of former Yugoslavia, including Serbia. Similarly in the southern Caucasus, Ukraine, and Moldova, leaders are beginning to identify EU membership as a national strategic goal. While the opening of accession negotiations with such countries is, to varying degrees, a distant prospect, it is not one that the EU dismisses out of hand. The process of conditionality in regard to domestic and foreign policy, as has been applied to Central and Eastern Europe, will therefore be applied to many other countries. In the long term the success of such conditionality can only be positive in terms of pan-European stability. The fact that Belarus is for the time being untouched by this process reflects the lack of democracy inside that country.

The promotion or export of democracy has become an explicit part of the EU purpose in contributing to rebuilding the societies of former communist countries. An example is the PHARE (Poland and Hungary Assistance for Economic Restructuring) democracy program, which provides financial assistance to institutions and NGOs contributing to the development of civil society and parliamentary democracy. Being a candidate in itself restricts a country from moving in any potentially antidemocratic direction. Although countries may dislike being dictated to by the EU, no country now participating wants to be excluded from the enlargement process. This would amount to a national humiliation and bring possible economic disadvantages or unwelcome domestic challenges. In a sense it can be argued that the Brezhnev doctrine of limited sovereignty has already been, in effect, replaced by new and more beneficent constraints on the sovereignty of any country seeking EU membership. As parliamentary democracy can now be said to be firmly established in the twelve countries participating in accession negotiations, the EU has switched the emphasis of its norm setting to the importance of a well-run public administration and judicial system. These are now the principal priorities in the assistance program agreed with candidate countries.

If the Brezhnev doctrine of the 1960s provided an uneasy stability in the heart of Europe, it can be argued that democratization and the drive for EU membership are now the main sources of security and stability for the countries concerned. For this reason many observers remain perplexed by some candidate countries' enthusiasm for early NATO accession. David Gombert, a former adviser to President George H. W. Bush, has argued that it cannot provide the economic advantages of EU membership. He added that "the main threat to Central and Eastern Europe is not of invasion but of internal instability."[10] EU enlargement should strengthen stability and thereby secure the democratic gains won by the people and countries of the regions. Suggestions that Brussels is becoming like Moscow in the Soviet era take the analogy too far because there is no monolithic party structure to back such centralization; moreover, Moscow was the capital of one country, Russia, which dominated the USSR as well as Comecon and the Warsaw Pact.

David Gow has identified very clearly[11] the main ways in which security and democracy have become irrevocably intertwined and of equal importance to both the EU and the candidate countries. He points out that the collapse of communism left behind societies "without the resources, capacities and institutions for autonomous decision making," adding that "a failure by the EU to reach out to Central and Eastern Europe would result in the EU's losing its meaning." This would not only reduce the benefits it provides to its existing members but also result in its missing the chance "to extend the zone of cooperation and integration as widely as possible" in a way that reduces threats to stability and security and creates the conditions favorable for trade and prosperity. The EU interest is not just to ensure that democracy succeeds as an end in itself but also that elections, accountability, transparency, and so on, create the conditions for domestic stability within neighboring (future member) countries.

The building of democracy in the EU neighborhood as part of the enlargement process is therefore in the interest of the EU itself, not least as a way of resolving problems that could have an impact inside the EU. The examples Gow provides of the Kurdish problem and the Yugoslav crisis are all too apposite as reminders of just how great the EU interest is in securing democracy and stability in as wide a geographical area as possible.

Discussions on enlargement sometimes miss these fundamental points as interest inevitably turns to economic and social issues, concerns about cheap labor or new competitive challenges as well as anxieties about immigration and the ability of the EU to function with a much wider membership. Such concerns are not new, but as Christopher Preston reminds us in his review of the four previous enlargements,[12] enlargement has always been part of the historic EC/EU mission. There is nothing new about this link between democratization and enlargement. Greece, Spain, and Portugal were obliged to democratize in order to achieve their ambition to join the Community, as it was then called.

Just as safeguarding democracy can be seen as one of the motives for enlargement, both from the EU and the candidate countries' perspectives, so the advancement of democratization can be seen as part of the preparation for enlargement now well under way in both the candidate countries and the EU itself. The successful advancement of these twin processes of democratization and public acceptance of their consequences may also be seen as conditions for the successful conclusion of the enlargement process. Given the controversy that has often occurred over institutional aspects of European political integration, it should come as no surprise that the completion of the enlargement process, bearing in mind these preconditions, has become problematic inside the EU and some of the candidate countries.

In the Candidate Countries

Attila Agh[13] has clarified the paradox whereby

> former members of the Soviet "external empire" had to be transformed into a new kind of limited sovereignty. This was forced upon them by the network of the all-European organizations as a mandatory adaptation to the New World Order and as an "entrance fee" to these organizations. Thus, the countries concerned regained their sovereignty in the early nineties and were expected to give it up immediately again, so to say, right after the pull-out of Soviet troops.

This was their rather rough introduction not just to the inevitable consequences of an open society and market economy in the era of globalization but also, as they pried open the door to the EU, to the fact that European integration implied the sudden abolition of the frontier between foreign policy and domestic politics, as well as a consequent drastic alteration of the balance between the internal and external aspects of sovereignty.

Some of the most dramatic lessons of this experience might seem uncontroversial: the tough message to Slovakia that unless it established a normally functioning parliamentary democracy and legal system it could not hope to take part in EU accession negotiations; EU insistence on the need for candidate countries to respect ethnic minority rights in Romania, Slovakia, and Latvia has been accepted by the countries concerned and this acceptance has been endorsed by voters in the countries concerned. The ambition of EU membership has similarly pushed forward programs of political decentralization or acceptance of sexual freedom in candidate countries. In short, all candidate countries have been firmly pushed toward consensual democracy. As Agh concludes:

> Democratic transition has not only chronologically coincided with the association to the EU, but there is a deeper connection between them as two sides of the same coin, the internal and external dimensions of the same project.[14]

The problematic stage of this process is now beginning, as the leaders and citizens of candidate countries have come to take their democracy for granted and begin to resent what they see as the excessive submission of their national sovereignty to Brussels. Similarly, as public opinion in the candidate countries becomes aware of some of the consequences of accession (e.g., agricultural reform, sale of land to foreigners), the threat of a possible populist challenge to elite ambitions for EU membership may well emerge. As inside the EU, the challenges will have to be faced up to and resolved through democracy (parliamentary votes, elections, referenda). National leaders in candidate countries delude themselves if they think that the EU member states will do them particular favors during the accession negotiations just because they face the kind of populist backlash that EU leaders faced and overcame in the early 1990s.

Some political leaders have chosen to ride on the waves of or even incite such a backlash. In June 2000 Vaclav Klaus, the chairman of the chamber of deputies of the Czech Republic, suddenly discovered that "Europe is now fundamentally challenging the nation state, particularly its sovereignty."[15]

The fact that he attacked both the temporary EU ostracization of Austria as well as NATO action against Yugoslavia during the Kosovo conflict says more about his attitudes and values than those of the EU. Hungary's prime minister, Viktor Orban, challenged the necessity of the EU action on Austria and openly sought to shore up his popularity with public challenges to the way Hungary was being treated in the accession negotiations. By challenging the

EU governments' action over Austria, such statements open a question as to how far common European values and commitments to integration have been internalized by the candidate countries, or whether the statements their leaders make to back up their accession demands are as much lip service as those that some EU leaders give to enlargement itself. The irony is that any political leader in a candidate country would challenge widespread concern about Haider's long-term goals. Hours after the "ostracizing" of Austria formally ended, he started a campaign for a referendum in Austria in order to block enlargement.

Orban and Klaus challenge the right of the EU to impose certain norms on its current and future members. As one journalist put it,

> Playing on fragile feelings of national pride, both have painted the EU as an overbearing big brother that should reduce itself to little more than a free trade zone if their countries are to join it.[16]

Leaders of EU countries have ridden out such backlashes themselves, but the game being played here is more dangerous. Leaders of candidate countries are in effect challenging not only the asymmetrical nature of the accession negotiations but openly questioning the need for institutional reforms as a condition for the EU itself to be able to enlarge. This, at a minimum, is a recipe for widespread public confusion in their countries and possibly could open up a gulf between themselves and the leadership of the EU at a time when the political goals of integration are being reasserted.

In the European Union: The Role of Parliaments

If the loss of the candidate countries' newly won sovereignty is one of the paradoxical consequences of coming closer to the EU, it is not the only paradox of the current situation. The very fact that twelve countries are queuing up to join the EU, which only recently enlarged from twelve to fifteen states and converted itself from a mere European Community into a monetary and would-be political union, is a clear confirmation of the success of the first forty years of political integration. It also contrasts with the media characterization of an almost permanent crisis of confidence in the EU in the 1990s. If the victory of democracy in Central and Eastern Europe has produced this paradox, it is equally paradoxical to point out that if the enlargement process is to be carried forward to a successful conclusion the EU will itself have to carry forward its own process of internal democratization.

This process has already advanced with a rapidity not expected a decade ago when the first reforms of the Treaty of Rome (by the Single European Act of 1987) were coming into effect. Since the end of the Cold War, three new treaty reforms have been carried out. These reforms have laid the basis for a single currency, a security and defense policy, and substantial extensions of majority voting.

By now the Union's leaders are well aware of the fact that the days when their decisions could be digested by a public opinion characterized by a benign indifference are over. In the first decades of integration its leaders faced few domestic challenges; populist nationalism and calls for greater democracy in the EU had no substantial political audience in the 1950s and 1960s. Early in 1999 the European Parliament forced the entire European Commission to resign after accusing it of mismanaging EU funds. The real issues at stake did not excite public interest and, as the *New Statesman*[17] put it, what Europe now needs is a mature public debate as to how it wishes to develop. Smothering such a debate inside or outside the EU risks a delayed explosion, whereas accepting the need to redefine the goals and methods for a much enlarged Union in a new historical era seems only common sense.

The "problem" in the candidate countries is that for the time being the pro-EU consensus among almost all political leaders means that it is only the opponents of integration who are initiating the kind of debate that has raged for years in, for example, France, Britain, and Denmark. With regard to the issue of enlargement, the public is only just becoming aware of what is involved. More controversy is inevitable as the concrete consequences of enlargement become more widely known. Parliaments are one of the frameworks in which these controversial issues can be aired. As all the countries involved in the enlargement process are parliamentary democracies and as the European Parliament also has to ratify each accession, the parliamentary dimension of the enlargement process exists at various levels. It both reflects and stimulates the necessary and inevitable debate among a wider public opinion on the contents of the accession process. This parliamentary dimension[18] of the enlargement process provides the opportunity for members of the European Parliament and the national parliaments of the candidate countries to work together in monitoring preparations for accession and negotiations on specific issues. The national parliaments of the EU member states are not involved directly in this process. But when the national parliaments and the European Parliament come to ratify accession treaties, they must be sure to reflect, not override, public opinion.

Each parliament has its own job to do. The national parliaments of the EU member states monitor the work of their respective governments. As EU accession negotiations involve, inside the EU alone, fifteen governments *and* the Commission, this will not be an easy task. The national parliaments of the candidate countries only monitor the work of one government, but as negotiations take place in what is in fact an intergovernmental accession conference of sixteen governments, this is only a small advantage, especially given the fact that accession negotiations revolve essentially around if, how, and when the candidates will accept existing EU legislation. It is not a negotiation between equal parties.

At least as parliamentarians, members of the national parliaments of the candidate countries take part in separate joint parliamentary committees (JPCs) with members of the European Parliament (MEPs), where the delegations on each side are of equal dimensions. The MEPs have the advantage of living their political lives inside the EU and therefore being informed about, as well as influencing, EU legislation, budget, and policy development. MPs from the candidate countries can use the JPCs to learn more about where the EU moving train may be headed, but they have no access to the engine room. National parliamentarians from the EU member states and the candidate countries meet regularly in the COSAC (Conference of Standing Committees of the national parliaments dealing with EU Affairs) framework to discuss general EU developments, but it is much too large a framework to deal with the details of the accession negotiations themselves. It is in the JPCs and the European affairs committees, established by the candidate countries' parliaments, that the negotiators and officials from the Commission and the relevant national governments come under pressure to provide details of the results of the screening process and of the outcome of the accession negotiations themselves. Since, however, nothing can be agreed in fact until the negotiations are definitely concluded, the national parliamentarians of the candidate countries will gradually come to terms with the very special kind of horse trading that characterizes EU negotiations. It is interesting to note also that just as the chief negotiators of the first six candidates that began accession negotiations in March 1998 meet regularly to compare notes, so too do the chairmen of the European affairs committees of the six national parliaments concerned. There are also regular meetings of the president of the European Parliament with the presidents of the thirteen countries involved in the enlargement process. These parliamentary contacts can be seen as part of the process of internalization of EU norms and even more as part of the socialization process referred to by Schimmelfennig in chapter 1 of this book.

The JPCs also test the depth of parliamentary democracy and pluralism, and in some cases the behavior of parliamentarians from candidate countries surprises their MEP colleagues. There is sometimes a widespread inability to differentiate between critical observation and hostility, as if questioning a minister's statement about his country's readiness to abide by EU rules challenged the honesty of the government or country as a whole. Similarly, parliamentarians from opposition parties, or media that use the JPC framework to criticize their country's government, have in Slovenia and Bulgaria come under attack for somehow letting down the national cause.

Frank discussion among parliamentarians can provide a firm reminder that there are no shortcuts to accession and that countries slowing down their accession preparations could easily be left behind as more countries join accession negotiations. The active participation of the presidency and the Commission in the work of the JPCs confirms their usefulness as a framework for sending clear messages outside the diplomatic framework and into the heart of the candidate countries' political systems, so that no one is left with any illusions. In this way surprises in the negotiations can be minimized.

Parliaments originally played a role of establishing new relationships with Brussels and Strasbourg in the early 1990s, particularly after the entry into force of the various Europe Agreements, but their role was enhanced once accession negotiations got under way. Once the negotiations end, parliaments and public opinion (including NGOs and representatives of sectoral interests) play the decisive role. Referendum experience in the most recent entrants shows that public opinion should never be taken for granted. Norway's and Switzerland's ambitions to join in European integration remained stillborn when their elites were unable to carry along public opinion. While Agh is right to argue that parliaments should be the chief intermediaries between governments and public opinion, even their active role is not a guarantee of success. There was during Norway's second abortive attempt to join the EU a functioning JPC and an active national parliament. The majority of citizens still voted no.

EU ENLARGEMENT: THE ROLE OF THE PUBLIC

Public attitudes to European issues are often analyzed in terms of such issues as sovereignty or identity. In reality, however, people tend to be more concerned about their personal economic and social prospects than about issues that excite and divide the elites. It may be expected that inside the EU attitudes to enlargement will depend on the general or regional economic situation. Such issues as the possible loss of jobs through cheap competition or the arrival of immigrants ready to work locally for lower wages are likely to have most impact. The possible loss of what is perceived as valuable EU financial assistance is already playing a part in the still nascent debate inside the EU on its prospective enlargement.[19] The salience of such issues also depends on geography. Concerns about the possible consequences of the free movement of labor are likely to be more important in countries and regions bordering on the countries hoping to accede to the EU. The decisions by the European Council in Berlin in March 1999 confirmed the national governments' hesitation to carry out the radical reforms of the CAP (Common Agricultural Policy) and the structural funds, as proposed by the Commission in its *Agenda 2000,* or to expand the EU budget as proposed by the European Parliament. The fact that decisions were taken at all reflected the EU determination to maintain the momentum of the enlargement process, but the absence of real reforms confirmed the views of those jaded observers of EU matters who point out that decisions to undertake fundamental policy or institutional changes are only taken when leaders find themselves up against immediate deadlines. Part of the reason for delay in this case is that leaders found themselves under pressure from sections of public opinion where particular interests were at stake. The regions receiving aid from the structural funds, the farmers and taxpayers in general, are examples. The key therefore for deeper understanding of public attitudes to enlargement inside the EU depends on sectoral or regional interests. By contrast, the political purpose of enlargement in relation to peace and security is the source of the pressure on EU leaders to act in a way intended to maintain the momentum of the enlargement process.

Public opinion will by definition be decisive during and just after the closing phase of negotiations. Unless national leaders inside the EU are confident that enlargement will be accepted by their respective publics (or at least not the subject of any major domestic challenge), they will be hesitant to sign any accession treaties at all. General economic circumstances and possibly (in light of the war in Yugoslavia) international events will influence public attitudes at the decisive moment when it occurs.

As recent studies of public opinion (mentioned above) confirm, EU governments are under virtually no domestic pressure whatsoever to enlarge the EU. In crude electoral terms it would be hard to identify any significant group of electors in any EU member state that would be seriously concerned by an announcement by the EU or its respective national government that enlargement had been indefinitely postponed. An exception could be found in Greece, which is keen to get Cyprus into the EU. Greek voters might be affected by the failure of their leaders to achieve this objective. In the countries of Scandinavia, leaders argued the case for accession or, for the two last EU treaties, in relation to the overriding importance of enlarging the EU to ensure peace and stability. Thus when Bulgaria's former prime minister Ivan Kostov denounced the EU for its lack of vision, its meaningless dictates, and the lack of urgency with which its leaders approach his country's EU ambitions, he would have been better advised to analyze the reasons for what he sees as this kind of discouragement.[20] Bulgaria faces tremendous problems, which have been aggravated by the conflict in the former Yugoslavia and the effective collapse of the Russian economy. This put Kostov under great pressure to improve his people's conditions and produce some progress in relation to EU accession. Unfortunately the leaders Kostov tried to influence in his outburst are not under any such pressure. When Bulgaria complains that the EU is being unreasonable in demanding the closure of a particular nuclear power station, he is right to point out the economic and social consequences and financial costs of such a step. But the public in neighboring Greece, which is at least sensitive to Bulgaria's concerns, is concerned at Bulgaria's unwillingness to close down what is considered to be a dangerous nuclear installation just across its frontier. Given that Bulgaria, along with Romania, will have the greatest difficulty in meeting the criteria for EU membership in the medium term, its leaders might better focus on creating the conditions to overcome public concerns inside the EU as to the consequences of enlargement rather than attack EU leaders for a lack of vision. Bulgaria and Romania are perhaps extreme examples to take, and their objective situation will always be confused in the public mind filled with images of endemic poverty, homelessness, pollution, and rising crime. These prejudices may anger the leaders of the countries concerned, but that is no reason for them to ignore their political consequences in terms of creating a potentially insurmountable barrier to their eventual accession.

Arguments about the cost of enlargement allow politicians to provide a mixture of facts and hyperbole to provoke debate or to score domestic political points, as the Socialist leader in Spain did in March 1999, when he accused Prime Minister Jośe Maria Aznar of selling out Spain's vital national interests in the *Agenda 2000* deal on the future financing of the EU. He argued that Spain would lose out in terms of its receipts in financial aid for structural economic reform in the framework of an agreement by EU leaders effectively fixing budgetary limits up to 2006 and announcing that as of 2003 the EU budget would be in a position to provide such aid to the newly acceding countries. Early in 2001 Aznar took a hard line (in public at least) as to the need to guarantee Spain's receipts from EU funds even after 2006.The candidate countries, which are naturally looking for a speedy conclusion of accession negotiations, have to bear in mind the fact that the EU governments cannot assume that public opinion will easily accept EU enlargement. The need for a cautious approach toward public opinion inside the EU is borne out by a summary of a special Eurobarometer survey on this issue,[21] which found for example that only 13 percent of EU citizens consider enlargement as a priority among the options facing the EU in its relations with countries seeking accession. Sixteen percent favored keeping the EU at its current size. Although only 5 percent wanted to leave the EU altogether, 55 percent felt that the EU should concentrate on its own internal problems. Eurobarometer also confirmed that there are great differences between public opinion in the various member states. Only in Denmark (61 percent) was a majority of public opinion clearly in favor of treating enlargement as a priority. In Greece (47 percent) and Sweden (49 percent) at least more people favored this as a priority instead of opposing it. In both Germany and France well under 20 percent took such a view, which suggests that the decisions taken by the European Council in Berlin and Nice could be considered as modestly courageous under the circumstances. EU leaders would have looked feeble if they had failed to agree on *Agenda 2000* within their announced timetable. Following the Santer Commission's resignation, decisive action was needed to restore confidence and a sense of direction, but on the specific issue of keeping up the pace of preparing the EU for enlargement the main leaders would not directly have lost any votes by failing to agree in Berlin or indeed in Nice.

Describing the future enlargement as a "controversial operation," the study found that the main lines of the current EU approach to enlargement were supported by public opinion. Sixty-seven percent of EU citizens could see that the EU would be more important in world affairs after enlargement. Sixty-one percent could see that Europe could be enriched culturally by enlargement. Nearly 60 percent felt an enlarged EU would give greater guarantees of peace and security in Europe. Fifty-four percent felt that EU institutional reform should take place before enlargement. Similarly, with regard to the criteria for accession, over 90 percent agreed that any future EU member state should respect human rights and democratic principles, and over 70 percent that new member states should be in a position to implement existing EU legislation (*acquis*) or have a level of economic development similar to that of current EU members.

In light of public attitudes for each of the countries seeking accession, it is interesting to note that of the six countries originally participating in the accession negotiations, four (Hungary, Poland, the Czech Republic, and Cyprus) are the only countries where a majority inside the EU clearly favored their joining. Slovenia and Estonia have recently gained or regained their national sovereignty and may be less well known as candidates. The fact remains that seven of the ten countries from Central and Eastern Europe that are seeking to join the EU cannot count on public support for their accession. Not surprisingly, attitudes toward each candidate country vary considerably among the publics of the EU member states. Greeks are almost 90 percent in favor of Cypriot accession while only 30 percent of French people are in favor. This difference of approach was reflected in statements made at the opening of the EU/Cyprus Intergovernmental Accession Conference in Brussels on March 31, 1998. A similar wide range of attitudes is apparent with regard to the accession of the Baltic states and Poland. This situation means that candidate countries seeking to speed up their accession will have to market themselves vis-à-vis the public of all the EU member states and not just rely on parliamentarians and the "friends" they may have sitting across the negotiating table at the accession negotiations.

Leaving aside such special relationships and the question of their real utility in such a complex series of negotiations, the basic fact remains that in only five of the fifteen EU member states is there a majority broadly in favor of the EU enlargement (Sweden, Denmark, Greece, Netherlands, Finland). In four countries less than 30 percent take a similar view. Most importantly France and Germany are in this group, as is Austria along with Belgium. In this context the European Council in Nice in December 2000 decided to aim to conclude some of the accession negotiations by the end of 2002 so that enlargement could begin in 2004.

This important political consideration is confirmed by the comparison with the degree of support within the EU for the enlargement now envisaged. In comparison, the last series of accessions in 1994, a few months before enlargement, were supported by an average of 75 percent within the EU. To ignore this reality would risk reigniting what is widely referred to as the Union's crisis of democratic legitimacy, a crisis that was only narrowly and with difficulty overcome in the early 1990s.

While the idea of enlargement is more widely understood, supported, and viewed with a sense of urgency in the candidate countries, it would be a serious oversimplification to assume that accession is or will remain an uncontroversial issue among the citizens of the candidate countries themselves. The Eurobarometer simply confirms the range of opinions that exists.

In the Baltic countries there is relatively low (around one-third) support for EU accession. In Romania 90 percent want to join the EU. The specific reasons for these differences can be analyzed, but the main lesson, particularly looking at the countries already in the accession negotiations, is that while in the candidate countries EU accession is considered more widely as a positive priority, the picture is complex and, as in any democracy, constantly evolving. A positive vote by, for example, Czech or Estonian voters in referendums on accession cannot be taken for granted, whereas in the four other countries such an outcome is more likely. In all the candidate countries, moreover, there is a large group of citizens without any clear opinion.

Eurobarometer already signaled a substantial decline of support for accession in the candidate countries between 1995 and 1996, just as the Europe Agreements were all beginning to function normally. The Commission study also suggested that citizens of the candidate countries had only limited and hazy knowledge of what joining the EU might actually mean. As Heather Grabbe and Kirsty Hughes[22] point out, this probably reflects the fact that "there is little serious debate in the Central and East European Countries about the desirability of joining the EU." Political leaders and the media see joining the EU as part of their countries' "return to Europe" and treat it as something inevitable and intrinsically linked with transition to parliamentary democracy and a market economy.

There are similarities here with the early days of European integration when the process was elite-led, uncontroversial, and highly political without any precise idea or worry about future developments. Discovering the EU as it is, with its forty years of *acquis,* its single currency, and its evolving political union, is therefore bound to be an unsettling experience to those who understandably take an idealistic, purely political approach of the kind that inspired the European project in the first place. As Agh points out,[23] sloganizing about the "return to Europe" quickly becomes meaningless and is based on a "low level of political and intellectual discourse" without any clear strategy to communicate to the public what EU accession might mean in concrete terms. In this way great expectations have led to quick disappointments, characterized by Agh as "postrevolutionary hangover" or "Eurofatigue" of the populations of the former communist candidate countries.

INSIDE AND OUTSIDE THE EU: DEMOCRATIC PRESSURE IN DIFFERENT DIRECTIONS

Public opinion on the different aspects of enlargement is profoundly unsettled inside and outside the EU. Because political leaders and the media have tended to present an excessively positive view of the political benefits of accession, a more balanced view has not emerged. As attention shifts to the practical questions (costs, sovereignty, identity, legal system, land acquisition, etc.), a major test of the strength of the emerging democracies will take place. The elites will have to handle the challenge from different sectors of society concerned about the possible negative consequences of accession, even as they come up against the tough and unbalanced reality of their accession negotiations. As the domestic debate heats up in the acceding countries, the relatively few sources of information about the EU (national governments, the Commission), which tend to present a very positive picture, will be supplemented by other sources of information (local authorities, industrial sectors, NGOs), which will be looking at accession in terms of their particular interests rather than in broad terms of national political destiny. Such issues as the impact on agriculture and the environmental and social costs will come to the fore. The sense of extreme urgency reflected by the candidate countries' governments and negotiations seems to suggest a fear that a delay could be accompanied by a further decline in public support for this objective. This is virtually the opposite of the situation inside the EU, where the democratic process is producing virtually no desire to speed up enlargement. The difference of approach on the different sides of the negotiating table does not suggest that one side is operating more democratically than the other; it is just that democracy is putting the two sides under completely different kinds of pressure.

Irena Brinar[24] has analyzed the passage from "Europhoria" to "Euro (realism)" in Slovenia. Between 1993 and 1996 there was a big drop in the number of Slovenians with a positive attitude toward the EU. This reflected an evolution from "high and rather idealistic expectations" to a recognition that the EU is not, in fact, an ideal association and that questions of differing national interests remain fundamental. Slovenians have merely come to a more balanced, informed, and realistic view of what the EU will mean for Slovenia. This would seem to be a positive assessment of Slovenia's test of democracy in relation to EU accession. Brinar is right to point out that such a pragmatic, oscillating view of EU membership is rather similar to that of most of the EU countries themselves, in which the EU is subject to substantial criticism without the idea of membership itself being called into question except by fringe parties. Additionally, European issues have been particularly controversial in Slovenia. Fears that Italians expelled by the communist regime in the 1940s might buy back their land at relatively low prices have stimulated parliamentary and public debate.

Poland has also been the scene of lively arguments in the government and the parliament, as well as demonstrations in the streets, as profound concerns about the precise economic and social consequences of accession replace the political aspect at the center of public interest in relation to EU accession. The use of PHARE money, restructuring of the steel industry, and respect for EU competition rules have all become regular subjects of concern. Some Church leaders expressed the fear that, inside the EU, Poland's Catholic identity could be threatened. Euro-skeptical elements have been present in the center-right government of Jerzy Buzek. Rural society feels deeply threatened by the prospect of EU membership. Since the majority in society and parliament remain committed to the aim of accession, however, controversy should be seen as a positive sign that democracy has firmly taken over in Poland.

Overselling of the advantages of membership, ignoring the inevitable problems, or, worse, pretending (as Chancellor Kohl and President Chirac used to do) that the year 2000 would have been the year of Poland's accession have proved counterproductive. This encourages Euroskepticism but, what is worse, it could in due course undermine the Poles' faith in their democratic system. This danger is unlikely to prove unmanageable precisely because most of the candidate countries plan referendums on accession. Democratization and enlargement will, in this way, be linked together as part of the same process. Positions taken by political parties will have to become more sophisticated, combining high politics and low politics. Any attempt to concentrate on the former in order to distract attention from the latter was, anyway, bound to fail. A defeat for pro-EU forces in any of the candidate countries would create the political uncertainty and basis for a purely nationalistic politics of a kind that could, in due course, undermine the democratic achievements of the last decade.

CONCLUSION: DEMOCRACY AND STABILITY

Controversy, divisions, uncertainty, and competition for public support are the normal characteristics of a democratic society. Inside the EU it is now taken for granted that each step forward in European integration will be challenged and that nothing involving public acceptance can be taken for granted. Countries emerging into a democratic dawn are bound to have a different outlook, and these differences between political life and recent history inside and outside the EU make for a gulf in understanding between elected representatives from the two sides.

As Gale Stokes has put it, since 1989 Eastern Europe has lived through the sudden reemergence of many problems that were not allowed to surface. Ethnic politics is just the most explosive of such problems and, as he points out, Western Europe has had generations of experience to cope with pluralism. Experience in Ireland or Corsica or the continuing problems of racism and xenophobia should lead to caution about the relative superiority of Western European democracy. Current EU member states such as Germany, Spain, or Greece fully understand how integration into Europe can be part of an irreversible process of democratization. Stokes is right, moreover, to point out that Central and Eastern European citizens and institutions are not just trying to adapt to the requirements of the market economy or the EU. They are recreating their constitutional systems, their political parties, their health, social security, and education systems, and "confronting many other issues that in major ways have long been regulated in the west. When one couples the sheer magnitude of the problems with the special shrillness in politics that comes from a compromised past, the wonder is not that the East Europeans are having difficulties, but that they are accomplishing anything at all."[25] He concludes that Eastern Europe is not (any longer) in transition but is now having to face the normal struggles and bitterness of pluralist political life.

Both sides can therefore be seen as being engaged in a common exercise involving redefinition of their national political systems in the context of a continuously changing European reality. The sacrifice of sovereignty required of countries joining the EU will never be easy. The fact that most of the twelve countries currently involved in the enlargement process are so small in relative terms brings them straight into the heart of intractable EU problems with democratization: the weighting of votes in the Council of Ministers and the makeup of the Commission. Whatever terms Lithuania, for example, manages to negotiate to join the EU, the basic political fact will remain that its population is equal to less than 1 percent of the current EU population (which is set to grow by 25 percent as a result of enlargement). Its economic weight is even smaller. This is bound to have political consequences, and when it comes under pressure from the EU to take the costly step of closing down its main domestic energy source (a nuclear power plant), the real balance of forces between itself and the EU is all too clear. It is also clear that public opinion cannot fail to see what is happening. As Michael Emerson has put it, "the forthcoming institutional reforms and enlargement of the EU boil down to a few numbers."[26] He is right, but they are very controversial numbers indeed.

Emerson's observation was sadly, if dramatically, confirmed by the embarrassing scenes at the European Council in Nice in December 2000, when EU leaders hammered out a deal on votes in the Council and seats in the European Parliament. A deal struck by the fifteen member states was presented as a fait accompli to the twelve candidates. A new date for a further effort at reform and redefinition was set for 2004, and the newly acceding countries will participate in this next step on the road to political integration. In this way they will become drawn into the ongoing EU constituent process and will have to clarify their own views as to the kind of Union that should evolve after enlargement.

The purpose of drawing attention to the controversial and uncertain democratic dimension of the enlargement process is not to undermine it but to remind all those committed to its success that an enlarged, democratized EU will require legitimization and acceptance by its citizens. The enlargement of the EU will indeed contribute to democratic stability in Europe. An enlarged EU should see the expansion of democracy in Europe as one of its principal objectives and indeed the purpose of its very existence.

This can only be achieved if enlargement is perceived as a process. The EU recognizes that it needs to change to enlarge, and the issues raised (from CAP to institutional reform) have been widely aired in the political system and in public debate for most of the past twenty years. The candidate countries may initially have underestimated the enormity of the step they were taking in presenting their applications for membership.

It is perhaps too easy to present the issues at stake in terms of a purely positive form of interdependence, where everyone emerges a winner. Agh[27] sees democratization, "marketization," and nation building as combined processes for the reorganization of society and as preconditions for Europeanization. The European Union's strategy for enlargement is based on the hope that these combined processes will prove successful and irreversible. It is too early to say whether a positive rather than a negative feedback between the different transformations taking place in former communist countries will always occur. As Europeanization becomes the dominant element, there could be challenges to previously achieved changes in the other transformation processes. The pressure for competition between political parties as well as an increased ability of sectoral interest groups to stand up for their particular interests could still threaten the whole process.

It is all too clear that failure to enlarge would be as damaging a failure for the EU as failure to stay on course for accession would be for any candidate country. The early years of the twenty-first century will show in an epoch-making way whether or not Europeans have learned the lessons of the twentieth century and are able to continue the process of stabilizing democracy and security in the framework of political integration: a process that was begun in the aftermath of a war caused by fascism and Nazism and has now found a new inspiration and sense of purpose following the collapse of communism.

In this context insistence on certain democratic norms as a condition for future EU accession is not just an exercise in the imposition of certain values but a way of ensuring that the project of political integration really is being carried forward on the basis of an irreversible process that will enhance and entrench both common interests and common values.

NOTES

1. Editorial, *Financial Times*, September 18, 2000.
2. European Commission, Enlargement Strategy Paper, August 11, 2000 (COM [2000] 700 fin).
3. "Agenda 2000 and the Accession Process to the European Union," European Parliament Task Force Paper, no. 36 (December 1999).
4. CEORG: Trends in EU, Czech, Hungarian, and Polish Public Opinion on Enlargement, Brussels, October 2000.
5. "Accession Negotiations: Selected Results," *European Integration Studies* 4 (2000). European Institute, Lodz, Poland.
6. "Democracy and Respect for Human Rights in the Enlargement Process of the EU," European Parliament Task Force Paper, no. 20 (April 1998).
7. M. Merlingen, C. Mudde, and V. Sedelmeier, "Constitutional Politics and the Embedded *Acquis Communautaire*," ConWEB 4 (2000) <www.qub.ac.uk/ies> (November 2000).
8. Mark Mazower, *Dark Continent: Europe's Twentieth Century* (London: Allen Lane, 1998).
9. Attila Agh, "The Role of ECE Parliaments in the Pre-accession Strategy," Hungarian Center for Democratic Studies, Budapest Papers, no. 21 (1992), p. 10.
10. *International Herald Tribune*, May 21, 1998, 8.
11. David Gow, "Security and Democracy," in *Back to Europe*, ed. Karen Henderson (London: UCL Press, 1999), 29.
12. Christopher Preston, *Enlargement and Integration in the EU* (London: Routledge/UACES 1997), 3.
13. Attila Agh, "Processes of Democratization in the Central European and Balkan States," Budapest Papers, no. 229 (1998), p. 27.
14. Agh, "Processes of Democratization," 18.
15. "Backlash Grows in Eastern Europe against EU," *International Herald Tribune,* June 29, 2000.
16. "Backlash Grows."
17. "Don't Panic: It's Democracy," *New Statesman*, March 19, 1999, 4.
18. "Enlargement of the Union: The Parliamentary Dimension" (paper presented to the Conference of the International Studies Association, Vienna, September 1998).
19. "Public Opinion and Enlargement," European Parliament Task Force Paper, no. 41 (April 1999).
20. Interview by Reuters, March 1, 1999.

21. Olga Gille-Belova, "Les enjeux de l'élargissement de l'Union européenne dans l'opinion publique," Study for the European Commission, DG 10, 1998.

22. H. Grabbe and K. Hughes, "Central and Eastern European Views on EU enlargement," in Henderson, *Back to Europe,* 188.

23. Agh, Budapest Papers, no. 22, p. 17.

24. Irena Brinar, "Slovenia: From Yugoslavia to EU," in Henderson, *Back to Europe,* 252.

25. Gale Stokes, *Three Eras of Political Change in Eastern Europe* (London: Oxford University Press, 1997), 202.

26. Michael Emerson, *Redrawing the Map of Europe* (New York: Macmillan, 1998), 230.

27. Attila Agh, *The Politics of Central Europe* (London: Sage, 1998), 216.

3

Transferring Transparency: The Impact of European Institutions on East-Central Europe

Alexandru Grigorescu

The growing literature on democratic consolidation emphasizes the accountability and "transparency" of governments as crucial elements needed for the survival of new democracies. In East-Central Europe the many legal provisions needed for transparency (e.g., "access to information" and "freedom of the press" legislation)—have been already put in place. Many of the countries in the area have adopted "access to information" laws before some of the traditional democracies have and thus, formally, are more transparent.

This chapter attempts to explain the impetus behind the adoption of institutions supporting government transparency in East-Central Europe. It suggests that (as in the case of other domestic institutions in the former communist states) domestic norms may be growing stronger but are still not powerful enough to explain the emergence of institutions of transparency. Furthermore, the usual explanations based on the role of "condition setters" or "norm exporters" of European international institutions, such as the EU and NATO, are also not convincing. Neither of these international institutions has made the adoption of comprehensive legislation allowing for transparency a condition for membership. Finally, the arguments linked to "export of norms" of transparency from such institutions to the new democracies is also weak, considering that some of the institutions, like the EU, have themselves been accused of lack of transparency.

This chapter will show how, despite the lack of preexisting domestic norms and of norms imported from the EU and NATO, domestic institutions supporting the free flow of information have nevertheless developed in the area. I argue that such developments are indeed related to the role of international institutions, but that they are unexpected consequences of mechanisms put into place for a variety of other reasons—not directly related to support of transparency and accountability. It is argued here that the states of East-Central Europe have become more transparent because of interactions and processes of providing information demanded by international organizations. Thus as these governments offer much sensitive information to international organizations, their cost-benefit calculations with regard to their "domestic transparency" also changes, leading to the appearance of legislation designed to increase transparency.

TRANSPARENCY AND DEMOCRATIC CONSOLIDATION

The last few decades of the twentieth century witnessed the most impressive "wave of democratization" yet. But the initial excitement of watching country after country shed its authoritarian system soon subsided as events in some new democracies pointed to the possibility of witnessing a "reverse wave" back toward authoritarianism.[1] In political science, the initial interest in transitions to democracy—discussed in the so-called transitology literature—soon gave way to an increased interest in democratic consolidation—reflected in the "consolidology" literature.[2] The growing body of work on democratic consolidation has emphasized that holding free elections, which had long been associated with the *emergence* of democratic systems, is only one of the necessary conditions for *furthering* of democracy. Various other elements—either institutions or norms—are identified as being relevant to the survival of new democracies.[3]

Among the factors identified as being essential to democratic consolidation is the accountability of governments toward the electorate. Democratic theory has long considered that "a key characteristic of democracy is the continued responsiveness of the government to the preferences of its citizens."[4] Such responsiveness should be continuous, that is, governments must be "accountable" to the electorate even between elections. They need to inform the public of their actions and intentions and offer mechanisms through which they can be punished for not being "representative." Thus the "transparency" of governments toward their societies is seen as a necessary factor of government accountability and responsiveness and, implicitly, of a truly democratic polity.

While the above argument for government transparency is a normative one, a second argument has emerged based on more "pragmatic reasons." The starting assumption of this second argument is that citizens' faith in the performance of any government (including democratic ones) is essential to its survival.[5] Thus, in order to maintain themselves, governments should pursue greater transparency in order to create greater understanding and support of their political and economic decisions.

Although the link between democracy and transparency has often been discussed in recent literature, the exact meaning of the latter remains murky. Transparency will be defined here as the ability of any citizen to gain access to information held by government.[6] For political science, the interest in transparency as a means of achieving government accountability has led to a focus on institutions that encourage a constant flow of information from governments to society. Thus political systems in which those who govern offer information only when it is in their interest, on an ad hoc basis, are not "transparent" or accountable. A transparent government is one that is bound by certain institutions or norms to offer information to citizens even when it would prefer not to.[7]

There are two main types of institutions that support government transparency: legislation on access to information[8] (similar to the Freedom of Information Act in the United States) and freedom of the press.[9] Both elements of transparency are crucial. Legislation on access to information has little impact on accountability of governments if the information accessed by one individual cannot be disseminated throughout society. Conversely, a "free press" with no direct access to government information needs to base its stories on back channels and anonymous sources.[10] This often leads to mistakes or distortions in reporting and eventually in citizens' lack of faith in the press which, in turn, affects the ability of the media to play an effective role in monitoring government actions and holding government accountable.

While both such institutions are essential for transparency and accountability of democracies, "freedom of the press" legislation appears to have always been more visible to both political scientists and policy makers. The reason for this may be that a free press has often been linked to "freedom of expression" which, beginning with its prominent role as the First Amendment of the U.S. Constitution, has always been seen as a cornerstone for democracy in countries around the world. Even in its simplest understandings, democracy has been associated with freedom of expression. In a well-known discussion on the simplicity of democracy, John Mueller argued, for example, that democracy is all about being able to "complain." "Democracy is at base a fairly simple thing—even a natural one. If people feel something is wrong, they will complain about it; and some complainers will naturally be led to organize and to try to convert others to their point of view."[11] Yet freedom of expression is not enough even in such a simple understanding of democracy. Before we are able to complain, we need to know what to complain *about* and thus we need to have access to information about government intentions, policies, and outcomes. An accountable and transparent government must allow its citizens access to official information.

While it may be difficult to understand why freedom of expression has been discussed more than freedom to access government information, empirical data show that the former has traditionally been better respected by governments than the latter. Thus, while freedom of the press has been protected by laws in traditional democracies for decades or even centuries, access to information legislation has only just recently emerged. Before 1980, there were only six countries in the world that had adopted such legislation.[12]

This chapter will assess the degree to which the two conditions necessary for government transparency (access to information and freedom of the press) exist in six countries in East-Central Europe: Bulgaria, Czech Republic, Hungary, Poland, Romania, and Slovakia.[13] I will show that the institutions supporting transparency have surprisingly been put in place very quickly, even if the practices and norms appear to be somewhat lagging. This encouraging development is not to be found in other areas of the third wave of democracy such as Latin America or most of the former Soviet Union. It is relevant, therefore, to study the emergence of institutions of transparency in East-Central Europe so we can better understand the factors that have allowed for them in this area of the world and not in others. The importance of transparency and accountability in all new democracies encourages us to ask what elements are present in East-Central Europe and are not elsewhere. The presence and role of European institutions are emphasized here as possible explanations of such developments.

Within the political science literature, there has been a growing interest in the role that norms "exported"[14] from international organizations have on the domestic changes within countries. Especially the European international organizations—with highly democratic members and, in some cases, with stated goals of promoting democracy—have been seen as generating and "exporting" norms of democracy to less democratic states. This study will discuss the possible appearance of a "norm of transparency" in East-Central European countries in the past decade and the role that international institutions may have had in generating and exporting such a norm. In doing so, it also discusses *what types* of international institutions are more likely to have an impact on domestic transparency, either through the mechanism of norm export or through other mechanisms. Since it emphasizes characteristics of organizations as "independent variables," the conclusion of this study should be viewed as relevant to other new democracies and should be considered as "transferable" to other parts of the world.

INSTITUTIONS SUPPORTING TRANSPARENCY
IN EAST-CENTRAL EUROPE

The countries of East-Central Europe emerged in 1989 from some of the most repressive political systems in the world. Although among these countries there were small variations in the degree of repression, under communism their policies with regard to information flow toward their societies were very similar. There is general agreement in the political science literature that communism was maintained in these countries by government force and that the government's control of all means of communication and information was necessary in order to maintain this control over the population.[15] It has been noted as far back as the writings of Barrington Moore that the control and deliberate manipulation of the media were essential functions performed by the Stalinist-type state.[16] Secrecy, use of rumors, and propaganda were necessary tools for this endeavor.

The government's need to control information in the communist system was well explained in Vaclav Havel's essay "The Power of the Powerless." Havel argues that in the communist era, ideology was a crucial "instrument of internal communication which assured the power structure of inner cohesion." Because ideology was built on lies, it was essential for communist governments to not allow dissent and alternative information flow, so as not to jeopardize their control on society.[17] In those days, individuals knew not only that they would not be given official information if they requested it, but that the simple act of requesting information would most likely be dangerous for them and their families. The press was completely controlled by government, and external sources were limited as much as possible. In many of these countries foreign broadcasts such as the VOA and Radio Free Europe—the last sources of external information—were jammed.

The overthrow of communism in East-Central Europe in 1989 brought about a rapid reduction in official restraints on the press. This permitted the media to take a lead role in the political changes in these countries. The number of newspapers, journals, radio, and television stations increased dramatically. In Romania, for example, the absence of official restraints led to a tripling of the number of publications from 1989 to 1991. Circulations also skyrocketed. The two main dailies in Romania published a combined 3.2 million copies per day (in a country with a population of about 22 million) less than a month after the overthrow of Ceausescu.[18]

The past decade has seen the adoption of laws with regard to freedom of the press in all of the former Soviet bloc countries. Although in some cases the legislation was sharply critiqued in civil society, by the free press, and by the West,[19] overall the general trend for the last years has been toward institutions supporting a free press.

The 2001 press freedom survey by Freedom House shows that of the six countries, five were in the category of having a "free press" by the end of 2000, while Romania was "partly free."[20] Together they score far better than the world average[21] and better than the vast majority of other countries of the "third wave of democracy" in other parts of the world. Most countries compare well with the traditional democracies and some (like Poland) score even better than countries like France and Italy.

If one focuses specifically on the rating these countries receive on "laws and regulations that influence media content," the six countries of East-Central Europe have just as good scores on this scale.[22] Furthermore, one can find more Western democracies that have lower scores than the best-scoring countries in East-Central Europe.

The Freedom House surveys indicate that the legislation supporting a free press in East-Central Europe has improved greatly in the past decade. Even if one considers that such scores are open to the biases of the evaluations, the differences between the six countries in 2000 and in 1989 are obvious. Other measures of freedom of the press support the Freedom House data.[23]

If one looks at the legislation regarding freedom of information, the trends in the six countries are even more astounding. In the past ten years, all of these countries have included the right to access information in their constitutions, and four of them (Hungary in 1992, Czech Republic in 1999, and Bulgaria and Slovakia in 2000) have also adopted specific freedom of information legislation. These figures are impressive considering that only eleven Western democracies had adopted such acts by 1990. Freedom of information acts were adopted by "traditional" democracies as late as 1990 in Italy, 1994 in Belgium, 1996 in Iceland, 1997 in Ireland and Norway, and 1999 in Japan. Others, like the United Kingdom, Austria, Luxembourg, and Germany (at the federal level)[24] have not adopted such a law even now. (Since the completion of this research, Poland, Romania, and the United Kingdom have also passed freedom of information laws.)

More specific laws supporting transparency have also emerged in some of the six countries in the past decade. All of them have adopted external audit and control mechanisms. Some (like Romania) have introduced the institution of ombudsman, which offers individuals the opportunity to request information about government abuses.[25]

Not only have these countries created institutions allowing for an increase in the amount of the information they are making available, they have also adopted institutions allowing for the improvement of the *quality* of such information. Their ability to aggregate the data that they hold has substantially improved through an overhaul of their economic and financial statistics systems. The Czech Republic, Hungary, Poland, and Slovakia (as well as Estonia, Latvia, Lithuania, and Slovenia) were among the first countries that volunteered to offer data on the IMF special data dissemination standard. They were considered by the IMF as meeting the specifications for quality, coverage, periodicity, and timeliness of information.[26] Bulgaria and Romania have also been praised by the IMF for their efforts to improve the quality of their data,[27] although they have not achieved the level of the aforementioned group of countries.

Some have adopted environmental laws that also include provisions detailing specific information that citizens can access. Others have enacted legislation for transparency in campaign financing which, in some cases, are more progressive than in established democracies.[28]

All of these examples show that the six countries discussed here have built a complex set of domestic institutions that encourage transparency. Such legislation should induce governments who collect and aggregate information from substate actors to offer it to the public. Furthermore, legislation on free press should allow for such information to be spread within society. Yet we should differentiate between the simple adoption of legislation supporting transparency and actual practices in these countries.

PRACTICES WITH REGARD TO TRANSPARENCY

The concept of democracy is among the most complex ones used in political science and has allowed for various definitions and uses. One of the principal distinctions between types of democracy has been the one between "formal" and "substantive" democracy. Formal democracy is defined by a set of rules, procedures, and institutions, while substantive democracy is defined in terms of the processes that allow the governed to influence the decisions of those that govern. More precisely, while the former is determined by institutions, the latter is determined by actual behavior and the way the institutions are implemented. The literature on East-Central Europe has emphasized that while in these countries institutional, formal prerequisites for democracy have generally been fulfilled, the level of democratic behavior and the necessary norms that come with democracy are still lagging.[29]

In the case of government transparency, one can point to various kinds of proof of such lags. For example, one indirect measure of behavioral levels of opaqueness is the level of corruption. Low corruption does not necessarily imply high levels of government transparency, as some closed authoritarian systems like Singapore with a very low level of corruption demonstrate. Yet, in most cases, high corruption clearly thrives in an environment of low transparency. The international nongovernmental organization Transparency International has issued a measure of corruption starting with 1995. Countries are rated yearly based on a series of surveys from different institutions reflecting perceptions of businesspeople, the general public, and country analysts. In the 1999 survey Hungary was ranked the thirty-first least corrupt country of ninety-nine surveyed, the Czech Republic thirty-ninth, Poland forty-fourth, Slovakia fifty-third, Bulgaria and Romania were among the five countries tied for sixty-third to sixty-eighth place. The average corruption score of the six was 4.05 (out of a possible 10 score for least corrupt countries)—lower than the average 4.44 for all countries. Even if one takes into account that the general average may be skewed by not including all countries and that corruption may also be related to low GDP, the East-Central European countries have clearly been identified as very corrupt by many different sources.[30] This indicates that behaviors related to transparency are not as high (relative to other countries) as the levels of institutions.

Focusing on the Freedom House measurement of the actual violations against the media (regardless of the institutional constraints) reveals a very different picture than the one depicted by institutional criteria alone. The average score of the six countries is about 2.5 out of a maximum of 10 (representing a maximum number of violations against the media)—very close to the average 2.8 of the entire set of countries. This is especially high considering that most of the Western democracies have almost perfect scores on this scale.[31]

One possible explanation for the less transparent practices in East-Central Europe is that the institutions of transparency that have been put in place may have simply been copied from Western models without having been accompanied by behavioral "norms of transparency."[32] Such lags in norms of transparency should be expected in societies emerging from the closed, secretive communist systems that still suffer from what some consider to be the lingering "culture of secrecy."[33] In Romania, the emergence of a draft law on "state secrets"—which states that access to public information is guaranteed only in exceptional cases[34]—sparked debate on the culture of secrecy. Critics of the state secrets law showed how the practice and culture of secrecy have persisted, although the postcommunist constitution allowed for access to information. The norms of secrecy were seen as being especially strong within the bureaucracy (in great part inherited by the post-1989 governments from the communist era).[35] Some have argued that such bureaucracies, socialized within the old culture of secrecy, are to blame for its perpetuation.[36] The degree of secrecy is so high that even Ludovic Orban, a top political appointee who ran the Romanian government's public information department in the late 1990s, complained about the bureaucratic red tape and difficulties he had in accessing information from other public institutions.[37]

The culture of secrecy is not limited to Romania, where one might expect a lingering effect of decades of repression under the infamous *Securitate* "secret police." Secrecy appears to be embedded in all of the six countries. A Freedom House study shows that data on budgets, economic statistics, public procurement, privatization, tax revenues, and court proceedings are difficult to obtain even in countries where comprehensive legislation for access to information is in place.[38] Even in the apparently more open political systems such as the Czech Republic or Hungary, one finds evidence of lagging norms of transparency. Hungarian Interior Ministry officials acknowledge that they, like most other bureaucrats, still have "a hedgehog reaction," refusing any comment to journalists who request information from them. Instead of using a press story as a basis for investigation, such officials are reluctant to follow up even detailed allegations.[39] The bureaucracy in Hungary is blamed—just as in Romania and other Central and East European countries—for much of the government's culture of secrecy. It is, for example, cited as the main cause for the slow pace with which the files of people who had been spied on by the Hungarian police during communism are currently being released.[40] Even the Czech Republic, considered in many ratings as the most transparent in East-Central Europe, is still plagued by lack of transparency in the economic realm.[41] Its system of military contracting is especially prone to corruption. Also, it has been noted that, although the national parliament's meetings are open to the public, the workings of local councils are often more opaque.[42]

The lack of transparency cannot be blamed entirely on "legacies of the past." Political scientists have argued that it is not only the old elites who can slow down the process of democratic consolidation but also the new ones.[43] Especially in countries in which the political changes take place simultaneously with the economic ones, the new elites have an interest in maintaining conditions that can potentially bring them material benefits. Stephen Holmes points out that in East-Central Europe there are important groups today, with ties to corrupt government officials, that have interests in the vagueness of laws and in lack of transparency. He notes that "successful office holders throughout the post-communist world have no immediate interest in the creation of political transparency or a rule governed polity and economy."[44]

If norms of transparency can be expected to be lacking among the elites who might have an interest in perpetuating secrecy, it is more interesting that the culture of secrecy appears to be present at the mass level as well, where one might expect to find interest in greater transparency. This is not to say that the public does not want more information from governments. The few studies that have been done on this topic show that, just like many publics in the world, East-Central Europeans are disappointed with the quality[45] and amount[46] of information they receive from their government. They generally want government to open up more and to offer more trustworthy information.

Although disappointed by the information they receive from their governments, the societies from this area still do not perceive as strongly as Western societies do that access to government information is a right they should have. One of the few surveys focusing on attitudes toward freedom of information found that more than half the population in the Czech Republic and Hungary supports even greater bans on access to information than are currently in place. For example, 56 percent of Czechs and 51 percent of Hungarians support a ban on "publication of embarrassing details about the private lives of government ministers." These figures are far higher than the ones in Western Europe—even higher than in countries like the United Kingdom that only adopted legislation on access to information in December 2000 (after four of the countries in this study already had adopted FOI laws).[47]

The conclusions that can be drawn from these few studies of norms of transparency are mixed. While societies still do not trust governments and seem to want more information about their inner workings, they are not willing to force their governments to improve their transparency. Moreover, although transparency and freedom of the press is an important issue for most societies, decision makers know that its relevance is minimal compared to other issues in an era of multiple reforms. They know that support or lack of support for access to information or freedom of the press legislation is not likely to weigh heavily in their ability to be reelected. Yet, even with a relative lack of domestic norms of transparency, institutions supporting the free flow of information have been adopted in most East-Central European countries. If the norms of neither elites nor publics can explain this outcome, the laws may be the result of external constraints.

THE ROLE OF EUROPEAN INSTITUTIONS
IN FOSTERING TRANSPARENCY

The fact that East-Central European systems have already adopted the institutions supporting transparency but not the norms may, at first glance, not be surprising. Many of the democratic institutions in these countries have been adopted under the pressure of some of the international institutions (especially European ones), even when domestic norms did not exist to support them.

Almost as soon as the Central and East European countries found themselves free of the Soviet dominance, they used their regained sovereignty to redirect their foreign policies toward European institutions and, ironically, to constrain their sovereignty once more by accepting conditions set out by the Council of Europe, the EU, and NATO. Their initial requests for membership were greeted with various degrees of readiness. While the Council of Europe quickly laid down a set of criteria that new members had to meet, it took NATO and the EU several years to offer the first guidelines for possible accession. Although their approach to enlargement was somewhat different, all three organizations eventually set out certain core conditions that had to be met before membership would be possible. These conditions reflected an intertwining of normative and pragmatic goals of the Western states.[48]

Perhaps no set of conditions reflects such intertwining as well as those pertaining to democracy. The Council of Europe, the first institution the East-Central European countries set out to join, tried to use the application process as a tool for furthering political changes in the area.[49] The EU, while not making clear at first if the countries of the area would or would not be accepted as members, used some of the mechanisms for cooperation with these countries to push for greater democracy. EU support for pluralist democracy in these countries was made explicit in the documents relating to the PHARE (Poland and Hungary Assistance for Economic Restructuring) program for assistance to East-Central Europe, in the Europe Agreements, as well as in the statute of the newly created European Bank for Reconstruction and Development.[50] NATO also set out conditions related to democracy both for Partnership for Peace (PfP) and later for full membership.[51]

On one hand, these three organizations based their support for democracy in the area on principles that had either explicitly or implicitly been included in their founding documents many decades ago. On the other hand, democratic principles such as tolerance and restraint from using violence were also seen as practical solutions to problems involving the stability of an unpredictable area of the world that was on Western Europe's doorstep.[52] Many felt that the greatest impetus for accepting EU and NATO enlargement came after the outbreak of war in the former Yugoslavia in 1991. With that war, Western powers realized that other parts of Eastern Europe could be engulfed by conflict if they were not induced to adopt more tolerant policies, both domestically and toward their neighbors.[53]

Because of the pragmatic importance of democracy as a source of stability in the area, much of the Western emphasis on democracy was on "consensual" democracy and the inclusion of large ethnic, religious, or political groups in the political process.[54] After the lessons of ethnic conflict in Yugoslavia and in some former republics of the Soviet Union, it is not surprising that much emphasis was set on minority rights. The Council of Europe as well as the Organization for Security and Cooperation in Europe (OSCE) adopted frameworks for the protection of minority rights.[55]

Of the three organizations, NATO was the one that focused on issues of security. While external factors had traditionally been the emphasis of NATO security concerns for the area, the internal ethnic conflicts that erupted early after the end of the Cold War made the alliance emphasize some domestic factors as part of its interest in East and Central Europe. Thus the Partnership for Peace was intended, in part, to bolster democratic reforms in the new democracies.[56] Although the prospect for joining NATO may have had an indirect effect on the domestic struggles between reformers and old elites, NATO had few direct requirements regarding institutional changes: civilian control over the military and making their defense budgets public.[57] The thinking behind the requirement of transparency of defense budgets was that they would "facilitate public scrutiny and legislative supervision, as well as reduce suspicions in neighboring states."[58]

While budget transparency is emphasized as an important factor in furthering democracy, NATO requirements targeted only the military realm. On one hand, this interest in a narrow component of government transparency can be interpreted as the organization's sense that requiring greater transparency in realms in which it is not designed to function is not "adequate." On the other hand, it can also be interpreted as an emphasis on the pragmatic goals of NATO members. One could, for example, argue that NATO was more interested in the openness of East European governments toward *other* governments (including Western ones) than to their own population.

The West's interest in increased transparency in the military realm increased in the early 1990s. During the Gulf War, Western countries sometimes found themselves fighting against weapons that they themselves had supplied. After the war, it became apparent how advanced Iraq had actually been in its programs for developing weapons of mass destruction. These shocks led in the early to mid-1990s to an even greater desire than before to reduce, where possible, the uncertainty of the international environment and an increased impetus for transparency in the military realm. Among the more successful results of the international push for greater transparency were the UN Register on Conventional Arms established in 1992 and the Chemical Weapons Convention, which entered into force in 1997. In this general context of increased emphasis on greater openness, it became even more important for NATO that former enemies from the now defunct Warsaw Pact should join PfP and begin offering an abundance of information on their military preparedness and on their programs. As PfP has developed, NATO officials have argued that the transparency and cooperation among members in the partnership is almost as great as for full NATO members.[59]

The European Union's complex programs for helping East-Central European countries prepare for accession had a greater democratic component than NATO's program for the area. One of the membership requirements of the Copenhagen European Council was specifically "stability of institutions guaranteeing democracy, rule of law, human rights and respect for protection of minorities."[60] The PHARE program, the main channel for the European Union's financial and technical cooperation with the countries of East-Central Europe, was set up in 1989 to support not only economic transitions but also political ones. The budget of the program for the 1990–1994 period was a hefty €4.2 billion. In the 1995–1999 period it was increased to €6.7 billion. A specific Democracy Program was built into PHARE, with a declared goal to "encourage non-governmental organizations that act to boost civic society and democracy in their countries by offering grants to projects that fulfill certain conditions."[61] The annual budget for democracy programs for all countries, however, is just slightly more than €10 million—far less than what is allocated for other purposes by PHARE.

The projects that have been funded through PHARE have rarely been intended to bolster a free press or "access to information." This is in part due to the recognition that the Council of Europe is the institution that deals with such issues. The EU typically funds through PHARE projects that help develop and coordinate NGOs, projects focusing on the improvement of the situation of ethnic minorities, and so on. But EU caution in requiring greater openness from member governments—or from prospective members—is also due to accusations about the lack of openness within *its own* workings.

The great success of the EU has been attributed by some to its opaque character as opposed to its democracy. Some observers point out that the "culture of secrecy" within the organization was the result of the initial design and that it was intended to offer greater efficiency by not publicizing dissent.[62] Yet the 1992 Danish "no" to the Maastricht treaty, as well as the close result in France and the British government's ratification problems in the House of Commons, were considered signs of the legitimacy problems the organization eventually developed and of the need for a more transparent policy-making process.[63] The first debates on the increase of transparency within the EU took place only in October 1992 at the Birmingham European Council. By 1994, both the Council and the European Commission adopted their own internal decisions on increased public access to their documents. With the 1995 accession of Finland and Sweden (both considered as representing some of the most "transparent" systems of government), there has been an even greater impetus for change with regard to the openness of the EU policy-making process.

Yet the process leading toward greater transparency and access to information generated by the European Union has only begun. The "culture of secrecy" is considered to remain deeply entrenched. An example of the opaque nature of the EU bureaucracy was recently offered. When the Council of Ministers drew up its first report on how the new code on access to public documents was working, for several months the report itself was kept secret at the insistence of just two member states: France and the Netherlands. Only after two months and much internal dissent was the report made public.[64]

Another example of the EU's lack of openness as compared to some of the most transparent governments in Europe was emphasized by a 1995 "test" conducted by a group of Swedish journalists. Twenty documents related to Europol were simultaneously requested by them from the Council and from the Swedish government. While the Council only issued four of those documents citing problems of confidentiality, the more transparent Swedish system issued eighteen of them.[65] Other similar examples have been cited as proof of a lingering culture of secrecy within the EU.

It is not surprising that an international organization itself accused of lack of transparency has not requested governmental transparency from member states or from prospective members. The EU has not emphasized the implementation of "access to information" legislation for either existing members or future members. Moreover, it is possible that EU norms of opaqueness have actually perpetuated the lack of transparency within countries where a culture of secrecy had existed prior to the accession to the EU or EC. For example, Antonio Barreto points out that in Portugal, although the European institutions played a decisive role in the first stages of democratization and democratic consolidation, their long-term impact in developing a modern transparent and participatory parliamentary democracy has been limited. He notes that "since Portugal acceded to the EC (now the European Union), contact with European institutions has brought pressure for modernization of surviving nondemocratic administrative and business practices. Such modernization, however, is markedly technical and moderately political; there has been no accompanying access to citizen participation. In short, modernization is not necessarily democratization."[66]

The one exception to EU indifference toward domestic transparency can be found in the environmental realm. In 1990 Council Directive 90/313 was adopted on the "freedom of access to information on the environment" specifying that member states must adopt legislation that ensures the freedom of access to, and dissemination of, information on the environment held by public authorities. Even such an act had great difficulties in being passed.[67] The adoption of this directive was only possible after almost all EU members (and especially the most powerful ones) had already passed national legislation supporting the release of information in the environmental realm. Adoption of a similar directive for general access to information (not just in the environmental realm) has not been possible because many member countries have only recently (and some have never) passed national laws supporting it. Thus it has been argued that the EU lack of will in pushing for greater transparency in East-Central Europe is also due to the lack of a "culture of transparency" in some major EU countries.[68]

Members of the EU with a less transparent culture have not supported much change in the institution's practices with regard to access to information. Thus Britain, France, and the Netherlands, for example, are said to pay lip service to the need for greater transparency in the EU but resist changes of the existing access to information policies.[69] As soon as the EU began discussing the possibility of opening up more to the public, the Dutch presidency argued that only documents originating in the EU should be made available to the public and not those that are received from other states. The Dutch influence, as well as that of other states, led to the adoption of Declaration no. 35, emphasizing that documents circulating within the EU but originating from member states can be requested by governments to remain confidential.[70] The struggle between groups advocating greater transparency in the European Union and those asking for less does not appear to be over. Until the EU adopts its own clear policies with regard to access to information, it will not be able to convince East-Central European states that they should become more transparent.

Of the three key European international organizations, the Council of Europe appears to have made the greatest effort for more transparency in East-Central Europe. This is not surprising, since it is the one organization of the three discussed here that has set down as its *main* mission the creation and endurance of parliamentary democracies respecting human rights and the rule of law among the European states.[71]

On paper, the Council has been, so far, the only European organization to adopt a common view on access to all government-held information—not just information in one particular field. As the protector of the European Convention of Human Rights, it is empowered to ensure that (among other rights) the "freedom to hold opinions and to *receive* and impart information" (emphasis added) is guaranteed. But this 1953 document has been criticized for its rather broad and vague limitations to this right. Thus the right may be circumscribed in the "interests of national security, territorial integrity or public safety, for the prevention of disorder and crime, for the protection of health and morals, for the protection of the reputation and the rights of others, for preventing the disclosure of information received in confidence, or for maintaining the authority and impartiality of the judiciary."[72] Much later the Council adopted a more specific view of access to information. In 1981 it adopted Recommendation R(81)19 on the access to information held by public authorities and in 1982 a declaration on the freedom of expression and information. But neither the Council's declarations nor its recommendations have a binding character (as, for example, the European Convention on Human Rights or the EU directive mentioned earlier). It may not be surprising, therefore, that the countries of the Council of Europe accepted such documents on access to information in this forum while they did not do so in the EU, where decisions have a much more binding character. This "lack of bite" of some of these Council of Europe documents can also explain the surprising fact, for example, that they were adopted in 1982, when only seven Council of Europe members had actually adopted specific access to information legislation and could technically fully abide by the principles in such a declaration. The lack of real power of such documents is reflected in the fact that, although the Human Rights Court has heard and expressed itself on cases involving abuses against journalists thus promoting greater freedom of press,[73] it has not been as adamant about "transparency" and actual access to information.

Some argue that we should take a broader view of the Council of Europe's role in pursuing greater government transparency, beyond simply focusing on those cases in which it chides governments for infringements of human rights. As Jeffrey Checkel points out, much of the compliance with Western procedures and norms is also the result of "policy dialogues, jawboning, learning, persuasion, and the like."[74] Such socialization would appear to be an important part of the Council's policy of "transferring transparency" to East-Central European countries.

The directorate general of human rights of the Council of Europe runs a series of cooperation and assistance programs in Eastern Europe, including one in the "media field." The activities for the development and consolidation of democratic stability (ADACS) include organizing seminars and roundtables, "study visits" for East European officials and experts to acquaint themselves with practices and legislation in West European countries, and expertise missions to help draw up media laws and access to information laws. Once again, the emphasis is on "freedom of the media" legislation rather than "access to information." Thus it is noteworthy that only 17 of the 373 aforementioned activities focus directly on access to information issues and, moreover, that this smaller set of programs has emerged only in the past several years. Of the six countries discussed here, only two of them have actually been the recipients of such programs (Bulgaria and the Czech Republic)[75] and only after they appeared committed to adopting such legislation in the first place.

Last but not least, the activities of the Council of Europe may be useful in supporting transparency by bolstering the reformers in East-Central Europe in their struggle with elements of the old elites.[76] The success of the reforms set down by the new elites depends in part on the help of international organizations. The economic and military successes of the West have led to the public perception in East-Central Europe that domestic policies supported by Western organizations such as the EU, NATO, or the Council of Europe, even in noneconomic and nonmilitary realms, are likely to bring long-term benefits to their new democracies. Elites in East-Central Europe use such perceptions to their own benefit by explaining many of their domestic policies and decisions (which often imply painful short- and medium-term sacrifices for their population) as "required" or "supported" by Western organizations. Thus, for example, the Croatian supporters of a law on access to information improved their chances of having it passed by presenting it as "based upon the Croatian Constitution and the documents of the Council of Europe."[77]

It is noteworthy that the Council does not organize any workshops and does not send expertise missions to countries lacking apparent initial interest in adopting legislation on access to information. Such expertise missions are only organized at the request of public authorities (i.e., governments or parliaments).[78] This raises the question of why there has been such an interest in legislation supporting transparency in so many countries in East-Central Europe in the first place.

The above observations indicate that if the European institutions had a *direct* impact on furthering transparency in these countries (through conditionality, export of norms, or supporting certain reformist groups), such influence was either minimal (as in the case of the Council of Europe) or related to a narrow issue area (such as the environment in the case of the

EU and military budgets in the case of NATO). We thus need to move beyond such "direct" mechanisms and consider an "indirect" mechanism that may have had an impact on the adoption of domestic legislation for access to information in East-Central Europe.

AN INDIRECT PROCESS OF EXPORTING TRANSPARENCY THROUGH EUROPEAN INSTITUTIONS

Even with such relatively low impetus from international organizations, and with relatively low levels of norms of transparency, the countries in East-Central Europe *are* adopting legislation for greater transparency. How can this apparent anomaly be explained?

One possible explanation focuses on the role of international organizations but not on the traditional mechanisms discussed in the literature. The process of accession to NATO and the EU, as well as to other international organizations, has at minimum obligated the Central and East European governments to generate and offer to international organizations (IOs) an enormous amount of information. Moreover, due to the uncertainty of some Western countries with regard to the usefulness of enlarging efficient organizations like the EU and NATO, additional mechanism and institutions were created in order to slow down the process of accession.[79] NATO created the North Atlantic Cooperation Council and the Partnership for Peace as an intermediary step to NATO accession. The European Union initiated, after several years of dialogue, the association agreements with East-Central European countries. All of the mechanisms and stages that were developed by the European institutions required the elaboration of numerous questionnaires and studies from prospective members.

For their part, the East-Central European countries saw the process of offering correct and timely information to these organizations as an important part of "the race" against one another to join the West.[80] The enormous bureaucracies that before 1989 were used to control the East-Central European societies and planned economies have been somewhat downsized. The remaining offices have shifted much of their effort from "regulating" the economy to writing up studies and generating data for international organizations. Entire "departments for integration" were created within ministries and, in many cases, "ministries of integration" emerged in these countries. All of these institutions are meant to interact and exchange information with the European institutions, especially with the European Union. Although the EU has not emphasized the norm or practice of transparency of governments, it has emphasized the quality of data generated by governments and received from them. "Statistics" is one of the thirty-one chapters of the screening process prospective members must go through before joining the EU.

Thus, although the "domestic transparency" of these countries has certainly improved, one can argue that their "external transparency" (i.e., the flow of information toward external actors—especially IOs) has improved dramatically and may actually be the driving force behind the legislation allowing for access to government information. As already mentioned, many of the political elites of these countries have attempted to use international institutions that were known for their success in bringing prosperity (EU) or security (NATO) in order to boost domestic support of their policies. For that, they were ready to "please" IOs and their bureaucracy by (among other actions) offering the suggested information and by offering it on time. The European organizations have generally been pleased by the amount of information coming from these countries. Although one may expect this because of the relevance of the European institutions for the six countries, similar external transparency can be found even toward other international organizations such as the World Bank, the IMF, and the UN.[81]

It is relevant that this increasing external transparency comes just as international organizations are themselves offering more information directly to domestic audiences. The 1990s saw increasing debate about the need for greater accountability and transparency to the general public of international organizations such as the EU,[82] the World Bank,[83] the regional development banks,[84] and the IMF.[85] Such debates resulted from the success and consequent impact that such international organizations had on societies.[86] Whether such arguments are credible or not, the result of these debates was a significant change in the 1990s of the public information disclosure policies of many of these organizations. Thus many international organizations, including the European ones, are now making more of the information that they receive from governments available to domestic audiences. The press in East-Central Europe, for example, often picks up information directly from IOs. Some of the information that comes back toward societal actors criticizes decisions and policies of the East-Central European governments.[87]

The East-Central European governments thus recognize that much of the information they used to control now has an indirect way of reaching their domestic audiences. This in turn leads to an understanding by the elites in these countries that they have little to gain by continuing to control it. There is an incentive to open up domestically even when "norms of transparency" are not yet fully rooted. It is the process itself of giving information to external actors that is key to changes in domestic politics of access to information.

The existence of institutions of transparency in East and Central Europe might thus be explained through a mechanism of "import of transparency" from the external realm to the domestic one. Yet such export is not the one suggested in other literature as being based on conditionality or norms. The link is of a different type and is possible due to the specific character of the subject under study: information. Information circulates between many different actors across different levels of analysis. Government elites are caught up in a "two-level informational game"[88] in which they need to take into account what information to make available to domestic audiences and to external actors. The decisions they make at one level have an impact at the other level. By deciding to offer more information to the large number of international organizations they are now dealing with, they are indirectly offering more information to their societies and thus creating conditions for greater domestic transparency.

A well-known example of this logic is the Soviet reaction to the 1986 Chernobyl accident. There are indications that Soviet president Mikhail Gorbachev initially wished to withhold information about the Chernobyl disaster from the Soviet society. Yet, due to the USSR's obligation to offer the International Atomic Energy Agency (IAEA) access to information—which in turn would have made it public—he decided to have his government offer the information about the disaster first to avoid loss of credibility. International organizations thus act as alternative sources of information for societies and alter the cost-benefit calculations of elites who wish to maintain greater opaqueness.

THE "LOGICS" BEHIND THE ADOPTION OF FOI LEGISLATION

The possible explanations for the surprisingly rapid adoption of access to information legislation in East-Central Europe can be organized in a two-by-two typology according to the "logic" one emphasizes and the relative role of domestic and international actors. March and Olsen suggest that the logic of any human action can be driven by either a "logic of anticipated consequences" or a "logic of appropriateness." According to the former, actors "choose among alternatives by evaluating their likely consequences for personal or collective objectives, conscious that other actors are doing likewise."[89] The "logic of appropriateness," on the other hand, involves "evoking an identity or role and matching the obligations of that identity or role to a specific situation."[90]

The second dimension used for the typology focuses on the relevance of international actors in the final decision of adopting access to information legislation. Thus, one could on one hand see the process as primarily an endogenous one, determined by the domestic cost-benefit calculations of domestic actors and/or of the domestic norms of "transparency" that have emerged among domestic elites or within society. On the other hand, one could emphasize the exogenous role that Western countries and institutions have had on the same domestic cost-benefit calculations or on the domestic norms. The result of such a classification is represented in table 3.1.

This chapter has shown (as demonstrated in table 3.1) that explanations based primarily on domestic, "homegrown" norms of transparency, (1), are

Table 3.1. Possible Explanations for Adoption of Access to Information Legislation in East-Central Europe

	Main Actor	
Logic of Action	*Domestic Actor*	*External Actor*
Logic of appropriateness	(1) Domestic norms derive from "legacies of the past" and/or from "culture."	(2) Domestic norms are being "imported" from Western countries and organizations.
Logic of consequences	(3) Domestic cost-benefit calculations are primarily based on consequences of actions of domestic actors.	(4) Domestic cost-benefit calculations are primarily based on consequences of actions of external actors.

among the least convincing. The countries of East-Central Europe have recently emerged from authoritarian systems emphasizing secrecy. The little work that has been done with regard to mass attitudes in the area shows that there is less support for institutions of transparency than there is in Western countries, where such a law does not yet exist.

Explanations based on the "import" of norms of transparency from European institutions, (2), also appear to be weak. As shown, while such norms are arguably present in many West European countries, the Western international institutions have not been efficient vehicles for transmitting them because of the lack of common understanding of the need for, or the practice of, transparency among all members. The "legacies" of these institutions have led to weak norms of transparency within their own bureaucracies. Moreover, if the cases of older "third wave democracies" such as Portugal are any indication of future trends in East-Central Europe, the norms that have been imported from the EU bureaucracy may actually perpetuate the opaqueness of government. Of the three international institutions discussed here, only the Council of Europe can be considered to have had an impact on the export of a norm of transparency but it has done so only where some initial interest in greater transparency already existed.

The "logic of consequences," viewed as involving only domestic actors, (3), is also not a powerful explanation of the adoption of access to information legislation. The fact that such legislation was not adopted worldwide until the 1980s supports the assertion that governmental actors have been powerful enough to maintain their "informational advantage" over societies. The cases in which access to information legislation has been adopted due solely to domestic cost-benefit calculations of governments (not including external actors) have involved some "exogenous shocks" such as was the case in the United States in the 1960s and 1970s during the Vietnam War and Watergate. In East-Central Europe there have not been any such shocks,[91] and the elections that have taken place have not included the issue of "transparency" on the agenda. Moreover, the simultaneous processes of privatization have arguably offered elites in power a supplementary motive not to open up domestically.

Many of the democratic institutions adopted in East-Central Europe can be attributed to the cost-benefit calculations involving international institutions, (4), such as the EU and NATO. Most often, the alteration of such cost-benefit calculations implies an element of "conditionality." International institutions that these countries desperately want to join, for security or economic goals, set conditions with regard to domestic democratic institutions. Yet, as noted, the European institutions did not set transparency as a condition for membership—except for narrower issues.

The above analysis suggests that all four types of explanations (captured in the four cells of the typology demonstrated in table 3.1), which are generally used by analysts to explain the appearance of institutions are, at first glance, not convincing. This chapter offered an alternative explanation, which would also fall into (4): the desire to join the European international institutions led to an increase in the "external transparency" of governments (i.e., toward IOs), which in turn has altered the costs and consequences of maintaining opaque institutions. Such an explanation resonates with the neoliberal institutionalist literature that emphasizes the existence of "unexpected consequences" of membership in international organizations. Whether they emphasize the role of international organizations or not, virtually all theories of international relations recognize that, at the minimum, international organizations have a role in facilitating the exchange of information. In an era in which countries are offering more information than ever before to international organizations,[92] there should be some domestic consequences of external information dissemination, for example, the increase of domestic transparency.

The plausibility of such an explanation is emphasized by a comparison with Latin American "third wave" democracies that have not adopted such legislation yet.[93] The role of the European institutions in demanding extraordinary amounts of information has no equivalent on the American continent or in other areas of the world with new democracies. Of all the "third wave democracies" very few outside of the former Soviet empire have adopted such legislation to date.[94]

Emphasizing one explanation from the typology does not necessarily mean discarding the other explanations. As March and Olsen point out, it is wrong to explain political action only in terms of the logic of consequences or of appropriateness. The two are not mutually exclusive, and any particular action usually involves elements of each.[95] In this chapter I have offered an additional piece to the general puzzle—one without which our understanding of transparency in this region would be incomplete.

NOTES

I would like to thank the East European Studies Program of the Woodrow Wilson International Center for Scholars for supporting this research through a short-term research grant.

1. The best-known discussion of the "waves of democracy" and the "counterwaves" can be found in Samuel Huntington, *The Third Wave: Democratization in the Late Twentieth Century* (Norman: University of Oklahoma Press, 1991).
2. For a discussion of the difference between the two strands of literature, especially as applied to East and Central Europe, see, e.g., Philippe Schmitter and Terry Lynn Karl, "The Conceptual Travels of Transitologists and Consolidologists: How Far to the East Should They Attempt to Go?" *Slavic Review*, 53, no. 1 (Spring 1994): 173–85.
3. For useful overviews of such literature, see, e.g., Juan Linz and Alfred Stepan, "Toward Consolidated Democracies," in *Consolidating the Third Wave Democracies*, ed. L. Diamond, M. Plattner, Y. Chu, and H. Tien (Baltimore: Johns Hopkins University Press, 1997); Bert Rockman, "Institutions, Democratic Stability, and Performance," in *Institutions and Democratic Statecraft*, ed. M. Heper, A. Kazancigil, B. Rockman (Boulder, Colo.: Westview, 1997).
4. Robert Dahl, *Polyarchy: Participation and Opposition* (New Haven, Conn.: Yale University Press, 1971).
5. Discussions of this assumption can be found as far back as Gabriel Almond and Sidney Verba, *The Civic Culture* (Princeton, N.J.: Princeton University Press, 1963), in which the survival of democratic institutions is considered to be affected by attitudes such as belief in one's ability to influence political decisions. Different facets of this argument can be found in more recent writings, for example, Richard Rose and Christian Haerpfer, "Democracy and Enlarging the European Union Eastwards," *Journal of Common Market Studies* 33, no. 3 (1995): 439; also in Linz and Stepan, *Toward Consolidated Democracies*, 16; Giovanni Sartori, "Rethinking Democracy: Bad Polity and Bad Politics," *International Social Science Journal* 43, no. 3 (1991): 437–50.
6. Increasing interest in the concept of transparency has led to its use in different subfields of political science based on different understandings and definitions. Thus the literature discusses transparency with regard to the information offered by governments to their societies ("domestic government transparency"), information offered by governments to external actors ("external transparency"), information offered by international organizations either to members or to societies ("transparency of an international organization"), and so on. A broader definition of transparency of actor A toward actor B is "the ability of B to receive information from A." See Alexandru Grigorescu, "The Conceptualization and Measurement of Transparency" (paper presented at the annual conference of the Northeastern American Political Science Association, Albany, New York, November 2000). This definition subsumes most of the existing definitions in the literature.
7. For an emphasis on this understanding of transparency, see, e.g., Robert Martin and Estelle Feldman, *Access to Information in Developing Countries* (Berlin: Transparency International, 1998), 5.
8. See, e.g., Ann Florini, "The Politics of Transparency" (paper presented at the annual meeting of the International Studies Association, Los Angeles, California,

March 2000). Florini takes the existence and completeness of access to information legislation as a main reflection of the transparency of governments.

9. For a discussion of transparency as freedom of the press, see, e.g., Douglas Van Belle, "Press Freedom and Peace: Theory and Findings," in *Power and Conflict in the Age of Transparency*, ed. Bernard Finel and Kristin Lord (New York: St. Martin's, 2000).

10. For a discussion of such problems in East-Central Europe, see "Media Responses to Corruption in the Emerging Democracies: Bulgaria, Hungary, Romania, Ukraine," Freedom House, 2000 <www.freedomhouse.org/reports/mediatxt.html> (October 12, 2000).

11. John Mueller, "Democracy and Ralph's Pretty Good Grocery: Elections, Equality, and Minimal Human Being," *American Journal of Political Science* 36, no. 4 (1992): 986.

12. A broad list of countries having adopted legislation supporting access to information can be found in the appendix of Florini, "Politics of Transparency."

13. The choice of cases was determined by two factors. First, almost all of these countries have adopted the institutions encouraging transparency and, as a group, offer some puzzling developments compared to other new democracies. As former states (or successors) of the Soviet Union's satellite countries, the six had relatively similar experiences both before and after their 1989 revolutions. Their similarity has been often cited as a useful tool for comparison with each other—as a "most similar systems" research design.

14. For comprehensive discussions and overviews of the generation and export of norms, see, e.g., Martha Finnemore and Kathryn Sikkink, "International Norm Dynamics and Political Change," *International Organization* 52, no. 4 (1998): 887–919; Ann Florini, "The Evolution of International Norms," *International Studies Quarterly* 40 (1996): 363–91.

15. See, e.g., L. Kolakowski, *Main Currents of Marxism* (New York: Oxford University Press, 1978), 465, cited in Peter Gross, *Mass Media in Revolution and National Development: The Romanian Laboratory* (Ames: Iowa State University Press, 1996), 10.

16. Barrington Moore, *Terror and Progress USSR: Some Sources of Change and Stability in the Soviet Dictatorship* (Cambridge, Mass.: Harvard University Press, 1954), 9–10, 168–70.

17. Vaclav Havel, "The Power of the Powerless," in *Without Force or Lies*, ed. William Brinton and Alan Rinzler (San Francisco: Mercury House, 1990).

18. See Gross, *Mass Media in Revolution*, 53–55.

19. The most comprehensive discussions of the problems of existing press legislation can be found in the annual press freedom surveys of Freedom House. See Freedom House, *How Free? The Web and the Press: The Annual Survey of Press Freedom* (New York: Freedom House, 2001).

20. The survey scores 186 countries on laws and regulations that influence media content, political pressures and controls on media content, economic influences over media content, and repressive actions. The total scores range from 0 (most free) to 100 (least free). The scores are also organized within three broad categories: free (0–30), partly free (31–60), and not free (61–100). In Freedom House, *How Free?*

21. On the scale from 0 (completely free) to 100 (not free), the six countries have an average score of approximately 29 for the year 2000. This is much better than the average score of 47 for the entire world. Reported in Freedom House, *How Free?*

22. Their average is 9.2 out of a maximum of 30 (least free).

23. See, e.g., Douglas Van Belle, "Global Press Freedom" <gopher://csf.colorado. edu/00/isa/data/datasets/Van_Belle.97.data.txt> (August 4, 2000). The data set measures freedom of the press from 1948 to 1994 on a scale from 1 (clearly free) to 4 (press directly controlled by the government). The six countries under discussion have almost all jumped from scores of 3 and 4 before 1989 to scores of 1 and 2 in the early 1990s.

24. Although Germany does not have a general access law, there are a large number of sectoral laws offering access to specific information. There are general access laws being prepared at the *Länder* level. See Florini, *Politics of Transparency.*

25. See "Am intrat in 2000 cu serioase lacune legislative: Interviu cu Paul Mitroi, Avocatul Poporului," *Romania libera* (Bucharest), May 3, 2000, 3.

26. Countries such as Austria, Belgium, France, Ireland, Spain, or Switzerland met such criteria later while others (e.g., Australia and Iceland) do not meet the criteria even now. See "Special Data Dissemination Standards, Subscribing Countries," IMF, 2000 <dsbb.imf.org/country.htm> (December 10, 2000; August 16, 2001).

27. See "FMI cere Guvernului sa dea bani pentru statistica," *Adevarul* (Bucharest), January 7, 2000, 4; "GDDS Participating Countries," IMF <dsbb.imf.org/gddsweb/country.htm> (September 8, 2000).

28. The Czech Republic's legislation regarding funding of political parties, for example, is considered to allow for greater transparency than, for example, the British one. While the British laws do not require donations to political parties to be declared (although there is currently a proposal to have all donations over $8,200 declared), the Czech law requires all donations to political parties that exceed $2,800 to be declared. See "Is Europe Corrupt?" *The Economist*, January 29, 2000, 57.

29. For a comprehensive discussion of the two types of democracy as reflected in East-Central Europe, see Mary Kaldor and Ivan Vejvoda, "Democratization in Central and East European Countries," *International Affairs* 73, no. 1 (1997): 59–82.

30. World Bank surveys rank corruption and unpredictable judiciaries in the area as some of the worst in the world. Also, see Freedom House, "Media Responses to Corruption," 4.

31. The most recent survey (for the year 2000) shows that the principal Western exceptions are the older "third wave democracies" (Greece with a score of 10 and Portugal with a score of 9).

32. Discussions of such a norm have recently emerged in the political science literature. See Florini, "Politics of Transparency"; Paul Nelson, "Transparency in International Organizations: Testing the Strength of the Norm in Regional and Global Multilateral Development Banks" (paper presented at the annual meeting of the International Studies Association, Los Angeles, California, March, 2000); and Arthur Stein, "Constrained Sovereignty: The Growth of International Intrusiveness" (paper presented at the annual meeting of the American Political Science Association, Atlanta, Georgia, September 1999). According to this perspective, governments find it increasingly appropriate to offer citizens greater access to information than in the past. Before 1970 only six countries in the world had any kind of "freedom of information" leg-

islation. Now almost fifty do, which is one sign of the spread of this norm. The vast literature on the "culture of secrecy" in the United Kingdom and the recent changes also emphasize the relevance of norms of transparency. See, e.g., David Vincent, *The Culture of Secrecy: Britain, 1842–1998* (Oxford: Oxford University Press, 1998).

33. See, e.g., discussions of the "culture of secrecy" with regard to the adoption of the Romanian state secrets law in "Trecerea de la o cultură a secretului la o cultură a transparenţei se dovedeşte extrem de anevoioasă," *România Liberă*, February 21, 2000, 3; and Eugen Vasiliu, "Nu avem o cultura a transparenţei," in *Douăzecişidoi*, 25 April–1 May 2000, 11.

34. Biancă Guruiţă, "The Cult of Secrecy Lives On," *Slavophilia*, May 17, 2000 <www.tol.cz/opinia/theculto.html> (May 18, 2000).

35. Guruiţă, "Cult of Secrecy," 2.

36. Vasiliu, "Trecerea."

37. Guruita, "Cult of Secrecy," 2.

38. Freedom House, *Media Responses to Corruption*, 5.

39. Freedom House, *Media Responses to Corruption*, 5.

40. See, e.g., Jane Perlez, "A Country Reluctant to Give Up Its Secrets," *New York Times*, September 6, 1997.

41. Stefan Wagstyl, "Comment and Analysis—Eastern Bloc," *Financial Times*, July 12, 2000, 16.

42. Freedom House, *Nations in Transit: Czech Republic* <www.freedomhouse .org/nit98/czech.html> (November 12, 2000).

43. See, e.g., Joel Hellman, "Winners Take All: The Politics of Partial Reform in Postcommunist Transitions," *World Politics* 50, no. 2 (1998): 203–34.

44. Stephen Holmes, "Crime and Corruption after Communism: Introduction," *East European Constitutional Review* 6, no. 4 (1997), 1 <www.law.nyu.edu/eecr/ vol6num4/feature/intro.html> (June 2, 2000).

45. Only about 46 percent of the population in the area trust the information they receive from national newspapers and 49 percent that from national television. Moreover, information published by governments is seen as reliable by only 37 percent of the population. See European Commission, *Eurobarometer: European Commission's Report CEEB 8—ZA—No. 3068* (November 1997) <www.za.uni-koeln.de/data/en/ eurobarometer/ceeb.htm> (October 22, 2000).

46. See Magda Boguszakova, Ivan Gabal, Endre Hann, Piotr Starzynski, and Eva Taracova, "Public Attitudes in Four Central European Countries," in *Perceptions of Security*, ed. Richard Smoke (Manchester, U.K.: Manchester University Press, 1996), 47.

47. See *Values and Political Change in Post Communist Europe*, ed. William Miller, Stephen White, and Paul Heywood (London: Macmillan, 1998), 143–45, 198.

48. For example, while NATO is formally an alliance of democracies, it did not emphasize the "democratic component" as much during the Cold War, when interests were shaped by the bipolar system. It accepted states that, at times, were not considered democratic (e.g., Portugal, Greece, and Turkey). See Laurence Whitehead, "Democracy and Decolonization: East-Central Europe," in *The International Dimensions of Democratization: Europe and the Americas*, ed. L. Whitehead (New York: Oxford University Press, 1996), 341–48.

49. See, e.g., Jean Manas, "The Council of Europe's Democracy Ideal and the Challenge of Ethno-National Strife," in *Preventing Conflict in the Post-Communist World*,

ed. Abram Chayes and Antonia Handler Chayes (Washington, D.C.: Brookings Institution, 1996).

50. For a discussion of the initial impetus of the EC (later EU) to support democracy in the area, see John Pinder, "The European Community and Democracy in Central and East Europe," in *Building Democracy: The International Dimension of Democratisation in East Europe*, ed. Geoffrey Pridham, Eric Herring, and George Sanford (London: Leister University Press, 1994).

51. See, e.g., NATO, "Chapter 1: Purposes and Principles of Enlargement," *Study on NATO Enlargement* (September 1995) <www.nato.int/docu/basictxt/enl-9502.htm> (November 27, 2000).

52. See Pinder, "European Community and Democracy," 125.

53. See, e.g., Antonia Handler Chayes and Richard Weits, "The Military Perspective on Conflict Prevention: NATO," in Chayes and Chayes, *Preventing Conflict in the Post-Communist World*.

54. Arend Lijphart, "Majority Rule in Theory and in Practice: The Tenacity of a Flawed Paradigm," *International Social Science Journal*, August 1991, 483–94, argues that there are two basic models of democracy: "majoritarian" and "consensus." The two differ fundamentally with regard to the question who is to govern and whose interests a government should be responsive to. In the first type of democracy "the majority of the people" govern while in the latter "as many people as possible" govern. Lijphart argues that newly democratized countries need consensual democracy because they tend to suffer from more serious internal cleavages and face more sensitive and divisive issues.

55. See Manas, "Council of Europe's Democracy Ideal"; Diana Chigas, Elizabeth McClintock, and Christopher Kamp, "Preventive Diplomacy and the Organization for Security and Cooperation in Europe: Creating Incentives for Dialogue and Cooperation," in Chayes and Chayes, *Preventing Conflict in the Post-Communist World*.

56. For a comprehensive discussion of the role the Partnership for Peace was designed to have on democratic consolidation in the area, see Charles Kupchan, "Strategic Visions," *World Policy Journal*, Fall 1994, 112–22. Kupchan served on the National Security Council during the first year of the Clinton administration, when the design for the Partnership for Peace was drawn up.

57. NATO, *Study on NATO Enlargement*.

58. Kupchan, "Strategic Visions," 114.

59. Jeffrey Checkel, "Compliance and Conditionality," Working Paper, no. 00/18 (Oslo: ARENA/Universitetet i Oslo, 2000).

60. European Union, *European Union Enlargement: A Historic Opportunity* (Brussels: European Union, 2000), 9.

61. European Union, "The Democracy Programme" <europa.eu.int/comm/enlargement/pas/phare/pt/mc/horizontal/democracy/democracy_prog11/18/00htm> (November 19, 2000).

62. See, e.g., Laurens Ian Brinkhorst, "Transparency in the European Union," *Fordham International Law Journal* 22 (1999): S128–S135; Martin Westlake, "Maastricht, Edinburgh, Amsterdam: The End of the Beginning," in *Openness and Transparency in the European Union*, ed. Veerle Deckmyn and Ian Thomson (Maastricht: European Institute of Public Administration, 1998), 131.

63. Westlake, "Maastricht, Edinburgh, Amsterdam."

64. Jacki Davis, "Access to and Transmission of Information: Position of the Media," in Deckmyn and Thomson, *Openness and Transparency*, 124.

65. See Alain Guggenbuhl, "A Miracle Formula or an Old Powder in a New Packaging? Transparency and Openness after Amsterdam," in Deckmyn and Thomson, *Openness and Transparency*, 21.

66. See Antonio Barreto, "Portugal: Democracy through Europe," in *Regional Integration and Democracy: Expanding on the European Experience*, ed. Jeffrey Anderson (Lanham, Md.: Rowman & Littlefield, 1999).

67. Brinkhorst, "Transparency in the European Union," S130.

68. For a comprehensive discussion of the lack of transparency in the British system, see Vincent, *Culture of Secrecy*.

69. Davis, "Access to Information," 124.

70. For a discussion of the efforts of some states to maintain a degree of opaqueness in the workings of the EU and of their own governments, see Deirdre Curtin, "Democracy, Transparency, and Political Participation: Some Progress Post-Amsterdam," in Deckmyn and Thomson, *Openness and Transparency*, 131.

71. Council of Europe, *The Council of Europe: Achievements and Activities* (Strasbourg: Council of Europe, 1995), 3.

72. See Robert Martin and Estelle Feldman, *Access to Information in Developing Countries* (Berlin: Transparency International, 1998), 6.2. The authors note that the right as mentioned in the European Convention on Human Rights is considered even weaker than the one in the Universal Declaration of Human Rights adopted half a decade earlier, which proclaims the right to "seek, receive and impart information."

73. It is noteworthy that a September 1999 court ruling against the Romanian government for infringements on the rights to free expression of journalist Ionel Dalban (for the fine and prison sentence he had received in 1995 on charges of libel) was actually the first one brought against the Romanian government—which, as already noted, is considered among the least free of the countries. See Corina Dragotescu, "Curtea Europeana a drepturilor omului recunoaste rolul presei," *Adevarul*, September 30, 1999, 15.

74. Checkel, "Compliance," 26.

75. For a complete listing of all such programs, see Council of Europe, *Council of Europe Co-operation and Assistance Programmes in the Media Field* (Strasbourg: Council of Europe, 2000); Council of Europe, *Assistance Programmes: Activities in the Year 2000* (Strasbourg: Council of Europe, 2000), both at <www.humanrights.coe.int/media/> (September 25, 2000).

76. For a recent discussion (and test) of this argument, see Jon Pevehouse, "International Organizations and Democratic Consolidation" (paper presented at the annual meeting of the American Political Science Association, Atlanta, Georgia, September 1999).

77. Actually, they presented it in such a manner even before the expert mission from the Council of Europe had come to fully study the law in July 1996 in Zagreb and months before the CoE offered its written comments on the law. See Vesna Antonic, "Croatia: Commentary Views Draft Law on Information Freedom," in *Zagreb VJESNIK*, June 8 1996; republished in *World News Connection*, June 12, 1996.

78. Author's correspondence of October–November 2000 with Cristophe Poirel, head of Media Division, Directorate General of Human Rights—DG II, Council of Europe.

79. On the creation of institutions for delaying the process of NATO enlargement, see, e.g., Nick Williams, "Partnership for Peace: Permanent Fixture or Declining Asset?" *Survival*, Spring 1996, 98–110; James Goldgeier, *Not Whether but When: The Decision to Enlarge NATO* (Washington, D.C.: Brookings Institution, 1999), 24–26.

80. Frank Schimmelfenning shows that the countries in the area used "swotting" strategies, through which they attempted to portray themselves as industrious students of the West's teaching programs and often as "the first" to fill out the needed paperwork for application. "International Socialization in the New Europe: Rational Action in an Institutional Environment," *European Journal of International Relations*, March 2000, 109–41.

81. The countries of the area were among the most active in offering information to the new U.N. Conventional Arms Register even when some (like Bulgaria) were later accused of offering incomplete or false information.

82. See Deckmyn and Thomson, *Openness and Transparency*; Brinkhorst, "Transparency in the European Union."

83. See, e.g., Lori Udall, "The World Bank and Public Accountability: Has Anything Changed?" in *The Struggle for Accountability: The World Bank, NGOs, and Grassroots Movements*, ed. Jonathan Fox and L. D. Brown (Cambridge, Mass.: MIT Press, 1998).

84. See, e.g., Paul Nelson, "Transparency Mechanisms in the Multilateral Development Banks," *World Development* 23, no. 11 (2001): 1835–47.

85. For an overview of the debate and changes with regard to transparency at the IMF as well as useful links, see especially International Monetary Fund, "Transparency at the IMF—Factsheet" <www.imf.org/external/np/exr/facts/transpar.htm> (June 5, 2000).

86. Robert Keohane and Joseph Nye, "The Club Model of Multilateral Cooperation and Problems of Democratic Legitimacy" (paper presented at the annual meeting of the American Political Science Association, Washington, D.C., August 31–September 3, 2000). The authors consider recent demonstrations against IOs (such as the ones in Seattle and Washington), as well as the Danish "no" in ratifying the Maastricht treaty, as proof of public disappointment with their accountability and transparency of organizations.

87. For example, the Polish media picked up the World Bank's public accusations against the Polish government for not dealing with corruption. The World Bank study was requested by the Polish government and was based on Polish data. Romanian media picked up EU data (which was initially produced using information offered by the Romanian government), noting that the country had one of the lowest indices of life expectancy and spending on education in Europe. Bulgaria's growing unemployment was signaled by the Bulgarian media after having been reflected in U.N. Economic Commission for Europe reports, also based on Bulgarian data. The three examples are mentioned in Delia Meth-Cohn, "Corruption in Poland Is Growing," *Business Central Europe*, May 2000, 44; Robert Veress, "România e ca după un război," *Adevărul*, December 23, 1999, 3; "EU Europe Commission Predicts 4 Percent Growth in 2000," *Sofia BTA*, December 14, 1999; republished in *World News Connection*, December 15, 1999.

88. See Robert Putnam, "Diplomacy and Domestic Politics: The Logic of Two-Level Games," *International Organization* 42, no. 3 (Summer 1988): 427–60.

89. James March and Johan Olsen, "The Institutional Dynamics of International Political Order," *International Organization* 52, no. 4 (Autumn 1998): 949.

90. March and Olsen, "Institutional Dynamics," 951.

91. The one exception in the area may be the Chernobyl accident in the Soviet Union, mentioned earlier.

92. See, e.g., Arthur Stein, "Constrained Sovereignty: The Growth of International Intrusiveness" (paper presented at the annual meeting of the American Political Science Association, Atlanta, Georgia, September 2–5, 1999).

93. The exceptions are Brazil (which included the right to access government information in its constitution), Belize, and Colombia. See Florini, "Politics of Transparency."

94. South Africa, Thailand, and South Korea, together with the Latin American countries mentioned above, are the exceptions. See Florini, "Politics of Transparency."

95. March and Olsen, "Institutional Dynamics," 952.

II

IMPACT ON COUNTRIES

4

Slovenia and the European Union: A Different Kind of Two-Level Game

Zlatko Šabič

The notion of two-level negotiations suggests a concern with the interplay of developments at domestic (intrastate) and international (interstate) levels.[1] This chapter, however, is about a different kind of two-level game, one that is played at the intergovernmental layer only but involves both multilateral and bilateral levels of negotiations. The argument is made that the bilateral level of such negotiations has a potentially significant influence on the outcome of what is normally perceived as multilateral negotiations. Since the process of Slovenia's accession to the European Union (EU)[2] has begun, the interplay between the bilateral and multilateral levels of negotiations has been revealed several times. It has demonstrated the potential impacts on the multilateral issue of EU accession of what are essentially bilateral problems between Slovenia and two of its neighboring states (and EU members), Italy and Austria. Slovenia is a particularly attractive case to study in the context of European integration because it is one of the smallest countries to have applied for full membership in the EU. Because of its size and limited resources, Slovenia could be perceived as being vulnerable—and thus easier to deal with—in the eyes of current EU members, who may be tempted to pursue their own interests vis-à-vis this country. It is important to evaluate Slovenia's ability as a small state to cope with such challenges, especially in view of the fact that most of the applicants for EU membership are, indeed, small states.

In April 1990, Slovenia, then one of the federal republics in the Socialist Federal Republic of Yugoslavia (SFRY),[3] held its first free elections. This was a tense period, when the scale of clashes with the federal government in Belgrade was increasing dramatically and the possibility of a military intervention was looming. Nevertheless, Slovenian public opinion was firm that

Slovenia should move toward independence. In fact, many remained quite optimistic about the prospects of Slovenia as an independent state.[4]

The optimism did not prove unfounded. In a mere decade, Slovenia has become a universally recognized sovereign state. The Yugoslav National Army, defeated in the so-called Ten Days' War (June–July 1991), left the country. Slovenians have welcomed many high-profile figures, including President Bill Clinton and Pope John Paul II, and they hosted the first official meeting of American and Russian presidents George W. Bush and Vladimir Putin. Slovenia was a nonpermanent member of the United Nations Security Council between 1997 and 1999. The small country with a population of just 2 million is by all accounts a strong candidate for a second round of NATO enlargement and appears to be well on track as far as the first eastern enlargement of the EU is concerned. Slovenia's economic performance has also been notable. In terms of its GDP per capita, for example, Slovenia is closing in on EU members such as Greece and Portugal.

One way to explain Slovenia's emergence and performance as a (small) state in the past decade is to look at the dialectic relationship between disintegration and integration processes in Europe that started at the end of the 1980s.[5] The dissolution of the Soviet Union, the breakup of the SFRY, and the reunification of Germany brought new items onto the European economic and political agenda. On one hand, it became clear that the link between France and Germany had to be preserved so that the dynamics of European integration could continue swiftly, as set by adoption of the Single European Act[6] and accomplished by the Maastricht treaty.[7] The latter was made possible by the unofficial quid pro quo between France and Germany on future steps toward an "ever closer European Union," which should include both economic and political integration.[8] On the other hand, the EU seized the chance of integrating the rest of the old Continent and thus creating a united Europe in the true sense of the word. The so-called Europe Agreements, which granted the status of associate membership to the applicants, were concluded with ten former communist countries in the 1990s. Various financial schemes designed to help restructure socialist economies (e.g., PHARE and Technical Assistance for the Commonwealth of Independent States [TACIS]) were offered to Central and Eastern European countries, including the newly independent states that emerged from the former Soviet Union. The accession process formally began on March 30, 1998, when negotiations were opened with the six most advanced countries from Central and Eastern Europe (including Slovenia). The disintegration-integration processes that began at the end of the 1980s are expected to consolidate Europe as a whole both economically and politically[9]—a scenario that dates back at least as far as the 1920s, when Richard Coudenhove-Kalergi, an ardent federalist, presented his case for European economic and political unification.[10]

Unification is a complex process, however, as are steps leading to it, such as the enlargement of the EU. The Commission frequently points out that "the enlargement facing the EU today poses a unique challenge, since it is without precedent in terms of scope and diversity: the number of applicants, the area (an increase by 34 percent) and population (an increase of 105 million), the wealth of different histories and cultures."[11] Both member states of the EU and applicant states may share the vision of a united Europe. However, to establish the terms on which the enlargement is to take place and, more importantly, determine when an applicant state shows enough "Europeanness" to become a member of the EU (i.e., is behaviorally compatible with the set of norms and rules applying in this institution) is not and never will be easy.

The EU has set the baseline for all applicant countries—the so-called Copenhagen criteria. In general terms, these criteria can be interpreted as corresponding to the operative definition of norms used by Katzenstein,[12] whereby norms are considered "collective expectations for proper behavior of actors with a given identity." In some situations, norms have "constitutive" effects that "specify what actions will cause relevant others to recognize a particular identity."[13] In other instances, norms have "regulative" effects, that is, they "operate as standards that specify the proper enactment of an already defined identity." "Norms," Katzenstein concludes, "thus either define (or constitute) identities or prescribe (or regulate) behavior, or they do both."[14]

The dual impact of norms describes the gist of the relationship between Slovenia and the EU during the accession process: meeting the Copenhagen criteria per se ("regulative" effect of norms) may not be enough for an applicant state to win a full EU membership. Because of the two-dimensional nature of accession negotiations—multilateral and bilateral—norms can also have "constitutive" effects. These effects may emerge from the bilateral level of negotiations, where an applicant state may need to make an extra effort to prove its "Europeanness" just to please individual EU members. The latter could employ the prospect of full membership in the EU as a means to solve open bilateral issues with an applicant state. If in addition they are able to translate what is essentially a bilateral problem into a "European issue" at the multilateral level of accession negotiations, the chances of reaching what they perceive as an appropriate solution to the bilateral problem with an applicant in question may increase considerably.

The result of accession negotiations is thus determined on one hand at the multilateral (Community) level: the EU, represented by the Council as the main negotiator vis-à-vis the applicant countries. On the other hand, the interests of individual EU member states may be confronted with those of the individual applicant countries at the bilateral level. The two levels may intersect, as the national interests of individual EU members have a natural tendency to be presented as European norms.

Being a state "worthy" of a status in the EU (whether associate or full membership) is therefore not solely dependent on the adopted norms and values, generated by the EU and embodied within its own negotiating stance. It also depends on the nature of bilateral issues perceived to be problematic by individual EU members. As will be seen in the analysis of Slovenia's relations with Italy and Austria in the light of accession negotiations, applicant states may be apprehensive of any such challenges emerging from the bilateral level of negotiations. One should therefore be prepared for some resistance from applicant states to the bilateral importing of European norms as a condition of joining the EU.

This chapter will proceed as follows. First, the concept of a small state is addressed and the possible perspectives are set out that can best account for EU-Slovenia relations during the accession negotiations. Slovenia as a newborn state is then briefly presented. The analysis of the negotiation process involving Slovenia and the EU follows, using the two-level character of negotiations as a starting point. In this respect, examples of outstanding bilateral problems that have emerged between Slovenia and, respectively, Italy and Austria, are examined briefly.

THE SMALL STATE AS A SUBJECT OF RESEARCH

Although often indirectly, small states and their role in the international community were part and parcel of analyzing the post-Westphalian society since its early stages.[15] When such studies centered around small states, however, authors tended not to focus on conceptualizing the small state phenomenon per se. They referred to small states or small powers only to distinguish them from the group of great powers. Consequently, the range of small states perceived as such by those authors was relatively wide. What they had in mind when referring to small states were not just small states like Switzerland. Their understanding of the term included states that (in geographical terms at least) were not small (e.g., Brazil).[16] More recent research on small states began to move away from this simplified categorization between big and small. The new direction of studying small states was already present in the interwar period,[17] but most research under this heading has been done after World War II. The main reason for researchers' growing interest in small states has been the considerable increase of smaller entities granted statehood via decolonization and/or self-determination. The formal status of smaller states and microstates in international institutions was even raised as an issue among politicians.[18]

While a detailed survey of the literature on small states is beyond the scope of this chapter,[19] a few remarks on the conceptualization of the term itself are in place. There are different perspectives from which to analyze the phenomenon of small states. The positivist approach, for example, in which smallness is defined with regard to measurable factors such as GDP of the state, the size of its population, territory, and so on, would seem to be prevalent in telling small states apart from big ones.[20] However, this approach covers only one dimension of a country's size and proves to be quite inaccurate as soon as the individual parameters that determine smallness are combined. Norway, a country of just 4 million inhabitants, could by the population criterion alone be considered a small state. But Norway has territory comparable to that of Poland, which has about 40 million inhabitants. Austria may have been perceived as a small state with regard to its territory and population, but never as far as its current economic strength is concerned; the 2000 OECD figures show that in terms of GDP per capita Austria ranked twelfth in the world.[21]

Other attempts to define small states have gone beyond distinguishing between small and other states solely by measurable parameters. In the social constructivist perspective, the definition of the smallness of a state depends on how it is construed by its members or others that relate to it.[22] A state may be considered small regardless of more tangible parameters that might suggest otherwise, if its own citizens consider it as such. The self-understanding of West Germans during the Cold War might serve as an example. Because of the consequences of the lost war and its diminished size, Germany construed itself and began to behave as a typical small state, looking for transnational cooperation and showing less concern for the loss of sovereignty due to the integration processes that began in Europe in the 1950s.[23]

But the construction of the size of a country from within may not necessarily correspond to the construction of that same country from without. Specifically, the citizens of West Germany might have perceived their country as small and acted accordingly, but this view was not shared by all others forming a relationship with the country. The French, for instance, were quick to demonstrate their own security dilemmas when the restoration of sovereignty and rearmament of Germany were proposed by the United States at the beginning of the 1950s, due to the escalation of conflict in Korea.[24] Similarly, when the creation of the European Coal and Steel Community was contemplated, smaller countries such as Belgium and the Netherlands were wary of an overwhelming influence in such an organization exercised by both France and Germany.[25] It would appear, therefore, that the social constructivist approach also fails the test of the multidimensionality of its definition approach.

An interesting perspective from which to observe and analyze small states was offered by Vital.[26] His approach is not based on an intention to come up with a precise definition of a small state, although the distinction between great powers and small states remains within his research interest. He instead looks for the so-called paradigm of the class. "The essence of such paradigm," according to Vital,[27] is that "it does not strictly purport to tell you how any member of its class will operate in particular circumstances. It tells you how a certain case, the paradigm, operates and wider uses then depend upon the extent to which examination of the paradigm throws light upon the likely behavior of others." In doing this, Vital operates with two variables: the so-called intrinsic (in terms of national attributes, e.g., size of the economy, size of the army) and contingent (i.e., the ability to recognize and capitalize on the state's importance in the international system) capabilities. The latter are of particular interest to him, given that smaller states—unlike great powers—cannot always rely on intrinsic capabilities to pursue national interests.

Another, call it a relational, approach builds on Keohane's[28] proposal that the smallness of a state should be defined according to its ability to influence affairs in the international system. That is, the ability of a small state to pursue its own national interests cannot be explained only as a potentially prosperous free rider. It seems more important that every state should be looked at as a political system that functions in various types of environments. Such an environment could be the international community as a whole or a very narrow field of cooperation in which the state might make its presence felt. The size of a state is then measured not in physical or geographical terms, but in relation to how successfully the state deals with matters relating to a specific issue area (e.g., finance, military, agriculture). In the final analysis, greater influence in an individual issue area might help such a state improve its overall image and influence in international relations. For example, Luxembourg is by general perception a microstate. But in the 1950s, when the European Coal and Steel Community (ECSC) was being negotiated, the production of steel in Luxembourg was not at all negligible—Luxembourg's steel industry ranked among the largest in Europe, which helped this small country exercise a tangible influence in the negotiations on setting up the ECSC.[29] Today, the role of Luxembourg in steel production still matters. Arbed, a company from Luxembourg, is now the largest steel producer in Europe and the third largest in the world.[30] Luxembourg also plays a relatively significant role in the international banking system; the city of Luxembourg has been ranked as the sixth largest world financial center.[31] In those sectors Luxembourg can be considered much bigger than some other parameters (size, population) might suggest. Similarly, Norway may not be such an important player in world finance, but when it comes to the oil sector, the picture is different. In 1998 Norway was the third largest oil exporter in the world,[32] and in 1997 the sixth largest oil producer.[33] The "size" of Norway in the oil sector may have strengthened Norwegian international influence in other issue areas such as human rights and development.[34]

The relational approach as introduced here will be used to partly explain Slovenia's way to the EU. Although it is still exploring the scope of its (cap)abilities, Slovenia faces a variety of challenges in many of its fields of cooperation. The last ten years show that Slovenia is well into trying to develop its own identity in international politics. The challenges have been many. Will Slovenia develop into a modern Western democracy? What will its relations be with neighboring countries? Should Slovenia become a member of international institutions such as the EU and, if so, on what terms? It was clear from the outset that Slovenia's place and role in Europe depend on how successfully these challenges are met. Before moving into the central point of our discussion—accession negotiations of Slovenia with the EU— I will briefly discuss Slovenia's first steps onto the European political stage.

SLOVENIA AS AN EMERGING EUROPEAN STATE

Independence

Slovenia achieved its independence in 1991, favored by developing circumstances in international affairs. At the same time, internal developments provided the context in which Slovenia's aim to secede looked less like an act of destroying the former Yugoslavia and more like the exercise of the right to self-determination. The Yugoslav Communist Party found it hard to sustain its legitimacy after the death of its leader, Josip Broz Tito, in 1980. By the end of the 1980s, political pluralism had grown in Slovenian political life. Along with that was increasing resentment against the federal, communist-dominated regime in Belgrade. The federal government, which seemed increasingly dominated by the Serbian leadership headed up by Slobodan Milošević, did little to restore confidence among political elites not only in Slovenia but also in some other republics.[35] On December 23, 1990, Slovenia held a referendum in which almost 90 percent of the population (with voter turnout of 93.5 percent) voted for independence. Pressure from the federal authorities, including an economic blockade by Serbia, was mounting. Slovenia remained undeterred, however, and declared its independence on June 25, 1991. The Yugoslav National Army attacked Slovenia almost immediately but gave up after ten days. Less than a year later, Slovenia was a member of the United Nations.[36]

Transition

Because of the loss of the Yugoslav market, Slovenia began its life as an independent state with a vulnerable economy. Its GDP per capita fell from US$8,658 in 1990 to US$6,052 in 1992. Inflation soared as high as 247 percent in 1991, with unemployment topping 8 percent (nearly three times the 1989 level), and continued to rise.[37]

Yet Slovenia's solid foundations allowed it to overcome these difficulties. The government was quick to exploit the benefits of the industrialization and modernization processes that had been taking place much faster in Slovenia than in any other former Yugoslav Republic. As part of the SFRY, Slovenia made a remarkable shift from a typical agricultural economy to one based on industry and services. In 1931 almost two-thirds (61 percent) of the Slovenian population was active in the agricultural sector; in 1991 the figure was only 15 percent.[38] In the same period, the share of those employed in industry rose from 21 percent to 45 percent, and in services from 12 percent to 40 percent.[39]

Unlike most countries in Central and Eastern Europe, Slovenia was not overwhelmingly dependent on the markets of the former Yugoslavia and former Soviet Union. In 1989 Slovenia was already sending 52 percent of its exports to the member states of the European Community (EC). This helped Slovenia maintain its status as the most economically developed republic of former Yugoslavia. Experience with Western markets made the Slovenian economy's transition somewhat smoother and, as a result, the share of Slovenian exports going to EC countries has been growing continuously since independence.[40] In 1993, after six years of recession, fueled by the slump in economic activity in the first years of independence, real GDP was again on the rise (then by a mere 1 percent). Inflation was brought down to 22.9 percent and continued to fall. Unemployment remained a considerable problem—it went up to 9.1 percent in 1993, and to 14.6 percent in 1994,[41] but the macroeconomic indicators showed signs of recovery being achieved without balance of payments problems.

Today Slovenia is regarded as a "functioning market economy."[42] Economic growth continues at a steady pace (see figure 4.1); real GDP growth

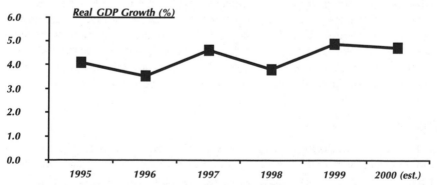

Figure 4.1   GDP Growth Rates in Slovenia, 1995–2000

Sources: "Favourable International Economic Environment Boosts Economic Growth in CEFTA." *Slovenian Economic Mirror,* March 2000 <www.sigov.si/zmar/arhiv/og0301/aog10300.html#amed> (November 28, 2000); "Strong Economic Growth in 2000 Driven by High Foreign Demand," *Slovenian Economic Mirror,* March 2001<www.sigov.si/zmar/arhiv/og0301/aog10301.html> (April 9, 2001).

ranged from 3.5 percent (1996) to a record 4.9 percent in 1999. In 2000, GDP growth was estimated at 4.8 percent.

In terms of GDP per capita at purchasing power parity Slovenia has already exceeded the US$10,000 benchmark. According to the 1998 figures, Slovenia's GDP per capita at purchasing power parity attained 65 percent of the EU average in 1998, and it was projected at 73 percent in 1999. In this respect, Slovenia was outperforming not only all of the Central and Eastern European economies but also two members of the EU: Greece (which in 1998 already had lower GDP per capita than Slovenia) and Portugal (whose GDP per capita was estimated to be lower in 1999).[43] Inflation and unemployment remain the biggest problems, however. Slovenia's inflation in 2000 stood at 8.9 percent, chiefly owing to the rising prices of oil and its derivatives and, consequently, the growth in prices of other product groups. The unemployment rate is around 13 percent (or between 7 percent and 7.5 percent according to the ILO definition of unemployment).[44]

The trend of redirecting the Slovenian economy toward the EU market continues and represents a vital foundation of the transition process in Slovenia. In 1999, 66 percent of Slovenian exports went to the EU. The EU share of imports to Slovenia is 69 percent. The remaining exports and imports, therefore, represent roughly one-third of Slovenian trade (see figure 4.2).

Slovenia's orientation toward the EU market would seem logical from a small state's point of view. Small states, as has often been pointed out, depend on big foreign markets.[45] A market of almost 400 million people, which may even increase to 500 million through enlargement, is a huge opportunity

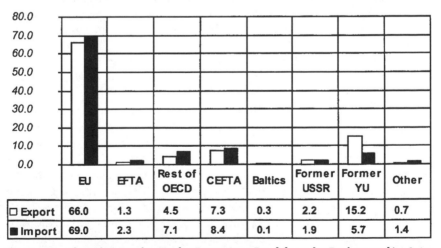

Figure 4.2 Slovenia's Foreign Trade: Percentage Breakdown by Regions and/or International Economic Organizations

Source: The Bulletin of the Bank of Slovenia 9, no. 8 (2000): 61.

for a small country like Slovenia. It is also a challenge, however, both economically and politically. Even as a non-EU member, Slovenia already faces tough competition in other EU member states when pursuing its own interests. It is therefore all the more important for Slovenia to be present in this market not solely as a commercial actor but also as a credible political member, so that it can influence decision making in the institutions that govern the EU. Slovenia learned fairly quickly that some of this credibility might well be gained—or lost—during the accession negotiations.

ACCESSION NEGOTIATIONS

The Two-Level Character of Negotiations

Although several EU institutions are involved in the accession process and the European Parliament must give its assent to admit a new member state, the core of negotiations takes place between an applicant state and the current member states of the EU. According to article 49 of the consolidated treaty on the EU, an application should be addressed "to the Council, which shall act unanimously after consulting the Commission and after receiving the assent of the European Parliament, which shall act by an absolute majority of its component members." Further, the conditions of admission "shall be the subject of an agreement between the Member States and the applicant state. This agreement shall be submitted for ratification by all the contracting States in accordance with their respective constitutional requirements."[46] Accordingly, while negotiating the terms of EU membership, an applicant state deals with the EU governments at two levels: with the Council as a collegiate body at the Community level and also with individual EU members.

There are many possibilities for individual EU member states to promote particular national interests during the course of accession negotiations with individual applicants and hide them beneath the cloak of "Europeanness," as figure 4.3 suggests. When negotiating the terms of EU membership, the applicant state is in a subordinate position as its ability to fulfill the membership criteria is under constant scrutiny by the Council and individual member states. Playing on this inferior position, a member state of the EU might try to present bilateral issues with a particular applicant that remain to be solved as European ones, thus hoping for a faster solution to the open problems. If the EU member succeeds in this, the applicant state must oblige if it wishes to stay on the road to accession. The applicant state therefore may face more difficulties when negotiating acceptable terms of accession because the latter might be subject to additional compromises, namely, those stemming from what could be considered essentially bilateral problems, and not necessarily part of, say, the Copenhagen criteria.[47]

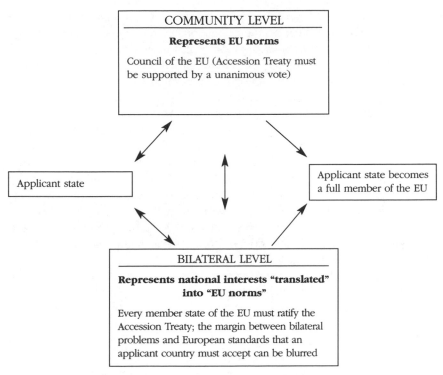

Figure 4.3   The Two-Level Character of Intergovernmental Negotiations between an Applicant State and the EU

As will be seen, Slovenia's challenges have indeed emerged not only at the Community level but also at the bilateral level, from Italy and Austria.

THE COMMUNITY LEVEL OF NEGOTIATIONS

The set of norms and values to be transported to states wishing to become EU members was determined at the 1993 Copenhagen European Council meeting. The governments of the EU agreed that "the associated countries in Central and Eastern Europe that so desire shall become members of the EU. Accession will take place as soon as an associated country is able to assume the obligations of membership by satisfying the economic and political conditions required."[48] These obligations—the membership criteria—referred to the stability of the institutions guaranteeing democracy: the rule of law, the respect of human rights, and protection of minorities (the so-called political criteria); the existence of a functioning market economy as well as the capacity to cope with competitive pressure and market forces within the EU (the economic criteria); and the ability of an applicant state to incorporate the *acquis,* that is, to "take on the obligations of membership including adherence to the aims of political, economic and monetary union."[49]

According to the European Commission,[50] Slovenia has made tangible progress in the first two sets of criteria. According to the Commission, two areas warranting further improvement are the streamlining and speeding up of the judicial and parliamentary processes. As for the economic criteria, Slovenia is regarded by the Commission as a market economy that should be able to cope with competitive pressure and market forces within the Union in the medium term, provided it continues to make further progress on structural reforms. The Commission has welcomed Slovenia's ability to maintain macroeconomic stability. Among other things, implementation of a major reform of the tax system together with the introduction of value-added tax are mentioned in the reports. But some issues remain to be solved, according to the Commission; the privatization of state assets, including the two state banks has been mentioned as a priority.

Clearly, the most important remaining work involves the third set of the Copenhagen criteria, although Slovenia has made progress there as well. The Commission has reported, for instance, that key parts of internal market legislation have been adopted (e.g., adoption of the law on value-added tax [VAT]). Important progress has been made in capital liberalization and the banking and securities sectors. Changes have been introduced in the company law with a view to further removing obstacles for foreign firms interested in doing business in Slovenia, although Slovenia retains its image of being not particularly friendly to foreign investment.[51] The Commission also reported progress in the field of justice and home affairs, as laws have been adopted on foreigners and asylum seekers and measures taken to combat organized crime and corruption. In the field of environmental protection, the adoption of laws in the areas of water, air, waste management, and nature protection are mentioned. But Slovenia lags behind in fields such as state aid, intellectual and industrial property laws, and the free movement of persons, capital, and services. Slovenia has been criticized in particular for making little progress in reforming the public administration[52] and the judiciary.[53]

The Commission's two recent progress reports have been accepted positively in Slovenia, despite criticism and the somewhat discouraging rankings, for example, as far as the state of its market economy and capacity to cope with competitive pressure and market forces within the EU are concerned.[54] Here Slovenia was ranked in the same league as the Czech Republic, but behind Cyprus, Malta, Estonia, Hungary, and Poland.[55] Nevertheless, Slovenia seems to be on its way to taking on the required values and norms that would align it with the EU and thus achieve compatibility.

The conclusions at the European Council in Göteborg in June 2001 suggest that the negotiations will proceed apace, and that the most successful applicant countries may be able to complete their negotiations by the end of 2002.[56] Slovenia, now in the group of applicant states that have made the biggest progress in negotiations (alongside Cyprus, Hungary, and the Czech Republic), may well be among the first ones ready to enter the EU. However, this does not mean that the remaining negotiations will be any easier for the applicant countries; on the contrary, the most difficult chapters have as a rule been left to the end. Agriculture is a particularly notable case in point. At the time of writing, negotiations on this chapter have not even begun.

Whether Slovenia will be one of the first applicant countries to complete the negotiating process at the Community level remains to be seen. One should also bear in mind that at this stage the chapters are deemed "temporarily closed" and may always be reopened.[57] The total workload is considerable, as the experience of applicant countries that are today full EU members suggests. Due to its accession to the European Economic Area, for instance, Austria had to incorporate into its domestic legal system some 1,400 legal acts of the EU (about 60 percent of the *acquis*) even before its accession negotiations started.[58] Besides the efforts, expected from Slovenia by the EU as a whole, the final score of negotiations will also depend on how Slovenia will be able to sell its own interests to the EU. The last three successful applicant states, Austria, Finland, and Sweden, had a better starting point in this respect. All of them were expected to be net contributors to the EU budget. The three newcomers did not seem to have any outstanding bilateral problems with any of the members of the EU.[59] Slovenia, by contrast, applied for EU membership as a future net recipient (from the EU budget), and it could not sidetrack open bilateral problems with individual EU members when it started to negotiate its status with the EU. Of course, Slovenia has seen the national interests of individual EU member states being present at the Community level as well, the most recent example being the request from Germany and Austria for a seven-year transition period for the free movement of workers. Afraid of the pressure of workers from applicant states on Austrian and German labor markets, these two governments have pressed for a seven-year transition period before the free movement of labor comes into effect. The transitional period would apply to all applicant countries becoming EU members, except for Cyprus and Malta.[60] But such demands apply to most if not all applicant countries. More difficult to deal with may be requests applying to individual applicants. With the existence of open bilateral issues between individual EU members and applicant states, however, the probability of demands arising that at the outset may not necessarily be part of the accession criteria established at the Community level increases. Slovenia is a witness to this, as it has already experienced the translation of particular national interests of individual EU members into European "norms."

THE BILATERAL LEVEL OF NEGOTIATIONS

Slovenian politicians had to learn very fast that politics is more about inter-ests than mutual sympathy. Support for and recognition of acquired state-hood was at hand soon after the declaration of independence, but so was the emergence of open issues, notably between Slovenia and its neighbors. Italy was quick to tackle such open issues. The Italian government did not hesi-tate to present those essentially bilateral problems as European ones, and it did not hesitate to put pressure on Slovenia to prove its "Europeanness."

The problems between Slovenia and Italy are interrelated and have their roots in the past, and the two states have reflected on them since Slovenian independence. The issues, which may still appear on the bilateral agenda of the two countries, include (1) border issues, (2) the status of minorities, and (3) the status of Italians who left Istria after World War II for Italy.

Slovenia and Italy do not have any outstanding border problems. However, they are considered an issue because in the past the territory called Istria[61] was claimed by both Italy and Slovenia (i.e., former Yugoslavia), and resolving this problem has affected both Italian and Slovenian populations. The Treaty of Rapallo (1920) confirmed Italy's possession of all of Istria. At that time, the so-called first Yugoslavia (the Kingdom of the Serbs, Croats, and Slovenians) was a new actor in the world. On the other hand, Italy was part of the victorious alliance, which it joined in May 1915, and sought rewards for its contribution to winning World War I. After World War II the status of Istrian peninsula was reopened. The Italians believed Istria was traditionally Italian territory. The SFRY, on the other hand, considered the Rapallo arrangement to be unfair. But the fortunes of war were different after 1945 and Yugoslavia, unlike Italy, was part of the victorious alliance. Still, this did not make it easy for the SFRY to dictate the border with Italy the way Italy appeared to do after World War I. In fact, the border was only finally agreed in 1975, when the so-called Osimo treaty was signed.[62] The 1975 settlement was a disappointment for Italian na-tionalists. Most of Istria formally became part of former Yugoslavia, and only a tiny portion in the Trieste region remained in Italy.

After the SFRY broke up, a small part of Istria became part of Slovenia and a much larger part went to Croatia. Italy was quick to accept Slovenia as an independent state and recognized the succession of Slovenia to all relevant treaties that Italy had concluded with the former Yugoslavia.[63] These in-cluded the Treaty of Osimo (1975), which thus determined the border be-tween Slovenia and Italy. While there might have been some pressure from the Italian nationalist-oriented public to question the validity of the Osimo treaty, given the new circumstances, it seemed obvious that within the cur-rent political constellation such a revision would in effect question the whole European order as set up in 1945—something Italy could hardly afford to do at that stage.[64] But Italy has tried to exercise an influence in the region, which not so long ago fell within its own jurisdiction. For a start, Italy pressed ahead in questioning the level of rights of its minorities in both Croatia and Slovenia, especially since the region in which they lived (Istria) was now to be divided between the two new countries.

Thus Italy prepared the tripartite memorandum of understanding, scheduled to be signed just before Slovenia's diplomatic recognition. The document contained the commitment of the two newly independent states to provide benefits for the Italian minority (e.g., free movement across borders of persons belonging to the minority). The Slovenian government accepted the trilateral agreement. The government, however, must have known that the agreement was unlikely to win the parliament's approval, since the latter was confident of the high standard of rights already enjoyed by the Italian minority in Slovenia, but was not sure whether the standards of rights for the Slovenian minority in Italy were at the same level. To obtain parliament's approval, the Slovenian government supplemented the trilateral agreement with a proposal for a bilateral treaty between Italy and Slovenia supporting the Slovenian minority in Italy. The latter refused to sign both agreements simultaneously, so the Slovenian parliamentary Committee on International Relations instructed the foreign minister not to sign the trilateral agreement.[65] Notwithstanding these developments, Italy recognized Slovenia as an independent state on January 15, 1992, and established diplomatic relations with it, but continued to complain about Slovenia's allegedly poor protection of the Italian minority, and even used the minority issue in trying to block Slovenia's entry to the Council of Europe.[66]

However, the Italian attempts were not successful. It has been clearly stated on several occasions that the standard of minority rights for Italians living in Slovenia can be taken as a role model in Europe.[67] Italy, for its part, managed to pass its own legislation on the protection of the Slovenian minority in Italy only in 2001.[68] The law had been awaited for three decades, and members of the Slovenian minority living in Italy look forward to seeing when and how it is going to be implemented.

But Italy was successful in its use of leverage on Slovenia with regard to a politically, legally, and historically contentious issue, namely, the property of Italians who opted to leave Istria (or were expelled, according to the Italian interpretation) at the end of World War II.[69] In the 1983 Treaty of Rome, Yugoslavia agreed to pay compensation for expropriated Italian property on the part of the territories that had come under its authority. The total amount, some US$110 million, was to be paid in thirteen annual installments, the first due on January 1, 1990.[70] Payment of the third installment was overdue because of the political events that tore Yugoslavia apart. Following independence, Slovenia was prepared to honor the agreement after agreeing with Croatia on their respective shares of the amount due. However, under the new government of Silvio Berlusconi Italy refused to accept the payments and instead challenged the Rome Agreement itself: "Italy invoked the principle of changed circumstances and demanded instead of material compensation the restitution of real property in kind (*in natura*)."[71] This was unacceptable to Slovenia, which considered itself a successor to the Treaty of Rome, something that Italy had itself recognized from the outset. Because Italy did not want to disclose the details of the account number to which the first two installments had been paid, Slovenia opened a fiduciary bank account at the Dresdner Bank in Luxembourg and continued to pay the installments as due there.[72]

At one point the Italian government's pressure on Slovenia almost yielded results. Lojze Peterle, the Slovenian foreign minister who was leaving office after resigning,[73] agreed to the terms of a draft joint statement signed in Aquilea, Italy, on October 10, 1994. The statement inter alia included a hint that Slovenia was prepared to negotiate the revision of all treaties between Italy and Slovenia, including the Treaty of Rome and even the Treaty of Osimo.[74] This led to serious internal disputes in Slovenia. The foreign minister was accused of overstepping his authority and the Slovenian government refused to honor the joint statement. The Berlusconi government then tried to portray Slovenia as an unreliable European partner.[75] Italy began claiming the right of preemption for ex-Italian property in Slovenian territory and began to demand that Slovenia liberalize its real estate market even before signing the Association (Europe) Agreement.[76] In so doing, the Berlusconi government succeeded in translating the bilateral problem into "European language."[77] Slovenian legislation at the time did not allow the acquisition of land by foreigners, nor did Slovenia wish to liberalize its real estate market overnight. As a consequence, Italy blocked any progress in signing the Europe Agreement with Slovenia. Not one of the other former socialist countries that (successfully) concluded Association Agreements had to face similar demands. An image was being created of Slovenia still needing to prove itself "worthy of Europe." It was difficult for the EU to sidestep Italy, a founding member of the European Community.

The deadlock was partly broken when Berlusconi fell from power in January 1995. The new government headed by Lamberto Dini showed a greater willingness to negotiate and agreed to a compromise that established the possibility of foreigners gaining access to real estate in Slovenia after a transition period of several years. That paved the way for entering into the Europe Agreement with Slovenia. When the new government headed up by Romano Prodi came to power in May 1996, Slovenia made further clarifications, namely, that four years after ratification of the Europe Agreement all those who had lived in Slovenia at any time for more than three years would have preferential access to Slovenia's real estate market.[78] That made it possible for Slovenia to conclude the Europe Agreement on June 10, 1996. Italy handed in its ratification on March 17, 1998.

The "constitutive" impact of the bilateral level on the shape of the Europe Agreement is tangible enough. Slovenia would eventually have to open up its real estate market—like all other applicants—but it was Slovenia alone that had to commit itself to do this early. What is more, Italy effectively arranged for its nationals who had left Yugoslavia after World War II to have the legal right to become the first buyers if they so wished. This was the way for Slovenia to prove its "Europeanness." Such a course of events would not have taken place without Italy's pressure.

In addition, the government in Ljubljana seemed to make it easier for Italian negotiators to expand their list of demands for Slovenia to prove its "Europeanness." In the early 1990s Slovenia declared itself ready to negotiate with Italy on everything except the borders.[79] For the Slovenian government this position became a boomerang insofar as Italy welcomed and tested Slovenia's willingness to actually do so. Finally, just before signing the Europe Agreement, Italy declared that "the problem between Italy and Slovenia relating to the restitution of compensation of former Italian property in Istria is not yet resolved, but that it was now only a bilateral matter no longer involving the EU."[80] Berlusconi's return to power in June 2001 again raises the question of whether this bilateral matter will be turned into another test of Slovenian "Europeanness." Italy will not be alone in such an undertaking, since Austria, the other EU member, has also strengthened its demands on Slovenia.

Austria, which in February 2000 received a new right-wing government (the so-called black and blue coalition, headed up by Chancellor Wolfgang Schüssel of the People's Party),[81] set an agenda of bilateral issues to be resolved with its neighbor Slovenia: closure of the Krško nuclear power plant; the status of the German-speaking population in Slovenia; the question of property of the German population who were dispossessed after World War II; and the status of certain so-called AVNOJ (Antifascist Council of the National Liberation of Yugoslavia) decrees, which provided legal basis for dispossession.

The problem of the Krško nuclear power plant apparently stems from Austria's concern about the safety of this complex. Austria feared the nuclear power plant was built in an earthquake-prone area, so it wanted the plant to close as soon as possible. The status of the German-speaking population in Slovenia, the problem of the dispossessed German-speaking population after World War II, and the AVNOJ decrees are interrelated. The German-speaking population was forced to move from many Eastern European countries, including former Yugoslavia, and could do little about the property they left behind. With the changed political circumstances after the dissolution of the Soviet bloc and with the SFRY falling apart, Austria seeks to represent the interests of those German-speaking persons and their descendants who wish to remedy the situation and, most importantly, seek the return of their property. In dealing with these issues, the Austrian government has shown that it has enough leverage to push Slovenia into making concessions.

The Krško nuclear power plant has from the outset been an issue dealt with at the Community level of negotiations within Chapter 14 (Energy). For a long time, there seemed little chance of a breakthrough in negotiations. The Austrian government indicated concerns about the seismic safety of Krško. To address these concerns, a study costing over EUR 700,000, financed by PHARE, was launched to evaluate the safety of the area in which the nuclear power plant is located. The Austrian government made it clear that it would not join the consensus of the EU members on closing Chapter 14 for Slovenia as long as the results of this study were unknown. Austria had the support of some other EU member states (Italy and Greece) in making this point.[82]

The research was made public in November and December 2000 and was considered good news for Slovenia. The analysis showed that there were no active faults in the area where Krško is located. It turned out, however, that all that glitters is not gold. Although the report indicated that the nuclear power plant was not situated in any earthquake-prone area,[83] the research could not entirely exclude the possibility of earthquakes.[84] Further, there were some dissenting opinions from Croatian and Hungarian experts concerning the research results. This was enough for Austria to express its own doubts about the study. Consequently, the Austrian government decided to continue its policy of not joining in a consensus to close Chapter 14 in EU accession negotiations with Slovenia. It was also pondering its own investigation of the Krško area.

The Austrian government tried to play down its moves, saying that in any case nothing is over until it is over, that temporarily closed chapters might still be reopened, and in this respect it was not really important whether Chapter 14 would be closed now or later.[85] But the Austrian reaction to the PHARE study caused considerable anger in Slovenia. Speculations about what was really behind the official Austrian position gained prominence. A question was raised, for instance, why Austria had agreed to temporarily close the Energy chapter with Hungary, even though the latter also has a nuclear power plant, with four reactors of Soviet origin,[86] as opposed to Slovenia's reactor in Krško, which was built by an American company. It is also worth noting that while Austria may have been concerned about nuclear power plants in Eastern Europe, it would seem to be somewhat less so as regards the transboundary effects of the many nuclear power plants throughout Western Europe, and therefore did not persist in their closure as it did with the Krško nuclear power plant.

Some saw the background of the Austrian position as involving attempts to dominate the electricity market in Slovenia. In September 1991, the Austrian government signed with its Slovenian counterpart a protocol on cooperation, which was supposed to lead to the construction of a set of hydroelectric power stations in Slovenia on the Sava River. The protocol inter alia required Slovenia to close the Krško nuclear power plant, which would effectively remove one of the main competitors from the market.[87] Such ideas could not be substantiated at the time, but they offered a possible explanation for the inconsistency in Austrian foreign policy on nuclear power plants, as well as the possible background of bilateral pressure on Austria to "Europeanize" Slovenia.

Austria eventually gave the green light, and in March 2001 it allowed the negotiations on Chapter 14 to be closed temporarily. Further, Austria decided not to launch any new investigation of Krško. It appeared to be pleased with the quality and transparency of new measures introduced by Slovenia to monitor the safety of the nuclear power plant.[88] At the same time, it became clear that the speculations about Austria's electricity interests mentioned before were not entirely unfounded. Austrian prime minister Schüssel later said that Austria had a continuing interest in becoming more present in the Slovenian electricity market by investing in hydroelectric power stations there.[89]

Thus Austria looks forward to realizing part of its own agenda with Slovenia concerning the electricity market of the latter, whereas Slovenia appears content to have removed one of the obstacles on its way to the EU. A more detailed understanding of the events that led to the temporary closure of the energy chapter, however, might suggest that the deal may prove to be fragile precisely because nuclear safety appears to represent only a part of the Chapter 14 problem between Austria and Slovenia. There is always a possibility of reopening the issue to check whether the "high standards" of nuclear safety in Central and Eastern Europe, as emphasized (but not clarified) by the 1999 Cologne European Council,[90] are being met in Slovenia.

Another issue on the Slovenian-Austrian agenda is the status of the German-speaking community in Slovenia. The roots of this bilateral problem go back to August 1991, when the president of the expelled Germans from Upper Styria asked the Speaker of the National Assembly of Slovenia to take into account the injustices done to the expelled German-speaking population and explore remedies through the denationalization law.[91] Diplomatic action followed in 1992. In a memorandum to the Slovenian government the Austrian government officially expressed its resolve to protect (and represent) the interests of the German-speaking minority in Slovenia.[92] This minority might have been small in current numbers,[93] but if it were reconstituted by returning Germans who had been expelled, it could include up to fifteen thousand people.[94]

The status of the German-speaking community is an issue whose existence Slovenia was at first reluctant to admit.[95] However, as the Austrian government was determined to press the issue, Slovenia became more willing to discuss it. Obviously, this could become yet another field in which the "Europeanness" of Slovenia could be tested.

The Austrian government took the initiative and in 1997 proposed an agreement to Slovenia clarifying the status and rights of the German-speaking population. Slovenia agreed to the proposal of the so-called Cultural Agreement soon after[96] but tried to draw the line in negotiations. Above all, it was not prepared to grant the German-speaking community the extent of (constitutional) rights that the Italian and Hungarian minorities enjoy in Slovenia when such demands appeared in Austria.[97] The Slovenian government claimed that, in line with the constitutional provision (article 61), each person is "entitled to freely identify with his national grouping or ethnic community, to foster and give expression to his culture and to use his own language and script."[98] Furthermore, the government recognizes cultural associations established by the German-speaking population of Slovenia and supports them financially.[99] The Slovenian government also argued that there could hardly be a comparison between the German-speaking community in Slovenia and the Slovenian minority in Austria. The latter is more like the Hungarian and Italian minorities in Slovenia, both considered autochthonous. Further, the German-speaking population in Slovenia has never claimed constitutional recognition for itself. The Austrian scholar Stefan Karner (who wrote the study on the German ethnic group in Slovenia commissioned by the Austrian government) pointed out that during his interviews with members of the German-speaking population it became clear that they sought the preservation of their culture and ethnic heritage, rather than minority recognition at the constitutional level.[100]

Slovenia tried to convince the Austrian side that, given such evidence, and as regards the Cultural Agreement, a reference to the German-speaking citizens in Slovenia would suffice. The Austrian government insisted, however, on using a more precise term—the German-speaking *Volksgruppe* (ethnic group). Although interpreted differently by the two parties, the term basically found its way into the final wording of both German and Slovenian versions of the agreement.[101] The Cultural Agreement was drafted early in 1999, but it took Slovenia two more years to eventually signal its willingness to the Austrian government to actually sign it. After further clarifications had been agreed between the two governments, the Cultural Agreement was signed on April 30, 2001.[102]

Reaching the end of negotiations, both sides appeared pleased with the outcome.[103] The Austrian government obtained explicit Slovenian recognition that a German-speaking minority exists in Slovenia. Without the possibility of EU accession for Slovenia, the negotiations on the Cultural Agreement might have been prolonged significantly. The Slovenian government, for its part, seemed pleased to see the reference to the Slovenian national minority in Austria in the Cultural Agreement. Explicit recognition of the German-speaking population could not be avoided. The Slovenian intransigence on this issue would have been a useful catalyst in creating the image of the Slovenian "non-Europeanness," which in turn could have represented an insurmountable hurdle in accession negotiations. Austria clearly used its leverage here, but from the Slovenian point of view at least the Cultural Agreement does not refer to the German-speaking population as a national minority with the potential to enjoy similar constitutional rights as do the Italian and Hungarian national minorities. Had it not been at least partly successful on the latter front, it would have been difficult for the Slovenian government to explain to other ethnic groups in Slovenia why they should not enjoy the same rights as the German-speaking persons.[104]

To improve the status of the German-speaking population in Slovenia is an important, but not a complete, step. The main issue here is the status of German (Austrian) property, which used to be owned by the German-speaking population on the Yugoslav territory. The reconstruction of the minority status of the German-speaking population completes the bilateral agenda between Slovenia and Austria only if coupled with possible restitution of the real property of the German-speaking citizens who left or were forced to leave Yugoslavia in the aftermath of World War II. In this respect, the so-called AVNOJ[105] decrees, which established the former Yugoslavia, but, among other things, also decisively determined the fate of its German-speaking population, played (and still play) an important role.

For Austria, two particular AVNOJ decrees—those adopted in November 1944—would seem to be the most disputable. One decree provided inter alia that all the property of persons of German nationality (with the exception of those who fought in the Allied forces or were neutral in the war) would be nationalized. The other decree stripped Yugoslav citizenship from members of the German minority.[106] The authorities of former Yugoslavia thought that the issue of the expelled German-speaking population had been resolved long ago, through adoption of the Austrian State Treaty in 1955. Article 27 of the treaty provides that Yugoslavia can confiscate or liquidate Austrian property, rights, and interests located in the Yugoslav territory, with indemnification to Austrian citizens to be paid by the Austrian government. Slovenia also considers this article as part compensation for the atrocities committed by Austrians against Slovenians and other nations in the former Yugoslavia during the war, since Austria was never subject to reparations. Yet these issues seem to be far from closed, as the present denationalization debate shows.

The problem of denationalization, as Austria sees it, lies in the fact that many German-speaking persons who are now Austrian citizens did not

receive any compensation under article 27 of the Austrian State Treaty because they were neither Austrian nor Yugoslav citizens during the postwar
years. The Slovenian law on denationalization of 1991 provides for the
possibility that members of the German speaking-population whose
property was confiscated under the AVNOJ decrees could request the
restitution of their property. But not all of the details were cleared up by
the law. Before 1997, non-Slovenian citizens were ineligible for restitution, and it was only in that year that the Slovenian constitutional court
ruled on the status of claimants of German nationality. Members of this
group of claimants had to prove their loyalty to the Yugoslav authorities
during World War II. If the requisite proof was at hand, they could become
eligible to claim their property.[107] Austria complained against this ruling,
arguing that Slovenia was operating from the premise of presumed (collective) guilt rather than the presumption of innocence. At the same time,
the Slovenian denationalization law did not seem to require such proof of
loyalty for others, for example, Slovenian nationals who were on the
wrong side during the war.[108]

The Austrian position about the injustice done by the 1991 denationalization law and about the 1997 constitutional court ruling remained firm,
and further activities from Vienna were likely to be expected. Indeed,
signs of moving this presumably bilateral issue onto a higher, European
level were soon visible. The Austrian government was careful not to tackle
the AVNOJ decrees head on, given that those decrees may indeed be perceived as embedded in the current European order. Instead, the government applied what may be called the delinking approach. When discussing the issue with its EU partners, Austria pointed only at the possibly
discriminatory practices of the Slovenian denationalization law. Such an
approach yielded results. In September 1999 the EU included denationalization on the agenda of accession negotiations with Slovenia, effectively
echoing the Austrian interests. Slovenia objected that denationalization
did not constitute part of the *acquis*[109] and was therefore not subject to
any accession negotiations.[110] Denationalization does not appear to be on
the agenda of any other applicant country, including the Czech Republic,
from whose predecessor (Czechoslovakia) the German population had to
flee en masse after the war.

The delinking approach and its emphasis on the discriminatory clauses
of the Slovenian denationalization law became ever more present in the
Austrian foreign policy rhetoric. The Foreign Ministry of Austria stressed
early in 2000 that "in the past Austria has dealt with the matter of AVNOJ
resolutions and their current legal effects bilaterally, without linking it to
the enlargement of the EU, and will continue to do so."[111] The Austrian embassy in Ljubljana has been even more clear on this issue, saying that "the
Austrian government never has and never will request a formal abolition of

the AVNOJ conclusions" and that "this is not the official view of the Austrian government and, consequently, Austria will not make this a condition for Slovenia's EU entry. What concerns Austria is the denationalization process in Slovenia."[112] Similarly, in his memorandum to Slovenian president Milan Kučan, Austrian president Thomas Klestil said that Austria did not demand that the AVNOJ decrees "be rescinded but that the discrimination contained in the Slovenian Denationalization Law of 1991 be removed," for the law "includes the principles of assuming collective guilt and the reversal of the burden of proof, which do not correspond to European legal standards."[113]

These arguments and the delinking approach itself did not appear convincing and found little sympathy in Slovenia. Šmidovnik, for example, argues that the Slovenian denationalization law would be discriminatory if interpreted separately from the AVNOJ decrees. Since it is not, and is thus based on those decrees, it can be interpreted only in the context of the European practice after World War II, which inter alia has been codified by the Austrian State Treaty. According to these terms, the enemy's property could be confiscated—with exemptions for those loyal to the allied forces.[114]

In July 2000, the European Commission sought to clarify its own position. During his visit to Slovenia in July 2000, the commissioner responsible for enlargement, Günter Verheugen, said that, in terms of property restitution, denationalization was not the subject of negotiations, but any proof of discrimination was, due to the general principle of nondiscrimination applied in the EU.[115] This statement was not good news for Slovenia, as it clearly follows the delinking approach applied by Austria. Denationalization has been therefore successfully brought onto the European level even though it is not part of the *acquis*. Now wrapped into the principle of nondiscrimination, denationalization might turn into an important argument for Austria in testing the "Europeanness" of Slovenia and consequently could have an impact on the outcome of accession negotiations between Slovenia and the EU.[116]

CONCLUSION

Finnemore has noted that "tensions and contradictions among normative principles in international life mean that there is no set of ideal political and economic arrangements toward which we are converging."[117] Much of this applies to negotiations between the EU and applicant countries. For Slovenia, considerable work at the Community level of negotiations remains to be done. Difficult chapters are still on the agenda. Even though the negotiations are progressing rapidly, it is too early to say how much Slovenia will lose or gain after this level of negotiations has been completed, and what the foundation will be on which Slovenia will start to build its position as a full EU member. The EU market as such is a challenge both economically and politically for any state, and particularly for a small state that depends and thrives on bigger markets. In economic terms, Slovenia will have become part of a common market that, by definition, offers ample opportunities for specialization and therefore an increase in the country's "size" in various fields of cooperation. In political terms, the advantages also seem obvious. When Slovenia is a full member, its relative political importance at the regional and global levels will increase.

In terms of Slovenia's taking on norms and values generated by the EU, the Community level of negotiations tells only a part of the whole story. The bilateral level of accession negotiations also warrants special attention. It is important simply because solving problems stemming from that level could be used as a test of an applicant state's compliance with European "norms and values," and can thus make the negotiations more complex, whereas for an applicant state the negotiating outcome becomes more uncertain. Here Slovenia has already faced the problem of being treated differently from other acceding countries. It was compelled to prove its "Europeanness" early in that it had to open up its real estate market sooner than initially anticipated. This was because during negotiations on Slovenia's Association Agreement, Italy had enough leverage in the EU to turn the essentially bilateral problem of property restitution into a European issue. Slovenia, for its part, did not seem to spend much energy exploring and making use of its own capabilities to promote its own interests. The desire to conclude the European Agreement sooner rather than later was stronger.

Relations between Austria and Slovenia indicate how powerful a small state can be in terms of its relative influence in certain fields of cooperation. The prize of EU membership is arming Austria with sufficient leverage over Slovenia to block any of its moves toward the desired goal unless bilateral issues are resolved satisfactorily. Slovenia, now more experienced with the bilateral side of accession negotiations, has been aware of this. For instance, it did some strategic thinking by not joining in political sanctions against Austria in January 2000, officially because it decided to judge the new government according to its deeds. Austria has publicly recognized that Slovenia continued its cooperation with Austria in spite of the EU sanctions.[118] However, Austria did not fail to continue promoting (rather successfully) its own interests vis-à-vis Slovenia. The problem with the Krško nuclear power plant appears to have been resolved, though at a price for Slovenia. Furthermore, the Slovenian desire for full EU membership has been instrumental in accepting the Cultural Agreement—a special bilateral arrangement that is particularly important to Austria because it addresses the issue of the German-speaking population in Slovenia.

On the other hand, the issue of denationalization remains open and may well prove an important test of Slovenia's "Europeanness." The Austrian government has already been able to translate this essentially bilateral problem into the issue of discrimination at the Community level of negotiations. This scenario has partly been possible since Slovenia has weakened its position, notably because of the lack of legal clarity as to those entitled to property restitution. Such internal weaknesses, combined with Slovenia's initial inability, as an applicant state, to envisage the different effects EU norms may have, might continue to backfire and make the Slovenian government less satisfied with the ultimate results of the accession talks than it might be hoping for.

NOTES

The author would like to thank Petra Roter for her reading of the earlier drafts of this chapter, her many useful comments and suggestions, and particularly her insights into the problematic relating to national minorities in Slovenia and neighboring countries. Thanks also go to the anonymous reviewer and particularly to the editor of this volume, Ronald Linden, for his meticulous reading of earlier drafts and valuable suggestions. Of course, the responsibility for the contents of this chapter rests solely with the author.

1. Robert D. Putnam, "Diplomacy and Domestic Politics: The Logic of Two-Level Games," *International Organization* 42, no. 3 (1988): 427–60; Peter B. Evans, Harold K. Jacobson, and Robert D. Putnam, eds., *Double-Edged Diplomacy: International Bargaining and Domestic Politics* (Berkeley: University of California Press, 1994).

2. The use of the term "European Union," which will be applied throughout this study whenever applicable, is correct insofar as the Treaty on European Union (TEU) signed at Maastricht (1992) and revised in Amsterdam (1997) is the result of the decision of member states to establish among themselves the "European Union" (article 1 of the TEU). Further, the EU shall be served by a "single institutional framework" (article 3 of the TEU). Thus the European Union does not have an institutional setup of its own but borrows it from the three European Communities, which have had a common institutional structure since the Treaty Establishing a Single Council and a Single Commission (the so-called Merger Treaty, which was signed on April 8, 1965, and came into force on July 1, 1967).

3. Where applicable, the term "former Yugoslavia" will also be used.

4. For example, in a survey of public opinion conducted between November and December 1990, almost three-quarters of respondents (74.4 percent) believed that living conditions in an independent Slovenia would improve in the following ten years. Niko Toš, *Vrednote v prehodu II: Slovensko javno mnenje 1990–1999* [Values in Transition II: Slovenian Public Opinion 1990–1999] (Ljubljana: Fakulteta za družbene vede, 1999), 18.

5. Bojko Bučar and Stein Kuhnle, eds., *Small States Compared: Politics of Norway and Slovenia* (Bergen: Alma Mater, 1994); Danica Fink-Hafner and Terry Cox,

eds., *Into Europe? Perspectives from Britain and Slovenia* (Ljubljana: Faculty of Social Sciences, 1996).

6. The Single European Act was adopted on February 17 and 28, 1986. It entered into force on July 1, 1987.

7. The Maastricht treaty was adopted on February 1, 1992. It entered into force on November 1, 1993.

8. Monetary integration has always been favored by France, which sees economic integration as instrumental to French interests in closely monitoring German economic progress. Further integration in the field of the economy, including the establishment of the Economic and Monetary Union (EMU), was the price for that, and apparently France was willing to pay it. But in 1989, things changed dramatically, with a unified Germany presenting a whole new dimension in Franco-German affairs. Forty-five years after World War II, Germany was on the brink of becoming the most powerful country in Europe and some states, notably France, saw this as a potential destabilizing element in the European integration process. The way to avoid any negative consequences of German unification was seen as firmly anchoring Germany within the European Communities. A formula acceptable to both the French and the Germans was sought. The French apparently believed the EMU would be instrumental in achieving this. The Germans, on a quid pro quo basis, seemed to want progress on a political union because it seemed hard to believe that monetary integration could survive without strong political institutions. A package deal was agreed between the Germans and the French and on April 19, 1990, Chancellor Kohl of Germany and President Mitterand of France sent a joint letter to the Irish presidency in which they expressed their wish that an intergovernmental conference (IGC) on European political union (EPU) be held parallel to the IGC on the EMU. The idea eventually found support at the Dublin summit of 25 and 26 June 1990. Zlatko Šabič, *Voting in International Organisations: Mere Formality or a Matter of Substance?* (Ljubljana: Scientific Library, 1999), 308.

9. Consider the speech of Romano Prodi, president of the European Commission, before the European Parliament in Brussels on May 13, 1999: "Now, as never before, and perhaps as never again, we have the chance to create a Europe in which all the peoples of this continent can live together in peace, security, freedom, justice and equality. A democratic Europe where human rights are respected and the rule of law prevails. An economically integrated Europe which offers growth and prosperity through a single market and a single currency." Speech 99/130 <www.europa.eu. int/rapid/start/cgi/guesten.ksh?p_action.gettxt=gt&doc=SPEECH/99/130 l 0 l RAPID& lg=EN> (September 17, 2000).

10. Richard N. Coudenhove-Kalergi, *Die Europäische Nation* (Stuttgart: Deutsche Verlags-Anstalt, 1953), 81; see also Richard N. Coudenhove-Kalergi, *Pan-Europa* (Wien: Paneuropa Verlag, 1924). The world seen from his perspective was divided into five main regions: Panamerica, the British Empire, the Soviet Union, East Asia, and Europe. He argued that while the first four regions functioned as single units, European *Kleinstäterei* did not allow for a common European policy. He remained convinced that if European states wanted to compete with other regions, they had to form a union among themselves. Of course, it may be argued that there have been many more or less elaborate plans on European unification before Kalergi's plan. For a brief overview, see, e.g., Zlatko Šabič, *In-*

ternational Parliamentary Organs in European Institutional Organisation: Selected Cases (Ljubljana: CIR, 1995).

11. "An Unprecedented Enlargement" <www.europa.eu.int/comm/enlargement/intro/index.htm#> (August 9, 2000).

12. Peter J. Katzenstein, "Introduction: Alternative Perspectives on National Security," in *The Culture of National Security: Norms and Identity in World Politics*, ed. Peter J. Katzenstein (New York: Columbia University Press, 1996), 1–32.

13. "Identity" is considered "a shorthand label for varying constructions of nation- and statehood." Katzenstein, "Introduction," 6.

14. Katzenstein, "Introduction," 5.

15. Natural theorists, for example, entertained the small state problematic from the perspective of the juridical equality of states. One of them wrote: "Since men are by nature equal. . . . Nations . . . are by nature equal and hold from nature the same obligations and the same rights. Strength or weakness, in this case, counts for nothing. . . . [A] small republic is no less a sovereign State than the most powerful Kingdom." Emeric de Vattel (1758), *The Law of Nations or the Principles of Natural Law* (Washington: Carnegie Institution of Washington, 1916), introduction, 18; bk. 2, chap. 3, 35–39.

16. Examples of such works include Edwin De Witt Dickinson, *The Equality of States in International Law* (Cambridge, Mass.: Harvard University Press, 1920); and F. C. Hicks, "The Equality of States and Hague Conferences," *American Journal of International Law* 2, no. 3 (1908): 530–61.

17. Peter J. Katzenstein, *Small States in World Markets: Industrial Policy in Europe* (Ithaca, N.Y.: Cornell University Press, 1985), 201.

18. On July 14, 1969, the U.S. representative sent a letter to the president of the Security Council of the United Nations, in which a new category called associate membership was proposed for consideration as to the formal status of very small member states. The new category would, according to the United States, particularly accommodate small countries, unable to assume the obligations of full membership (S/9397 and S/8296). The matter was debated at the 1,506th meeting of the Council. Speaking on behalf of his country, Spain, the president of the Council recognized the need to deal with this issue. He stated, however, that article 4 of the charter imposed no limitations about the size of an applicant. Consequently, it would be difficult to judge whether, for economic reasons or because of the excessive economic burden involved, a state can be barred from full membership (S/PV.1506, 6).

19. Besides the works referred to in this chapter, a wealth of literature is available in the field of small state research. See, among many, David Vital, *The Inequality of States: A Study of Small Power in International Relations* (Oxford: Clarendon, 1967); Wilhelm Christmas-Møller, "Some Thoughts on the Scientific Applicability of the Small State Concept: A Research History and a Discussion," in *Small States in Europe and Dependence*, ed. Otmar Höll (Vienna: Wilhelm Braumüller, 1983), 35–53; Colin Clark and Thomas Payne, eds., *Politics, Security, and Development of Small States* (London: Allen & Unwin, 1987); Michael I. Handel, *Weak States in the International System* (London: Frank Cass, 1990); Milan Jazbec, "Security and the Diplomacies of Small States" (unpublished paper, 1999); and Marjan Svetličič, "Implications of Globalization for Small Transition Economies in Central and Eastern Europe," *Global Focus* 12, no. 1 (2000): 51–64. An excellent survey of the small state literature in Europe

can be found in Richard Griffiths and Helge Pharo, "Small States and European Integration: Literature Survey and Evaluation," Arena Working Papers, no. 19 (Oslo: Research Council of Norway, 1995).

20. Jennie Harre Hindmarsh, "How Do We Define *Small* States and Islands? A Critical Analysis of Alternative Conceptualizations," *Convergence* 29, no. 2 <http://ehostweb15.global.epnet.com/fulltext.asp?resultSetId=R00000001&hit Num=2&booleanTerm=Hindmarsh> (July 6, 1999).

An example of defining a small state by measurable parameters only is Marjan Senjur, "The Viability of Economic Development of a Small State Separating from a Larger One," in *Slovenia: A Small Country in the Global Economy,* ed. Marjan Senjur (Ljubljana: Centre for International Cooperation and Development [CICD]/International Center for Economic Growth [ICEG], 1993), 17–31, 19. He defended his arbitrary decision on defining a small state for operational reasons. In his view, a small state should have a surface area of between 10,000 and 100,000 square kilometers and should have a population of 1–10 million.

21. "Gross Domestic Product 2000," Organisation for Economic Co-operation and Development <www.oecd.org/publications/figures/2001/anglais/012_013_GDP.pdf> (May 15, 2001).

22. Hindmarsh, "How Do We Define."

23. Hans Geser, "Kleinstaaten im internationalen System," *Kölner Zeitschrift für Soziologie und Sozialpsychologie* 44, no. 4 (1992): 627–55, 629; Katzenstein, *Small States in World Markets,* 200–201. Chancellor Adenauer of Germany believed that it would take some time before Germany would be able to lead an independent foreign policy again, and that "only through abstaining from national sovereignty in several fields, could Germany develop normal relations to its neighbors." Bjørn Otto Sverdrup, "Odysseus and the Lilliputians? Germany, the European Union, and the Smaller European States," Arena Working Paper, no. 27 (Oslo: Research Council of Norway, 1997).

24. M. Jansen, "History of European Integration, 1945–1975," Occasional Papers of the Europa Institute, no. 1 (Amsterdam: University of Amsterdam, 1975), 40.

25. Michel Dumoulin, "La Belgique et les débuts du Plan Schuman (mai 1950–février 1952)," in *Die Anfänge des Schuman-Plans 1950– 51,* ed. Klaus Schwabe (Baden-Baden: Nomos Verlag, 1988), 271–85, 281–82.

26. David Vital, *The Survival of Small States: Studies in Small Power/Great Power Conflict* (London: Oxford University Press, 1971).

27. Vital, *Survival of Small States,* 7.

28. Robert O. Keohane, "Lilliputians' Dilemmas: Small States in International Politics," *International Organization* 23, no. 2 (1969): 291–310.

29. Sasha Baillie, "A Theory of Small State Influence in the European Union," *Journal of International Relations and Development* 1, no. 3–4 (1998): 195–220, 199–200.

30. Alan Osborn, "Banking on the Euro," *Europe Magazine* March 1999 <www.eurunion.org/magazine/9903/luxembourg.htm> (September 20, 2000).

31. Osborn, "Banking on the Euro."

32. U.S. Energy Information Administration, "World Oil Market and Oil Price Chronologies: 1970–1999" <www.eia.doe.gov/emeu/cabs/chron.html> (September 8, 2000).

33. Arild N. Nystad, "Perspective on Oil and Gas Developments on the Norwegian Continental Shelf," *IAEE Newsletter,* Summer 1997 <www.iaee.org/newsltr/97sum4.asp> (September 1, 2000).

34. Jan Egeland, *Impotent Superpower—Potent Small State: Potentials and Limitations of Human Rights Objectives in the Foreign Policies of the United States and Norway* (Oslo: Norwegian University Press, 1997).

35. Laura Silber and Allan Little, *The Death of Yugoslavia* (London: Penguin/BBC Worldwide, 1996).

36. Irena Brinar and Stein Kuhnle, "Perspectives on European Integration in Smaller Democracies: Norway and Slovenia Compared," in *Small States Compared: Politics of Norway and Slovenia,* ed. Bojko Bučar and Stein Kuhnle (Bergen: Alma Mater, 1994), 1–28, 14–15. There are several works that, from different perspectives, analyze the emergence of Slovenia as an independent state. See, for instance, Jill Benderley and Evan Kraft, eds., *Independent Slovenia: Origins, Movements, Prospects* (Basingstoke, U.K.: Macmillan, 1994); Frane Adam and Gregor Tomc, eds., "Small Societies in Transition: The Case of Slovenia: Transformation Processes in a Small Post-Socialist Society," special issue of *Druzboslovne Razprave* (Ljubljana: Slovenian Sociological Association, 1994); Danica Fink Hafner and John R. Robbins, eds., *Making a New Nation: The Formation of Slovenia* (Aldershot, U.K.: Dartmouth, 1996); and Milan Brglez, "Diplomatic Relations, Modern Law of Diplomacy, and the Republic of Slovenia: Selected Aspects," *Journal of International Relations* 3, no. 1–4 (1996): 54–69.

37. The figures are taken from Branko Hvastija, ed., *Gospodarski kazalci držav sveta* [Economic Indicators of the World's States] (Ljubljana: Center za mednarodno sodelovanje in razvoj—CMSR, 1993), 271; and *Bulletin of the Bank of Slovenia,* October 1994; June–July 1994.

38. According to other sources, even as low as 5.3 percent. See Hvastija, *Gospodarski kazalci,* 271.

39. Ivan Svetlik, "Slovenia: A Portrait of a New European Country," in Ivan Svetlik, ed., *Social Policy in Slovenia* (Avebury, U.K.: Ashgate, 1992), 1–14; Brinar and Kuhnle, "Perspectives on European Integration," 17.

40. *Bulletin of the Bank of Slovenia* 6, no. 10 (1997): 51.

41. *Bulletin of the Bank of Slovenia,* October 1994; June–July 1994.

42. "Regular Report from the Commission on Progress toward Accession—Slovenia" (1999), sec. C <http://europa.eu.int/comm/enlargement/slovenia/rep_10_99 aa.htm> (April 2, 2001).

43. The data are from the Vienna Institute for International Economic Studies (Wiener Institut für Internationale Wirtschaftsvergleiche). They were presented in "Foreign Analysts Forecast around 4 percent Economic Growth in Slovenia in 2000 and 2001," *Slovenian Economic Mirror,* July 2000 <www.sigov.si/zmar/arhiv/ og0700/aogl0700.html> (November 28, 2000). See also "Favourable International Economic Environment Boosts Economic Growth in CEFTA," *Slovenian Economic Mirror,* March 2000 <http://www.sigov.si/zmar/arhiv/og0300/aogl0300.html#amed> (November 28, 2000).

44. The figures about the inflation and unemployment are from the Slovenian government <www.sigov.si/vrs/ang/slovenia/the-economy.html> (July 15, 2001). For analysis, see "Annual Edition 2000," *Slovenian Economic Mirror,* 2000, 4/S

<www.sigov.si/zmar/arhiv/aletno00/aleo2000.html> (March 16, 2001); and "Economic Reform Monitor no. 1. Country Notes: Slovenia," European Commission, March 2000, ECFIN/D.1 <europa.eu.int/comm/economy_finance/document/eesuppc/2000_1/sloven.htm> (September 7, 2000).

45. Katzenstein, *Small States in World Markets*, 25.

46. Article 49 of the consolidated treaty on the EU.

47. As already mentioned, the European Parliament must also give its assent to the Accession Treaty. Because only the intergovernmental part of accession negotiations is discussed here, the role of the European Parliament has not been included in the figure.

48. "Presidency Conclusions," Copenhagen European Council, June 21–22, 1993, section 7/A.

49. "Presidency Conclusions," Copenhagen European Council, section 7/A.

50. The following section, which presents a brief overview of Slovenia's progress in its efforts to accede to the EU from the Commission's perspective, is based on the following documents: *Regular Report from the Commission*; *Slovenia 2000: Regular Report from the Commission on Slovenia's Progress toward Accession* <www.sigov.si/svez/uk/_doc/_arhiv/report2000.pdf> (April 2, 2001); and the 2000 Slovenian government's *Report on Slovenia's Progress toward Accession* <www.sigov.si/svez/uk/_doc/_arhiv/SVEZreport2000.pdf> (April 2, 2001).

51. The reasons for this seem to be structural. Slovenia is a small market and as such is not always attractive to foreign investors. At the same time, protectionism seems well established in Slovenia. According to *World Competitiveness Yearbook* (2000) data, as presented by *Slovenian Economic Mirror*, "Slovenia's legislation is very open and Slovenia adopted a program of lifting barriers to foreign investors. However, the downward trend of foreign direct investment is one of the most convincing pieces of evidence showing that national protectionism does exist. . . . Slovenia ranks the lowest in investment initiative, which is too weak to attract foreign investors. Slovenia ranks the second lowest place in the area of controlling foreign investors in domestic companies: the level of control is almost twice the level of Ireland." "Is Protection in the National Interest?" *Slovenian Economic Mirror*, February 2001 <www.sigov.si/zmar/arhiv/og0201/aogl0201.html> (June 17, 2001).

52. In this respect several problems have been mentioned. The Commission believes that Slovenia must strengthen its public employment service, as well as the public administration and enforcement structures in areas such as social policy, health, and safety at work. Reform is also needed in managing the labor market and employment policies. Also, "the institutional, judicial and administrative capacity to implement co-ordination rules in the field of social security of migrant workers needs to be improved further through strengthening of the social security administration and the further training of officials." "Slovenia 2000," 55.

53. The European Commission pointed out several outstanding issues to be solved. For example, the Commission criticized the slowness of the judicial process. Although the Commission recognized improvements in reducing the size of backlogs (mostly in district and local courts), the number of pending cases was still considered high. At the end of June 1999, the number of pending cases (local courts were considered particularly overburdened) was 566,000. Of the total number of pending cases, 64 percent concerned the land register and the enforcement

of decisions. Such an overload inter alia reduces the capacity of domestic courts to integrate the EC law into the domestic legal order, but Slovenia has been trying to minimize the problem by adopting additional legislation (e.g., new civil procedure law, adopted in April 1999, that shortens and rationalizes legal proceedings in courts and offers additional protection to victims), providing for additional training of judges, modernization/computerization of the land registry, and so on. "Regular Report from the Commission," sec. B/4; "Slovenia 2000," 15. As for public administration (especially its ability to implement the *acquis*), the Commission has sent out even more critical tones. The Commission believes that reforms in this area have been weak due to the lack of consensus on fundamental issues (such as the scope of civil service and salaries), but also because of a lack of political commitment. According to the Commission, the Slovenian government appears to underestimate the implication of EU membership for the domestic public administration, which in its present state will find it very difficult to cope with the demands of implementing the *acquis*. Slovenia, for its part, recognizes the problem and has reported on several measures such as the adoption of framework legislation (in particular within the field of the internal market), recruitment, and training of staff needed for implementation of the EU legislation. "Regular Report from the Commission," sec. B/4; "Report on Slovenia's Progress," 200–201. The Commission recognizes these efforts, although it has insisted that "the excessive duration of court procedures continues to be a problem in Slovenia." "Slovenia 2000," 15.

54. These somewhat unusual rankings caused irritation not only in Slovenia but also in the Czech Republic, both ranked behind Poland. "Ugodno kljub nekaterim kritikam" [Commission Report Favorable, Despite Some Criticism], *Dnevnik*, November 9, 2000 <www.dnevnik.si/cgi/view.exe?w=dn.9.11.2000.1huat> (November 22, 2000); "EU Notes Improvements in Czech Republic," *RFE/RL Newsline*, November 10, 2000 <www.rferl.org/newsline/2000/11/091100.html> (November 24, 2000). The ranking approach is part of the so-called new enlargement strategy proposed by the Commission on November 8, 2000, which aims at stepping up the negotiation process. The new enlargement strategy was endorsed by the member states at their December 2000 summit in Nice. "Presidency Conclusions," Nice European Council, 7–9 December 2000, para. 5 <www.europa.eu.int/council/off/conclu/dec2000/dec2000_en.pdf> (March 10, 2001).

55. The operative head of negotiations for Slovenia, Janez Potočnik, said that the conclusions in the last report of the Commission were hardly surprising, since the Commission relied on data by and large supplied by Slovenia in its own 2000 report. But he remained optimistic about the prospects of Slovenia entering the EU in the first round, as did the Slovenian government. For the statement of the government of the Republic of Slovenia on the occasion of the release of the third Commission report, see <www.gov.si/svez/svez1ang.htm> (June 2, 2000). See also "Portret tedna: Dr. Janez Potočnik" [Portrait of the Week: Dr. Janez Potočnik], *Delo—Sobotna Priloga*, November 11, 2000, 3.

56. The EU member states pledged: "Provided that progress toward meeting the accession criteria continues at an unabated pace, the road map should make it possible to complete negotiations by the end of 2002 for those applicant countries that are ready. The objective is that they should participate in the European Parliament

elections of 2004 as members." "Presidency Conclusions," Göteborg European Council, June 15–16, 2001, para. 9.

57. The status of the temporarily closed chapters has been described by the Slovenian negotiating team as follows: At the intergovernmental conferences on accession, "the Committee of Permanent Representatives (COREPER) of the Council and an applicant country discuss the negotiating positions on both sides, bring their positions on the substance of individual negotiating chapters into line and—provided there are no outstanding issues with regard to a given chapter—establish that negotiations on that chapter may be temporarily closed. Since the principle that nothing is agreed until everything is agreed applies to negotiations, the temporarily closed chapters may still be reopened by the conference on accession." "Negotiations" <www.gov.si/ops/ang/organizacija/index.html> (September 19, 2000).

58. Ulrike Hiebler, "Austria's Accession to the European Union: Impacts on the National Legal Order," *Journal of International Relations and Development* 2, no. 2 (1999): 187–215, 188.

59. These problems were not encountered during the accession process of Austria, Finland, and Sweden to the EU. For analysis, see "Lessons and Experiences from the European Union's Latest Newcomers," *Journal of International Relations and Development* 2, no. 2 (1999): 126–215. Special issue with guest editor Bojko Bučar.

60. According to the Commission's proposal issued in April 2001, there would be a general five-year transition period that could be extended for a maximum of two years for individual countries. "Enlargement: Commission Proposes Flexible Transitional Arrangements for the Free Movement of Workers" <www.europa.eu.int/rapid/start/cgi/guesten.ksh?> (June 17, 2000).

61. Istria is a small peninsula divided between three countries: Croatia, Italy, and Slovenia. Between 1918 and 1943 it belonged to Italy.

62. Ivo Murko, *Obmejna problematika, posledice vojne in tehnična vprašanja sklepanja pogodb* [Border Problematic: Consequences of War and Technical Questions of Concluding Agreements] (Ljubljana: Fakulteta za sociologijo, politične vede in novinarstvo, 1983).

63. Bojko Bučar, "The International Recognition of Slovenia," in *Making a New Nation: The Formation of Slovenia*, ed. Danica Fink-Hafner and John R. Robins (Aldershot, U.K.: Dartmouth, 1997), 31–45, 41.

64. Bojko Bučar, "The Issue of the Rule of Law in the EU Enlargement Process: Aspects of Slovenian-Italian Relations," in *Development and Developing International and European Law: Essays in Honour of Konrad Ginther on the Occasion of His Sixty-fifth Birthday*, ed. Wolfgang Benedek, Hubert Isak, and Renate Kicker (Frankfurt/Main: Peter Lang, 1999), 339–53, 343.

65. Bučar, "Issue of the Rule of Law," 341–42.

66. Bučar, "Issue of the Rule of Law," 342. See also "Motion for a Resolution on Unity and Respect for the Rights of Italian Minority in Slovenia and Croatia," Council of Europe, Parliamentary Assembly, doc. 6795, 1993.

67. The following are excerpts from "Opinion on the Application of the Republic of Slovenia for Membership in the Council of Europe" Parliamentary Assembly of the Council of Europe, doc. 6823, 1993 (Rapporteur: Mr. Hörcsik, Hungary, Democratic Forum): "My impression is that Slovenia . . . has modern legislation on civil and penal law—and in many other fields—and modern institutions, some of which do not

(yet) exist in all Council of Europe member states (constitutional court, ombudsmen, and special representatives of minorities in elected bodies) . . . Both [Italian and Hungarian] communities are relatively privileged. . . . The way [Slovenia] protects the rights of minorities is a model and an example for many European States (both east and west)."

68. The so-called Global Protection Act for the Slovenian Minority in Italy was adopted by the Italian senate on February 14, 2001.

69. It is of interest that two expressions are used for the group of people who left Istria after World War II. In Slovenia they are called *optanti* ("optants," i.e., those who opted to leave a country); in Italy, the word *esuli* (meaning "the exiled," i.e., those who were forced to leave their own homes) is preferred.

70. Bučar, "Issue of the Rule of Law," 344.

71. Bučar, "International Recognition of Slovenia," 41.

72. Bučar, "Issue of the Rule of Law," 344.

73. He resigned in September 1994 due to internal rows within the ruling coalition, composed of left- and right-wing parties.

74. Mojca Drčar-Murko, "Some Legal Aspects of Relations between Slovenia and Italy," *Journal of International Relations* 3, no. 1–4 (1996): 70–84, 71.

75. Bučar, "Issue of the Rule of Law," 344–45.

76. The problem of liberalizing the real estate market and how it affected the people living in areas where Slovenia borders on other countries was certainly not unknown to European institutions. Mr. Hörcsik, a Hungarian representative in the Council of Europe, pointed that problem out quite clearly in his 1993 report, when discussing the status of the minorities in Slovenia. "For instance, the Italian community drew my attention to legislation which prohibits the acquisition of real property near the borders, a provision clearly detrimental to them." *Opinion on the Application of the Republic of Slovenia for Membership in the Council of Europe,* Parliamentary Assembly of the Council of Europe, doc. 6823 (Rapporteur: Mr. Hörcsik, Hungary, Democratic Forum).

77. "For the first time a link arose between a (legally nonexistent) bilateral question and the multilateral relations between Slovenia and the institutions of European integration." Drčar-Murko, "Some Legal Aspects," 72.

78. "Slovenia Applies for Membership in EU," *Together in Europe: European Union Newsletter for Central Europe*, July 15, 1996 <europa.eu.int/en/comm/dg10/infcom/newspage/news-93.html> (August 13, 2000).

79. Drčar-Murko, "Some Legal Aspects," 73; Bučar, "Issue of the Rule of Law," 343.

80. "Slovenia Applies for Membership in EU," *Together in Europe: European Union Newsletter for Central Europe*, July 15, 1996 <europa.eu.int/en/comm/dg10/infcom/newspage/news-93.html> (September 8, 2000).

81. Schüssel's partner in making the coalition government was Jörg Haider, the populist leader of the Freedom Party. Although eventually forced to distance himself from the government and renounce the leadership of the party due to international pressure, Haider is still considered an influential figure within the Freedom Party. "Haider's Party Sworn into New Austrian Government," *New York Times on the Web*, February 4, 2000 <www.unc.edu/depts/eucenter/articles/000204austria_nyt.html> (August 2, 2001); "Haider's Resignation Meets Skeptical Response," *FT.com Financial Times*, February 29, 2000 <www.unc.edu/depts/eucenter/articles/000228austria_ft.htm> (August 2, 2001).

82. "Nach Temelin nun Krsko: Wien blockiert Beitrittsverhandlungen," *Die Presse*, November 11, 2000 <www.diepresse.at/archiv.taf?_function=read&_UserReference= D00B1179B71744463A46074D&_id=710893> (December 16, 2000).

83. "Slovenian Nuclear Power Plant Safe from Earthquake," Government of the Republic of Slovenia, Public Relations and Media Office <www.uvi.si/eng/new/background-information/jek> (January 9, 2001).

84. "Der Reaktor darf ein bisschen wackeln," *Der Standard*, November 28, 2000 <http://derstandard.at/dyn/archiv/archarchiv.asp?artfn=/Archiv/20001128/56.HTM> (January 12, 2001).

85. "AKW Krsko: Laibach wegen Wiens neuer Bedenken verstimmt," *Die Presse*, December 2, 2000 <www.diepresse.at/archiv.taf?_function=read&_UserReference=D00B1 179B71 74 4463A46074D&_id=714704> (January 12, 2001).

86. The data obtained from the IAEA, "Power Reactor Information System" <www.iaea.org/cgi-bin/db.page.pl/pris.powrea.htm?> (August 21, 2000).

87. "Slovenia, zakaj ne vpiješ" [Slovenia, why don't you Yell], *Dnevnik*, December 12, 2000 <www.dnevnik.si/doc/dn/2000/12/2/nndac.hts> (January 12, 2001).

88. "Avstrija ne bo ovirala vstopa Slovenije v EU" [Austria Will Not Impede Slovenian Entry in EU], *Delo*, March 17, 2001, 1.

89. "Na trdnih tleh vzajemnih koristi" [On Solid Ground of Mutual Benefits], *Delo*, March 17, 2001, 1.

90. "Presidency Conclusions," Cologne European Council, June 3–4, 1999, para. 60.

91. Igor Mekina, "Slovenia and Austria: A New Minority," *AIM Press,* January 22, 2000 <www.aimpress.org/dyn/trae/archive/data/200001/00122-001-trae-lju.htm> (October 18, 2000).

92. For the text of the memorandum, see Dušan Nečak, ed., *"Nemci" na Slovenskem 1941–1955: Izsledki projekta* ["Germans" in Slovenia 1941–1955: Project Findings] (Ljubljana: Znanstveni inštitut Filozofske fakultete, 1998), 9.

93. The term "German-speaking population" as used here refers to those Slovenian citizens who declare themselves as Germans or Austrians, or have declared German as their mother tongue. According to the 1991 national census, 546 inhabitants of Slovenia declared themselves Germans and 199 said they were Austrians. In the total population of Slovenia, this accounts for 0.03 percent and 0.01 percent, respectively. At the same time, 1,543 persons declared German as their mother tongue. *Ethnic Minorities in Slovenia* (Ljubljana: Institute for Ethnic Studies/Information Bureau of the Government of Slovenia, 1994), 8.

94. Mekina, "Slovenia and Austria." It is worth noting that there is a sizable Slovenian minority in Austria numbering between twenty thousand and sixty thousand (Bučar, "Issue of the Rule of Law," 350). Legally speaking, the Slovenian minority enjoys protection under the Austrian State Treaty.

95. In 1997, the foreign minister of Slovenia, Boris Frlec, stated publicly that he did not know of any German minority in Slovenia. Igor Mekina, "Slovenia and Austria: The Scare of Indiscriminate Denationalisation," *AIM Press,* September 24, 2000 <www.aimpress.org/dyn/trae/archive/data/200009/00924-003-trae-lju.htm> (November 28, 2000).

96. "Wien-Laibach: Fast ein Meilenstein," *Die Presse*, January 17, 1998 <www.diepresse.at/archiv.taf?_function=read&_UserReference=43B2487437BBEED 63B553383&_id=28783> (September 14, 2000).

97. In major part the demands for recognition of the German-speaking population as a national minority under the Slovenian constitution originated from Jörg Haider, the ex-leader of the Freedom Party. Had these demands gained prominence at the governmental level, the issue of the rights of the German-speaking population in Slovenia might well have turned into another trouble spot in accession talks between Slovenia and the EU. "Želje eno, pogoji drugo" [Between the Wishes and Conditions], *Dnevnik*, April 14, 1999 <www.dnevnik.si/cgi/view.exe?w=dn.14.4.1999.2zbqj> (September 14, 2000).

98. The constitution of the Republic of Slovenia is available at <www.us-s. si/en/basisfr.html> (July 7, 2001).

99. Miran Komac, "Evropska listina o regionalnih ali manjšinskih jezikih v luči ohranjanja manjšinskih jezikov v Sloveniji" [The European Charter for Regional or Minority Languages in the Light of the Preservation of Minority Languages in Slovenia] (unpublished paper, 2000).

100. "Kulturni sporazum? Dobra rešitev" [Cultural Agreement? A Satisfactory Solution], *Dnevnik*, April 8, 1998 <www.dnevnik.si/cgi/view.exe?w=dn.8.4.1998.y5er> (October 11, 2000). See also Stefan Karner, *Die deutschsprachige Volksgruppe in Slowenien: Aspekte ihrer Entwicklung* (Klagenfurt: Hermagoras–Mohorjeva, 1988); and Nečak, *"Nemci" na Slovenskem*.

101. In Austria, the term *Volksgruppe*—an ethnic group—refers to national minorities. Upon ratifying the Framework Convention for the Protection of National Minorities (ETS no. 157, in force since February 1, 1998; declaration contained in the instrument of ratification deposited on March 31, 1998), Austria declared that the term "national minorities" within the meaning of the Framework Convention for the Protection of National Minorities is understood to designate groups that come within the scope of application of the Law on Ethnic Groups (*Volksgruppengesetz*, Federal Law Gazette no. 396/1976) and live and traditionally have had their home in parts of the territory of the Republic of Austria and are composed of Austrian citizens with non-German mother tongues and with their own ethnic cultures. By contrast, the Slovenian legal order distinguishes between national minorities, which are entitled to special constitutional protection, and other ethnic groups (*etnične skupine*; the term used in the Slovenian version of the agreement).

102. Before the Cultural Agreement entered into the ratification procedure in both countries, the Austrian and Slovenian governments agreed to attach an interpretative statement to it. The statement clarifies that the German *Volksgruppe* is entitled to protection within the framework of article 61 of the Slovenian constitution, not article 64, which refers to the Italian and Hungarian national minorities in Slovenia.

103. "Visit by the Federal Minister for Foreign Affairs of the Republic of Austria to Slovenia," Ministry of Foreign Affairs of the Republic of Slovenia <www.gov. si/mzz/eng/news_room/news/01043001.html> (May 30, 2001). For the official Austrian view, see "Ferrero-Waldner: Beziehungen mit Slowenien besser als Zeitungsberichte behaupten," Austrian Federal Ministry for Foreign Affairs <www.bmaa.gv. at/presseservice/aussendungen/x1eu00pa_Laibach_3004_20010430.html.de> (May 30, 2001).

104. "Am Wort 'Volksgruppe' schieden sich die Geister in Laibach und Wien," *Die Presse*, April 30, 2001 <www.diepresse.at/archiv.taf?_function=read&_UserReference=43B2487437BBEED63B553383&_id=741486> (June 2, 2001).

105. The acronym AVNOJ stands for Antifašističko Veče Narodnog Oslobodenja Jugoslavije (Antifascist Council of the National Liberation of Yugoslavia).

106. Mekina, "Slovenia and Austria: The Scare of Indiscriminate Denationalisation." The original of the latter decree was not found (i.e., it has not been published in the *Official Gazette*), but there is a decree on the transfer of the enemy's property into state property, published in the *Official Gazette* in 1945. Janez Šmidovnik, "In vendar kontinuiteta" [Still, Continuity], *Delo—Sobotna priloga*, September 23, 2000, 9.

107. The Constitutional Court of Slovenia, Decision on Case U-I-23/93, published in the *Official Gazette of the Republic of Slovenia* 23/1997. For the full text of the decision, see <www.us-rs.com/search/show_full.php?id=1246&problem=1&legalbasis=1&fulltext=1&tekst=1&> (April 7, 2001). See also Mekina, "Slovenia and Austria: The Scare of Indiscriminate Denationalisation."

108. "Ukinitev sklepov ni mogoča" [The Annulment of Decrees Is Not Possible], *Dnevnik*, September 7, 2000 <www.dnevnik.si/cgi/view.exe?w=dn.7.9.2000.m8xk3> (September 16, 2000).

109. Article 295 of the Treaty on the Establishing the European Community reads as follows: "This Treaty shall in no way prejudice the rules in member states governing the system of property ownership."

110. "Nevihtni oblaki nad Slovenijo" [Storm Clouds over Slovenia], *Dnevnik*, October 16, 1999 <www.dnevnik.si/cgi/view.exe?w=dn.16.10.1999.o6uep> (October 1, 2000). For the Slovenian position on this issue, see "Additional Explanations concerning the Negotiating Position to Chapter 4: Free Movement of Capital—Denationalisation," Government of the Republic of Slovenia, Public Relations and Media Office <www.sigov.si/uvi/eng/new/backgrthundarround-information/denationalisation> (October 23, 2000).

111. "Foreign Ministry: No Linking of AVNOJ Resolutions and Slovenia's EU accession," *Press Release*, February 10, 2000, Austrian Federal Ministry for Foreign Affairs <www.bmaa.gv.at/presseservice/index.html.en> (September 30, 2000).

112. "Austrian Diplomat: Dispute over AVNOJ Conclusions 'Misunderstanding,'" *BBC Monitoring International Reports,* September 5, 2000 <www.globalarchive.ft.com/search-components/index.jsp> (September 30, 2000).

113. "Austrian President Tries to 'Defuse' Recent Problems with Slovenia," *BBC Monitoring International Reports*, September 8, 2000 <www.globalarchive.ft.com/search-components/index.jsp> (September 30, 2000).

114. Šmidovnik, "In vendar kontinuiteta," 9.

115. "EU potrebuje Slovenijo" [EU Needs Slovenia], *Dnevnik*, July 19, 2000 <www.dnevnik.si/cgi/view.exe?w=dn.19.7.2000.4d24z> (October 25, 2000).

116. According to the Slovenian government, Austria's complaints are unfair not only from the legal point of view but also as far as the practical dealing with denationalization requests are concerned. At the time of writing, out of 1,611 denationalization requests from Austria, more than one-third have been complied with in their entirety and more than one-half are being dealt with. "Popravljanje kulturnega sporazuma" [Setting the Cultural Agreement Right], *Delo*, March 7, 2001, 5.

117. Martha Finnemore, *National Interests in International Society* (Ithaca, N.Y.: Cornell University Press, 1996), 135.

118. In her statement on Austrian television in September 2000, the Austrian foreign minister Benita Ferrero-Waldner was critical of the Czech lack of cooperation in discussing the status of the Czech nuclear power plant Temelin. She complained that "Prague had exploited EU sanctions on Vienna to reject dialogue with it" about nuclear energy. She said that "the Czech Republic's position was totally opposite to that of Slovenia which had permanently provided Vienna with information about its Krsko nuclear power plant." "Austrian Minister Says Czechs Used EU Sanctions to Reject Nuclear Debate," *BBC Monitoring International Reports*, September 17, 2000 <www.globalarchive.ft.com/search/components/index.jsp> (November 30, 2000).

5

Which Way to Progress? Impact of International Organizations in Romania

Annette Freyberg-Inan

Focusing on Romania, this chapter explores the roles played by international organizations and the norms and rules they advocate for domestic economic and political development. It begins with an overview of theoretical suggestions concerning the domestic impact of international norms. After a survey of Romania's present situation, the chapter then reviews the projects of four highly relevant international organizations: the European Union, the IMF, the World Bank, and NATO. It analyzes the combined impact of those organizations on Romanian politics and raises a number of critical questions concerning the legitimacy of the policies pursued as well as the accountability of their instigators to the Romanian electorate. In conclusion, it develops some implications presented by the Romanian case for international relations theorizing on the domestic impact of international norms.

WHAT WE MIGHT EXPECT: THEORETICAL PERSPECTIVES ON THE DOMESTIC IMPACT OF INTERNATIONAL NORMS

International organizations can influence a nation's policies and codetermine its path of development by communicating their norms and rules to domestic decision makers and by familiarizing them with the "carrots and sticks" that are associated with compliance and rejection of those norms and rules.[1] In recent years, considerable progress has been made in the study of how international norms affect domestic politics. A number of studies have shown that international norms do indeed influence state behavior. These works have identified patterns of correlation between such norms and state actions which are apparently guided by them.[2] Such research has, however, been criticized for failing to shed light on the causal links between the existence of international norms and domestic policy choices.[3] The exploration of such causal links requires a closer look at the domestic political arena and at the actions of domestic decision makers, who function as the agents of norm transfusion.

International relations scholarship has identified a number of pathways that may lead to the domestic institutionalization of the norms propagated by an international organization. First, such norms can infuse the values and beliefs of domestic decision makers.[4] Second, they may become enshrined in the standard operating procedures of domestic bureaucratic agencies.[5] Third, international norms may be incorporated into domestic laws, a process referred to by Robert Keohane as "institutional enmeshment."[6] Fourth, "government officials and societal actors can invoke an international rule to further their own particularistic interests in domestic policy debates."[7]

In an important exploration of the fourth of the above-sketched pathways in particular, Andrew Cortell and James Davis have found that "government officials and societal interest groups can appeal to international rules and norms to further their own interest in the domestic political arena" and that "through these appeals, international rules and norms become incorporated into domestic debates, under some conditions influencing national policy choices."[8] Observing that the domestic impact of international norms varies both across countries and across issue areas, Cortell and Davis identify two conditions "as affecting the extent to which a domestic actor's appropriation of an international norm will influence state behavior: the domestic salience of the norm; and the domestic structural context within which the policy debate transpires."[9]

In a more recent article, Cortell and Davis further explain that domestic salience "requires a durable set of attitudes toward the norm's legitimacy in the national arena."[10] Salient norms "give rise to feelings of obligation by social actors and, when violated, engender regret or a feeling that the deviation or violation requires justification."[11] Clearly, the higher the domestic salience of the international norm, the more likely its adoption by domestic actors is, ceteris paribus, to affect state behavior.

The two relevant components of domestic structure are the organization of decision-making authority, which ranges from centralized to decentralized, and the pattern of state-society relations, which ranges from distant to close. While the domestic structural context, thus defined, is expected to vary across issue areas, it is worthwhile noting at this point that state-society relations in Romania are generally distant, as civil society development is stunted and societal actors and their interests are not effectively integrated into the policy-making process. What is theoretically expected under such conditions is that "state officials serve as the primary means by which international norms and rules affect national policy" and "societal actors' ability to use international rules and norms to their advantage in the national arena is limited."[12]

The degree of centralization of decision-making authority in Romania shows more variation across issue areas. It is theoretically expected that in a decentralized structure the success of appeals to an international norm depends more strongly on the domestic salience of that norm. This is simply because in this type of structure a greater degree of consensus is needed to enable individual decision makers to achieve their goals. Independent of decision-making structure, however, political agents are expected to follow the same basic logic: "By appealing to a salient rule or norm, the official's interests are associated with the rule's domestic legitimacy, making them difficult to challenge." Thus "a policy maker's appropriation of a salient international rule helps to empower her position in the national arena."[13]

At this point it becomes necessary to introduce a distinction between norms and rules, as the salience of an international norm should not simply be assumed to be proportional to the salience of the accompanying rules. In the case of Romania, for example, the salience of the norms propagated by major international organizations in the domestic political arena is extremely high. As Cortell and Davis observe, "repeated declarations by authoritative political actors are indicative of the state's commitment" and can lead to the association of international norms "with the advancement of the country's national interest or core values."[14] Such commitment can, in the words of Caldeira and Gibson, create a "durable set of attitudes toward the legitimacy of the institution."[15] Such a development is clearly apparent in the case of Romania. Although the basic norms propagated by the EU, IMF, World Bank, and NATO generally enjoy the resulting domestic acceptance, the salience of many accompanying rules is contested. During the process of domestic institutionalization of international norms in Romania, problems thus occur primarily at the implementation stage, when the lack of consensus on concrete rules of norm adaptation becomes apparent to policy practitioners.

One result of disassociation between international norms and rules in their transmission to domestic structures can be developmental stagnation. While the putting into practice of reform measures is constantly inhibited by the lack of a genuine consensus about concrete policies which would serve to institutionalize international rules, the development of normative alternatives as well is stunted. As Thomas Risse-Kappen has explained, "when actors regularly refer to the norm to describe and comment on their own behavior and that of others, the validity claims of the norm are no longer controversial, even if the actual behavior continues violating the rules."[16] The salience of international norms in the domestic context "puts an extra burden of proof on regime opponents because . . . the regime structure serves automatically as frame of reference" in political discourse.[17] In the case of Romania, continuous appeals to the norms propagated by those international organizations most relevant to Romania's development have enabled leaders to cling to power whose actual policy preferences have become quite irrelevant. At the same time, the degree of distance in state-society relations has prevented those international norms, even though highly salient for domestic politics, from truly becoming rooted in Romanian society.

The following case study will shed some light on the impact major international organizations have had in Romania through the norms and rules they propagate. Its purpose is thus to open up "the black box of domestic politics in an effort to offer a better understanding of how international norms and rules affect state behavior."[18] The following section will introduce Romania's present-day political and economic situation in an effort to clarify the conditions under which and against which international organizations operate in this country; the next section will then provide a survey of the main activities of EU, IMF, World Bank, and NATO in Romania.

ROMANIA TODAY: POLITICS AND ECONOMICS

Between 1997 and 2000, the government of Romania was reformist, at least in reputation.[19] The new government elected in November 1996, headed by president Emil Constantinescu, took office in a climate of hopes for change, after living conditions had failed to improve during the six-year reign of the Partidul Democraţiei Sociale din România (PDSR) and its former communist leader Ion Iliescu. Yet, more than most other nations in the region, at the time of the next general elections in the year 2000 Romania found itself still at a critical juncture in its political and economic development. Constant infighting, lack of progress, and accusations of corruption had marred the image of the reformist governing coalition. In July 2000, Constantinescu unexpectedly declared that he would not run for reelection, professing despair at his failures, especially to beat corruption in the country.

The third prime minister of the reformist government, Mugur Isarescu, an economist who had been head of Romania's Central Bank since 1990, at the time enjoyed the reputation of a politically independent technocrat. Fall 2000 opinion polls granted him an unusually high approval rating of over 50 percent.[20] As the last-ditch attempt of the governing coalition to achieve performance, the Isarescu government showed some determination to try to effect the positive change voters had long desired. Isarescu's ascent to power had generally received cautiously favorable comments from business leaders, who expected him, above all, to take measures to improve the investment climate, and the new cabinet members were widely judged to be more "professional" than their predecessors.[21]

In response to EU demands, the Isarescu government formulated a medium-term economic development strategy for 2000–2004, which provides a window for strategic planning until 2010. The strategy focuses on limiting deficits and inflation, tightening public spending, and improving income policy, the business climate, and market functioning. To achieve these goals, it calls for large cuts in government employment and administrative expenses. The overarching economic task faced by the government has been to achieve noninflationary growth, as inflationary growth became unsustainable after 1993, when efforts to close nonprofitable companies began. Projected growth for the year 2000 was initially set at 1.3 percent, with 27 percent inflation. While the inflation target had to be revised, and inflation stood at 40 percent at the end of 2000, the GDP surpassed expectations, achieving almost 2 percent growth after three straight years of contraction.[22] In September, the 2000 state budget was revised in response to new inflation estimates. Additional expenses of some 17 trillion lei increased the consolidated deficit from initially 3 percent to the IMF-agreed target of 3.5 percent.[23] Average gross and net income have been increasing slightly, continuing a mild stimulation of consumption, which rose by 1.7 percent over the January–September 2000 period.[24] Exports have been on the increase as well, apparently driven largely by a rise in industrial output.[25] Analysts' judgments are summed up by Raluca Nicolescu of Demir Securities: "no material deterioration in economic fundamentals by the year 2000."[26]

Inflation targets for 2001 and 2002 were initially set at 18 percent and 12 percent, respectively, with one-digit figures hoped for beginning in 2003. The 2001 inflation forecast was subsequently adjusted up to 20–25 percent.[27] A Reuters poll of analysts conducted in November 2000 projects GDP growth in the year 2001 to reach nearly 3 percent, the target agreed on with the EU under Romania's medium-term economic strategy.[28] Isarescu predicted during his term that GDP per capita, at $3,500 in mid-2000, would reach $10,000 by the year 2010.[29]

The country's financial needs for the year 2000 lay at about $3 billion, including an account deficit of $1.8 billion plus debt repayment obligations. Credit inflow had to reach $1 billion, much needed cash being contributed by external loans, prominently the 650 million grant for 2000 pledged by the EU to aid Romania in the accession process.[30] Romania was at no risk of default on its foreign debt in this year, when the country had to service around $1.5 billion, as compared to $2.6 billion in 1999. Central Bank hard currency reserves had increased to reach $1.69 billion (not including gold) by the end of January 2000.[31] This increase was triggered mainly by the bank's hard currency purchases from the local interbank market and constituted a recovery from low levels in mid-1999, when Romania was forced to repay part of its foreign debt to avoid default.[32]

In order to succeed in its current development strategy, Romania still faces a desperate need to attract capital. As pressure to privatize state-owned companies has continued to increase while domestic capital accumulation has remained low, foreign investment becomes ever more important to keep the Romanian economy afloat. Romania's privatization agency, the State Ownership Fund (SOF), attempted to sell the shares of all remaining companies in its portfolio in the year 2000. As of February 2000, these were 3,150 companies, 2,870 of which were to be put up for sale, while 280 were expected to be restructured or liquidated. They include over 640 state-owned farms and almost 100 research and development institutes. Sixty-four big state-run companies (the "Fabled 64," including the Romanian airline Tarom and aluminum producer Alro Slatina) are due to be sold or liquidated in the context of a World Bank private sector adjustment loan (PSAL) program. The head of SOF, Radu Sarbu, reportedly expected that 1,700–1,800 companies would be privatized in the year 2000 alone.[33] The SOF also hoped that most state-owned banks would be privatized in 2000, even as some banks protested rapid privatization, asserting their successes and arguing that their specific responsibilities would not be met by private players.[34] While several large state-owned companies have indeed been privatized recently or seem to be well on the way (Banca Agricola, Sidex), other important deals look likely to fail (Oltchim, CS Resita) for the time being, and loss-making state-owned enterprises are still numerous, despite extremely low asset prices.

As of February 2000, the SOF held another $2 billion in share capital but expected to receive only some $500 million through its sale. In light of such desperate deals, it is impossible not to question the wisdom of continuing the privatization drive under present investment conditions. The main obstacles to investment in Romania in the last few years have been bureaucratic red tape and corruption, the limited availability of investment finance, constant change in laws and regulations, a lack of respect for contractual obligations,[35] low confidence in the judiciary,[36] restrictions against foreign ownership of land,[37] and excessively high income and social benefits tax rates. Theoretically, Romania could now profit from the fact that the markets of the Eastern European frontrunners have become saturated, and profit margins in those markets have decreased due to increasingly high competition. The country still maintains a huge unmet demand for practically all kind of services and goods. If investment conditions were improved, these opportunities would certainly attract capital, both foreign and domestic, and invite the competition needed to make privatization more profitable. However, Romania has not seemed to be moving closer either to properly regulating its market or to making it more attractive.

In early 2000, the Isarescu government initiated a set of fiscal reforms which proved additional cause for worry. A report by the Economic and Social Council (CES) on the economic and social impact of the reform package observed that these new measures favored the export of raw material over technologies and the use of imports instead of domestic products.[38] The state's attempts to raise money for refinancing the budget deficit have involved prohibitively high added value taxes. In spite of the realization that "a strong and growing medium size and small enterprise sector is essential for stable, sound development,"[39] they have also tended to result in crowding out small and medium enterprises (SMEs) and cutting them off from affordable loans.

In response to the high credit risk in the Romanian banking sector, the Central Bank established the Banking Risk Center to better monitor lending practices. New securities and collateral legislation has been passed to enable banks to extend financing to smaller companies.[40] Legal and institutional progress in the financial sector was, however, offset by a series of scandals, culminating in May 2000, when several anonymous phone calls to investors in the Romanian Commercial Bank (BCR) began a run on the bank that led to the collapse of its partner, the state-run National Investment Fund (FNI). In the illegal and highly precarious position of keeping only 4 percent of its $164 million in assets liquid, the fund collapsed, leaving tens of thousands of small investors stripped of their savings. At the time, Stratfor's *Global Intelligence Update* speculated that the FNI collapse may be costing the Romanian government not only an estimated $49 million, but also the upcoming general elections.[41] Undoubtedly, this scandal (which broke, probably not coincidentally, immediately before local elections) contributed to the shockingly bad performance of the governing Convenţia din Democrată România (CDR) and helped the opposition PDSR gain control of a plurality of municipalities, including the mayorship of Bucharest. This placed the PDSR in the strategic position of being able to influence voters at the local, while continuing to expose government corruption at the national level, thus being able to affect voter sentiment in time for the November general elections.

In countless opinion polls Romanians have expressed support for genuine economic reform. Their majority has shown a willingness to undergo economic shock therapy. Yet they have clearly been running out of patience as their leaders have failed to agree on basic goals, adopt long-term or even medium-term policies, or stick by them in spite of possible short-term problems. According to a preelection poll conducted by the Metro Media Transylvania Institute, 51 percent of Romanians believed in November 2000 that their families were better off in the period before 1990. Twenty-one percent judged their standard of living to be highest between 1990 and 1992, as compared to only 9 percent for the period of 1997 to 2000. Only 1 percent of the population claimed to be very satisfied, 17 percent to be reasonably satisfied with their lives. In comparison, 45 percent professed to be "not so" satisfied and 36 percent to be not satisfied at all. Thirty-four percent of Romanians apparently expected no improvements for their lives within the next year. Twenty percent expected to become worse off.[42] Given such widespread dissatisfaction and pessimism, Isarescu showed little sensitivity to the social impact of reforms, speaking out against strikes and protests and asking Romanians to simply accept the inevitable hardships associated with the reform process. In the face of growing disbelief he continued to maintain that, if the government managed tight control of the fiscal deficit and current account, Romanians would begin to feel the positive effects of reform by the end of 2000.[43] They did not.

Before the 2000 elections, the mainstream business media found the government "between a rock and a hard place: Staying the course on reforms, or even quickening them, will only sink their opinion poll scores lower, while stalling in favor of election-year populist measures will ruin the currently-good relations Romania enjoys with the international institutions they desperately need."[44] While strongly supportive of the medium-term strategy, President Constantinescu admitted that there had been insufficient government-citizen communication, leaving Romanians at a loss as to why they should have to make the sacrifices demanded by their politicians and inhibiting the growth of social solidarity.[45] While, in the words of Steven Roper, "the population was experiencing all of the shock but none of the therapy of reform,"[46] the government's strategy toward achieving political consensus was doomed to fail. The medium-term strategy was, for example, subjected to debates by three working groups: one technical, composed of economists; one political, including the government, parliament, banks, and privatization agencies; and one composed of civic NGOs. The latter were expected to create a popular consensus. This approach might well constitute a misuse of the NGO sector to help "sell" government policies and clearly failed to bridge the communication gap. Instead, it was indicative of the persistent distance in Romanian state-society relations.

As in other countries of the region, the suffering associated with privatization, restructuring, and the drastic reduction of social services explains the appeal of political rhetoric that pledges to cushion the effects of reforms. The quasi-egalitarian ethos espoused by many citizens and their expectation to be looked after by a paternalistic state only reinforces this posture. As a consequence, populism has been on the rise in Romania. It has contributed to developmental stagnation by defending the majority consensus represented by international norms while eschewing any unpopular measures to actually achieve their realization. Determination and integrity have been chronically wanting among the Romanian political elite, as critical decisions needed to be made to pull the country out of economic crisis, yet decision makers appeared paralyzed by the threat of popular displeasure with the potential results of their decisions.

Campaigning reformists generally argued that the previous Iliescu government ran up deficits that drove the country close to bankruptcy, and that their own cost-cutting and privatization measures were what would eventually save the day. In spite of a still widening trade deficit, at the end of the year 2000 it was judged that during Isarescu's time in office the Romanian economy did indeed enjoy a small recovery, and that conditions for foreign investment had improved slightly.[47] However, these developments appeared to amount to "too little too late." According to Isarescu, the two pillars of recovery had been rising exports, with increased added value, and increasing investment. He admitted, however, that this recovery was not "felt by the average citizen because we didn't focus on stimulating consumption."[48] The average voter retaliated. As a technically independent candidate in the presidential elections of November 2000, Isarescu achieved only fourth rank at under 10 percent of the vote. The reformist governing coalition performed abysmally in parliamentary elections. Centrist and liberal forces all but disappeared from the party spectrum—a shocking development indicative of the lack of consolidation of the Romanian party system.[49]

As suggested by preelection polls, former president Iliescu, of the opposition PDSR, took a clear lead in the presidential election, polling 36.35 percent of the vote.[50] According to the CURS/CSOP exit poll conducted at the request of the Pro Institute and a study performed by the IMAS marketing and research institute, Iliescu was strongly supported by older voters, particularly pensioners, and the rural population. His supporters are found disproportionately among the less educated, in the regions of Moldova and Muntenia, and among the Roma population. Significantly less support for Iliescu came from young voters, larger towns and cities, Romanians with an academic background, Transylvania, and ethnic Hungarians. Iliescu won in twenty-four counties, including some former CDR strongholds. The PDSR slate took 36.61 percent of the vote for the chamber of deputies and 37.09 percent of the vote for the senate.[51]

The great shock of the 2000 election was the success of the extreme right populist Corneliu Vadim Tudor and his nationalist Partidul România Mare (PRM). Tudor received 28.34 percent of the presidential vote. His PRM received 19.48 percent of the vote for the chamber of deputies and 21.01 percent of the vote for the senate.[52] Tudor, director and owner of the publications *România Mare* and *Politica,* is a former senator and a writer. Known as "the judge" for tirelessly judging his political opponents' mistakes, he is infamous for his hateful tirades directed against ethnic Hungarians, Jewish Romanians, and Roma. His campaign strategy relied on acrid criticism of his political opponents, poetic appeals to God and nation, attribution of blame to minorities, and promises for tough crackdowns on criminal activity and corruption. He appears to have convinced his voters that corruption does not affect the PRM and its leader.

According to IMAS studies, Tudor supporters tend to be male and, surprisingly, young. Tudor beat Iliescu by 5 percent in Transylvania, which does not bode well for relations between ethnic Hungarians and Romanians in the region. Neither the size of voters' towns nor their educational background seemed to matter in regard to their support for Tudor, who won in fourteen counties, some of which were former CDR strongholds. However, his lowest levels of support were found among voters with a university background and those over sixty.[53]

As none of the twelve candidates in the presidential elections received a simple majority, a runoff election took place on December 10, 2000, between the two frontrunners. Romanians now had the choice between a former communist and a right-wing extremist. Panic was widespread among moderates in Romania, especially as a few pre-runoff polls suggested that Tudor might just win the presidency. While official reactions from foreign governments, international organizations, and foreign investors were mostly cautiously moderate, the international media joined in a choir of condemnation of Tudor, and some intergovernmental and nongovernmental organizations as well as numerous academics issued explicit warnings to the Romanian electorate. For example, the Romanian-American Chamber of Commerce shed its usual political neutrality, stating that Tudor's "ascendancy would not only terminate the nation's accession plans for the European Union, but drive virtually all foreign investment away from Romania and turn this great European nation into a pariah state."[54] Allusions to the fate of Yugoslavia were made, and students and other groups organized public protests against extremism.

To the great relief of the majority of the population, Iliescu won the runoff elections with 68 percent of the vote, Tudor polling a still worrisome 33 percent. The PDSR formed a minority government based on cooperation with centrist liberal, social democratic, and the ethnic Hungarians' parties. In June 2001, it merged with the Partidul Social Democrat Român (PSDR) to form the Partidul Social Democrat (PSD). The PSD has officially ruled out cooperation with the PRM, which is also not represented in the cabinet. The new prime minister is Adrian Nastase, sociologist, foreign minister in the first postrevolutionary government, and president of the house of deputies during the Iliescu/Vacaroiu government of 1992–1996.

The resurgent popularity of the former president and his party was due in large part to the overall failure of the governing coalition to improve standards of living or achieve significant economic recovery. Polls have consistently identified price controls and unemployment as the most important issues on voters' minds. As observed in 2000, during Constantinescu's term in office, "foreign investment has fallen, unemployment has risen in the wake of a World Bank–induced privatization program, and spending on public services has been severely reduced in a number of austere budgets designed to keep government expenditure to a minimum."[55] The average monthly wage fell continuously after 1996 and was considerably below $100 at election time. Constantinescu also lost ground for his coalition through his support for the NATO bombing of Yugoslavia during the Kosovo war, which was incompatible with majority opinion in the country. Many Romanians were also disappointed by the failure of the anticorruption crusade he launched at the beginning of his mandate as well as the lack of follow-through on campaign promises to clear up the mysteries surrounding the revolution of 1989.

During the campaign, Iliescu argued that, as a result of Ceausescu's legacy, the economy took a nosedive at the beginning of his first term in office, but that his regime began turning it around by cutting subsidies and government contracts gradually. He blamed the reformist governing coalition's shock therapy for sending Romania's economy spinning downward again. As the top-priority concerns of their new government, Iliescu and Nastase identified the drawing up of an economical yet socially acceptable budget for 2001 as well as far-reaching fiscal and legal reforms aimed at attracting investment. Specifically, the PDSR has identified excessive taxation, unstable and unfair legal codes, and excessive bureaucracy as the main obstacles to both foreign and domestic investment, and it has proposed some specific reforms to address each.[56] Iliescu has also promised greater sensitivity in his government's handling of restructuring and privatization: "Restructuring and the privatization of state enterprises and utilities must be continued, but we ought to be more careful about how these are handled, not just do things for the sake of having them done." Specifically, "restructuring or privatizing doesn't always mean firing hundreds of thousands of people without making sure better economic results will follow."[57]

The PDSR made campaign promises to poor Romanians that conflict with the aim to balance (or at least almost balance) the Romanian budget. The new government immediately found itself under pressure from the IMF and the World Bank not to carry out those promises. However, a failure to speedily improve living standards in the country, where 44 percent of the people now live under the EU poverty line, is likely to further increase public support for extremists, perhaps enabling them to take control in the next term. On the other hand, a failure to achieve drastic structural reform will likely do the same in the medium term, as genuine recovery depends on such reform. In their relations with the PSD government, the IMF and World Bank initially adopted a wait-and-see stance; further support from the EU depended in large part on the development of Romania's relations with the two lenders.[58] In the meantime, the new government has not introduced any radical changes of course. Slight economic growth has continued and, combined with lower levels of unemployment and inflation, gives some reason for hope to government planners, even as its effects are not yet felt by the population at large.

On its westward quest, Romania has become "tied up" in international obligations that restrict the range of possible domestic political developments and national policies for better or for worse. It is widely assumed that the pressure applied on Romania by international organizations such as the IMF, the World Bank, the EU, and NATO aids the country's progress, especially in the economic realm. This fact is reflected in statements by rating agencies that expressly identify "orthodox economic policies and reform" with "Romania's IMF program and EU accession efforts."[59] Especially "the overriding objective of EU accession . . . will put constraints on any new government's policies, and provide both pressure and incentives to move reforms ahead in the medium term."[60] The intervention of international organizations in Romanian politics is thus commonly judged to be beneficial, and only a small minority of Romanians strive for disassociation from those organizations, which have come to symbolize the country's westward orientation. Even the return to power of Iliescu and the PDSR, with their traditional reluctance to apply shock therapy, have not made Romania swerve off its course of integration into the EU and Euro-Atlantic Alliance structures.[61] Instead, the Nastase cabinet has clearly given priority to addressing the reform issues raised by the European Union.[62]

INTERNATIONAL ORGANIZATIONS OPERATING IN ROMANIA

The European Union

The number one declared goal of all relevant political players in Romania is full participation in the European Union.[63] A Europe Agreement has been implemented successfully in the interim since March 1993 and in final form since February 1995. In its context, EU-Romanian bilateral trade has increased significantly.[64] An associate member since 1995, Romania was admitted to accession talks at the Helsinki summit in December 1999. The Department for European Integration was established in the Foreign Ministry, and on January 5, 2000, the foreign and European affairs minister, Petre Roman, held his first press conference, identifying as his top policy priority European integration and his country's efforts to fulfill EU criteria for membership. In the new cabinet, two separate ministers, Mircea Geoana, formerly Romania's ambassador to the United States, and Hildegard Puwak, head the Foreign Ministry and the Ministry for EU Integration, respectively. The first five chapters of preaccession negotiations, from a total of thirty-one, were opened in late March 2000 and have been closed.[65] The next round of chapters is presently under negotiation.[66] The government continues to be confident that Romania can meet its January 1, 2007, target date for entering the EU and aspires to close negotiations and sign the accession treaty by July 1, 2005.[67]

Established at the Copenhagen European Council of June 1993, the so-called Copenhagen criteria for EU membership lay out political and economic conditions as well as guidelines for alignment with the *acquis communautaire*, the body of law that defines the Union. An "accession partnership" functions like a roadmap to accession for each applicant country.[68] The Copenhagen political criteria for membership state that an applicant country must achieve "stability of institutions guaranteeing democracy, the rule of law, human rights and respect for and protection of minorities." How does Romania fare? The EU considers Romania to fulfill the Copenhagen political criteria at this time. Improvements have recently been noted with respect to the crisis in Romania's child care institutions, affecting over 100,000 children in institutionalized care. However, having observed past failures to act to ensure adequate funding for the children, the European Commission is keeping a close eye on child care reform in the country.[69]

The EU also remains concerned about the use of executive ordinances and about deficiencies relating to the independence and efficiency of the judiciary, although some progress in judicial reform is noted. Other priority areas include the fight against corruption, where the EU holds that institutional responsibilities and functions must be consolidated.[70] The EU is also monitoring the situation of the Roma and other minorities, pushing for their inclusion in the sociopolitical system and against racism and discrimination.[71] The issue is highlighted in the accession partnership, and the EU has provided €2 million to help the Romanian government develop and implement a strategy to improve the situation of the Roma.

The Copenhagen economic criteria ask for a functioning market economy and the capacity to cope with competitive pressures and market forces within the Union in the medium term. Here Romania clearly fails, lagging far behind Poland, Hungary, the Czech Republic, and Estonia, which as of mid-2001 have realistic chances of joining the Union. The 2000 *Report on Progress toward Accession* by the European Commission, which was published on November 8, dealt a severe blow to the Constantinescu/Isarescu government. Placing Romania at the very bottom of the list of aspiring EU members, the report observed little progress toward a functioning market economy, concluding that "Romania is not able to cope with competitive pressure and market forces within the Union in the medium term and has not substantially improved its future economic prospects."[72] At present, the report states, "Romania cannot be regarded as a functioning market economy," since "the vulnerability of the macroeconomic environment, the uncertain legal and institutional framework and uneven commitment to sustained reforms have hindered the development of economic activity."[73]

Isarescu reacted promptly, pointing out that the report failed to take into sufficient account progress made in the year 2000, in which the economy began to show modest signs of recovery after three years of contraction.[74] On the positive side, the EC report observes a "broad consensus on the need to establish a market-based economy,"[75] improved macroeconomic stability, "largely due to strict fiscal and monetary policies,"[76] tightened fiscal policy, liberalized prices and trade, an improving financial situation of the largest public banks, and an increase in exports. On the negative side, however, the report criticizes the GDP decline of 3.2 percent in 1999; little progress on reforms and transparency of public finances; difficulties of business creation stemming from uncertainty about property rights, changes in the legislation, and difficulty of access to financing; and the weakness or nonexistence of institutions that could enforce the existing legal framework.

Like the report of October 1999, the 2000 EC progress report singles out macroeconomic imbalances and financing problems, pointing out that instability and legal uncertainty are continuing to deter foreign investment, which is needed to modernize supply. The EU observes that, above and beyond the medium-term strategy, determined and sustained efforts will be necessary to restore growth and improve living standards. It urges financial discipline, the swift restructuring of the large loss-making state enterprises, and the creation of a transparent and business-friendly environment.[77]

Another set of Copenhagen criteria concerns Romania's progress toward alignment with the *acquis*. Judgment on all three groups of criteria—political, economic, and alignment with the *acquis*—depends also on the capacity of the country's administrative and legal systems to put into effect the principles of democracy and market economy and to apply and enforce the *acquis* in practice. The EU regularly examines progress in applicants' ability to take on the obligations of membership, including adherence to the aims of political, economic, and monetary union. Here, Romania's record is mixed. An area of particular concern is the environment. In general, the process of alignment is severely hindered by lack of funds and overall weak administrative and judicial capacity.[78]

While Romania has begun to address certain aspects of administrative capacity in regional development and the internal market, adopt measures to restructure the banking sector, reform public procurement, and regulate state aids, other short-term priorities of the accession partnership have not been met. These include certain aspects of the justice system and home affairs, such as the fight against organized crime and corruption as well as the demilitarization of the police and border control, and environment priorities. At present, the EU considers none of the medium-term priorities of the accession partnership to be fully met.[79]

So far, the main EU instrument for supporting Romania's preaccession strategy and convergence to the Copenhagen criteria has been the PHARE program. Between 1990 and 1999, PHARE allocated €1.2 billion to Romania. Around 30 percent of PHARE allocations are used for "institution building," that is, to help improve the country's capacity to implement the *acquis*. The remaining 70 percent are used for financing investments with the aim of both strengthening the regulatory infrastructure needed to ensure compliance and reinforcing economic and social cohesion affected by restructuring. PHARE has concentrated on transferring know-how, equipment, and financial resources in fields such as industrial restructuring and privatization, SME development, trade and investment promotion, energy, and land registration. Of particular relevance in the Romanian context is PHARE support to agriculture and SMEs, which aims to develop sector strategies and initiate essential institutional and financial mechanisms servicing enterprises in these crucial sectors.[80] Romania has been the second biggest beneficiary among the central and eastern European states (after Poland) from PHARE agricultural aid, receiving €85 million from 1989 through 1998.[81]

Following the decision at the Helsinki summit to begin accession talks with Romania in the spring of 2000, the head of the local EC delegation, Fokion Fotiadis, stressed that "improvement in the investment climate is a priority in the short term."[82] The EU now assists Romania in the accession process with financial help of some €640 million in grants per year. This is almost five times more than in previous years. The money is disbursed under three programs: PHARE and the new ISPA (Instrument for Structured Policies for Preaccession) and SAPARD (Special Accession Program for Agriculture and Rural Development). The RICOP (Enterprise Restructuring and Employment Conversion Program) grants €100 million for backing reforms with social protection measures. In addition, the European Investment Bank offers loans of up to €500 million per year for infrastructure development.[83]

The crucial criterion on which Romanian qualification for EU membership depends is its capacity to cope with competitive pressures and market forces within the Union. At the present time, no reliable trend toward this end can be observed, as productive capacity and exports have only cautiously picked up (in spite of a real depreciation of the leu), and purchasing power and living standards stagnate. The EU warns that a participation of Romania in the third stage of EMU as a nonparticipant to the Euro area could pose serious problems due to its precarious economic situation. Under these conditions no target dates for accession can realistically be established. The EU expects the Romanian government to contribute its own realistic strategies for approaching accession criteria and to create the conditions necessary for their implementation. This is frequently a problem, as illustrated by the case of the national development plan for 2000–2006. After the European Commission had judged the draft document to be neither sufficiently explicit and detailed nor financially realistic, it had to exert considerable pressure to ensure its revision by May, when funding decisions for PHARE 2000 were made.[84]

In response to EU demands a medium-term economic development strategy supported by a majority of parties was formulated in 2000. Yet following EU guidelines creates political problems for Romanian officials inasmuch as the necessary reform efforts force tradeoffs and cause hardship among the population. The most difficult talks with the EU in the near future will cover the areas of agriculture and the supersize steel and petrochemical sectors that are the legacy of Ceausescu's industrialization strategy. Romania is pushed to keep its budget deficit at or below 3 percent of GDP by both EU accession plan demands and by the international financiers. To fulfill this expectation, loss-making companies in the iron and steel industries, agriculture, heavy and chemical industries will have to be shut down rapidly, and there will be little money available for social protection measures. The medium-term strategy has been severely criticized by trade union leaders for not addressing social protection concerns. The suffering associated with rising unemployment in the old sectors combined with the "fiscal discipline" demanded under accession and financing plans has aided in the return to power of the more "gradualist" opposition.

The IMF

The declared goal of the International Monetary Fund is to act as a monitor of the world's currencies by helping to maintain an orderly system of payments between all countries and to facilitate a multilateral payments system between member countries. The IMF makes loans to all its members to ease their short-term balance of payments difficulties and seek full convertibility of their currencies through a flexible exchange rate system in force since 1973. While the World Bank makes loans for both policy reforms and projects, the IMF concerns itself with policies alone.

Romania has been a member of both the IMF and the World Bank since December 1972. Its quota in the Fund amounts to SDR1,030.2 million, or 0.5 percent of total quota.[85] Since 1972, Romania has used IMF resources on eight occasions in support of the government's economic programs by making use of two types of facilities, stand-by arrangements and extended fund facility.[86] Total Fund credit and loans outstanding by the end of June 2000 amounted to SDR395.4 million (roughly $530 million). The IMF has provided Romania with technical assistance in a number of areas, including taxes and customs, monetary policy and central bank organization, banking supervision, and statistics. The Fund has also provided training to Romanian officials in financial programming, analysis, and policy, external sector policies, public finance, monetary and exchange operations, and statistics.

In November 1994, the IMF approved a standby arrangement for Romania over $439.9 million. Under this arrangement, the country actually received $129.4 million. IMF involvement in Romania, just like that of the World Bank, picked up after the launch of the Constantinescu government's reform program in February 1997. This program was supported with a new standby arrangement of over $413.8 million, of which Romania received $165.5 million. In August 1999, the IMF observed that Romanian authorities had renewed their efforts to correct severe economic imbalances and long-standing structural weaknesses. In light of this commitment, the Fund reacted to Romania's foreign debt crisis of spring 1999 by approving a new standby arrangement in an amount equivalent to SDR400 million (about $535 million, or 39 percent of quota) to support the government's economic stabilization and reform program. The loan was made available in four installments; the first installment was drawn in August 1999 and amounted to SDR53 million (about $71 million).

Completion of the first performance review, originally scheduled for October 1999, was delayed considerably, and the second tranche, $200 million, of the originally scheduled loan was thus never issued. According to the IMF, this was due mainly to slippages in policy formulation and implementation, notwithstanding an acknowledged turnaround in Romania's external position. Given that Fund guidelines hinge on the implementation of a tight fiscal policy, which is expected to lower budget deficits and slow down inflation, the government's decision to raise some public wages became a particular concern to the Fund. IMF negotiator Emanuel Zervoudakis, in town during a wave of strikes in early 2000, professed to be "confused about wage policy in Romania" and expressed concern with several specific features, such as an increase in the salaries of army personnel by 80 percent, which significantly increased defense spending as a percentage of GDP.[87] A sudden cabinet reshuffle in December 1999 did little to alleviate worries about potential political instability. Moreover, during preparation of Romania's budget for the year 2000, the government's judgment diverged from the Fund's with respect to several key indicator targets. Concerning the targeted level of inflation, the IMF requested that inflation be brought down to 18 percent while the government judged 25–30 percent to be a more realistic expectation (down from 54.8 percent in 1999). Concerning targeted economic growth, the IMF fixed its expectations at 3 percent while the government hoped for 1.3 percent (up from -4 percent in 1999 and -5.4 percent in 1998). The fiscal reforms initiated by the Isarescu government in early 2000 also met with some reservations, as the IMF continues to monitor their potentially adverse effects on the budget deficit.

On the positive side, however, the IMF has lauded the large reduction of Romania's current account deficit, which had fallen to under $1.2 billion by the end of 1999, from $3 billion in 1998. This decrease came after a significant adjustment of the trade balance, initially driven by a decline in imports of about 15 percent. More recently, exports have finally begun to increase, supported by an increase in industrial output.[88] Another welcome development was an increase in foreign exchange reserves, which totaled US$1.55 billion at the end of 1999. Following the meeting of the IMF Board in June 2000, the Fund stated that Romania had made economic progress and improved its external position since mid-1999 by stabilizing the economy, reducing its current account deficit, increasing exports, boosting reserve levels, and laying the basis for renewed growth and declining inflation. It now judges that the country will not need to restructure its debts in the near future, as was expected in 1999, by "bailing in" the private sector and forcing private lenders to take on part of the burden of international rescue deals.

In early 2000, Romanian authorities designed and began to implement a program for the year that formed the basis for requesting waivers for nonobservance of several performance criteria, completion of the first review, and an extension of the $547 standby arrangement (negotiated in 1999 and initially set to end in March 2000) for eleven more months to the end of February 2001. On June 6, 2000, the IMF completed the first review under the current standby arrangement and approved the extension of the credit to February 28, 2001, with an associated rephasing of purchases. As a result, Romania was able to draw the equivalent of SDR87 million (about US$116 million). The program had review deadlines of August 15 and November 15, 2000, and provided for performance criteria for end-June, end-September, and end-December 2000. According to the revised schedule of purchases, the three remaining installments would each have amounted to the equivalent of SDR86.75 million (some $113 million), pending completion of the quarterly reviews and observance of performance criteria. However, failure to meet targets on the reduction in domestic arrears and public sector wages prevented the conclusion of the second review.[89] Consequently, the program expired in February 2001, Romania having made only two purchases amounting to SDR140 million (about US$187 million).

At present, the most discussed issues in negotiations with the IMF remain public sector wage policies, intercompany arrears, and the growth of debt to the state by state companies, as well as privatization and budget policy more generally.[90] Arrears have become a chronic problem in the Romanian economy, estimated to amount to 40–50 percent of GDP.[91] There are some indications that relations between Romania and the IMF might have become slightly strained by the change in government, as the PSD announced that it will attempt to negotiate a "more flexible" accord with the Fund.[92] A new accord, which would allow for a budget deficit of 4.5 percent of GDP, up from the previously agreed on 3.5 percent, has not been concluded as of this writing.

The World Bank

Through its main institution, the International Bank for Reconstruction and Development (IBRD), the World Bank grants loans to member developing countries or those in transition to a market economy both for specific investment projects and to improve policies in certain fields. The World Bank's declared aims are to help borrower countries use their resources more effectively, reduce poverty, and better manage long-term growth.

Romania belongs to the group of World Bank members that are judged able to pay near-market interest rates. It thus qualifies for loans carrying an interest rate of about 6.5–7 percent and having a fifteen- to twenty-year maturity with a five-year grace period. The first World Bank loan to Romania was approved in June 1974. Eventually, World Bank commitments to Romania reached $4.9 billion under fifty-six loan projects. The greater part of that debt was repaid by the Ceausescu regime following a unilateral decision, which caused tremendous suffering to the Romanian people during the 1980s.[93]

Since 1990, when Romania joined the International Finance Corporation,[94] the country has received a series of World Bank structural adjustment loans (SALs).[95] The first SAL, in the amount of $400 million, was made in 1994 for a wide range of economic reforms: macroeconomic stabilization, trade liberalization, privatization, investment, and social protection. After the 1996 elections, the World Bank approved four new structural adjustment loans. One was a $50 million social protection adjustment loan; another was a $280 financial and enterprise sector adjustment loan, of which $180 million was disbursed; a third was a $350 million agricultural sector adjustment loan, of which 300 million had been disbursed by the end of 2000. The last SAL was approved in June 1999, a private sector adjustment loan of $300 million dollars, successfully completed in May 2000. A new two-phase structural adjustment loan is presently being prepared. In its context, a second private sector adjustment loan (PSAL 2), currently under negotiation, builds on the same four areas as PSAL 1: "privatization of banking, privatization of state companies, social security reform and improvement of the business environment."[96] PSAL 2, which is expected to bring new loans amounting to some $500 million, also supports privatization and monitoring of institutions in the nonbanking sector, including unit trusts, insurance firms, and credit cooperatives.[97]

During the transition period, the World Bank has built up a portfolio of thirty IBRD-financed projects in the country, totaling commitments of over US$3 billion, of which around US$1 billion are still being disbursed through twenty-one active projects. Two global environmental facility (GEF) grants, of which one is currently active, amount to an additional $10 million. The new country assistance strategy (CAS) for Romania, which was recently presented to the Romanian government and covers the period from 2001 to 2004, envisages further financial support of up to US$1.5 billion, depending on implementation capacity and progress in reform and restructuring.[98]

World Bank disbursements to Romania presently stand at $2 billion, making the World Bank Romania's largest creditor. Many reform objectives pursued by Bank projects are considered to have been met by the institution, including transparent subsidization (which helped bring inflation down), price liberalization, direct farmer subsidies, social safety measures such as increasing the child allowance, compensation packages for layoffs, and others. Less successful was the drive for privatization and financial discipline, as persistently loss-making state-owned enterprises are still numerous.

Technical assistance is generally part of project implementation. The Bank provides financing for expert advice and staff training projects, and trains individuals from borrower countries to design and implement development programs. The Bank also plays the role of a catalyst in mobilizing grant funding from bilateral donors. Many Bank projects in Romania are co-financed by the EU, the governments of the United States, Japan, or others, through special assistance programs. Another significant function of the World Bank is to mobilize additional resources through trust funds for member countries. Major projects are financed with trust fund disbursements. A Romanian example is the Danube Delta biodiversity project, which is financed through the Global Environmental Facility Trust Fund, of which the Bank is a repository. Since 1990 the World Bank has mobilized $10.5 million in grants to Romania that were used to prepare support projects for technical assistance operations and institutional development.

Romania is now included in the pilot group of countries for a new World Bank initiative known as the comprehensive development framework (CDF). The CDF is intended to provide a holistic approach to the challenges of development that attempts to integrate the macroeconomic and financial aspects of development with the structural, social, and human dimensions. The consensus-building process for this initiative is under way. Consultations in its context have informed the articulation of the country's long-term priorities as well as the current country assistance strategy established in co-operation with the Romanian government.

Whereas the early World Bank projects in Romania largely addressed structural reform issues and problems in the core sectors of the economy, with the passage of time the Bank's assistance strategy has shifted its focus to social issues in response to government demand to cushion the impact of transition to a market economy. This tendency to balance economic reform and social protection shows in several projects that are new or in various preparatory stages. The World Bank's program for the next three fiscal years focuses, largely in agreement with government priorities, on promoting structural reform and private sector development, fighting poverty and developing human capital, strengthening and rationalizing the role of the state, and protecting and enhancing the environment. Priority is given to advice and financing for EU accession-related programs.[99]

NATO

A member of the NATO Partnership for Peace (PfP) program since its inception in 1994, Romania continues to seek full membership in the alliance. NATO is interested in Romania primarily because of its strategic geographic position close to Caspian and Black Sea oil reserves. It is a friendly neighbor to the crucial NATO outpost and growing multiregional power, Turkey. It borders an unpredictable region full of potential dangers that stretches from Russia to the Middle East. Last but not least, it is Yugoslavia's next-door neighbor and forms the northeastern edge of the ever troubled Balkans. In the case of continuing NATO expansion, Romania is a probable candidate for the next round. However, no crucial decisions on the subject are likely to be made until a high-level NATO session on the future of expansion, which is scheduled for the year 2002.

According to NATO, the Partnership for Peace program should, in the meantime, help Romania to "facilitate transparency in national defense planning and budgetary processes; ensure democratic control of defense forces; maintain the capability and readiness to contribute, subject to constitutional considerations, to operations under the authority of the UN and/or the responsibility of the OSCE; and develop cooperative military relations with the Alliance for the purpose of joint planning, training, and exercises, in order to strengthen the ability of the participating states to undertake missions in the field of peacekeeping, search and rescue, humanitarian operations and in other areas."[100] Cooperative activities in the context of the program benefit NATO and perhaps Romania by "assisting in the development of Partner forces better able to operate with those of the members of the Alliance."[101] The Washington summit of April 1999 confirmed NATO's assessment of Romania as a serious membership aspirant. It also initiated the Membership Action Plan program, designed to intensify NATO support to aspirant countries by giving advice, assistance, and practical support to and tightening cooperation with countries aspiring to membership.

Romania has clearly demonstrated its commitment to integration in the Euro-Atlantic institutions by initiating internal reforms, building regional ties, and deepening cooperation with the rest of the Euro-Atlantic community.[102] By 1996, Romania had already participated in 960 activities with NATO members forces and signed thirty-one bilateral military agreements in the context of the PfP.[103] The country has since continued to strive for full cooperation under the PfP and has contributed to the Implementation and Stabilization Forces in Bosnia. Cordial relations with the Western Alliance received a boost with Romania's cooperation during the war in Kosovo, during which the nation supported NATO both politically and practically. For instance, Romania volunteered to participate in NATO's Operation Eagle Eye to help verify the pullout of Yugoslav security forces from Kosovo. After the war broke out, Romania permitted the alliance to use Romanian airspace. Now Romania is participating in the KFOR.[104] The Pentagon in particular also appreciates the fact that Romanians have dutifully striven to transform their military from a large, badly educated force more suited to manual labor than to fighting into a smaller, better-trained force organized along flexible Western command lines. Romania's 1999 strategy of national security and concept on the restructuring and upgrading of the armed forces were in line with NATO expectations, and the Romanian Defense Ministry envisions transforming the army's rapid reaction force, which was set up in 1997, into the nucleus of Romania's future modernized army.[105] In return for this rather costly commitment, the Romanian military continues to receive both flattery and support from the U.S. military, as well as confirmation in its hope for eventual NATO membership.[106]

A SOVEREIGN NATION? THE IMPACT OF INTERNATIONAL ORGANIZATIONS IN ROMANIA

The types of policies pursued by decision makers in Romania are in many cases affected by appeals to international norms and reminders of the "carrots and sticks" held out by the organizations that espouse them. The prospect of joining the EU and NATO in the near future has operated as an anchor for reform policy in Romania. Domestic polls and those taken by Eurobarometer and Eurostat show the tremendous desire of Romanians to join these two institutions, which are presumed to guarantee economic prosperity and security, respectively. When asked in 1995 whether they would vote for EU membership in a referendum, 97 percent of Romanians responded yes, the highest figure in all of Eastern Europe. Similarly, 95 percent of the population supported membership in NATO.[107]

As Romania has continued to strengthen its commitment to pursuing EU and NATO integration and has increased its reliance on IMF and World Bank funding in its quest for this and related ends, compatibility with the associated conditions has emerged as a dominant criterion for political acceptability in mainstream domestic politics. Everyone is a reformist in name in today's Romania. The EU decision at the Helsinki summit to open accession negotiations with the country effectively empowered President Constantinescu to dismiss his second prime minister, Radu Vasile, and pull Mugur Isarescu into the government. The fact that Isarescu was on good terms with the IMF and World Bank benefited his government internationally, especially as he tended to be contrasted with the specter of former communism in the person of Ion Iliescu. However, Iliescu and the PSD are declared supporters of accession to the EU, and their success in the fall 2000 elections seems largely due to voters' hopes that theirs is a more comfortable route toward this goal. After a pre-election meeting with Iliescu, EU enlargement commissioner Gunther Verheugen commented that "the PDSR's view was realistic and compliant with that of the European Commission,"[108] and events since then have borne out this judgment.

The Helsinki summit constituted an important moment for Romania, with respect not only to Euro-Atlantic integration but also with respect to its internal development. Before the summit, Romania perceived itself in a marginal position. Since a more concrete integration perspective has materialized, interest in Romania has risen, the nation enjoys increased support from the EU, and Romanians are finding themselves engaged in concrete preparation. These developments have an important impact on Romanian domestic affairs. Romanian political analyst Dorel Sandor observes that "the negotiations are an additional mechanism to stimulate reform [and] modernization" inside the country.[109] As David Dessler has noted, used as domestic political resources, international norms and rules may be viewed not as "concrete girders constraining action but, instead, are media through which action becomes possible."[110] To be engaged in the integration effort is perceived as positive by many observers for having a disciplining effect on policymakers and government and motivating decision makers "to be more effective, efficient, and pragmatic."[111] In turn, their proaccession course is rewarded by improved prospects for investment, particularly by EU-based companies that offer hope for the future to voters and thus lend domestic political support. This support plays a part in the fact that Romanian political parties have for the most part rallied behind the idea of adopting the reform measures necessary for accession.

Together, EU, IMF, and World Bank provide essential means to achieve what they advertise, and membership in Euro-Atlantic security structures both profits from and lends support toward this end. During the Kosovo war, public opinion in Romania did not support NATO attacks on neighboring Yugoslavia. However, following the logic offered by their elites, the majority of Romanians accept their government's pursuit of NATO membership as a necessary part of integration with the West. To be sure, levels of popular sympathy for Western nations and the United States in particular are very high. Yet, significantly, Romanians also pursue integration into NATO as a backdoor to economic integration with the West. It is widely expected that Romania will become a member of NATO before it will be able to join the EU, and that participating in NATO will help advance Romania's other, mainly economic objectives. As Steven Roper points out, "while EU membership entailed significant economic reforms that were politically difficult, NATO membership required military modernization and interoperability that were much easier to finance and sustain."[112] While the clear priority for Romania is accession to the EU, admission to NATO has been pursued at least partly as a shortcut to this end.

Despite public statements to the contrary, it is highly unlikely that Romania will actually be admitted into the EU anytime soon. The government's target date of 2007 appears rather optimistic. Rapid accession may not even be advisable. While Romania can profit from preaccession assistance now, as a member it would soon become aware of the associated costs. The country has significant export potential, not least in the agrarian sector. It is an open question whether Romania should be bound by EU norms and regulations when it might find easier markets elsewhere. Such questions would have to be publicly discussed for citizens to be able to make informed judgments on accession strategy. A referendum on membership will be held at the close of negotiations with the EU, but Romanians hardly possess enough information on the subject to make an informed decision. While expressions of optimism increase motivation and discipline in the accession process, it is a more basic requirement that Romanians be accurately informed about and encouraged to debate what striving for accession does and EU membership would actually mean for their country.

According to Dorel Sandor, Romanians have "a very paternalistic attitude" toward the EU, as they traditionally would toward their state: "They will come here to help us. They will come here with money, with investment. They will come here to protect us." Basically, "people expect from the EU . . . to have similar conditions as in Germany as soon as possible."[113] As they remain unaware of both the difficulties and the real opportunities associated with the nation's present development strategy, the prospect of EU membership remains a "virtual reality" for much of the population. Their support for the necessary reform measures is motivated by the vague hope that things will get better and by the psychological mechanisms of wanting what one cannot have and wanting what others, like Hungary or Poland, do have or are about to get. In the short term, there is public support for EU integration, and the necessary measures can provide public support for parties and officials, but in the long run these measures are likely to become sources of frustration, as expectations are inevitably disappointed.

It is unclear whether the Romanian government actually has a popular mandate to pursue EU integration. This pursuit appears rather an ambition of the political elite in their search for additional resources to maintain and consolidate their power in the country. In Romania, political capital can be acquired by shaking hands with Western leaders, and politicians frequently consider the power gained this way a personal resource, transferable across positions, affiliations, and issue areas. The pursuit of integration at this level is motivated by "political vanity and ambition" and is played out as a competition between political parties and leaders for recognition and favors from the west.[114] This is a picture book example of how, in the words of Cortell and Davis, "international rules can become power resources, helping domestic actors to translate their preferences into policy."[115]

Significantly, increased hopes for EU membership since Helsinki also serve to deflect public pressure from those domestic political elites. The prospect of joining the EU in the near future is an important factor contributing to the remarkable patience and stoicism of the poor in Romania, whose numbers have not declined. The often illusory hopes associated with the promise of accession enable Romanian decision makers to delay or avoid necessary reform efforts in praxis. At the same time, they create conditions under which such decision makers can get away with representing international organizations in theory more effectively than they represent their voters. While Romanians' obvious desire for rapid accession lends a degree of legitimation to the government's professed quest to establish the necessary conditions, the widespread ignorance of the true circumstances involving integration, combined with the often disastrous consequences of the means with which it is (or is not) pursued, at the very least continue to raise doubts concerning the state of democracy in Romania. Moreover, as Strang and Chang have pointed out, norms are more effective "when they serve as resources that reinforce the purposes domestic actors are already aligned around."[116] Thus, paradoxically, international organizations active in Romania might be better served by the domestic status quo, however questionable, than they would be by the effects of those political reforms they themselves tend to advocate.

International organizations have a strong impact in Romania at least partly because popular sovereignty remains crippled. The norms, principles, and guidelines propagated by the international organizations most relevant for Romanian politics are generally mutually reinforcing. The European Union, World Bank, and IMF are all encouraging rapid economic liberalization complete with practically identical guidelines on how to achieve it. Romania is pressured to dramatically speed up privatization and restructuring. However, conditions for investment are too poor to allow for lucrative sales, and the state has neither the funds nor the expertise to support those whose livelihoods are threatened and destroyed by the restructuring process. While stamping out the black economy would significantly increase the amount of taxable income, the prevalence of corruption makes this task seem all but unachievable.[117] Romania desperately needs a sweeping reform of its civil service, which is notorious for both corruption and inefficiency. Yet corruption is sure to persist while civil servants are not paid a living wage.[118] But there is no money for higher wages. Besides, as Isarescu put it, "the IMF representatives consider that salary progress, even in the public utility entities, is an inflationary factor."[119] In fact, the strictly anti-inflationary guidelines upheld by the IMF effectively rule out a demand-driven recovery.

According to its Central Bank, Romania required $5 billion in foreign financing during the year 2000, of which about $2 billion could come from technical assistance and privatization receipts and thus not generate debt. "Borrowed growth" works only on the condition that funds are used to finance projects that enhance productivity. In the nine years following the revolution, Romania borrowed in excess of $8.6 billion. For the most part, the money seems to have simply disappeared, or perhaps it bought time for political elites to stay in power. Borrowed funds have also supported the maintenance of an overvalued currency. The results have been cheap imports, expensive exports, a ballooning trade deficit, and an unsustainable current account deficit. According to financial analyst Matei Paun, the year 2001 found Romania between a rock and a hard place, forced to either accelerate depreciation of the leu to capitalize on productivity gains and facilitate medium-term productivity recovery (thereby inviting increased inflation) or accept a widening trade deficit, which must be financed with hard currency. This would increase Romania's dependency on international moneylenders.[120]

The policies encouraged by the international organizations active in Romania are hardly beyond criticism. While World Bank and EU programs address issues of social protection, they tend to be treated as side effects of economic management rather than incorporated into macroeconomic planning. The IMF choice of strategy to narrow external imbalances on the basis of domestic demand restraint is at the very least questionable.[121] Another critical issue is the hurried sale of government property under pressure to privatize. In many cases it remains unclear why Romania should accept the concomitant losses. These problems are not specific to Romania, of course, yet they have considerable political relevance in a country where the benefits of economic transition as propagated by the external funds remain elusive to most citizens. Still, policies that are pursued with the aim of appeasing these international organizations are never seriously debated. Alternatives are not usually taken seriously, and citizens seem to feel that they really have no choice. This is perhaps not too surprising, given Romania's totalitarian legacy. Yet the lingering effects of public disenfranchisement is hardly the only reason for the utter lack of public debate on matters so vital for the nation.

Another reason can be found in the convergence of parties and leaders on a discourse that employs the norms propagated by international organizations toward tactical ends by identifying them with the national interest. Most Romanians continue to accept this logic, yet at the same time they have grown increasingly frustrated with the lack of economic progress and the hardships resulting from reform measures. The international organizations examined, individually as well as through their combined impact on policy making in Romania, have thus unwittingly served to revive the popularity of the "gradualists" in Romanian politics. At the same time, however, they have led the "gradualists" to move ever closer to the "reformist" position. As a result, the outcome of the 2000 general elections has had practically no effect on Romania's development goals and strategies.

Independent of judgments on the norms fostered by the main international organizations active in Romania, it is clear that their shared goals and largely overlapping prescriptions introduce a bias into Romanian politics. This bias remains largely unquestioned as a fully democratic civil society has had no chance to develop and political elites have shown little interest in helping to create a democratic political culture. The government's approach to integration with the West, which, significantly, has viewed integration as "a coherent, all inclusive process" which could not proceed on an "issue-by-issue basis" has never been truly publicly debated.[122] At stake in such a debate would have been not only long-term political and economic progress but a people's very identity. A series of political leaders has placed Romania firmly in Central Europe, fearing that a psychological association with the Balkan region might hurt the country's chances for Euro-Atlantic integration. Nationalists have contested some features of this newfound identity, and, as Steven Roper has pointed out, ordinary Romanians may be rather "less clear about which geographic zone Romania belongs to."[123]

The shocking success of the extreme nationalists in the 2000 elections may well be partly attributable to the fact that mainstream political forces have avoided all criticism of the norms underlying the intervention of international organizations. This has left Vadim Tudor and parties like the PRM with a monopoly on the expression of disagreement. Steven Roper puts it bluntly: "Romania does not possess a civil society in which conflict and disagreement can be resolved through negotiation without the threat of violence."[124] International organizations have failed to problematize and address this issue, instead relying on the docility of a de facto disenfranchised population in pursuing their agendas. While the lofty goal of supporting the development of democracy in this postcommunist country is invoked in countless documents and speeches, sadly, the one norm that is unmistakably communicated to the Romanian people as a result of the joint intervention of the EU, the World Bank, the IMF, and NATO is the norm of compliance.

THEORETICAL IMPLICATIONS AND CONCLUSION

According to Cortell and Davis, three signs indicate the domestic impact of an international norm or set of norms: their "appearance in the domestic political discourse," corresponding changes in national institutions, and corresponding changes in state policies.[125] All three criteria clearly point to the impact of the developmental norms propagated by the main international organizations active in Romania on the country's domestic politics.

The introductory section of this chapter identified four ways to the domestic institutionalization of the norms and rules propagated by an international institution. The first pathway, the internalization of international norms by domestic decision makers, is sure to play a role in Romanian politics, but the extent of its significance is difficult to determine. The main reason for this difficulty lies in the extent of the structural changes experienced by the country. It is difficult to compare the values held by today's decision makers with those of the members of the Ceaușescu regime. To be sure, many formerly important personalities have clung to positions of power. However, since they were not free to pursue their own political agendas in the past, it is difficult to ascertain which values they held at the time. Thus value change across the two historic periods becomes exceedingly difficult to determine. For ten years after the revolution, Romanian politics witnessed a progressive strengthening of the consensus represented by the values associated with westward development. Judging from official statements, former communists indeed underwent a considerable change of heart. Whether such statements can be believed might become more clear in the near future, as the government might face increasing extremist pressure.

The second pathway to the domestic institutionalization of international norms suggested above is of lesser significance in the Romanian context, for the simple reason that bureaucracy in the country has proven practically immune to any efforts of reform. In fact, standard bureaucratic procedures are one of the major obstacles to institutionalizing the norms and rules advocated by the EU and other international organizations, and a complete overhaul of Romanian bureaucracy has become one of the preconditions for the success of the proposed reforms.

The third pathway to the institutionalization of international norms, their incorporation into domestic laws, is presently of greater importance in the Romanian case. The preparation for accession to the EU but also the creation of conditions to safeguard continuing support from the IMF and World Bank as well as the goodwill of NATO in effect forces the Romanian government to push forward the adoption of the required norms and rules into Romanian law. Clearly, bureaucratic reform will have to follow for this strategy to be successful.

The fourth way for international norms to succeed domestically is of enormous influence in the Romanian context. It is everywhere apparent in Romania how "a domestic actor can use the existence of an international rule to justify her own actions or call into question the legitimacy of another's."[126] Cortell and Davis have raised the possibility that, in this way, "government officials . . . may appeal to international norms to legitimate unpopular decisions."[127] Indeed, successive Romanian governments have been making such appeals since the year 1990. The third and fourth ways in which international norms become institutionalized domestically operate in conjunction as the main road on which Romania is traveling toward membership in the European Union.

The case of Romania confirms the need to focus on domestic structure as an intervening variable affecting the domestic impact of international norms. It also delivers considerable support for Cortell and Davis's theoretical suggestions concerning the creation of this impact. The nature of the domestic impact of international norms in Romania is observed to be conditioned by two main factors. The first does not come as a surprise: The distance of state-society relations in Romania leads to a situation in which the impact of international norms on domestic policy is determined exclusively by political elites. This calls into question the democratic legitimacy of the government's pursuit of those norms and policies. The second factor which conditions the domestic impact of norms in Romania contributes to this democratic deficit.

While a decentralized decision-making structure may seem inherently more democratic than a centralized one, the impact of international norms actually becomes more easily distorted and out of step with popular consent where decision making is decentralized. This is due to the role played by salient international norms in domestic political discourse. Domestic players appeal to international norms to defend their own decisions or to attack those of others. Such appeals only serve to further increase the domestic salience of the norm. As Cortell and Davis have pointed out, "when a norm is salient in a particular social discourse, its invocation by relevant actors legitimates a particular behavior or action, creating a prima facie obligation, and thereby calling into question or delegitimating alternative choices."[128] As the level of general acceptance of the norm rises, alternative positions increasingly lose political viability. This can happen without any constructive debate and assessment of different policy options and without the involvement of society in the consensus-building process.

This study clearly confirms Cortell and Davis's suggestion that "the effects of an international norm cannot be understood independent of the norm's salience in the domestic political discourse."[129] It remains true that reform policy has become anchored in Romania through the salience of international norms and their tactical use in domestic political debate. It is also indisputable that Romania needs reform. However, the present impact of international organizations in Romania sadly serves less to transmit relevant norms to the population and thus to provide a political-cultural foundation for progress than it does to subvert their own express purpose of true reform by helping to consolidate state-society relations as well as political culture and institutions at levels unfit for a functioning democracy.

A final observation concerns the effects of dissociating international norms and rules within the Romanian domestic context. While all important domestic players profess to supporting the basic norms propagated by the four organizations discussed here, there is much less agreement on the exact rules associated with the pursuit of those norms. In fact, the relative freedom from domestic political pressure which results from the rhetorical salience of international norms enables elites to pursue particularistic interests in everyday decision making. The result is developmental stagnation. The relevance of this phenomenon in the Romanian context suggests that the potentially diverse impact of different levels or types of international norms is a fruitful field for further study. While norms may represent a highly salient minimal consensus, rules may be less salient or more contested and may thus require different structural conditions to be successfully put into practice. At the very least, this possibility illustrates the difficulties involved with theorizing about the domestic impact of international norms at a high level of generalization.

158 *Annette Freyberg-Inan*

NOTES

1. Norms can be defined as "standards of behavior defined in terms of rights and obligations," while "rules are specific prescriptions or proscriptions for action" that serve the application of norms. Stephen Krasner, "Structural Causes and Regime Consequences: Regimes as Intervening Variables," in *International Regimes*, ed. Stephen Krasner (Ithaca, N.Y.: Cornell University Press, 1983), 2, 5.

2. See, for example, Krasner, "Structural Causes and Regime Consequences" and "Global Communications and National Power: Life on the Pareto Frontier," *World Politics* 43 (1991): 336–66; A. Stein, "Coordination and Collaboration: Regimes in an Anarchic World," in Krasner, *International Regimes*, 115–40; Robert Keohane, *After Hegemony: Cooperation and Discord in the World Political Economy* (Princeton, N.J.: Princeton University Press, 1984); Jack Donnelly, "International Human Rights: A Regime Analysis," *International Organization* 40 (1986): 599–642; Alexander Wendt, "The Agent Structure Problem in International Relations Theory," *International Organization* 41 (1987): 335–70; Nicholas Onuf, *World of Our Making: Rules and Rule in Social Theory and International Relations* (Columbia: University of South Carolina Press, 1989); and L. Martin, "Interests, Power, and Multilateralism," *International Organization* 46 (1992): 765–92.

3. See, for example, Friedrich Kratochwil and John G. Ruggie, "International Organization: A State of the Art on an Art of the State," *International Organization* 40 (1986): 763–69; S. Haggard and B. Simmons, "Theories of International Regimes," *International Organization* 41 (1987): 491–517; and Helen Milner, *Resisting Protectionism: Global Industries and the Politics of International Trade* (Princeton, N.J.: Princeton University Press, 1988).

4. See, for example, Joseph Nye, "Nuclear Leaning and U.S.–Soviet Security Regimes," *International Organization* 41 (1987): 371–402; E. Nadelmann, "Global Prohibition Regimes: The Evolution of Norms in International Society," *International Organization* 44 (1990): 479–536; and J. S. Duffield, "International Regimes and Alliance Behavior: Explaining NATO Counter Force Levels," *International Organization* 46 (1992): 819–55.

5. See, for example, Nye, "Nuclear Leaning"; Duffield, "International Regimes"; and Oran Young, *International Cooperation: Building Regimes for Natural Resources and the Environment* (Ithaca, N.Y.: Cornell University Press, 1989).

6. Keohane, *After Hegemony*.

7. Andrew P. Cortell and James W. Davis Jr., "How Do International Institutions Matter? The Domestic Impact of International Rules and Norms," *International Studies Quarterly* 40, no. 4 (1996): 451–78, 453. See also Robert McElroy, *Morality and American Foreign Policy* (Princeton, N.J.: Princeton University Press, 1992); Peter Haas, "Do Regimes Matter? Epistemic Communities and Mediterranean Pollution Control," *International Organization* 43 (1989): 377–403; David Strang and Patricia M. Y. Chang, "The International Labor Organization and the Welfare State: Institutional Effects on National Welfare Spending, 1960–1980," *International Organization* 47 (1993): 235–62; and C. Lipson, "The Transformation of International Trade: The Source and Effects of Regime Change," in Krasner, *International Regimes*, 233–71.

8. Cortell and Davis, "How Do International Institutions Matter?" 452.

9. Cortell and Davis, "How Do International Institutions Matter?" 452. See also Jeffrey Checkel, "Institutions, Norms, and Domestic Politics: Citizenship and National Identity in the New Europe" (manuscript, University of Pittsburgh, 1994).

10. Andrew P. Cortell and James W. Davis Jr., "Understanding the Domestic Impact of International Norms: A Research Agenda," *International Studies Review* 2, no. 1 (2000): 65–87, 69.

11. Cortell and Davis, "Understanding the Domestic Impact," 69.

12. Cortell and Davis, "How Do International Institutions Matter?" 455.

13. Cortell and Davis, "How Do International Institutions Matter?" 457.

14. Cortell and Davis, "How Do International Institutions Matter?" 456.

15. Gregory Caldeira and James Gibson, "The Legitimacy of the Court of Justice in the European Union: Models of Institutional Support," *American Political Science Review* 89 (1995): 356–76, 357.

16. Thomas Risse-Kappen, "Principled Ideas, International Institutions, and Domestic Policy Change: The Case of Human Rights" (manuscript, University of Constance, 1995), 10.

17. Harald Mueller, "The Internalization of Principles, Norms, and Rules by Governments: The Case of Security Regimes," in *Regime Theory, and International Relations*, ed. Volker Rittberger (Oxford: Clarendon, 1993), 361–88, 383.

18. Cortell and Davis, "How Do International Institutions Matter?" 452.

19. The term "reformist" is used of those who believe in the benefits of rapid economic liberalization in accord with IMF guidelines, while the "gradualists," who were in power until 1996 and have now partially returned, prefer more gradual and in some areas less sweeping reform. The distinction is increasingly less relevant in today's Romania.

20. Craig Turp, "Where Is the New Blood?" *In Review*, August 2000, 10–11, 17.

21. "Business Leaders Assess PM," *Bucharest Business Week*, December 20, 1999 <www.bbw.ro/index.cfm> (January 16, 2000).

22. Figures according to the National Statistics Board, as quoted in "Economic Notes," *Bucharest Business Week*, December 4–10, 2000, 6.

23. "Budget Revision Approved," *Bucharest Business Week*, September 25–October 1, 2000, 16.

24. "Average Net Salary Up in October," *Business Review*, December 4–10, 2000, 2; "GDP Up in Real Terms," *Business Review*, December 4–10, 2000, 2.

25. "Economic Notes," *Bucharest Business Week*, October 2–8, 2000, 6.

26. "Poll–Romanian Analysts See No Economic Slippage," *Business Review*, December 4–10, 2000, 6.

27. "Economic Notes," *Bucharest Business Week*, October 2–8, 2000.

28. This prediction is supported by rating agencies, which believe that up to 3 percent GDP growth in 2001 is possible, due to export recovery. See Cristina Vasiloiu, "Rating Romania," *In Review*, August 2000, 5.

29. *The Economist* Intelligence Unit recently predicted that it will take fifteen years for Romania's GDP to double. See Vasiloiu, "Rating Romania."

30. The EU also concluded a €200 million loan agreement with the Romanian government. With this money, the Finance Ministry is opening euro deposit accounts at the Central Bank, from which funds can be transferred into the foreign currency

reserve as necessary. See Tim Judy, "Gov't Presents Economic Plan for EU Accession," *Business Review,* February 7–13, 2000, 1, 6.

31. Gold reserves, which amount to over $800 million, cannot be sold or pledged as collateral due to legal clauses on previously made loans that have not matured. The IMF and World Bank have insisted that the gold not be sold or pledged in order to bolster the Bank's reserves.

32. The IMF had a part in helping Romania avoid default in May 1999. The Fund made it clear that its decision to step in was not economically but politically motivated.

33. Bogdan Marchidanu, "SOF to Shed 200 Employees," *Business Review,* February 7–13, 2000, 6.

34. An example is the Romanian Savings Bank, headed by Camenco Petrovici.

35. Business contracts are often not enforceable.

36. A July 2001 survey by the CURS polling institute, sponsored by the Romanian Association for Freedom and Development (ARLD), and the June Metromedia Barometer of Opinion, sponsored by the Open Society Foundation, show alarmingly low levels of trust in public institutions, especially the judiciary.

37. Foreigners may lease but not own land.

38. "CES Report: Ostensible Fiscal Reform Will Trim Population's Incomes and Purchasing Power," *Romania Libera,* January 24, 2000, 4.

39. Foreign Investors Council, *Investment Climate in Romania: Proposals for Improvement,* White Book, December 1999, 3.

40. Foreign Investors Council, *Investment Climate in Romania.*

41. Stratfor, "Stratfor.com's Global Intelligence Update," June 6, 2000 <www.stratfor.com> (June 7, 2000).

42. "More Than Half Romanians Were Better Off before 1990," *Business Review,* November 20–26, 2000, 2.

43. "Romanian Premier Says Romania Should Stop Strikes," *Business Review,* January 31–February 6, 2000, 3.

44. Bill Avery, "The End Game," *In Review,* December 1999, 5.

45. Judy, "Gov't Presents Economic Plan."

46. Steven D. Roper, *Romania: The Unfinished Revolution* (Amsterdam: Hardwood Academic, 2000), 102.

47. According to data produced by the National Statistics Board, as quoted in "Economic Notes," *Bucharest Business Week,* December 4–10, 2000. There have been a few positive signals in the area of foreign investment. For example, Hungarian investment interests have been growing significantly, in spite of setbacks from a decision in 1999 to temporarily cancel customs facilities with the Central European Free Trade Agreement. Swedish investment, brought to a halt by government-level disputes over a $3 billion Romanian debt, is poised to pick up as Swiss-Swedish technology giant ABB proposed a series of projects in the context of an "investment for debt" program. Romania is also enacting a bilateral treaty on investment and business with the United States. Since the Helsinki summit, increased foreign capital inflows into Romania come especially from the EU.

48. Quoted in Bogdan Marchidanu, "Isarescu Confident about Economy," *Business Review,* November 20–26, 2000, 4.

49. Compare Roper, *Romania.*

50. Election results presented here are as announced by the Central Electoral Bureau (BEC) and reported in "Tudor Challenges Iliescu," *Bucharest Business Week*, December 4–10, 2000, 6.

51. Raluca Topliceanu, "Romania: Where Next?" *Bucharest Business Review*, December 4–10, 2000, 1, 10; Bogdan Marchidanu, "Ion Iliescu," *Business Review*, December 4–10, 2000, 10.

52. Topliceanu, "Romania: Where Next?"; "Tudor Challenges Iliescu."

53. Bogdan Marchidanu, "Corneliu Vadim Tudor," *Business Review*, December 4–10, 2000, 10.

54. Quoted in Tim Judy, "Tudor's Rise Sends Chills Up Investors' Spines," *Bucharest Business Week*, December 4–10, 2000, 2.

55. Turp, "Where Is the New Blood?" 11.

56. "Growing Fears That Reforms Will Slow Further," *Business Review*, December 11–17, 2000, 12–13.

57. Quoted in "Growing Fears," 12.

58. "Romania Enters the Danger Zone?" *Bucharest Business Review*, December 4–10, 2000, 10.

59. Vasiloiu, "Rating Romania," 5.

60. Vasiloiu, "Rating Romania," 5.

61. See PDSR, "Political Program of PDSR," n.d. <www.pdsr.ro/eng/PP_en_sum.html> (February 25, 2000). It must be observed, however, that while Iliescu appears keen to publicly discuss the EU accession process, he is less outspoken about his views on NATO.

62. "PDSR Pledges EU Priority," *Bucharest Business Week*, December 4–10, 2000, 6.

63. See Ministry of Foreign Affairs of Romania, "EU Integration Process," 1999 <domino.kappa.ro/mae/> (February 2, 2000). Compare also the documents available at the Web site of the Department of European Affairs <servernt1.exec.gov.ro/die/en/defaulten.htm>.

64. The second essential element of the preaccession strategy is a white paper of May 1995 on the internal market.

65. The first five chapters address education, training and youth development, science and research, SMEs, international economic relations, and the common foreign and security policy.

66. The current chapters include statistics, consumer protection, transport, customs union, telecommunications, competition, company law, and culture.

67. Aurel Ciobanu Dordea, "EU Accession: What's in It for Romania's Economy," *In Review*, June 2000, 8–9. Interview by Ilianca Burlan.

68. See EC, *Accession Partnership—Romania*, October 1999, Draft <europa.eu.int/>; EC, *Enlargement: Preparation for Accession: Partnership for the Accession of Romania* (1998) <europa.eu.int/>.

69. EC, *Regular Report from the Commission on Progress toward Accession by Each of the Candidate Countries: Romania, November 8, 2000* <http://europa.eu.int/comm/enlargement/dwn.report_11_00/pdf/en/ro_en.pdf> (December 11, 2000).

70. EC, *Regular Report: Romania,* November 8, 2000.

71. Europen Council document provided to the author in the context of an interview at the EC delegation in Romania, January 31, 2000. See also, the EU enlargement briefing, "EU Support for Roma Communities in Central and Eastern

Europe," May 2002 <http://europa.eu.int/comm/enlargement/docs/pdf/brochure_roma_may 2002.pdf> (August 5, 2002).

72. EC, *Regular Report: Romania,* November 8, 2000, 35.

73. EC, *Regular Report: Romania,* November 8, 2000, 32.

74. Marchidanu, "Isarescu Confident."

75. EC, *Regular Report: Romania,* November 8, 2000, 28.

76. EC, *Regular Report: Romania,* November 8, 2000, 29.

77. EC, *Regular Report from the Commission on Progress toward Accession by Each of the Candidate Countries: Introduction* and *Romania,* October 13, 1999 <europa.eu.int/comm/enlargement/report_10_99/intro/index.htmIP/99/751> (February 2, 2000).

78. EC, *Regular Report: Romania,* November 8, 2000.

79. EC, *Regular Report: Romania,* November 8, 2000.

80. EC, *Regular Report: Introduction* and *Romania,* October 1999.

81. PHARE, "An Evaluation of Phare Financial Agricultural Reform Programmes in the Candidate Member States," November 1999 <europa.eu.int/comm.scr/evaluation/reports/phare/951493_final.pdf>.

82. Teodora Hasegan, "Romania Gets Closer to EU," *Bucharest Business Week,* December 20, 1999 <www.bbw.ro/index.cfm> (January 16, 2000).

83. Hasegan, "Romania Gets Closer to EU."

84. In 2000 PHARE planned to spend €60–80 million on regional development projects and about €15 million on institutional construction and National Development Plan (NDP) implementation. PHARE support requires a regional development program that targets SMEs (25 percent), the development of local and regional infrastructure (50 percent), and human resources development (25 percent). "European Commission Recommends Romania to Revise Its National Development Plan," *Romania Libera,* February 21, 2000, 3.

85. The special drawing right (SDR) is the IMF accounting unit. As of March 31, 2000, SDR 1 equaled US$1.34687. On joining the IMF, each member contributes a certain sum of money called a "quota subscription." The IMF total quota amounts to SDR 210 billion (almost US$300 billion), following a 45 percent quota increase effective January 22, 1999.

86. Standby arrangements are designed to provide short-term balance of payments assistance for deficits of a temporary or cyclical nature, typically for twelve to eighteen months. Drawings are phased on a quarterly basis, with their release made conditional on meeting performance criteria and the completion of periodic program reviews. Repurchases are made three and a quarter to five years after each purchase. The extended fund facility is designed to support medium-term programs that generally run for three years, aiming at overcoming balance of payments difficulties stemming from macroeconomic and structural problems. Performance criteria are applied, similar to those in standby arrangements, and repurchases are made in four and a half to ten years.

87. Quoted in "Government under Pressure," *Business Review,* January 31–February 6, 2000, 2. Salaries in the Romanian armed forces are still low.

88. "Promising Export Figures," *In Review,* August 2000, 7.

89. "Growing Fears That Reforms Will Slow Further."

90. "Economic Notes," *Bucharest Business Week,* October 2–8, 2000.

91. "Economic Notes," *Bucharest Business Week,* October 2–8, 2000.

92. "Growing Fears," 12.

93. On this period in Romanian history, see, for example, Trond Gilberg, *Nationalism and Communism in Romania: The Rise and Fall of Ceauşescu's Personal Dictatorship* (Boulder, Colo.: Westview, 1990); Edward Behr, *Kiss the Hand You Cannot Bite: The Rise and Fall of the Ceauşescus* (New York: Villard, 1991).

94. A World Bank affiliate, the IFC was established to make private sector investments at higher risk and assist governments in privatizing state-owned enterprises, help raise private funding for business ventures, and provide legal and regulatory advisory services.

95. SALs are meant to support the efforts of a member country to achieve structural reforms in the economic and social fields, leading to long-term sustainable development. The financial support is meant to sustain the balance of payments, and the only constraints on spending are on the Bank's objection list, including items such as military technology or luxury imports.

96. Tim Judy, "Pushing Forward, Slowly," *Bucharest Business Week*, October 30–November 5, 2000, 10.

97. "PSAL 2 Launches Soon," *Bucharest Business Week*, September 25–October 1, 2000, 16.

98. The *Country Assistance Strategy* (CAS) is a document that outlines the main areas for which the government seeks assistance and loans from the Bank. It provides the basis for the government to prepare, with or without Bank assistance, structural reform programs or investment projects, for whose implementation structural adjustment loans or investment loans are then requested. As opposed to SALs, investment loans address specific goals.

99. World Bank, "About Romania," n.d. <www.worldbank.org> (January 26, 2000).

100. NATO, "Welcome to NATO," December 1, 1999 <www.nato.int/welcome/home.htm> (January 17, 2000).

101. NATO, "Welcome to NATO."

102. Xavier Solana, Opinion/Editorial, *Romania Libera,* July 7, 1999. Also available in NATO Online library, NATO News Articles, July 22, 1999.

103. Roper, *Romania.*

104. Solana, Opinion/Editorial.

105. Solana, Opinion/Editorial. See also Ministry of Foreign Affairs of Romania, "Romania's Integration into NATO," November 1999 <domino.kappa.ro/mae/> (February 2, 2000).

106. Robert D. Kaplan, "The Fulcrum of Europe," *Atlantic Monthly*, September 1998, 28–36.

107. Quoted in Roper, *Romania*, 115.

108. "Iliescu Met Verheugen," *Nine O'Clock*, September 28, 2000, 2.

109. Dorel Sandor, director, Center for Political Studies and Comparative Analysis, interview by author, Bucharest, January 27, 2000.

110. David Dessler, "What's at Stake in the Agent Structure Debate?" *International Organization* 43 (1989): 441–73.

111. Sandor, interview by author.

112. Roper, *Romania*, 121.

113. Sandor, interview by author.

114. Sandor, interview by author.

115. Cortell and Davis, "How Do International Institutions Matter?" 457.

116. Strang and Chang, "International Labor Organization," 244.

117. According to a recent Gallup poll on corruption in Bucharest, 91 percent of city residents view corruption as a general phenomenon, with 80 percent reporting that civil servants ask for bribes, and the health care sector pocketing the largest portion, 37.4 percent, of bribes paid. Bogdan Tudorache, "Corruption Reigns in Bucharest," *Bucharest Business Week,* July 31–August 6, 2000, 6.

118. A promising civil service reform law was passed in 2000 but still needs to be successfully implemented.

119. Quoted in "IMF to Discuss Romanian Accord by End-October," *Romanian Economic Daily,* September 28, 2000, 1.

120. Matei Paun, "Fooled Most of the Time," *Vivid,* August 2000, 14.

121. See IMF, "IMF Approves Stand-By Credit for Romania," press release no. 99/38, August 5, 1999 <www.imf.org/external/np/sec/pr/1999/PR9938.htm> (February 1, 2000).

122. Roper, *Romania,* 113–14.

123. Roper, *Romania,* 113.

124. Roper, *Romania,* 84.

125. Cortell and Davis, "Understanding the Domestic Impact," 70–71.

126. Cortell and Davis, "How Do International Institutions Matter?" 453.

127. Cortell and Davis, "How Do International Institutions Matter?"

128. Cortell and Davis, "Understanding the Domestic Impact," 69.

129. Cortell and Davis "Understanding the Domestic Impact," 86.

6

NATO Standards and Military Reform in Poland: A Revolution from Without

Andrew A. Michta

Military reform in Poland after the collapse of communism offers a powerful testimony as to the importance of Western norms in the institutional transformation of postcommunist civil-military relations. The need to meet these external standards as the condition for membership, presented to Poland by the NATO alliance in the years leading to enlargement, proved instrumental in transforming the Soviet-era army into a NATO-compatible military. NATO procedures and practices often ran counter to the historical pattern of civil-military relations in Poland. Nevertheless, the incentives to change as the price of entry into the trans-Atlantic alliance proved more powerful than the national ethos, and by 1999 they had reshaped the institutional framework sufficiently to warrant Poland's inclusion in NATO.

NATO offered Poland a Western pattern of civil-military relations, which guided the practical side of Polish military modernization in the areas of planning, procedure, equipment compatibility, and training. NATO guidance was especially important to the structural reform of the Ministry of Defense and the General Staff. Although Polish military modernization remains a work in progress, the institutional foundation established during the years leading to NATO enlargement constitutes the framework for the current and future rounds of reform.

The question of civil-military relations in NATO candidate states also had a larger political dimension. For Poland, like for the other two new members, the requirement for democratic civilian control over the military was an integral part of its postcommunist systemic transformation. Hence, during the first round of enlargement, the norm defining civil-military relations put forth by NATO was part of a larger process of the institutionalization and consolidation of democracy in Central Europe. The difficulty of this transition and its larger systemic implications were especially highlighted by the Polish case. These lessons are critically important for the next batch of NATO aspirants, as they prepare for the 2002 enlargement decision.

This chapter reviews the criteria used to institutionalize the basic tenets of the Western liberal standard for civilian control over the military in the 1999 NATO entrants. It treats the "norm-institutionalizing" goal—the democratization of civil-military relations in postcommunist states—as the enduring objective of civil-military relations in the new NATO for the foreseeable future. It describes the adjustment of the existing legal and administrative framework in Poland to meet NATO criteria, as well as the importance of NATO standards to Polish military modernization, both before and after the country's membership in the alliance was achieved. It concludes with a discussion of the prospects for continued reform and the short-term prospects for developing the requisite sense of professionalism among the military in Poland and its suitability for NATO missions.

DEMOCRATIC CIVILIAN CONTROL OVER THE MILITARY

As the key condition for NATO membership, the Poles were required to adhere to democratic civilian control over the military because the liberal model was considered part of the democratization process in transitional postcommunist states. From the start, then, the norm of civil-military relations was presented to NATO aspirants in terms of institution building. In 1995 Jeffrey Simon of National Defense University offered a practical definition of effective democratic civilian control over the military for the candidates for NATO membership. Simon's formulation remains the effective standard to be met by the partners left out of the 1999 round of enlargement. Simon outlined four conditions that a country aspiring to membership in NATO had to meet in order for the Western standard to be established: (1) a clear division of authority between the president and the government (prime minister and defense/interior minister) in the constitutions or through public law; (2) parliamentary oversight of the military through control of the defense budgets; (3) peacetime government oversight of general staffs and military commanders through civilian defense ministries; and (4) restoration of military prestige, trustworthiness, and accountability for the armed forces to be effective.[1] In Simon's definition, while key policy decisions on the use of military force must remain in the hands of civilian authority, the government must also fulfill its part of the bargain by giving the army the resources needed to perform the specific tasks assigned to it.

The question of civil-military relations concerns, in the final analysis, the nature of a country's political system. In that broader sense, the pattern of civil-military relations not only establishes the military's subordination to civilian authority but also, more importantly, frames the mechanism employed in the security policy-making process. The criteria offered to the NATO aspirants have combined the traditional precepts of the Western understanding of civilian oversight with a new emphasis on the shifting balance between political priorities and military professionalism prior to 1999. This aspect of Simon's definition, focusing on the perpetual tension between military professionalism and civilian oversight and control, became a central issue as the new NATO moved in 1999 to assume tasks outside the territory of its members. It proved particularly troublesome in Poland, where historically the armed forces had played a uniquely political role.

TRADITION AND COMMUNIST LEGACY IN POLISH CIVIL-MILITARY RELATIONS

In the interwar period the Polish military ranked among the most prestigious institutions of the Second Republic. The army drew on the "insurrectionary tradition" that emerged after the third partition of the Commonwealth of Poland-Lithuania among Russia, Prussia, and Austria in 1795. Throughout the nineteenth century Polish nationalism evolved under the conditions of statelessness, punctuated by a series of failed national uprisings. In the process, the Poles began to view the soldier as the embodiment of the highest national values, the favored "son of the motherland," committed to the restoration of national independence. The Polish insurrectionary tradition was further validated by the experience of World War I and the role played by the Polish Legions, led by Marshal Jozef Pilsudski, in restoring an independent Polish state. The custodial role of the army was strengthened by the victory in the 1919–1920 Polish-Soviet war during which the Poles defended their newly regained independence and determined the country's eastern borders. As a result, the Polish officer corps saw itself as the progenitor and defender of national independence. In 1926 Marshal Jozef Pilsudski moved the military to center stage after a coup that made him the country's central political figure until his death in 1935. The 1926 coup eviscerated Polish democracy. After Pilsudski's death, Poland moved further in the direction of military-dominated government, as Marshal Edward Smigly-Rydz and the "colonels" took the reins of the Polish state.

The disaster of the 1939 defeat at the hands of the Germans (assisted by a Soviet invasion of Polish territory) discredited Smigly's regime, but it did not fundamentally alter the popular perception of the Polish military's role in society. The heroic albeit hopeless fight in 1939, the subsequent guerrilla resistance, and the contribution of the Polish army in the West led by General Wladyslaw Anders fit well with the tradition of the Polish soldier fighting yet again "for your freedom and ours." The creation of the Polish People's Army

in 1943 (like the Anders army on Soviet territory but this time under the aus-
pices of the communist-led Union of Polish Patriots) added a new element
to the country's military ethos. Loyalty to the communist regime became the
core of the Polish officer's creed. In the process, the military found itself
deeply enmeshed in the country's politics, as it was used to capture and then
consolidate political power for the communists.

Throughout the communist era, the Polish military played an important
role in domestic politics. In 1956 demonstrations of support by some senior
officers for Wladyslaw Gomulka's national communist faction contributed to
the Soviet decision to accept a political solution to the Polish October crisis.
In 1968 the appointment of General Wojciech Jaruzelski as defense minister
prefigured a further increase in the military's involvement in domestic politics. In 1970 the army took part in the suppression of workers' demonstrations on the Baltic coast. In 1976 General Jaruzelski had an indirect, albeit
powerful, impact on the resolution of the crisis by signaling the army's reluctance to partake again in the police crackdown against striking workers.
Finally, in 1981 the military moved directly to replace the disintegrating Polish communist party by introducing martial law to suppress the Solidarity
trade union.

As this brief survey of Polish civil-military relations between 1945–1989
shows, the communist legacy offers little that could be construed as the
foundation for a relationship between the military and the civilian authority
that embodies the values of a democratic polity. The lesson of the communist era for the Polish military was that the only way to ensure military professionalism was to build a wall between the army and the civilian authority
of the state. Otherwise, the army would be used over and over again by the
ruling elite for domestic political purposes. At the same time, the Polish officer corps retained a clear sense of a special responsibility for the fate of the
nation. Even Jaruzelski's martial law was presented by the military in terms
of Polish *raison d'état,* as the only solution that could prevent an all-out Soviet invasion.

In short, the military in communist Poland was highly politicized, even as
it strove to insulate itself from politics. The Polish United Workers' Party (the
country's communist party) controlled the armed forces, and communist
party membership was essential to the officer's professional success. The
party exercised control over the military through the Main Political Directorate, an agency of the Communist Party within the armed forces. This contributed to a sense of disconnect between the Polish officer corps and the
civilian structures of government. More importantly, the Polish parliament
(Sejm) had no oversight powers, and all key matters related to the professional military side were left either to senior Soviet officers within the Warsaw
Treaty Organization (WTO) Joint Command or to Polish officers themselves.[2]
At the same time, the system retained a clear distinction between the civilian

and the military areas of policy, with practical national defense matters relegated to the military. This reflected Moscow's policy toward all its satellites, which limited the East European commanders to the implementation of WTO plans, the organization and the release of the operational forces to the WTO Joint Command, and territorial defense and support operations.

The communist pattern of civil-military relations produced three generations of Polish officers who had little experience in the area of strategic planning and security policy making, and, more importantly, only a limited experience interacting with the government as either advisers on policy or as advocates for the armed forces. During the forty-five years of communist control this established a deeply held belief among Polish officers that professionalism was incompatible with civilian control, as the latter was associated with the manipulation of the army for domestic political purposes.

Notwithstanding the constraints imposed by the communist regime and the Warsaw Pact, the national esprit de corps remained largely intact. During the communist era the Polish military thought of itself as first and foremost a national army. In the 1960s in particular, the Polish military made a concerted effort to increase its autonomy within the Warsaw Pact. At the time Generals Jerzy Duszynski and Boleslaw Chocha argued for the creation of a "Polish front" within the WTO structure in order to keep some control over the Polish forces within the Polish command structure in case of war. Although this program failed because of the subsequent Soviet-imposed WTO reforms, it was a telling sign of how the Polish military saw its role in society and its place in the Warsaw Pact. Because party membership was a prerequisite for senior appointments, Polish officers considered it as irrelevant to their professional ethos. This approach carried into the postcommunist era, when communist party membership was not considered a sufficient cause for the officer's dismissal from active duty, with the exception of officers who worked in the Main Political Directorate or spied for the Soviet Union.[3]

THE CORE ISSUE AFTER 1989: "THE LAW ON THE OFFICE OF DEFENSE MINISTER"

The early years of postcommunist reform in Poland witnessed a deepening crisis in civil-military relations. Between 1991 and 1995, the principal problem was the progressive decoupling of the military and civilian authorities, as President Lech Walesa and the parliament struggled over who would control the Polish general staff. In effect, Walesa rejected the Western norm. He argued that the president should exercise control over the armed forces through the direct subordination of the chief of the general staff to the president, bypassing the defense minister. The parliament insisted that the only acceptable pattern would be to subordinate the military to the government through the office of the defense minister. The first serious clash between Walesa and the defense minister (the so-called Parys affair) came in the spring of 1992, after Defense Minister Jan Parys had alleged the existence of a conspiracy inside the military linked to the president. Parys, whose sometimes erratic actions were ostensibly aimed at "decommunizing" the officer corps through a purge of the senior ranks, was in effect engaged in a struggle for control of the armed forces. The confrontation between the president and the defense minister resulted in a parliamentary inquiry, which eventually cleared Walesa and contributed to Parys's resignation. The Parys affair set the stage for the subsequent three-year struggle over who would control Poland's armed forces and in what form.[4]

The issue soon became a matter of personal loyalties. Walesa turned to the chief of the general staff, General Tadeusz Wilecki, and in the process marginalized the defense minister. Emboldened by the presidential sanction, senior general staff officers began to challenge the defense minister's authority. The fight culminated in a confrontation, in September 1994, between general staff officers and Defense Minister Piotr Kolodziejczyk during a dinner at the proving grounds at Drawsko. In the presence and with the approval of President Walesa, the officers took a de facto no-confidence vote in the continued leadership of the defense minister. The Drawsko affair set off alarm bells in the West that Poland was moving dangerously close to a constitutional crisis that could undermine the country's aspirations to join NATO. To make matters worse, no disciplinary action against the Drawsko generals was ever taken. The sense that Poland was moving in the wrong direction in the area of civil-military relations was compounded by Walesa's veto in July 1995 of a draft law that would subordinate the army to the control of the defense minister. Inflammatory statements by the chief of the general staff, General Tadeusz Wilecki, Walesa's confidante, further aggravated the crisis. Walesa vetoed the law on the office of the defense minister because (as he put it) it "failed to address the issues of the presidential prerogative, the status of the [president's] National Security Office, and the National Defense Committee."[5] In response, Washington and Brussels sent a strong and unequivocal message that Walesa's approach to civil-military relations and General Wilecki's continued tenure as chief of staff endangered Poland's prospects for NATO membership.[6]

A breakthrough in Polish civil-military relations came after the 1995 election of Aleksander Kwasniewski, a former communist and the leader of the Democratic Left Alliance (SLD), as Poland's president. Kwasniewski signed the new law on the office of the defense minister and subsequently removed Wilecki from the general staff. The promulgation of the new law, which unequivocally subordinated the general staff of the Polish armed forces to the authority of the civilian defense minister, proved central to the transformation of civil-military relations in Poland. The law, first presented on July 12,

1995, and then approved by the Sejm (parliament) on December 14, 1995, reflected the Western standard of democratic civilian control over the military.[7] It also constituted a breakthrough in the history of Polish civil-military relations. It defined specifically twenty-three prerogatives of the defense minister, thereby unequivocally settling the debate over who controlled the general staff and in what way. According to the new law, the chief of the general staff could command the Polish armed forces only in the name of and on the authority of the defense minister.[8] The new law proved an important step in the development of Poland's parliamentary democracy. The direct subordination of the general staff to the defense minister made it impossible for the president to claim a special prerogative over the senior military. Since it reduced the power of the general staff, the law was decisive to the depoliticization of the Polish armed forces. The change in civil-military relations in Poland is also reflected in the country's new "large constitution," finally adopted by the National Assembly on April 2, 1997, and approved by the referendum on May 25, 1997. While article 134 of the new constitution affirms the president's role as the supreme commander of the armed forces, it also specifically makes the defense minister the direct superior of the military in peacetime.[9]

MILITARY REFORM IN PREPARATION FOR NATO MEMBERSHIP

Polish official contacts with NATO began on March 21, 1990, with a visit to NATO headquarters in Brussels by Foreign Minister Krzysztof Skubiszewski. By August 1990 working relations between Warsaw and Brussels were established, followed by contacts between the Polish parliament and the North Atlantic Assembly. In 1991 President Walesa visited Brussels. This "declaratory phase" in Polish-NATO relations paved the way to more structured cooperation within the framework of the North Atlantic Cooperation Council in late 1991.[10] These first contacts marked the beginning of Western guidance in the area of civil-military relations. Though not yet a requirement for membership, the advice provided to Poland served to map what would be expected of Poland in terms of institutional reform as it democratized its political system. Though this early form of cooperation with NATO was limited, and at first had a negligible impact on the institutional structures of the defense ministry, it was the first necessary step on Poland's road to NATO membership.

A much more important development was Poland's 1994 decision to participate in the Partnership for Peace program (PfP). The PfP expanded the country's cooperation with NATO from the political to the military area. At first the Poles expressed considerable misgivings about the value of the PfP initiative, but they soon moved to take full advantage of it, signing it on

February 2, 1994, and then becoming the first NATO partner to turn in its PfP presentation document to Brussels on April 25, 1994. Between Poland's 1994 access to the PfP and the 1997 NATO invitation to the three first entrants to join the alliance, Poland was guided by NATO military advice in the areas of command and control, defense planning, standardization, infrastructure, and training.

Poland's initial three years of participation in the PfP program constituted the first sustained exposure of the Polish armed forces to NATO standards. The joint military exercises within the PfP in particular had a lasting impact on changes in the Polish military's professional ethos. They exposed a rising generation of Polish officers to the values and practices of NATO armies, making it easier for them to accept the unquestioned primacy of civilians on matters of policy. Poland's participation in the PfP also moved to the top of the agenda the need to adjust the legal framework of the country's armed forces to make them compatible with NATO's. Although the 1991–1995 crisis in civil-military relations was at the center of the news, a less visible but equally important change took place in the country's legal norms applied to the military. Polish laws governing the conditions under which national forces could be deployed outside of the country, and/or foreign troops deployed on Polish territory, were rewritten to meet NATO requirements. For example, the new law outlined procedures for authorizing foreign troop transit or deployment, procedures for dealing with criminal offenses committed by foreign troops, procedures for issuing the permission to station NATO troops on Polish territory, and the like.[11] These modifications reflected both NATO and PfP standards. Likewise, Poland moved to increase the transparency of the defense budget and to provide for effective parliamentary oversight, as required by NATO.

Another area where NATO norms drove military reform in Poland was force interoperability. The Polish forces relied on NATO standards to assess the readiness of the Polish units earmarked for future NATO assignment for joint operations. As the government identified selected Polish units assigned for joint operations with NATO within the PfP framework, gradually these "interoperability goals" were expanded to cover command and control, tactics, logistics, air traffic control, and support. Beginning in 1997, after the invitation to Poland to join the alliance had been issued, these PfP standards were replaced by NATO itemized objectives the country would have to meet. The specific sixty-five goals were classified, but they continued to emphasize the overall interoperability requirements, this time at a higher level expected of a future NATO member. On December 20, 1997, the Polish Defense Ministry received from NATO the list of sixty-five goals that Poland was to implement in preparation for membership. These covered the defense doctrine, training, planning, command and communications, air defense and air traffic control, equipment modernization, and infrastructure and logistics. Of the sixty-five goals, twenty-six were general goals applicable to the Polish armed forces as a whole, while the balance applied specifically to individual services. Poland committed to meet sixteen of these goals by the time it entered the alliance, and a further eighteen by the end of 1999.

As final negotiations with NATO on Poland's membership began in earnest, in January 1997 Warsaw set up a coordinating team to prepare the accession talks. After the July 1997 Madrid invitation to Poland, Hungary, and the Czech Republic to join NATO, a Polish negotiating team arrived in Brussels for a briefing at the NATO headquarters on the norms, procedures, and goals for membership. Officially, the accession review procedure was set in motion after the Sejm voted to authorize the government to initiate the formal accession talks.

The four rounds of the accession talks between Warsaw and Brussels set a number of specific criteria Poland had to meet in four areas: legal reform, military reform, financial commitments, and procedural requirements for accession. The talks gave Poland the first opportunity to move beyond the PfP requirements and be briefed in detail about NATO standards and operating procedures, NATO military requirements for units assigned to or earmarked for allied operations, and NATO standards for the protection of classified information. Upon the completion of the accession talks, Polish foreign minister Bronislaw Geremek delivered a letter to Brussels affirming his country's readiness to meet the alliance standards and obligations outlined in the course of the accession negotiations. From this point on, the strategic requirements of the alliance would provide the overall direction for military reform in Poland. The negotiations phase concluded with the November 27, 1997, letter from NATO Secretary-General Javier Solana to Polish prime minister Jerzy Buzek declaring the readiness of the sixteen NATO member governments to admit Poland as a new member of the alliance. On December 16, 1997, the NATO foreign ministers submitted Poland's protocols of accession to their parliaments for ratification; the ratification process began in February 1998.

Beginning in 1998, NATO standards for interoperability were applied across the Polish force structure, from the levels of defense planning, through force restructuring, to hardware modernization. In the process, NATO standards laid the foundation for a Western-style military in Poland. In addition to providing interoperability with NATO forces, the norms have begun to change the professional ethos of the Polish military. In 1996 the Poles created a special service to coordinate the work of several existing agencies, including the Office of Military Standardization and Military Codes, the Commissions of Military Standardization, and the Commission for the Standardization of Armaments and Military Equipment, with the specific objective to translate and introduce NATO standards into the Polish armed forces and defense industry. When the job is completed, the Polish armed forces will have translated and implemented close to twelve hundred NATO standardization agreements (STANAGs) and related alliance norms. The process began in earnest in 1997, with the translation and distribution of some seven hundred STANAGs and 130 allied publications among the Polish armed forces and in the defense sector of Polish industry.[12] Finally, NATO standards in the area of interoperability, as well as NATO expectations for Poland's contribution to security projecting missions in the Balkans, shaped the Polish military's reform program. The Northeastern Multinational Corps, headquartered in Szczecin, became the first command on Polish territory to be operating fully according to NATO standards and using English as its official language—a lingua franca for its Polish, Danish, and German personnel.[13] The priorities for 1998–2002 targeted further improvements in the Polish air defense and air traffic control systems, as well as communications and control systems, and transition from analog to digital systems, as required by NATO. Likewise, the modernization of selected Polish harbors and airfields was guided by NATO interoperability standards for receiving reinforcements.

Finally, as they prepared for NATO membership, the Poles accepted NATO advice to create a separate land forces command. They also invested the three service commands—the land forces, air and air defense forces, and the navy—with the responsibility for training their personnel, and the responsibility for each service's infrastructure and logistics. In line with the Western model, this approach has moved the Polish general staff away from the command functions toward strategic planning. The existing Polish military commands and staffs have been reorganized based on NATO standards. In a decisive departure from the Warsaw Pact practice, the Polish army divisions have been reorganized from the regiment-based into the brigade-based system preferred by NATO.

CONCLUSION

Between 1991 and 1995, as Poland prepared for NATO membership, the legacy of undemocratic communist-era civil-military relations aggravated the problem of military reform. The Polish "soldier-citizen"[14] during the early postcommunist democratic consolidation saw himself as a narrowly defined professional officer who shared the general democratic values of the state but rejected the Western norm of civil-military relations. The military's goal in postcommunist Poland was to achieve a large degree of autonomy vis-à-vis the state. This internal struggle was exemplified by President Lech Walesa's efforts to subordinate the chief of the general staff directly to the authority of the president through a 1995 draft legislation that would bypass the civilian defense minister altogether. In the end, the Polish crisis in civil-military relations was resolved largely because of the conditions set forth by Brussels for Poland's membership in NATO. The prospect of NATO membership proved a strong enough inducement for the Poles to accept the Western norm of civil-military relations.

As it prepared for entry into the alliance, Poland committed to the depoliticization of its armed forces along the Western standard. This was accomplished through legislation and through several rounds of senior personnel reductions. The forced retirement had another benefit: it brought down the postcommunist "officer overhang" inherited by the Poles from the Warsaw Pact era. The Polish government created the civilian defense ministry and, after the 1996 legislation, ensured the civilian control over the military in the defense minister's office. The transparency of the defense budget was increased. Parliamentary oversight and supervision were established through the Sejm commissions, although the level of expertise of the commission staffs, both in the areas of foreign policy and national security policy, has remained spotty.

The key to the establishment of civilian democratic control over the military in Poland was the subordination of the general staff to the authority of the defense minister. In addition, the government moved to limit the tenure in office of the senior officer corps and introduced periodic rotation of the chief of the general staff. The cashiering of General Tadeusz Wilecki symbolized this change.

Institutional reform based on the Western model has been largely successful, but Polish military modernization continues to be a work in progress. Warsaw has found it difficult to integrate the units earmarked for NATO operations with the larger army because of continued shortfall in the defense budget. Aware of the urgent need to build a better equipped military, in January 2001 the Polish government adopted a six-year program that stipulates a reduction of the armed forces to 150,000 personnel and commits 1.95 percent of GDP a year for defense over the six-year period.[15] The Polish case suggests that "democratic" civilian control over the military is more difficult to achieve than civilian control alone, and, furthermore, that military modernization tends to lag behind institutional reform.

Still, what has transpired in Polish civil-military relations between 1991 and 1999 is nothing short of a revolution. The Polish case suggests that the norm-setting value of the Western standard is of utmost importance for the democratizing polities aspiring to join Western security institutions. Civilian democratic control over the military means the primacy of democratically elected governments and legislatures on budgetary issues, as well as intelligence operations, strategic planning, arms acquisition, force structure development, and military promotions. However, while the key policy decisions remain in the hands of the legitimate civilian authority, the government must provide the army with the resources required to perform the tasks assigned by the policymakers. In other words, democratic civilian control over the military requires a high degree of professionalism on the part of the military. As the Polish case shows, this can only be achieved when institutional reform has been augmented by equipment modernization and training.

Most importantly, the story of Polish military reform after communism demonstrates how effective Western normative influence can be if the nation shares a broad-based consensus on its key national security and foreign policy objectives. The goal of joining the NATO alliance as the ultimate guarantee of Poland's continued independence proved strong enough to do away with its historical pattern of a politicized military. Ultimately, it was this general consensus that gave the Western norm the power to change not just the military institutions, but in the long run, the culture of civil-military relations in Poland as well. Polish officers have shared the national consensus on the need for democracy and integration with the West. Hence, they were willing to trade their former political influence for the new standard of military professionalism offered to them by NATO. The process was turbulent, and (like any such cultural changes) the completion of the transformation of the Polish military ethos will take time. Nevertheless, there is little doubt that military reform in the 1990s, in preparation for Poland's NATO membership, has wrought a lasting change in the country's pattern of civil-military relations.

NOTES

1. Jeffrey Simon, *NATO Enlargement and Central Europe: A Study in Civil-Military Relations* (Fort McNair: National Defense University, 1996), 26–27.

2. See, for example, Timothy J. Colton and Thane Gustafson, eds., *Soldiers and the Soviet State: Civil-Military Relations from Brezhnev to Gorbachev* (Princeton, N.J.: Princeton University Press, 1990).

3. Apparently Polish officers saw no contradiction in accepting the planners of the 1981 martial law as honorable enough to serve in the new democratic army. In 1992 I encountered Colonel Tadeusz Puchala, one of the key planners of Jaruzelski's martial law, in the Defense Ministry in Warsaw.

4. See Andrew A. Michta, "The Presidential-Parliamentary System," in *Transition to Democracy in Poland,* ed. Richard F. Staar, 2d ed. (New York: St. Martin's, 1998).

5. "Weto prezydenta: Ustawa o ministrze obrony narodowej," *Rzeczpospolita,* August 18, 1995.

6. U.S. government officials, interview by author.

7. "Przed podpisem prezydenta RP: Cywilna kontrola nad armia," *Rzeczpospolita,* December 15, 1995.

8. "Przed podpisem prezydenta RP." For the complete text of the new law, see *Dziennik Ustaw Rzeczypospolitej Polskiej,* no. 10, Warsaw, January 30, 1996.

9. The Constitution of the Republic of Poland as Adopted by the National Assembly on 2nd April, 1997 <www.sejm.gov.pl/english/konstytucja/kon1.htm>.

10. Marek Tabor, "Polska na drodze do sojuszu polnocnoatlantyckiego," in *Polska w organizacjach miedzynarodowych,* ed. Stanislaw Parzymies and Irena Popiuk-Rysinska (Warsaw: Wydawnictwo Naukowe Scholar, 1998), 178. Tabor provides a detailed description of the stages of reform leading to Poland's accession to NATO.

11. See "Ustawa 1063 z dnia 23 wrzesnia 1999 r. o zasadach pobytu wojsk obcych na terytorium Rzeczypospolitej oraz zasadach ich przemieszczania sie przez to terytorium," *Dziennik Ustaw Rzeczypospolitej Polskiej,* no. 93 (Warsaw) November 20, 1999.

12. Tabor, "Polska na drodze do sojuszu polnocnoatlantyckiego," 189.

13. A briefing by General Edward Pietrzyk, deputy corps commander, during the author's visit to the Northeastern Corps headquarters in the summer of 2000.

14. For a discussion of the concept, see Andrew A. Michta, *The Soldier-Citizen: The Politics of the Polish Army after Communism* (New York: St. Martin's, 1997).

15. "Gonimy sojusznikow," *Rzeczpospolita,* January 31, 2001.

7

Security and Identity in Southeast Europe: Bulgaria, NATO, and the War in Kosovo

Ronald H. Linden

Bulgaria is no longer the best student in Brezhnev's class.

Trud, 1997

FOREIGN POLICY CHANGE: THE OTHER TRANSITION

The post–Cold War world has stimulated theorizing about international relations and rethinking assumptions derived from a bipolar world.[1] Much of this work has retained a systemic-level focus, but some studies of foreign policy, especially of the major powers, have emerged.[2] The states of East Europe provide an enticing experimental field to draw on for studies of national-level policy, utilizing either a cross-regional or cross-time comparison. This is because, just as we might hope for in a laboratory experiment, some factors in this region have changed, some have not, yet behavioral outcomes have varied. Across the region, one-party communist governments have been overthrown, their accompanying state-commanded economic systems dismantled, and their enforced system of international orientation eliminated. In the last decade new, more open political processes, economic dynamics, and media environments have been created and new leaders and parties (as well as some old ones) have come to power. On the other hand, for most of the states, fundamental national attributes (e.g., geographic position, resource endowment, precommunist and communist past) have stayed the same. For all of them the external environment changed dramatically, with the collapse of the Soviet Union, the disengagement and then reengagement of the United States, the vertical and horizontal growth of the EU, and the expansion of and use of force by NATO in the Balkans. In this situation not all governments have embraced economic change with similar enthusiasm, the path back to power for communist party descendants has varied, and, most significantly for our purposes, policies toward the external environment have varied.[3]

Under these circumstances, the foreign policy orientation and behavior of these states should be a natural magnet for study. In fact, though, studies of the domestic "transition" dominate the new literature on the region.[4] There are several reasons for this, including the inherent fascination with the process of democratization and the change from a state-dominated to privately owned economy; a legacy of low interest in the foreign policies of the East European states (as opposed to the USSR) during the communist period; and, not least, the dominance of the realist paradigm in international relations theory and foreign policy studies. According to the logic of power on which this approach is based, there are few degrees of freedom for the East European states. The collapse of the Soviet Union/Russia and the dominance of the United States and its allies make the region's states "price takers" with few options but to conform to the demands of NATO, the EU, or the Council of Europe. The long line of applicants outside the doors of the dominant institutions seem to confirm this expectation. But several problems with this level of explanation remain. First, the power explanation has proven a poor predictor in general of post–Cold War foreign policies in both west and east Europe.[5] Second, it is not clear which expectations from a power approach are most appropriate. After all, realism's logic might point in the other direction, namely, toward balancing, not bandwagoning.[6] In that case we might expect to see evidence that the East European states are searching for a way to counter rather than join with the dominant power. Third, whatever they do, we still want to know how and why they choose the path they do to negotiate the environment provided for them by the new international power structure. Following Katzenstein, we can view the international power structure as providing the "outer boundary" for national behavior.[7] We still want to find the explanation for the varying approaches states take to the world within those boundaries.

Before doing that, we must address two preliminary questions: (1) Has there been enough variation in these states' foreign policies—even within the strictures of a realist world—to warrant our attention? and (2) Where should we look for other, more fulsome explanations of foreign policy behavior?

On the first question, the evidence is clear. The foreign policy actions and orientations of the East European states have shown substantial variation, even within the relatively circumscribed area of alliance orientation. For example, among the Central European states, views of the advantages of and need for pursuing a separate alliance, through the "Visegrad" process, for example, varied greatly.[8] Further, not all East European states pursued NATO membership with equal ardor or consistency over the decade. Even among those applying, the enthusiasm, reasons behind the policy orientation, level of interest in alternative arrangements, and level of public support varied greatly.[9]

Some states, such as Macedonia and Albania, have acted at times (such as the spring of 1999) like virtual NATO members, though their prospects of actually joining are in fact weaker than those of Bulgaria and Romania. Still others, like Slovakia, were seemingly in the front of the queue to join NATO and the EU but found themselves, as Timothy Garton Ash says, "jumping in and out of Central Europe."[10] The cases of Slovakia and Romania demonstrate such changes in security orientation. Under Vladimir Meciar (1993–1998, except for a brief period in 1994), Slovakia moved from a position of progress on democratic developments, and thus proximity to Western goals, to movement away from these. At the same time, some in this government made it clear that other international alliance alternatives, including ties with the former hegemon, Russia, were possible and even preferable.[11] Once Meciar was defeated in September 1998, movement in this direction abruptly ceased and progress toward rapprochement with the West resumed. In Romania, President Ion Iliescu hastily signed a treaty of friendship with Russia in early 1990, provoking domestic protest. In 1995 Iliescu moved to accommodate the West by pursuing improved relations with Hungary, a choice that fragmented his governing coalition and critically diminished his chances in the elections of 1996.[12] Whether it is farmers in Poland, nationalists in Hungary, or socialists in Bulgaria, substantial political forces in the region argued for— and in some cases practiced—other policies.

What is the cause of such potential and real variations? Why and under what circumstances do the applicants seek to join these institutions and behave in ways that enhance their prospects of joining? If realism is an uncertain guide to the foreign policy actions of states (at least these states), what other approaches at the international level might be utilized to gain some insight into how to explain foreign policy change?

The institutional approach has been very influential in explaining foreign policy change, especially toward cooperation. An outgrowth of the "new institutionalism" in the study of domestic politics and especially economics, institutional approaches basically fall into two categories, each of which is relevant for our case. Liberal institutionalists accept the argument of realists that the world is basically anarchic and a struggle for power and security. Theorists in this area argue that institutions are created or joined by states to help them ease the "security dilemma" in which they all exist. Institutions lower the "transaction costs" of and increase the gains from international cooperation and reduce incentives for desertion or cheating. The institutions, in this view, have little power on their own but provide payoffs that serve states' needs.[13] An interesting offshoot of this approach suggests that even if institutions such as international organizations arise that way, they soon take on power of their own because of their ability to rationalize and legitimize power, and through their control of expertise.[14] Furthermore, because of a number of things they do both for states and on their own, international organizations can evolve into independent actors.[15]

The constructivist approach takes the role of international institutions further and focuses on the role and impact of international institutions in norm creation and dispersion. Constructivists argue that international institutions, including international organizations such as the EU and NATO, are part of an international structure that creates certain norms of behavior for states. These norms, according to the "logic of appropriateness" favored by organizational theory, confront the behavior and identity of the actors, that is, states. These norms could arise in the area of human rights,[16] the conduct of war,[17] or any number of areas.[18] In the course of this interaction, according to this approach, states do not simply cave in to the demands of actors more powerful than themselves (in this case international institutions). They create a new conception of their own interests, even a new identity. Unlike realism or liberal institutionalism, constructivism argues that a state's interests are not given, fixed, or largely predictable from the international power distribution, but are a product of the state's interaction with its environment, are malleable, and are subject to a process of internal adjustment. From this self-conception are derived policies consistent with that self-conception.[19] In the area of security policy, constructivists reject the realist argument that all states act on the basis of a view of the world as anarchical. Rather, as Wendt puts it, "anarchy is what states make of it," that is, they view the threats and opportunities presented to them differently and adopt policies accordingly.[20]

This seems a promising approach to investigating the security policies of the East European states. But to explore why some norms are accepted and adapted into policy in some states and not others, or at some point in one state but not before, we must consider explanations at the national level. Advocates of a liberal theory of foreign policy accept the idea that a state's self-concept and foreign polices are malleable, but they see the source of that change as domestic political battles, which reflect competing societal interests.[21] They reject what they see as privileging international-level factors and argue that the key to understanding foreign policy behavior is to find out who has "captured" the state and what their interests are. This will lead to an understanding of foreign policy change. A nuanced blending of these two approaches accepts the "intersubjective" (between national and international) nature of norms and norm creation but argues that whether and how they diffuse domestically depends on other factors, such as the structure of the state in question, that is, whether it is dominated by its elites or whether the elites run before public pressure,[22] or its own "organizational culture."[23]

Taking this approach not only offers the hope of a more complete explanation of norm adherence, but it takes advantage of the richness of the East European cases. If there ever was a time and place when the line between international and domestic politics is blurred, it is now in East Europe. For the states of this region, international orientation and foreign policy mean confronting the need for changes in virtually all aspects of the domestic political, economic, and even social systems. The EU "Copenhagen criteria," evaluative *avis,* and yearly reports on adoption of its massive *acquis communautaire,* as well as NATO's *Study on Enlargement* make it clear that what these states do, how they define themselves, and what policies and structures they adopt to authenticate that identification—domestically and internationally—are foreign policy decisions.[24] Thus it is logical to ask, Are the variations that we see in orientation toward Western alliances a function of the international structure, institutional norms, competing domestic interest groups worried over material gains and losses or, possibly, of competing concepts of national identity and the country's place in the world?

BULGARIA AND NATO AS A CASE

As already noted, there have been some investigations of post–Cold War foreign policies, mostly of the major powers, some utilizing or evaluating explicitly theoretical approaches. For East Europe, such studies have been few and have predominantly focused on Central Europe.[25] The foreign policies of the states of southeast Europe in general and Bulgaria in particular have not been subjected to close examination despite their proximity to the scene of the most significant conflict in Europe since the end of World War II.[26] An additional attractive feature about Bulgaria and all the East European states is that as medium-size powers their attributes more closely resemble those of most of the states of the world; thus, findings related to foreign policy changes are more likely to be generalizable than those for a superpower.

The potential explanatory factors suggested by the various theoretical approaches obtain in this case. Like the other East European states, Bulgaria has seen its domestic and external environments change dramatically. On the international level powerful international organizations in the political, economic, and security realms dominate the horizon and make clear their behavioral norms. What is especially intriguing about Bulgaria is that during the communist period constancy rather than change was the hallmark of Bulgarian foreign (and domestic) policy. Bulgaria did not challenge Soviet hegemony and was not threatened or invaded by Moscow. Unlike any of the other East European states, it embraced a positive cultural and historical orientation toward Russia. Yet since 1989 the country's security orientation and related policies have shown significant change, not just from the communist period but within the postcommunist decade. The country has not yet been invited to join NATO, so membership is still an open question. Sharing a border with Yugoslavia, Bulgaria found itself in the direct path of NATO military actions against that state, calling into question the country's security orientation.

We can accept realism's premise that states are primarily concerned with their security while also utilizing the constructivist notion that each state, as Wendt says, tries to make something of it. How did the leaders of a small state like Bulgaria envision their security? What did they see as the source of threats to the country's security? Were these primarily international or domestic? From the East or the West? Are there social and economic aspects to their views of security? Given that violent conflict broke out right next door, a key focus of this part of the work should be the effect of the fighting in Kosovo on Bulgarian notions of security.

How did the country's leaders propose to ease their security dilemma? Specifically, did they see a role for Western international institutions? What gains and costs were involved? Chief among the latter category would be relations with their former patron, Russia. This is especially crucial given NATO intervention in Kosovo, the support sought for this action from countries like Bulgaria that do not belong to the alliance, and Russia's hostility toward this action and toward NATO expansion.

More broadly, and to test constructivist notions, we need to see if such policies are related to a change in the state's concept of itself. We can assess this by looking at two questions, one related to the present and one the past. (1) How did the Bulgarian foreign policy leaders define themselves and their *drushtvo*, or international community? What role did they see themselves playing in their region and globally? Whom did these states' leaders identify as their natural international community? (2) Given the significance of both the region's history and the importance of defining the "other" for defining the "self," it is important to assess changes, if any, in the country's attitude toward its newly independent and ethnically related neighbor, Macedonia.

Finally, even without the nudging of the liberal approach, we must recognize that, now in democratic Bulgaria, there is no single foreign policy attitude or definition.[27] There are instead competing goals and attitudes and, maybe, competing identities.[28] This investigation will need to be alive to differences among political elites and, to the extent possible, between them and the public. In doing so, we can explore both the diffusion of norms, should there be any, and the battle of political forces, which the liberal approach tells us will be decisive.

With these approaches guiding us to certain dynamics and factors (e.g., norms, interests, identity), we can begin to examine the case of Bulgaria.

BULGARIAN FOREIGN POLICY DURING THE COMMUNIST ERA

Todor Zhivkov ruled Bulgaria for an astonishing thirty-five years, during which time Bulgaria earned a reputation as the most loyal of Soviet satellites. By most indicators and across most key foreign policy areas this was true. Bulgarian trade was overwhelmingly concentrated on the USSR and CMEA, and links to the global capitalist world were small, tentative, and volatile.[29] The Bulgarian party leadership defined the country unequivocally as part of the socialist commonwealth, as a fraternal comrade of the USSR and as deeply hostile to the imperialist, aggressive machinations of, inter alia, NATO, Germany, and the United States. As Todor Zhivkov reported to the Tenth Congress of the Bulgarian Communist Party in 1971:

> The Bulgarian Communist Party and the Bulgarian people need Bulgarian-Soviet friendship the way all living things need the sun and air, it is a centuries-old friendship and a friendship to last centuries, it is one of the main motive forces of our development, it is a prerequisite and guarantee for the future upsurge of our socialist country and of its morrow.[30]

At times of crisis the Bulgarian Party clearly sided with Moscow, as in the split with China during the 1960s and the crisis over Czechoslovakia in 1968. Though not the most ferocious in condemning domestic heresy there or in Poland during 1980–1981, Bulgaria was clear in its preferences and, in the case of Czechoslovakia, even participated in the invasion designed to end the reform movement there.[31]

Though practicing what J. F. Brown calls "demonstrative servility" in its relations with the USSR,[32] Bulgaria was willing to take advantage of times of détente to explore ties with the West, as it did in the 1970s and again in the 1980s, and even to get itself overextended in Western loans when petrodollars were being recycled.[33] The leadership was also quite willing to utilize nationalist appeals in its policies toward neighboring Yugoslavia and toward its own Turkish minority.[34] Especially in the former case, the regime seemed careful not to exceed guidelines set and enforced from Moscow.[35]

BULGARIAN FOREIGN POLICY AFTER 1989

As elsewhere, the change in regime in Bulgaria at the end of 1989 produced a lot of talk about a "return to Europe." Both NATO and the EU were generally cool to overtures from East Europe at this time and the opportunity to do more than declare intentions was slow in coming. With regard to NATO, in 1993 the Bulgarian legislature declared formally its readiness to try to cooperate with the alliance.[36]

In January 1994 NATO announced its Partnership for Peace plan, offering the opportunity for bilateral cooperation not only to the East European states but also to those states in the area of the former Soviet Union. There was a great deal of grumbling at first, especially from states in Central Europe that saw themselves as being first in line to join the alliance, but also from Bulgaria.[37] Still, all the prospective members signed on; Bulgaria joined in 1994.

Actual progress toward joining NATO was slow, however. After the end of one-party rule, Bulgaria endured a series of weak coalitions and caretaker governments with only one government able to secure a parliamentary majority, that of the Bulgarian Socialist Party (BSP) and its allies. This government lasted from 1994 to 1997 and oversaw a precipitous slide in Bulgarian economic fortunes, a virtual halt to reform, and movement off the radar screen of Western allies as a possible new member.[38] In terms of NATO membership, one study refers to the entire postcommunist period to that point as "7 lost years."[39]

Until 1997 the one political force unambiguously committed to the kind of changes Western organizations were demanding—the Union of Democratic Forces (UDF)—had not been in a position to put them into effect. The view of the world held by the ruling BSP reflected a great deal more skepticism about the benefits—and costs—of joining these organizations. In an interview in 1995, for example, Bulgarian foreign minister Georgi Pirinski was asked, "What is best for Bulgaria's national security?" His response was:

> An unequivocal answer cannot be given at present, because the European structures are developing, and so are the realities around us. What could clearly be said is that the initial impulse of finding simpler solutions—for example, becoming a member of a certain organization and expecting this to solve everything—is over. Now people are talking about the need to find a more complex attitude about developing the West European Union and NATO and expanding the economic structures within the EU. What is meant here is not only a dialogue, but also agreements with partners of Europe and NATO such as Russia, something that could create more security and not a new tension.[40]

The BSP and its partners made it very clear that they were suspicious of NATO and wary of what its expansion would mean for the security of Bulgaria.[41] The BSP argued that Bulgarian society was not ready to accept some of the costs of NATO membership, such as stationing of nuclear weapons or foreign troops on Bulgarian territory or the use of Bulgarian troops in other countries.[42] They defined themselves as the true defenders of Bulgaria's national interest, which they saw as being served by an approach that combined "a Western and a Eastern policy. . . . Only a Bulgarian politician who is able to combine Bulgaria's interests with the interests of Europe and Russia could claim greatness."[43]

This view defines Bulgaria as part of a distinct community, not necessarily tied to western Europe, with continued close ties to the country's historical protector, Russia:

> because Russia exists and will continue to exist, and because Europe—yes Europe itself, regardless of its consolidation—cannot exist without Russia. If any Bulgarian politician thinks that by entering NATO—whenever this happens—we will solve our national security problem, he is either naive or stupid. Despite the historical changes taking place on the continent, Russia will inevitably play a role in Bulgaria's destiny.[44]

The ruling party consistently argued for a "security architecture" based on more than just NATO. According to Prime Minister Zhan Videnov, for example,

> Relations with NATO, WEU and OSCE . . . have assumed crucial importance for us. We are trying to avail ourselves of the opportunities that the enlargement of NATO and WEU afford. Along with that, we are convinced that the future security architecture of Europe can be built only if the isolation of individual countries and the existence of zones with a varying degree of security are avoided.[45]

> A security system should develop through integration with the involvement of all interested parties, Bulgaria included, and not in the form of unilateral enlargement westwards and unilateral democratization eastwards.[46]

The issue of membership in NATO was moot in any case, at least until the Partnership for Peace program was announced. As noted, Bulgaria joined this program, but its participation was minimal and military ties with Russia remained strong.[47] Bulgaria joined the alliance's North Atlantic Cooperation Council and President Zhelev spoke out in support of joining NATO.[48] But after 1994 the BSP-led government was more suspicious. At this time Bulgaria was operating in a period characterized aptly as one of "dual foreign policy."[49]

BULGARIAN ELECTIONS AND THE NEW DEBATE

Presidential elections in Bulgaria in late 1996 produced an overwhelming victory for Petar Stoyanov of the UDF.[50] Stoyanov's election gave hope to the UDF and associated parties that for the first time, they would have a chance to control both the presidency and the parliament. Popular dissatisfaction with the policies, economic slide, and widespread corruption produced large-scale street demonstrations at the beginning of 1997. Elections were held in April 1997, and the UDF, in coalition with the People's Union Party, won more than 52 percent of the vote and was able to secure a parliamentary majority on its own.[51]

Almost immediately, this new government demonstrated its desire to breathe life into the nominal commitment toward NATO. It articulated and submitted for approval a new national security concept, which was duly adopted by the parliament in 1998. According to the now official view, the country could still be threatened by traditional means (i.e., military aggression), but Bulgaria's security needed to be seen in much broader terms. Specifically, three kinds of threats were to be addressed by Bulgarian policy to afford the country protection. First, Bulgaria's isolation from the "international financial and commercial structure" was itself a danger to the country. Hence Bulgaria should not be left a part of a "blank zone" outside the "European integration processes." Second, what happens domestically is critical to national security. As the security concept stated it:

> National security is such a condition of State and society, where: the State is not threatened by a change of constitutional order, armed invasion, political dictate or economic enforcement; the basic individual rights and freedoms are protected; democratic functioning of state and civil institutions is guaranteed. As a result society keeps and enlarges its welfare along with its growth.[52]

Third, organized crime posed a new, dangerous threat to all of the countries of Central and East Europe, Bulgaria included. The new concept stated: "A real danger for the frail democracies of Central and East Europe exists. It is not the military forces of counterparts' armies, but the illegal criminal groups, specialized in organized violence, smuggle of goods, traffic of people, drugs, and arms."[53]

According to this view, Bulgarian foreign policy had as its priority goal the integration of the country with both the EU and NATO. "Only full membership in these structures will entirely guarantee its security," the national security concept stated. Closely related to this was the view that Bulgaria's national security was provided for to the extent that its neighbors were secure. Hence, an important central aim of Bulgaria' policy should be to work for regional security (i.e., that in Southeastern Europe). Finally, the new security concept included a prominent role for the country's economy. "Stabilization, restoration, and growth of Bulgaria's economy" are seen as central to the country's well-being.[54]

A variety of specific policies followed from this concept, for example, the need to change the composition, orientation, and operation of the country's armed forces to provide for civilian control and a smaller, more flexible force.[55] In addition, regional initiatives in the Balkans, the Black Sea, and Southeastern Europe also were supported by this view.[56]

Above all, this integrated national security concept blended the domestic and the international and linked Bulgaria's overall social economic policy to its national security. This made the country particularly open to the importation of norms from norm-generating organizations like the EU and NATO. Not only foreign policy orientation and policies of national defense but those affecting democracy, treatment of minorities, and rule of law were seen as linked to the country's security orientation.

The new leaders of Bulgaria thus defined the country as linked inextricably to developments in western Europe. "In terms of geography and culture," said President Stoyanov in Madrid, "Bulgaria has always been a part of Europe, and the Euroatlantic security cannot be whole and sound without it."[57] Both the president and the government talked about NATO as serving the country's strategic interests and as being the right place for Bulgaria, which shared the values of democracy, pluralism, and individual and group rights exemplified in their systems and the institutions they created.[58] As the pro-UDF paper *Demokratsia* put it:

> NATO is not only a collective system for defense but also an alliance of democratic countries. Through this reasoning it becomes obvious that the acceptance of the project of a military doctrine is a continuing step for affirming Bulgaria's strategic choice toward unity with NATO and through that with the democratic world.[59]

The leaders of the UDF consistently pointed out that their policies were not directed against any other state and that the country had much to gain from ties with Russia; but the contrast between the UDF-led notion of Bulgaria's *drushtvo* and that of the Socialists was clear. The latter fretted that

> our relations with Russia have seriously deteriorated. The conflict forebodes long-term strategic consequences for Bulgaria. . . . In Russian society, the erosion of the cordial feelings toward Bulgaria is gathering pace like an avalanche. The gas war may come and go, but it is shortsighted to foolishly squander the social capital represented by the benevolent disposition of the Russians toward our country.[60]

The BSP argued that the country's security could better be advanced by an all-European organization such as OSCE or even by "active neutrality."[61]

In contrast, the UDF government's view of the world meant a renewed and invigorated effort was needed to join Bulgaria to NATO. From the time of his election, President Stoyanov made it clear this was the direction he favored for the country. While not fundamentally different from the views of the previous president, Zhelju Zhelev, after a few months Stoyanov had a majority government that shared similar views, something not available to Zhelev.

In pursuit of this goal, Bulgaria actively pursued regional diplomacy, including improved ties with Romania, Greece, and Turkey and an enthusiastic response to U.S.-sponsored initiatives on regional stability.[62] In 1997 the country hosted a meeting of eight southeast European defense ministers, who approved the establishment of a crisis prevention center in Sofia.[63] The next year plans were laid for a multilateral Balkan peacekeeping force, to include military from both NATO members and nonmembers, with headquarters initially in Plovdiv.[64] These initiatives were designed explicitly to impress NATO, as Bulgaria's leaders began to emphasize the contribution the country could make to regional stability, as a net gain for NATO in its goal of general European security.[65] The UDF also argued for a policy of "differentiation" from the West, that is, one in which their contribution would be appreciated.[66] In 1998 the UDF government announced and began to implement plans to sharply reduce the size of the Bulgarian army and take other steps to bring the army into line with NATO forces.[67] The BSP was sharply critical of these moves.[68]

The Fighting in Kosovo

The real opportunity for the country to demonstrate its association with the values of the NATO community and its own strategic importance came with NATO's challenge to Slobodan Milošević over his policies and actions in Kosovo. The debate over Kosovo revealed sharp differences (as well as some similarities) in notions of the country's identity and related policies as well as the costs and dangers to it. This was seen in debates over (1) the values that were seen as in conflict in Yugoslavia; (2) the nature of the danger to Bulgaria; (3) the cost to the country of the conflict, in terms of its boycott of Serbia and expenses for supporting refugees; and (4) the possible impact of the conflict on the country's relationship with Russia.

The UDF leadership unhesitatingly characterized the conflict as a struggle between democracy and dictatorship, between the pluralistic, "civilized" future represented by West Europe and "dictatorship and totalitarianism."[69] Along these axes, the government wanted there to be no doubt where Bulgaria stood:

> We have a collision of two models—one is the pursuit of "great nations" establishing ethnically clean states, which is absolutely impossible, given the distribution of the people from different ethnicities and religions on the maps of each state. The other model is the true European alternative—states in which there is ethnic peace, religious tolerance protection of individual rights and freedoms; states in which governments do not abuse personal rights and freedoms, or the security of their citizens. This is the model that Bulgaria is following.[70]

The opposition saw it as a question of sovereignty and national interests in a more narrow, immediate sense. Referring to President Stoyanov's address to the nation just before the NATO summit in Washington, *Duma* said:

The absurd thing is that Mr. Stoyanov's address reveals no interest in the opinion of the Bulgarian nation. Although addressed to this nation, it is written for someone else's attention. This other person lives in Brussels, and his name is Solana [secretary-general of NATO at the time]. He is the real addressee. Solana, not the ordinary Bulgarian man or woman, has to be convinced that Bulgaria is ready to lick NATO's boots in any way necessary, even at the cost of a fratricidal quarrel. Here, the national interest is completely trampled underfoot by political mania.[71]

The UDF saw the country and the region as threatened by the failure of democracy in Yugoslavia.[72] They saw NATO as stepping in to provide the necessary force to prevent Milošević from achieving his aims and thus offering security to all the states around Yugoslavia.[73] While the UDF tried to reassure the public that the country would not get involved militarily,[74] they saw the danger in much broader terms than military spillover. In contrast, the opposition saw the danger coming from NATO's actions—including stray bombs—not those of Yugoslavia and that the attack on sovereignty and the formation of a new empire by NATO was much more threatening.[75] "The Balkan power keg fuse is smoking," wrote *Duma*.[76] "NATO is preparing a strike against sovereign Yugoslavia in the name of 'humanitarian' goals. In totally logical fashion, our neighbors are preparing to defend themselves." They linked this to the danger of the country being drawn into a conflict[77]— a prospect that threats from Yugoslavia[78] only served to underscore—and to the danger of isolating Russia.[79]

When it was eventually asked to provide overflight rights for NATO air strikes, Bulgaria (along with Romania) did so despite not only political opposition but a public apparently overwhelmingly hostile to the action. The parliamentary vote to provide the air corridor fell along party lines: the ruling coalition gaining 154 votes and the BSP and Euroleft producing seventy-five votes against (plus five independents and one abstention).[80] The UDF saw this as a cost the country should be prepared to bear, especially as a future NATO member, in order to demonstrate its willingness to contribute. The Socialists railed at this "national betrayal."[81] "This is no longer politics" said *Duma* "but servility."[82] On the other hand, when Russia asked for overflight permission to provide peacekeepers in Kosovo, this request was refused—which prompted further criticism from the opposition.[83]

The UDF shared with the Socialists concern about the cost to the country. The boycott of the country during the previous conflict was estimated to have cost the country the equivalent of three years of the national debt.[84] Now a new blockade was necessary and, more seriously, the danger of large numbers of refugees pouring over the border from Macedonia was seen as very real.[85] For the UDF this was the price one pays to join a community; for the Socialists, this was the fruit of NATO's aggression.

Policy toward Macedonia

Along with orientation toward NATO and Kosovo, attitudes and actions toward Macedonia represent the clearest illustration of a redefinition of the country's identity offered by the UDF-led government. Bulgaria had been one of the first countries to recognize Macedonia after it emerged from a disaggregated Yugoslavia, but its recognition had extended only to the state, not its people or language. This orientation stemmed from a long-standing view, held by both precommunist and communist governments, that the region of Macedonia had been ripped from its rightful place as part of twentieth-century Bulgaria, as a result of big power meddling going as far back as the Congress of Berlin.[86] Macedonians were viewed as ethnically and linguistically Bulgarian, and thus their place was within the Bulgarian state. The establishment of communist Bulgaria had not eliminated this view. Rather it was transmuted into a special brand of Bulgarian hostility toward Tito's Yugoslavia and pointed nonacknowledgment of the separate Macedonian republic Tito created.[87]

Despite the change to democratic government in Bulgaria and the emergence of a new independent Macedonia, little progress was made on improving or expanding bilateral relations. Skopje and Sofia could not even agree on what to call the language in various treaties. But the UDF government elected in 1997 articulated a worldview in which the stability and health of neighboring Macedonia was central to its own security.[88] As part of its broad redefinition of Bulgaria's place in Europe and with admission into NATO now high on the agenda, the UDF put the language/nation issue behind it and offered a range of treaties and agreements in February 1999. Against fierce opposition from the Socialists,[89] the UDF government moved ahead with a range of treaties, normalizing relations[90] and later providing Macedonia with tanks and howitzers.[91] Given the history of this conflict, stretching across decades and various types of regimes, it is hard to overestimate the significance of the new Bulgarian government's actions and hard to avoid the conclusion that what the UDF was offering was not simply a modification at the margins of the country's foreign policy, but a new conception of the country and its place in the world and in its own neighborhood. Speaking on Bulgarian television, Prime Minister Kostov appealed for a new Bulgaria: "Let Bulgaria once in this century, at the end of this century, take a responsible attitude to Macedonia."[92] To the wider external audience, he could not resist a boast:

> Speaking about the Bulgarian model, I would like to say to the Europeans that there is no need to import anything in SEE, because all these successful models are already here. I would like to emphasize for example the way that governments—the Bulgarian and the Macedonian, overcame some disputes, which have lasted for 50–60 years. The so-called "language dispute" is a mystery, but

it was obvious for every experienced political analyst that there are contradic-tions deriving primarily from the attempts for ethnic domination, pretensions, and confrontations. Bulgaria is a perfect example of how everything of this type could be resolved.[93]

CONCLUSION: A NEW BULGARIAN IDENTITY?

It is tempting to conclude that what we are seeing in Bulgaria is a change of national identity, of national self-perception. Further, the changes seemingly apply to both the country's notion of its domestic governing values and its place in the wider world. This is because membership in the target interna-tional community involves more than simply being able to make a military contribution or draw on protection as traditionally defined. It involves, specifically and explicitly, adopting the values propagated by that commu-nity. Like the EU, NATO has made its criteria very clear, including dimen-sions of democratic political process and social pluralism as well as geostrategic contributions. Viewing NATO in strictly geostrategic terms, the socialist opposition had all but rejected membership outright; embracing the value orientation of the alliance, the UDF government eagerly sought it.

There are several caveats to be entered before accepting the construc-tivist argument. First, identities may be intersubjectively created, but it helps if the national-level actor begins from a point closer to the values pro-claimed by the dominant international structures. In the Bulgarian case, clearly the UDF favored the domestic political and economic processes en-couraged by NATO and the EU. Its philosophy and policy orientations were more inclined in this direction than were those of the BSP. But the rational calculations suggested by the institutionalists have not been absent from the interactions. Clearly a geostrategic calculus has been operating as well. The UDF leaders, for example, have not argued their case *solely* on the ba-sis of values; they see the gains from institutional membership in both the EU and NATO.[94] Nor should we expect it to be otherwise. Human beings are not solely creatures of values, any more than they are solely creatures of utilitarian calculation. Indeed, the constructivist approach is based on the idea that the interactions between state and international institutions, often begun from utilitarian motives, nonetheless have the effect of chang-ing the self-concept of state. Schimmelfennig, for one, has sensibly and per-suasively reminded us that constructed changes take place in a rationalist environment.[95] This allows us not to worry (from an analytical point of view) if Bulgaria—or, more properly, its leaders—changed what they *really* believe (if that were knowable). They manifestly offered a changed defini-tion of the country and its place in the world and acted on that. That they did so in an environment that offered them clear and valuable incentives (membership in the alliance) does not diminish the significance of the process or its results.

This points to another trimming of the constructivist argument. The UDF may have brought a NATO-oriented value system to the international arena and certainly seems to have worked hard to create a new identity for Bulgaria and the world. But it had to get to power in the first place. Here is where the liberal argument weighs in, along two dimensions. First, those willing to engage in the dialogue and begin the process of identity change had first to "capture the state." In the UDF case, this was not accomplished by holding only the presidency; the government needed to share the philosophy as well. This did not happen until 1997, and trying to gauge the changes in Bulgarian identity without recognizing the timing of domestic change would be pointless. Second, by focusing on the internal battle among competing interests, the liberals remind us of the domestic component of the identity struggle. In the elections of 1996 and 1997 the UDF did not decisively defeat the BSP on the basis of positions on NATO; they did so because of BSP mismanagement of the economy, corruption, and a lack of movement on reform. Once this "capture" happened, however, the UDF was in a position to reframe the image of the country and move it closer to NATO. Third, the liberal argument reminds us that this is an ongoing process—there will be continuing struggles and new elections. But these might or might not produce a reformulation of the country's foreign policy identity. In the spring of 2000 the BSP shifted its view to accept the government's policy on both the EU and NATO (with reservations among some), making future foreign policy change less likely.[96] Then, when the elections of 2001 did produce a new government, it was led not by the socialists or the UDF but by Bulgaria's former king, Simeon Saxecoburgotski, and his National Movement Simeon II. This government is, if anything, even more strongly committed to joining Europe's key organizations.[97] Thus, while government changes make foreign policy changes possible, who holds the power and how they see themselves matters a great deal.

Realists would argue, however, that bandwagoning—lining up with the most powerful states or groups—has more to do with the shift in Bulgaria's position than any change in identity. This view would seem to be supported by the BSP's shift. But this argument does not explain why the BSP, when it was in power, did not show any but nominal movement toward NATO despite the organization's powerful position in those years. The change only came when a UDF government came in. At the same time, the UDF-led shift occurred despite the country's proximity to Russia and its considerable dependence on that country for energy, something a realist argument would emphasize. Perhaps there is a threshold within Schimmelfenning's "rationalist environment" (operationalized by a victory in war) above which the power of the external group is irresistible. A true test, of course, of the role of both the (external) power and (internal) identity explanations for shifts in foreign policy would require seeing what the BSP did once it returned to the government.[98]

This would also allow us to gauge the importance of domestic interest groups and public opinion, dimensions insufficiently accounted for in both explanations. The Democratic Left faction of the BSP, for example, continued to support a full referendum on NATO.[99] At the same time, public opinion polls, though volatile, repeatedly showed (1) the public roughly divided on NATO membership (though not on EU membership)[100] and (2) overwhelmingly opposed to the country's involvement in the war in Kosovo, including the granting of an air corridor.[101] In other words, if a new Bulgarian identity is being constructed, its roof does not yet cover everyone. In part, this is a natural result of the polarization that has beset Bulgarian politics since the end of communist rule.[102] In part, it is the result of the government's own clumsy handling of the issue of risk to the country and its involvement.[103] In any case, it reaffirms the notion that this new identity construction is a *process,* one involving both domestic and international constituencies.

NOTES

An earlier version of this chapter was delivered at the Annual Convention of the International Studies Association, Los Angeles, California, March 14–17, 2000. I would like to thank Gergana Noutcheva for her careful reading of this chapter and Alexander Grigorescu, Jivko Kirov, and Daniela Trajkovska for their assistance in research. Trajkovska also translated some articles from Bulgarian newspapers.

1. See, for example, Pierre Allan and Kjell Goldmann, eds., *The End of the Cold War: Evaluating Theories of International Relations* (The Hague: Kluwer Law International, 1995); Richard Ned Lebow and Thomas Risse-Kappen, eds., *International Relations Theory and the End of the Cold War* (New York: Columbia University Press, 1995); Ethan Kapstein and Michael Mastanduno, eds., *Unipolar Politics: Realism and State Strategies after the Cold War* (New York: Columbia University Press, 1999).

2. Jeffrey Checkel, *Ideas and International Political Change: Soviet/Russian Behavior and the End of the Cold War* (New Haven, Conn.: Yale University Press, 1997); Ted Hopf, ed., *Understandings of Russian Foreign Policy* (University Park: Pennsylvania State University Press, 1999). See also chapters 5–10 in Kapstein and Mastanduno, *Unipolar Politics.* Philippe G. Le Prestre, ed., *Role Quests In the Post–Cold War Era* (Montreal & Kingston: McGill-Queen's University Press, 1997).

3. These developments are reviewed in Stephen White, Judy Batt, and Paul G. Lewis., eds., *Developments in Central and East European Politics 2* (Durham, N.C.: Duke University Press, 1998).

4. "Post-Communist Transformation in East Europe," *Comparative Political Studies,* July 1995, special issue; Jon Elster, Claus Offe, and Ulrich Preuss, *Institutional Design in Post-Communist Societies* (Cambridge: Cambridge University Press,

1998); Fritz Plasser, Peter Ulram, and Harald Waldrauch, *Democratic Consolidation in East-Central Europe* (London: Macmillan, 1998).

5. On East Europe and Ukraine, see Mark Kramer, "Neorealism, Nuclear Proliferation, and East-Central European Strategies," *International Politics* 35, no. 3 (1998): 253–304. On Germany, see John S. Duffield, "Political Culture and State Behavior: Why Germany Confounds Neorealism," *International Organization* 53, no. 4 (1999): 765–803; Emil Nagengast, "Germany's New Ostpolitik and the Ideology of Multilateralism," *International Politics* 35, no. 3 (1998): 305–31.

6. Randall L. Schweller, "Bandwagoning for Profit: Bringing the Revisionist State Back In," *International Security* 19, no. 1 (1994): 72–107.

7. Peter Katzenstein, *Cultural Norms and National Security: Police and Military in Postwar Japan* (Ithaca, N.Y.: Cornell University Press, 1996), 22–25.

8. Andrew Cottey, *East-Central Europe after the Cold War* (London: Macmillan, 1995), 126–35; Adrian Hyde-Price, *The International Politics of East Central Europe* (Manchester, U.K.: Manchester University Press, 1996), 122–35; Matthew Rhodes, "Post-Visegrad Cooperation in East Central Europe," *East European Quarterly* 33, no. 1 (1999): 51–67.

9. Armand Clesse and Lothar Ruhl, eds., *Searching for a New Security Structure in Europe* (Baden-Baden: NomosVerlagsgesellschaft, 1990): pt. 3, B; Andrew Michta, *East Central Europe after the Warsaw Pact* (Westport, Conn.: Greenwood, 1992); Richard Smoke, *Perceptions of Security: Public Opinion and Expert Assessments in Europe's New Democracies* (Manchester, U.K.: Manchester University Press, 1996); Stephen White et al., "Eastern Publics and Western Enlargement," *International Politics* 37, no. 3 (2000): 323–43.

10. Timothy G. Ash, "The Puzzle of Central Europe," *New York Review*, March 18, 1999, 20.

11. A. Duleba, "Pursuing an Eastern Agenda," *Transition* 2, no. 19 (1996): 52–55.

12. Ronald Linden, "Putting on Their Sunday Best: Romania, Hungary, and the Puzzle of Peace," *International Studies Quarterly* 44 (2000): 121–45.

13. Robert Keohane, *International Institutions and State Power* (Boulder, Colo.: Westview, 1989); Robert Keohane, Joseph Nye, and Stanley Hoffmann, eds., *After the Cold War: International Institutions and State Strategies in Europe, 1989–1991* (Cambridge, Mass.: Harvard University Press, 1991).

14. Michael Barnett and Martha Finnemore, "The Politics, Power, and Pathologies of International Organizations," *International Organization* 53, no. 4 (1999): 699–732.

15. Kenneth Abbott and Duncan Snidal, "Why States Act through Formal International Organizations," *Journal of Conflict Resolution* [electronic version] 42, no. 1 (1998): 3–33.

16. Thomas Risse, "International Norms and Domestic Change: Arguing and Communicative Behavior in the Human Rights Area," *Politics and Society* 27, no. 4 (1999): 529–59.

17. Jeffrey W. Legro, "Which Norms Matter? Revisiting the 'Failure' of Internationalism," *International Organization* 51, no. 1 (1997): 31–63.

18. For a discussion of the development of the norm against assassination, see Ward Thomas, "Norms and Security: The Case of International Assassination," *International Organization* 25, no. 1 (2000): 105–33.

19. Martha Finnemore and Kathryn Sikkink, "International Norm Dynamics and Political Change," *International Organization* 52, no. 4 (1999): 887–917.

20. Alexander Wendt, "Anarchy Is What States Make of It," *International Organization* 46 (1992): 391–425; Ted Hopf, "The Promise of Constructivism in International Relations Theory," *International Security* 23, no. 1 (1998): 171–200.

21. Andrew Moravcsik, "Taking Preferences Seriously: A Liberal Theory of International Politics," *International Organization* 51, no. 4 (1997): 513–53.

22. Jeffrey Checkel, "Norms, Institutions, and National Identity in Contemporary Europe," *International Studies Quarterly* 43, no. 1 (1999): 83–114.

23. Legro, "Which Norms Matter?"; Katzenstein, *Cultural Norms*.

24. On the EU, see Heather Grabbe and Kirsty Hughes, *Enlarging the EU Eastwards* (London: Royal Institute of International Affairs, 1998); Alan Mayhew, *Recreating Europe: The European Union's Policy towards Central and East Europe* (Cambridge: Cambridge University Press, 1998); on NATO, see Linden, "Putting on Their Sunday Best."

25. In addition to Kramer, "Neorealism," see Ilya Prizel, *National Identity and Foreign Policy: Nationalism and Leadership in Poland, Russia, and Ukraine* (Cambridge: Cambridge University Press, 1998).

26. On southeast Europe, see Paul S. Shoup, ed., *Problems of Balkan Security* (Washington, D.C.: Wilson Center Press, 1990). On Romania, see Daniel N. Nelson, ed., *Romania after Tyranny* (Boulder, Colo.: Westview, 1992), pt. 2. On Bulgaria, see John D. Bell, "Bulgaria's Search for Security," in *Bulgaria in Transition*, ed. John D. Bell (Boulder, Colo.: Westview, 1998), 305–23; Ekaterina Nikova, "Bulgaria in the Balkans," in Bell, *Bulgaria*, 281–304.

27. The democratization of foreign policy is discussed in Ronald Linden, "Liberalization and Foreign Policy in East Europe," in *Liberalization and Foreign Policy*, ed. Miles Kahler (New York: Columbia University Press, 1997), 165–92. For a review of public opinion on security in Central Europe, see Smoke, *Perceptions of Security*.

28. Katzenstein, *Cultural Norms*, 3.

29. Aurel Braun, *Small-State Security in the Balkans* (Totowa, N.J.: Barnes & Noble Books, 1983), 200–208; Roger Kanet, "East-West Trade and the Limits of Western Influence," in *The International Politics of East Europe*, ed. Charles Gati (New York: Praeger, 1976), 192–213.

30. Bulgarian Communist Party, "Report of the Central Committee of the Bulgarian Communist Party to the Tenth Congress of the Party, Delivered by Comrade Todor Zhivkov," in *Under the Banner of Internationalism: Materials from the 10th Congress of the Bulgarian Communist Party* (Sofia: Sofia Press, 1971).

31. John D. Bell, *The Bulgarian Communist Party from Blagoev to Zhivkov* (Stanford, Calif.: Hoover Institution Press, 1986), 144; Ronald Linden, *Bear and Foxes: The International Relations of the East European States, 1965–69* (Boulder, Colo.: East European Quarterly/Columbia University Press, 1979), 153–76.

32. J. F. Brown, *Nationalism, Democracy, and Security in the Balkans* (Aldershot, U.K.: Dartmouth, 1992), 113.

33. CIA, "East Europe Faces up to the Debt Crisis," in *East European Economies: Slow Growth in the 1980s*, vol. 2, *Foreign Trade and International Finance: Selected Papers Submitted to the Joint Economic Committee* (Washington, D.C.: U.S. Congress, March 28, 1986), 151–85.

34. Brown, *Nationalism*, 114–21.

35. Braun, *Small State Security*, 21–30.

36. Khorizont Radio Network, December 21, 1993 (Foreign Broadcast Information Service [hereafter FBIS], December 22, 1993).

37. See "Interview with Bulgarian President Zhelyu Zhelev," *Liberation*, May 2–3, 1994 (FBIS May 2, 1999).

38. Garabed Minassian, "The Road to Economic Disaster in Bulgaria," *Europe-Asia Studies* 50, no. 2 (1998): 331–49. Bulgaria was not among the five states invited in 1997 to begin negotiations for membership in either the EU or NATO. In the latter case, both Slovenia and Romania, though not invited, were singled out for praise for their progress; no such comments were made about Bulgaria. "Madrid Declaration on Euro-Atlantic Security and Cooperation," *NATO Review*, Documentation, no. 4 (1997): 2.

39. Jeffrey Simon, "Bulgaria and NATO: 7 Lost Years," *Strategic Forum* 142 (1998).

40. *Standart News*, July 5, 1995 (FBIS July 10, 1995, 3–4).

41. *Duma*, May 3, 1996 (FBIS May 8, 1996, 4–5).

42. See the statements by Prime Minister Zhan Videnov in *Trud,* April 18, 1995 (FBIS April 24, 1995, 8–9).

43. *Duma*, April 19, 1995 (FBIS April 24, 1995, 7–8).

44. *Duma*, April 19, 1995 (FBIS April 24, 1995, 7–8).

45. BTA, 26 April 1995 (FBIS, 3 May 1995, 1). See also the remarks of Defense Minister Dimitur Pavlov in *Chasa,* March 19, 1996 (FBIS 26 March 26, 1995, 10).

46. BTA, April 18, 1995 (FBIS April 25, 1995, 2).

47. John D. Bell, "Bulgaria's Search for Security," 308.

48. Dimitar Tzanev, "Bulgaria's International Relations after 1989: Foreign Policy between History and Reality," in *Bulgaria in a Time of Change*, ed. Iliana Zloch-Christy (Aldershot, U.K.: Avebury Ashgate, 1996), 183.

49. Evgenni Dainov, "Foreign Policy and Domestic Politicians," *Standart News*, December 12, 1995 <www.osf.acad.bg/dg-piper/ins10/konsens.htm> (December 12, 1995).

50. Stoyanov won 44 percent of the vote in the first round, with the Socialist candidate, Ivan Mazarov, winning 27 percent; in the second round Stoyanov defeated Mazarov 62.1 percent to 37.9 percent. See John D. Bell, *Bulgaria in Transition* (Boulder, Colo.: Westview, 1998), 331.

51. Stefan Krause, "Winds of Change Sweep Bulgaria," *Transitions on Line,* Country Files, Bulgaria: Annual Report 1997 <www.tol.cz/session/highlight&url=/countries/bular97.html> (March 7, 2000).

52. *National Security Concept*, May 1, 1998, e-mail from NATO Information Center, Sofia.

53. *National Security Concept*, May 1, 1998, e-mail from NATO Information Center, Sofia.

54. *National Security Concept*, May 1, 1998, e-mail from NATO Information Center, Sofia.

55. Nadezhda Mihailova, "Security in South-East Europe and Bulgaria's Policy of Nato Integration," *NATO Review* 1 (1998): 7; see also the statements by the Bulgarian defense minister, Georgi Ananiev ("We Are Basing Ourselves on a 50,000-Strong Army," *Trud,* March 17, 1999 [FBIS March 17, 1999]), and by Prime Minister Ivan Kostov ("The Government Never Doubted and Does Not Doubt the Loyalty and Competence of Its Military Personnel," *Bulgarska Armiya,* February 22, 1999 [FBIS April 14, 1999]).

56. *Bulgaria 2001: Program of the Government of the Republic of Bulgaria 1997–2001,* n.d. <www.bulgaria.govrn.bg/eng/oficial_docs/index.html>.

57. Petar Stoyanov, President of the Republic of Bulgaria, Address, Madrid, July 9, 1997 <hq.natoint/docu/speech/1997/s970709p.htm> (March 3, 1998).

58. *Le Monde,* Interview with Bulgarian president Petar Stoianov, May 2–3, 1999 (FBIS 2 May 2, 1999); *Trud,* Interview with Bulgarian foreign minister Nadezhda Mikhaylova, January 29, 1999 (FBIS, January 29, 1999).

59. *Demokratsia,* April 8, 1999, 11.

60. *Standart News,* February 3, 1998 (FBIS February 3, 1998).

61. *Duma,* December 29, 1997 (FBIS December 29, 1997); Lisa McAdams, *Bulgaria: Sofia Looks to Nato,* RFE/RL, February 18, 1997 <www.rferl.org/ncs/ncs/features/1997/02/F.RU.970218172416.html>.

62. Khorizont Radio Network, "Three Balkan Foreign Ministers to Meet in Sofia," May 14, 1999 (FBIS May 14, 1999); "Nadezhda Mihailova, statement at EAPC meeting of foreign ministers, December 17, 1997" <www.nato.int/docu/speech/1997/s971217t.htm> (March 3, 1998). Radio Romania, "Report by Sorine Croitoresiu on the Conclusion of the Romanian-Bulgarian-Turkish Presidential Summit in Sinaia on March 12," March 12, 1999 (FBIS March 12, 1999).

63. *Standart News,* October 6, 1997 (FBIS October 6, 1997, 6–7).

64. AFP, September 26, 1998 (FBIS September 26, 1998). Stefan Krause, "A Year of Consolidation," *Transitions on Line,* Country Files, *Bulgaria. Annual Report 1998,* 1998 <www.tol.cz/countries/bular98.html> (March 7, 2002).

65. *Kontinent,* April 13, 1998 (FBIS April 13, 1998); Ivan Kostov, interview by Deutsche Welle, *Demokratsia,* May 14, 1999.

66. "Nadezhda Mihailova, Secretary of State Madeline K. Albright with Bulgarian foreign minister Nadezhda Mihailova, Remarks at Joint Press Conference, Sofia, Bulgaria, June 22, 1999" <secretary.state.gov/www/statements/1999/990622.html> (July 15, 1999).

67. According to Konstantin Ivanov, this was done in accordance with explicit NATO direction and with EU financial support. The United States also provided funds. Konstantin Ivanov, "Thinning the Ranks," *Transitions on Line,* February 2, 2000 <www.tol.cz/jul99/specr0200.html> (March 7, 2000).

68. "Reform and the State of the Bulgarian Army," *Duma,* March 9, 1999.

69. AFP, April 16, 1999 (FBIS April 16, 1999); "No One Gives Free Tickets in History," *Demokratsia,* May 6, 1999.

70. Kostov, interview by Deutsche Welle.

71. "He Sold His Own Soul before He Sold Our Skies," *Duma,* April 19, 1999 (FBIS April 19, 1999).

72. See the statement by Foreign Minister Mihailova in *Oesterreich Eins,* "Report by Karin Koller on Statements by Bulgarian Foreign Minister Nedezhda Mikhaylova," May 19, 1999 (FBIS May 19, 1999).

73. Ivan Kostov, interview by Bulgarian National Radio, *Demokratsia,* March 25, 1999.

74. "169 Deputies United for Kosovo, BSP Strays Away," *Demokratsia,* March 26, 1999.

75. "Kosovo, Kostov, and the Bulgarian Political Iceberg," *Duma,* October 12, 1998 (FBIS October 12, 1998); *Duma,* May 5, 1999.

76. "Where Are We?" *Duma,* October 10, 1998 (FBIS October 12, 1998).

77. "Would We Allow It?" *Duma*, April 2, 1999 (FBIS April 2, 1999).

78. On April 25, 1999, the Yugoslav chargé d'affaires stated, "Bulgaria will become an accomplice in the aggression if your parliament approves an air corridor for NATO airplanes in a military operation against neighboring sovereign FR Yugoslavia" (Tanjug, April 25, 1999; FBIS April 25, 1999). *Trud* reported a threat to all Yugoslavia's neighbors by Deputy Prime Minister Vojislav Seselj (*Trud*, March 2, 1999; FBIS March 2, 1999); see also the statement by the Yugoslav embassy in Sofia (Tanjug, April 18, 1999; FBIS April 18, 1999).

79. "Duma Asks: What If Russia Also Demands Air Corridor?" *Duma*, October 12, 1998 (FBIS October 12, 1998).

80. *Demokratsia*, May 10, 1999.

81. "The Bitter 'Silent Majority,'" *Duma*, May 15, 1999.

82. *Duma*, April 2, 1999 (FBIS April 2, 1999).

83. Interfax, June 15, 1999 (FBIS June 15, 1999); "Our Statesmen Should Look More Often at the Map," *Pari*, June 15, 1999 (FBIS June 15, 1999).

84. *Oesterreich Eins*, "Report by Karin Koller."

85. Ivan Kostov, "Statement Given by Prime Minister Ivan Kostov Addressing the Parliament on May 4," *Demokratsia*, May 6, 1999; "Refugee Move Could Prompt Dissatisfaction in Bulgaria," *Trud*, April 13, 1999 (FBIS April 13, 1999). The IMF estimated the overall effect of the Kosovo crisis as reducing Bulgaria's GDP by 2.5 percent; International Monetary Fund, *The Economic Consequences of the Kosovo Crisis: An Updated Assessment*, May 25, 1999 <www.imf.org/external/pubs/ft/kosovo/052599. htm> (July 23, 1999).

86. Robert Lee Wolff, *The Balkans in Our Time*, rev. ed. (New York: Norton, 1974), 87–91.

87. Braun, *Small-State Security*, 219–24.

88. *Trud*, "Interview with Prime Minister Ivan Kostov," May 3, 1999 (FBIS May 3, 1999).

89. RFE/RL, *Newsline*, February 11, 1999.

90. MIC, February 22, 1999 (FBIS, February 22, 1999).

91. "We Are Sending First Tanks to Macedonia by End of April," *Trud*, April 14, 1999 (FBIS April 14, 1999).

92. *Bulgarska Televiziya*, April 22, 1999 (FBIS April 22, 1999).

93. Kostov, interview by Deutsche Welle.

94. See, for example, the remarks of President Zhelev in *Bulgarska Armiya*, June 9, 1994 (FBIS June 15, 1994, 1).

95. Frank Schimmelfennig, "International Socialization in the New Europe: Rational Action in an Institutional Environment," *European Journal of International Relations* 6, no. 1 (2000): 109–39.

96. Bulgarian Radio, May 26, 2000 (*BBC Summary of World Broadcasts*, May 29, 2000); "Positano Approves Position on NATO," *Trud*, June 5, 2000 (FBIS June 5, 2000).

97. "We Will Get into NATO during Current Term," *Standart News*, July 26, 2001 (FBIS July 26, 2001); "Bulgaria: A Fresh Start?" *Transitions Online*, July 30, 2001 <www.tol.cz/look/TOLnew/article.tpl?IdLanguage=1&IdPublication=4&Nr Issue=22&NrSection=6&NrArticle=1759&ST1=body&ST_T1=wir&ST_PS=3&ST_max =1> (August 1, 2001). The prime minister appointed Solomon Pasi as foreign minis-

ter, the president of the Atlantic Club of Bulgaria, and the first East European to become a vice president in the Atlantic Treaty Association of Paris.

98. In November 2001 Georgi Purvanov, chairman of the BSP, was elected president, a position that is more representational than powerful, as leader of the Coalition for Bulgaria. He announced that the country's strategic objectives were membership in the EU and NATO. *BTA,* November 19, 2001 (FBIS November 19, 2001).

99. Bulgarian Radio, May 26, 2000.

100. *Demokratsia*, May 10, 1999.

101. Zoia Lubenova, "The Kosovo Crisis as a Provocation to Bulgaria's Governmental, Political, and Societal Choices" (unpublished manuscript, 1999).

102. Petur-Emil Mitev, "Popular Attitudes toward Politics," in Bell, *Bulgaria in Transition*, 39–64.

103. In February 1999 Prime Minister Kostov declared that the country would "not participate directly or indirectly in NATO's military operation" (*Trud*, February 13, 1999; FBIS February 13, 1999). In March the UDF coalition secured passage of a resolution to that effect in parliament (*Demokratsia*, March 26, 1999). In May, the government sought and received approval for a NATO air corridor. Further discussion of this aspect is found in Lubenova, "Kosovo Crisis."

III

IMPACT IN POLICY AREAS

8

Transformation, Accession to the European Union, and Institutional Design: The Fate of Tripartism

Elena A. Iankova

The transition literature has widely acknowledged the search for Western models in postcommunist Europe (often denoted as "imitation") in the immediate aftermath of 1989, for the sake of quick establishment of market-oriented institutional structures (Elster et al. 1998, 235–38; Lijphart and Waisman 1996). The institutional restructuring under way was not a simple process of imitating the Western institutional highways, however (Jacoby 1998). This chapter focuses on the institution of tripartism—government-union-employer talks as a bargained exchange for the more equal distribution of the pains and rewards of transition—with the aim of tracing the rationale, channels, and extent to which postcommunist tripartism was shaped by western European influences.

The question about the foreign modeling of the institution of tripartism is especially important in light of the fact, first, that tripartism did not exist in state socialist Europe before 1989 but emerged everywhere in the region at the very opening of the transition process. By 1998 it was consolidated as an enduring institution (Iankova 1998). Second, the "model" of tripartism is especially characteristic, even seems to be "reserved" for western European corporatist countries (Schmitter and Grote 1997). It is also actively promoted—though with dubious results—at the European level (Gorges 1996; Falkner 1998) or, as students of multilevel governance assert, in a framework of European multilevel decision making (Grande 1996). Finally, with the European Union's (EU) opening of accession talks with ten central and eastern European (CEE) applicants for EU membership—in March 1998 with Poland, Hungary, the Czech Republic, Slovenia, and Estonia, and in February 2000 with Bulgaria, Romania, Slovakia, Latvia, and Lithuania—the EU has been singled out as the most important and influential source of foreign institutional design in the postcommunist region.

These developments raise questions about the Europeanization of post-communist tripartism, as part of an increasingly evolving process of the Europeanization of postcommunist politics, policies, and institutions (Agh 1999). The term "Europeanization" has been mostly used in European regional integration theory in regard to EU member states—to delineate the definition of national state and interest group interests in an international and institutional context that includes the EU (Ladrech 1994). The Europeanization of domestic politics, policies, and institutions in non-EU member states, and especially in nation-states aspiring for EU membership, as a result of general processes of regionalization, has been only sporadically explored. Research in this area has predominantly stemmed from studies of the southern enlargement of the EU (Greece in 1981; Portugal and Spain in 1986), which required much greater preaccession and postaccession change and adaptation to the requirements of EU membership, in contrast to the more recent 1995 enlargement, which included economically much more developed and politically much more consolidated nations, for example, Sweden, Finland, and Austria (Borras et al. 1998; Featherstone 1998; Borras-Alomar 1999). The Europeanization of postcommunist politics, policies, and institutions is an area that has only recently attracted academic attention, with the advancement of the EU eastward enlargement project, and remains generally embedded in studies about the consequences of EU eastward enlargement on EU institutions, governance rules, and policies (Mayhew 1998; Grabbe and Hughes 1998; van Brabant 1999; Curzon Price et al. 1999).

Based on interview data,[1] analyses of documentation and various program materials and protocols, in this chapter I provide a detailed historical account of the process of emergence and development of tripartism in Bulgaria, and the institutional implications of the "European" factor from the very beginning of the post-1989 reconstruction of the country. Bulgaria, like most of the other postcommunist countries, developed tripartite-corporatist structures very early in its transition (Hethy 1994; Iankova 1998). By now it has thirteen different tripartite bodies at the national level (see table 8.1 on p. 216), some of them with decision-making powers over the management of social funds and labor affairs in general, and Bulgaria's tripartism encompasses virtually all levels of bargaining (e.g., national, sectoral, and regional) (Iankova 2000).

After the 1989 breakthrough, tripartite collaboration had ensued in the postcommunist region—remarkably early in the transition away from state socialism, and to a remarkably encompassing extent. It incorporated labor and emerging business in political and economic processes. Tripartism, in broad terms, aimed to preserve social peace by distributing the burden and pain of transformation across the population as fairly as possible, with successful political and economic restructuring the anticipated reward. Thus while ruling elites, new opposition movements, and the society at large all agreed to disentangle themselves from the old practices of state socialism, successful accomplishment of this goal was largely contingent on their commitment to maintain social peace. This meant a continuous societal effort to balance the dynamic and intensifying conflicts between the "high" public interest in transforming the old social order and the "low" group and individual interest in keeping wages and living standards at high levels. Societal and multitier bargaining developed to cope with this difficult transformational task. By helping to consolidate independent worker and business organizations so as to obtain their representation and participation, and by helping the state to diminish its (formerly overwhelming) intervention in the economy and control over society, tripartism also aimed at correcting the institutional fusion that had characterized the old state socialist arrangement, in which the state and party became one with labor and business.

The overwhelmingly communitarian culture and the basically corporatist character of politics under state socialism (Bunce 1983; Chirot 1980), as well as the importance of corporatist settlements in the demise of communist regimes (Ost 1989), facilitated but did not directly cause the establishment of tripartite arrangements immediately after the collapse of the regime. The vulnerability of the postcommunist economies encouraged the CEE countries to follow tripartite arrangements similar to those chosen by the western European states in the aftermath of World War II (Schmitter 1974). A strong domestic effort to cope with regime change and transition to a market economy is what, in the short run, determined the emergence of tripartite adjustments in the postcommunist region. International lending actors and especially the anticipated accession to the European Union is what, in the long run, helps preserve and maintain social dialogue structures.

This chapter traces four consecutive steps of increasing institutional transfer from the European Union: (1) the search for foreign models for the preservation of industrial and social peace in the conditions of a market economy—"lesson drawing" from the western European experience; (2) the conditionality of international financial institutions; (3) the learning experience under the EU PHARE social dialogue project; (4) the establishment of temporary tripartite institutions such as the Council for the Ratification of the European Social Charter (Revised) and the Joint EU-Bulgaria Consultative Committee on Economic and Social Issues, as tripartite institutions serving specific needs of the EU integration process; and (5) attempts to establish an economic and social council as an enduring, accession-driven institutional structure of tripartism.

IN SEARCH OF INSTITUTIONAL SOLUTIONS: LESSON DRAWING

Tripartism and collective bargaining can operate as viable mechanisms for the regulation of the terms and conditions of employment where there is a market economy, especially labor markets, and where there are clearly differentiated social groups with contrasting interests containing labor and social issues. In

November 1989–March 1990, in the context of a severe strike wave in Bulgaria, a process of genuine, bottom-up search for institutional solutions to the problem of mounting industrial unrest was spontaneously initiated. Union activists at various levels became involved in "lesson drawing," that is, the interpretation and adaptation of Western achievements with collective bargaining, and its active promotion in the emerging market conditions of Bulgaria. They looked for Western models with the aim not of copying them, even for administrative expedience, but to build on them a "return to normalcy" under the conditions of a market economy, while catching up with the advanced practices of collective bargaining in the most developed market economies in the world.

In early 1990, when people in Bulgaria started searching for Western experience in combating strikes and other industrial unrest, the search was for Western experience, not necessarily in tripartism but in collective bargaining. The latter was an institution familiar to the Bulgarian actors from the pre–World War II past, though with profascist elements between 1936 and 1941 (Tseneva 1991). The practice of tripartism, or social partnerships among unions, employers, and the state that developed across western Europe as part of the postwar settlements, was unknown to the Bulgarian actors in the industrial arena. Yet in practice, given the domestic conditions of a prevailing state property and an overwhelming state involvement in the economy, it was *tripartism* that was established in Bulgaria by March 1990.

In order to secure political legitimacy and favorable conditions for the implementation of the reform package, the two governments of the former communists (constituted as the Bulgarian Socialist Party, BSP, after 1989) entered into regular negotiations and consultations with the old unions, constituted as the Confederation of Independent Trade Unions in Bulgaria (CITUB). The Socialist government needed public support on the eve of the June 1990 elections, and the CITUB needed public legitimacy in the new conditions of rapid union pluralization. Following the 1989–1990 winter strike wave, the CITUB and the government of A. Atanassov began bilateral negotiations.[2] In February 1990, they agreed to regular consultations between the government and the CITUB on problems of vital importance to working people, such as rising unemployment and rapidly falling living standards.[3] Later agreements were reached to include the National Union of Economic Managers and other actors (chiefly the new union Podkrepa).

The first normative documents prepared by the Bulgarian "social partners" to regulate their interrelationships included the elaboration of the law on the settlement of collective labor disputes, adopted by the Grand National Assembly on March 6, 1990; the signing of a general agreement on urgent social and economic problems by the government, the CITUB, and the National Union of Economic Managers (NUEM) (March 15, 1990); and the adoption by the social partners of general guidelines for the conclusion of collective contracts and agreements in 1990 (April 5, 1990). The creation of the National Commission for Coordination of Interests on April 5, 1990, marked the institutionalization of this sort of social dialogue in Bulgaria.

Founding members of the commission became the signatories of the general agreement—the government, the CITUB, and the Union of Economic Managers.[4] The commission was open to other parties, without any legitimization or recognition requirements, as long as they signed the general agreement. Equal numbers of representatives—three—from each member participated in the sessions of the commission. The government was represented at the level of deputy prime minister, while the social partners sent deputy leaders. Participation by interested political and other organizations as observers was also regulated. Decisions became final only when consensus was reached.

The National Commission for Coordination of Interests aimed at mutually acceptable decisions concerning economic reforms and the social consequences of the reforms. These included labor relations issues, social security and living standards, and the resolution of important labor conflicts, including those in which strike actions were legally forbidden. It also coordinated the activities of its founding members covered by the general agreement and was responsible for preparing a new general agreement and other agreements on more specific issues.

The Agreement on Indexation of Incomes, concluded in August 1990,[5] marked a step forward in the institutionalization of social dialogue by forming standing working groups at the commission on living standards, unemployment, wages, privatization, economic legislation, labor law and social security, rest and recreation, conditions of work, and health and safety.

THE CONDITIONALITY OF INTERNATIONAL LENDING INSTITUTIONS

After a year of stagnation and mass shortages in 1990, the Socialist government led by Andrej Lukanov was toppled by a nationwide strike organized by Podkrepa Confederation of Labor (CL) in December 1990. The new coalition government (BSP, the democratic opposition—Union of Democratic Forces [UDF] and Agrarians) was formed in December 1990 as a government of compromise led by Dimiter Popov. For the success of its stabilization program, the government needed not only political consensus within parliament but also broad mass support, including the cooperation of trade unions. Social dialogue, which had been cut short in October 1990 by the nationwide strike that toppled the Socialist government, was restored in January 1991. Following the recommendations of the IMF, the government signed two social peace agreements and reached a temporary six-month consensus with the social partners.

To coordinate the activities of the partners in securing social peace in the course of macroeconomic stabilization, the National Standing Tripartite

Commission for Coordination of Interests was established on January 15, 1991. Founding members of the commission became the signatories to the Social Peace Agreement. The commission was also open to other interested organizations and institutions, and initially the National Student Confederation participated in its sessions. The commission's goal was to establish dialogue and negotiation as the basis of social partnership in the resolution of major labor conflicts.[6] Seven subcommissions were set up, covering financial and credit policy and banking; employment, layoffs, and training of the labor force; social minimum wages and income compensation; industrial conflicts; privatization, expert evaluation, and autonomization of state and municipal property; social insurance and social care; and labor and social legislation. Discussions in the subcommissions (the expert level) were a precondition for official negotiations in the commission (at the leadership level).

The reception given the neoliberal reforms when they were initiated in February 1991[7] showed that Bulgaria enjoyed a broad sociopolitical consensus on the need for radical change. Despite a drastic fall in living standards of 40–45 percent, there were no major industrial conflicts or civil unrest. The number of labor conflicts and strikes dropped from 1,300 in 1990 to 850 in 1991.[8] For the nine-month period of its existence (until October 1991), the Tripartite Commission functioned actively and regularly, meeting forty-six times, or more than once a week.[9]

The commission and its subcommissions discussed all important issues regarding labor, social insurance, and standard of living. Topics included the introduction of wage bargaining at national, industrywide, and enterprise levels and the adjustment of wages and other income with price liberalization. Discussions focused specifically on price liberalization and income adjustment, procedures for layoffs in enterprises, guidelines for collective bargaining in 1991, the introduction of wage bargaining and a procedure for legitimization of the partners in collective bargaining, the process of collective bargaining in the public sphere, privatization issues and development of small business, employment issues, and amendments to the labor code. The reduction of personnel in state enterprises was counterbalanced by a procedure to prevent chaotic and unjustified layoffs. The guidelines on collective bargaining for 1991 fostered the development of collective bargaining at the enterprise level and forced enterprise managers to bargain with unions.

The shift in power from the Socialists to the opposition that began with the Popov coalition government was consolidated in the second free parliamentary election in October 1991. These elections brought a modest victory for the UDF movement. The UDF formed a minority government led by Filip Dimitrov and continued to carry out the economic reforms. Its platform was more distinctly neoliberal than those of the previous governments had been. Determined to continue shock therapy on a large scale, it sharpened the restrictive financial and income policy. The strategy was to keep wages down and to create macroeconomic conditions that would both stimulate the spontaneous development of private enterprises and allow the rapid privatization of the state sector.

The Dimitrov government had firm neoliberal commitments; it favored a U.S.–U.K. pluralistic and adversarial model of relations between government and labor. Although Podkrepa was one of the founding members of the umbrella organization UDF, it was not as bound to it as the Solidarity union was to the Solidarity movement. Thus, while in Poland the Solidarity-led government, despite its firm neoliberal orientation, was involved in an informal social dialogue with the Solidarity union, in Bulgaria the UDF government's strong antiunion policies threatened to push trade unions to the periphery of the political process. For example, the government declared that trade unions were the main obstacle to the creation of a free market economy and that the tripartite structure was an unnecessary second center of power in the country. The government decided to replace the National Tripartite Commission with consultations at the level of the Ministry of Labor instead of at the council of ministers.

In official declarations, both Podkrepa and the CITUB protested the government's abandonment of tripartism and initiated bipartite actions with the major employers organizations in the country. The social partners' opposition to the UDF government resulted in increased tensions and the pluralization of union structures. The government attack on social dialogue and tripartism continued with the adoption, on December 19, 1991, of a law mandating the confiscation of the remaining property of totalitarian organizations; the CITUB was included in its list as the successor of the Bulgarian trade unions.[10] These antiunion policies and the disastrous fall in wages and rise in unemployment provoked the CITUB to organize, in January 1992, a national "warning" strike favoring the renewal of the activities of the National Tripartite Commission and opposing any confiscation of union property.

The revival of tripartism in mid-1992 was also closely linked to negotiations with the IMF (Thirkell and Tseneva 1992). Thus under pressure from the IMF, the UDF government reconsidered its social partnership policy. By early summer 1992, the government had reshuffled the Ministries of Finance and Industry and appointed a new deputy prime minister, N. Vassilev, who was charged with maintaining contact with the trade unions. At several of its sessions the government discussed a draft proposal for reviving the work of the social partnership system. It also proposed introducing works councils in enterprises as a means to weaken the unions. This brought a new element of hostility into relations among the social partners. Podkrepa CL and the CITUB, joined by the employers organizations, refused to engage in any negotiations with the government until social partnership was again institutionalized. Podkrepa CL backed up its demands with a national miners strike in March 1992.

On May 29, 1992, the guidelines for the activities of the national social partnership system were signed by the government, Podkrepa CL, the CITUB, the

Bulgarian Industrial Association, and the Union for Private Economic Enterprising.[11] The National Council for Social Partnership was created as its "supreme organ." The council was to discuss and adopt agreements concerning social insurance, living standards, the definition of the poverty level, the rate of unemployment, the resolution of labor and social conflicts, and national aspects of the conditions of labor.[12] The parties were the government; unions, represented by Podkrepa CL and the CITUB; and employers organizations, represented by the Bulgarian Industrial Association, the Vazrazhdane Union of Private Producers, the Association of Free Entrepreneurs "Alternative 2000," and the Union for Private Economic Enterprising. Like the previous forums, the council had standing commissions and working groups denominated by function: labor force (labor, employment, training, and retraining); incomes and prices; collective labor disputes; social insurance and social aid; privatization and restructuring of the economy; financial, tax, and credit parameters of social partnership; and specific problems of employees in the budgetary/public organizations. The regulations for the functioning of the council regulated the formation of branch and regional councils.

As the Bulgarian case of tripartism reveals, international lending institutions have turned into external policy-making centers for setting up the guidelines for a market economy in CEE; they have played the role of "shadow partners" in domestic policy making and national tripartism (Petkov 1996). This has been part of a broader shift in recent IMF policies from providing temporary financing to countries to achieve sound money, stable exchange rates, and open markets, toward offering assistance for policy initiatives addressing a wider range of issues, including increased spending on basic human needs, on adequate social protection for vulnerable groups, and, most importantly, on the promotion of a more effective dialogue on economic policy among governments, labor, business, and the rest of civil society (Camdessus 1998).

LEARNING EXPERIENCE: THE EU PHARE
SOCIAL DIALOGUE PROJECT

It was at least a few months after the creation of the first tripartite body in Bulgaria in April 1990 when experts from the ILO were mobilized in numerous seminars and workshops with all actors to clarify the concept and meaning of the Western mechanism of collective bargaining. And much later, in 1993, after the adoption of a new labor code that made tripartism mandatory, the EU developed a special social dialogue project under its PHARE assistance program for the region.

The project was part of PHARE's Democracy Program aimed at building institutions and civil society in the countries of CEE. The funding for the Democracy Program has been relatively small: only 0.4 percent of total PHARE assistance to CEE (Commission of the EC 1997). The social dialogue project, which ran until 1998, had as its major goal the strengthening of the organizational capacity of the social actors and educating them in social dialogue and negotiations as an alternative to spontaneous strike actions in the emerging market environment (ISA and PHARE 1994). Expert assistance and office equipment were provided to the social partners under this program. In order to promote social dialogue in Bulgaria and across CEE countries, arrangements were made for representatives of the social partners and governments in both western and eastern Europe to visit one another. For example, the Bulgarian social partners made study visits not only to some western European countries with developed social dialogue structures, but also to Poland and Hungary. Such trips, which involved briefing sessions beforehand and group learning sessions afterward, were aimed at giving CEE social partners concentrated exposure to other countries' approaches to equivalent work.

A series of policy seminars was also organized under the social dialogue project. To develop social dialogue at branch and regional levels, training became the crucial element of the project. Different courses were set up at different levels, covering the major areas of skills the social partners needed, such as the structure of the market economy and industrial relations, labor and social welfare legislation, privatization and employment contracts, negotiation skills, development of a local economy, employer and trade union structures and organizations, conflict management, and general technical skills for use at the base organization.

The project aimed also at strengthening and professionalizing the structures of the social partners in order to ensure the adequate functioning of social dialogue, developing an arbitration and conciliation service and strengthening the structures and processes of the industrial court, and establishing an information and resource base to meet the social partners' needs. A major emphasis was put on training the trainers, with expert assistance from western Europe. The social dialogue project within the EU PHARE program thus significantly *strengthened* tripartite institutions in Bulgaria and across postcommunist Europe.

ON THE ROAD TO EU ACCESSION

In early 1993, following the adoption of a new labor code that made social dialogue and social partnership mandatory, the National Council for Tripartite Cooperation (NCTC) was formed. It continues to this day and comprises representatives of the government and of the organizations of employees and employers recognized by the council of ministers as being nationally representative. On the union side, these are the CITUB and Podkrepa CL. On the employers side, these include the Bulgarian Industrial Association, the Bulgarian

Chamber of Commerce and Industry, the Union of Economic Enterprising, and the Vazrazhdane Union of Private Producers.

The tripartite council focuses much of its attention on wages. The social partners have to agree on the national minimum wage and other protected payments—monthly additional children's payments and unemployment benefits—which are calculated as a percentage of the minimum wage. Strategies and policies in the area of employment and unemployment are also regularly discussed by the tripartite council, and important laws and normative documents eventually issued by the government often have been prepared by the council. The goals, principles, criteria, and mechanisms of income policy have also been a major area of discussions within the tripartite forum, as well as most aspects of the economic reforms. These included price controls on selected basic goods and other goods produced by state monopolies, legislation concerning the financing of small and medium enterprise development, and privatization and industrial restructuring.

The Bulgarian economy deteriorated sharply in 1996, as a result of mismanagement by the Videnov government—a Socialist cabinet formed in January 1995 following the general parliamentary elections of December 18, 1994—and social dialogue within the National Council was discontinued. Massive protest actions and strikes across the country in December 1996 and January 1997 led to the resignation of the Socialist government and to early parliamentary elections in April 1997. In July 1997, following the April 1997 general elections, the UDF-based cabinet led by Ivan Kostov was formed. At IMF insistence, a currency board was also formed that pegged the Bulgarian currency, the lev, to the German mark. Although the currency board substantially reduced government control of the economy, it helped establish sound financial discipline and financial and economic stability in the country.

With the introduction of the currency board, the role of the IMF has become particularly important in Bulgarian tripartism. The currency board stabilized the Bulgarian currency. Consumer price inflation dropped to only 1 percent in December 1998, from 578.5 percent a year earlier, and stood at 1.7 percent in the twelve months prior to July 1999 (Wyzan 1999; Done 1998, 11; Agency for Economic Analyses and Prognoses 1998). The currency board arrangement also challenged the government and the social partners to work closely with the international financial institutions that became an important part of the revised social dialogue system. Under the conditions of the Charter for Social Cooperation and Memorandum for Priority Common Action (signed in October 1997 between the prime minister and the social partners), the unions agreed to allow the currency board to start working. The social partners recognized the need to preserve the social peace, under the condition that there would be a deeper social dialogue.

Through a series of laws adopted in 1997–1998, the Kostov government created additional tripartite organs to complement the NCTC in all major areas of the social sphere, in accordance with the priorities set in the government program Bulgaria 2001 for 1997–2001.[13] The program emphasized the social market economy as the economic guarantee for the development of industry and for the rights and freedoms of individuals (Bulgarian Government 1997). The social market order included private property and the creation of markets, free bargaining, and a well-developed social security system. Government policy in the social sphere included several major high-priority goals, among which were a panoply of reforms—in the social security system, in incomes policy and social assistance, and in health and safety at work, for example—and the creation of labor markets. The government program emphasized the tripartite character of the management and control of a variety of social funds.

Consistent with the social dialogue orientation of the new government, thirteen corporatist structures arose in Bulgaria after 1997—eight tripartite forums and five tripartite boards for the management of social funds (Ministry of Labor and Social Policy 1998a). Many of the tripartite organs departed from their classical tripartite character and became multipartite, including nongovernmental organizations and various professional organizations. Moreover, the tripartite organs developed not only as organs of consultation but as organs through which social groups became directly involved in the decision-making process in the respective sphere.

In addition to the NCTC, the social partners created the following specialized national tripartite forums to facilitate the conciliation of interests on a broad variety of social issues: the National Council on Unemployment Protection and Employment Promotion (to regulate unemployment insurance policy, employment promotion, and vocational training of persons of working age); the National Council on Vocational Training (to approve the state policy in the area of vocational training); the Supervisory Board of the National Employment Office (to approve basic guidelines on the implementation of the state policy on employment promotion, organization of professional training and retraining, and unemployment protection); the National Council on Working Conditions (for coordination of state policy for the promotion of health and safety at work); the Managing Board of the Working Conditions Fund (to exercise control over the management of the Working Conditions Fund); the Council on Social Assistance (to analyze the development of social assistance in the country); the Managing Board of the Social Assistance Fund (to exercise control over the fund); the Supervisory Board of the National Social Security Institute (to exercise control over the National Fund on Social Security); the National Council on Rehabilitation and Social Integration (a consultative organ to the council of ministers in the area of rehabilitation and social integration); the Managing Board of the Rehabilitation and Social Integration Fund (to exercise control over the Fund); a tripartite Meeting of Representatives as a governing body of the National Health Insurance Bank; and a Consultative Council for Legislative Initiatives at the Bulgarian Parliament (with the aim to improve the quality of the social dialogue in Bulgaria and to guarantee transparency of public debates on the most important areas of social legislation: social reforms, and harmonization of Bulgarian social and labor legislation with European common law).

The expansion of Bulgarian tripartism in 1997–1998, while provoked by a purely domestic need to preserve social peace following a drastic financial crisis in the fall of 1996, nonetheless reflected the increased impact of the process of eastward enlargement of the EU, and Bulgaria's aspirations for membership in the club. It also marked a shift from "soft" to "hard" Europeanization of tripartism.[14] According to the Charter for Social Cooperation signed by the social partners in October 1997, the goal already was to bring social dialogue *"in the style that takes place in many European countries"* (Ministry of Labor and Social Policy 1997, my italics).

With the launching of the EU enlargement project, the EU indirect impact on the institutional structure of Bulgarian tripartism was more evidently man-

Table 8.1.   The Institutional Design of Bulgarian Tripartism

Tripartite Forums	Year of Establishment
A. Domestic Innovation, "Lesson Drawing," and Learning Experience	
1A. National Commission for Coordination of Interests	1990–1991
1B. National Standing Tripartite Commission for Coordination of Interests	1991–1992
1C. National Council for Social Partnership	1992
1D. National Council for Tripartite Cooperation	Since 1993
2A. Supervisory Board of the Vocational Training and Unemployment Fund	1991–1996
2B. Supervisory Board of the National Employment Office	Since 1998
3. National Council on Unemployment Protection and Employment Promotion	Since 1998
4. National Council on Vocational Training	Since 1998
5. National Council on Work Conditions	Since 1998
6. Managing Board of the Work Conditions Fund	Since 1998
7. Council on Social Assistance	Since 1998
8. Managing Board of the Social Assistance Fund	Since 1998
9. Supervisory Board of the National Social Security Institute	Since 1998
10. National Council on Rehabilitation and Social Integration	Since 1998
11. Managing Board of the Rehabilitation and Social Integration Fund	Since 1998
12. Meeting of Representatives of the National Health Insurance Bank	Since 1998
13. Consultative Council for Legislative Initiatives at the Bulgarian Parliament	Since October 1997
B. Impact of EU Accession	
14. Council for the Ratification of the European Social Charter (Temporary)	1998
15. Joint EU-Bulgaria Consultative Committee (Temporary)	1999
16. Economic and Social Council	2001 (to be est.)

ifested with the establishment of temporary, EU accession-driven tripartite institutions such as the Council for the Ratification of the European Social Charter (Revised) (1998) and the Joint EU-Bulgaria Consultative Committee on Economic and Social Issues (1999).

Council for the Ratification of the European Social Charter (Revised)

The EU Agenda 2000, the accession partnership agreement with Bulgaria concluded in 1998, and the EU decision to open accession negotiations with Bulgaria in February 2000 have determined Bulgaria's future direction and the priorities of the Kostov government. Since 1997, the process of European integration has developed domestically at the level of institutional infrastructure and judicial norms—all draft laws require special certificates that show the degree of their harmonization with European standards and directives (Center for the Study of Democracy 1998).

Directly linked with the European integration process was the creation of a fourteenth social dialogue forum—the Council for the Ratification of the Social Charter (Revised). One of the few firm accession requirements of the EU in regard to the harmonization of national legislation with the European common law—as one of the accession conditions set up by the EU—in the social sphere has been the ratification by each applicant country of the social charter (revised) of the Council of Europe. On September 21, 1998, Bulgarian minister of labor and social policy, Ivan Neikov, signed the European social charter, and national preparation began for its ratification.

The Council for the Ratification of the European Social Charter (Revised) was established in the fall of 1998. Its aim was to give voice to the social partners' opinions regarding the ratification of the social charter by mid-2000, and the implementation of the obligations following the ratification. The ratification council must work to win acceptance not only of specific articles that need to be ratified according to the requirements for ratification, but also of an additional number of articles or numbered paragraphs, to make a total of not less than sixteen articles or sixty-three numbered paragraphs (Council of Europe 1998). In the course of its work on the ratification of the European social charter and the fulfillment of all obligations subsequent to ratification, the ratification council must follow the social policy of the Council of Europe. It thus plays the role of intermediary for all adopted European measures, for the European facets of Bulgarian social cohesion, and for full harmonization of Bulgarian social legislation with the basic standardizing and coordinating documents of the Council of Europe. One of the strategic goals of the ratification council is to increase the transparency in its activities and to promote mutual trust between state institutions and civil society.

The ratification council includes representatives of state institutions, organizations of employers, organizations of workers, professional organizations, nongovernmental organizations, local authorities, and research institutions and organizations—some forty different institutions and organizations. This is the widest institutional structure among any of Bulgaria's tripartite organizations to date. Each organization participating in the council's work nominates one representative to the council. The council is chaired by the minister of labor and social policy. Members of the council can form factions or working groups, according to various group interests. Opinions on finished draft documents are voted on at a plenary session of the council and are adopted by a three-fourths majority (Ministry of Labor and Social Policy 1998b).

The ratification council had four sessions by mid-1999, on January 13, 1999, February 3, 1999, February 24, 1999, and April 19, 1999. The third session was a joint meeting with representatives of the Council of Europe. The work of the council focused on the selection of articles for ratification in three major groups of social rights: protection of employment, protection outside the workplace, and social protection (e.g., unemployment benefits and health insurance) for the population.

The screening of social legislation as part of the overall screening process initiated by the EU in 1998 was an area in which the Bulgarian social partners became actively involved, through the elaboration of a joint action plan with the Ministry of Labor and Social Policy (Neikov 1999). Moreover, when accession negotiations opened in early 2000, the government decided to include the social partners from the National Council for Tripartite Cooperation in the EU accession negotiations, specifically in the discussions on the free movement of people, social policy, and employment. The social partners will also take part in the management of the resources of the EU preaccession funds (*Pari*, January 11, 2000).

In regard to compliance with EU social *acquis*, virtually all influential groups in Bulgaria have come to accept the need for harmonization of Bulgarian social legislation with the EU common law because they expect an improved living standard to follow harmonization. Problems thus arise not between the EU and Bulgaria and not among the various social interests in Bulgaria, but rather between those working in the financial sphere and those working in the social sphere within Bulgarian government.[15]

Conflicts also arise between the EU requirements and the IMF and World Bank conditions for granting loans. For example, while effective oversight of health care will require extensive administration, the IMF and World Bank require a 4 percent layoff of all administrative personnel, including administrators in agencies charged with oversight and control. More tension arises between the EU *acquis* and the ratification of some of the ILO recommendations. For example, ILO conventions require the abolition of female work in mines for the purpose of preserving women's reproductive function. The EU, however, insists that Bulgaria denounce these conventions because they contradict the principle of equal opportunity.[16]

Joint Consultative Committee on Social and Economic Issues

The formation of the EU-Bulgaria joint consultative committee was another major tripartite development in Bulgaria initiated by the process of European integration. The decision to form the consultative committee was made by the EU-Bulgaria Association Council on September 15, 1998, and the committee's inaugural meeting was held in Bulgaria on January 17, 1999. It is multipartite, comprising six representatives from the economic and social interests of the EU (the Economic and Social Committee of the European Communities, ESC) and six from Bulgarian economic and social interests.

Among the more than two hundred advisory bodies to the major EU institutions, the Economic and Social Committee of the European Union plays a special role in the accession process. Although it has not been seen as a powerful EU institution, the committee has played a prominent role in enforcing social dialogue in the region. It has drawn up and adopted numerous opinions and reports to offer constructive advice to the EU authorities facing the challenge of enlargement (Economic and Social Committee of the EC 1998a, 1998b). In these opinions the committee has insisted that a broader public within the applicant countries should be involved in the accession process, not just political, economic, and legal experts.

The Bulgarian part of the EU-Bulgaria joint consultative committee was constituted at the end of October 1998. It comprises three groups: employers (the Bulgarian Industrial Association); trade unions (the CITUB and Podkrepa); and various interests (the Federation of Consumers in Bulgaria; the Bulgarian Women's Union; the Federation of Consumers; and a farmers' Federation of the Cooperatives in Bulgaria). The ESC part of the joint consultative committee also comprises three groups: employers (the Assembly of French Chambers of Commerce and Industry, ACFCI; the General Italian Confederation of Commerce, Tourism, and Services, Confcommercio; and the Confederation of Finnish Industry and Employers); employees (the Netherlands Trade Union Confederation, FNV, and the French Democratic Confederation of Labor, CFDT); and various interests (the Greek Economic Chamber, and the Central Union of Agricultural Producers and Forest Owners MTK, Finland). The Bulgarian secretariat to the JCC is administered by the Bulgarian Industrial Association, and its chairman was elected chairman of the Bulgarian part of the committee. The ESC Division of External Relations organizes the secretariat of the ESC part of the committee.

The purposes of the committee are to prepare the ground for enlargement of the EU by promoting dialogue and to support the professional organizations of the partner country in their efforts to create a functioning society in which their consultation by the government is an integral part of the decision-making process. This is particularly important with the start of accession negotiations between the Bulgarian government and the EU. Another task of the committee is to assist and consult the EU-Bulgaria Association Council on the promotion of dialogue and cooperation between the economic and social interest groups in the EU and those in Bulgaria. The dialogue covers all economic and social aspects of EU-Bulgaria relations in light of the Association/Europe Agreement and the Accession Partnership Agreement between the EU and Bulgaria.

BECOMING EUROPEAN? TOWARD AN ECONOMIC AND SOCIAL COUNCIL

A "loose" EU requirement in terms of social dialogue in applicant countries is for the establishment of an economic and social council as a purely consultative organ, whose recommendations need not necessarily be followed by the government. Still, according to EU recommendations and government regulations, all draft laws have to be submitted beforehand to the economic and social council for review. The latter directly corresponds to the European standards for economic and social councils. The creation of the council was envisaged under the PHARE program, and its formation became part of the Kostov government program in the social sphere, under recommendations from EU experts.[17] A draft law for the economic and social council was to have been adopted by parliament in 2001. The council is to expand to overlap civil society and develop as a multilateral interinstitutional structure, with representatives of trade unions, employers, women's organizations, consumer organizations, and organizations of cooperatives, and a chair jointly appointed by the council of ministers, the chairman of the parliament, and the president (Daskalova 1999).

In light of the extensive tripartite system that has developed so far in the country, the creation of an additional tripartite structure—economic and social council—challenges Bulgarian tripartism in important ways. Despite the fact that the idea about the creation of this council was launched as early as 1993 through the EU social dialogue project, the Bulgarian social partners are still debating its creation. Some of them argue that there is no real need to create an additional tripartite structure that at its best will come to duplicate already existing tripartite forums. The NCTC already satisfies the minimal EU accession requirement of social dialogue as government consultations with social groups, and even goes beyond purely consultative functions to add some important decision-making responsibilities of the social partners in the areas of minimum wage and the social sphere. At the same time, twelve additional tripartite institutions have already established tripartism's outreach to society at large, as suggested by the economic and social council.

The EU experts participating in the screening of the Bulgarian social legislation were "surprised" by the proliferation of so many tripartite institutions at the national level in Bulgaria.[18] Since Bulgaria has so far developed the most elaborate system of national, regional, and sectoral social dialogues in the CEE region, it is striking that in its evaluation on the implementation of the Community *acquis* by the CEE applicant countries, the Commission of the European Communities has assessed the development of social dialogue in Bulgaria as "still embryonic, although the Government and the employers and workers organizations have signed a Charter on Social Partnership" (Commission of the EC 1999).

CONCLUSION

As far as the birth and initial development of the institution of tripartism is concerned, "lesson drawing" and "learning experience" (Rose 1991) prevailed over any direct institutional transfer and imitation of existing western European tripartite structures. Initially tripartism was mostly shaped by twin domestic necessities—the need to secure social peace and legitimate the actors in times of rapidly falling living standards and uncertainty, as a result of economic, political, and legislative reforms. That domestic effort, had it not been a product of domestic sensibilities alone, would have gained high priority because of pressure from international lending institutions and the European Union, which offered to make loans to the region only provided that certain conditions of social peace were met. Overall, the initial developments with Bulgarian tripartism reveal a trend of "soft" Europeanization in an international and institutional context that included not only the EU and the western European model of capitalism but also global lending actors such as the IMF.

Bulgaria is a classic example of how a variety of domestic and international actors and pressures were pushing in the same direction, toward tripartite concertation. As early as March 1990, the social partners established a tripartite forum as a predominantly domestic innovation to cope with rising social tension and help organizational restructuring and consolidation along economic, as opposed to ideological, lines. As soon as a more neoliberal government came to power, however (1991), the normative foundations of tripartism were shaken by the government's firm antitripartism, as an ideological stand and well-articulated public policy. This challenge to tripartism was short-lived, however, chiefly because of the interference of international lending institutions. The IMF required the government to restore and maintain social dialogue as a condition for its revitalizing financial injections. Reluctantly, the government did so in the summer of 1992.

With the advancement of transformation and the European integration process, direct institutional transfer from Europe has become more prominent. With the stepped-up harmonization of CEE countries' laws with the EU common law, the *acquis communautaire*, the applicants for EU membership have become also subject to the requirement to "establish and maintain social dialogue" as a precondition for their entry. While this EU requirement or norm is not stringent with respect to details, it is nonetheless viewed as important for defending tripartism against potential attempts by neoliberal governments to abolish it, and may as a result lead to the "hard" Europeanization of tripartism and its further development as an enduring institutional structure.

This gradually expanding trend toward "hard" Europeanization of tripartism raises another, much broader issue: to what extent will this *permanent* social dialogue be fully *meaningful?* The difficulties with establishing an economic and social council in Bulgaria point toward an institutional bifurcation and duplicity of tripartite structures during accession—one set of institutions for actually serving domestic purposes and another set of institutions for serving the mere purposes of accession to the EU, without any meaningful vitality beyond the formal accession procedures.

An additional international challenge to a *meaningful* postcommunist tripartism is the fact that social dialogue, as practiced in most of continental western Europe, is itself changing. Searching for new solutions to the challenges of globalization and European integration, western European countries have recently combined established national corporatist schemes with the "neoliberal" regime, resulting in the tentative emergence of a new socioeconomic order and a new model of capitalism (Rhodes and van Apeldoorn 1997). This transnational form of capitalism does not simply replicate an Anglo-Saxon neoliberal regime on a grand scale, but rather integrates elements of Anglo-Saxon corporate governance and economic organization with established national institutions, norms, and rules.

It may well be that EU experts, EU integration, and EU norms regarding the establishment and maintenance of social dialogue as part of advanced accession requirements since 1997 have fortified social dialogue in Bulgaria by preventing the advent of a strict neoliberal government with no commitment to social partnership. A compromise consensus on accession already exists. Even L. Balcerowicz, prominent Polish and CEE neoliberal, while raising concerns about EU imposition of its social standards in its eastward expansion, has nonetheless acknowledged that little can be done to counterbalance this trend in the Central and Eastern European applicants, as long as they wish to become EU members (Balcerowicz 1999).

NOTES

I acknowledge financial support for this research from the National Council for Eurasian and East European Research. For their helpful comments on earlier versions of the chapter, I would like to thank Heather Grabbe, Geoffrey Harris, Andrs Inotai, Wade Jacoby, Peter Katzenstein, Ronald Linden, and Margit Williams.

1. Persons interviewed include, among others, Aleksander Bozhkov, deputy prime minister, minister of industry and chair of the National Council for Tripartite

Cooperation, July 28, 1999; Ivan Neikov, minister of labor and social policy, July 15, 16, 28, 1999; Dimiter Manolov, vice president of the union Podkrepa Confederation of Labor (CL), July 21, 1999; Grigor Gradev, director of the Institute for Trade Union and Social Studies and executive secretary of the Confederation of Independent Trade Unions in Bulgaria (CITUB), July 21, 1999; Vikran Tebeian, vice president of the Bulgarian Industrial Association, July 28, 1999; and Svetlana Djankova, vice president of the Parliamentary Group of the UDF and chairman, Permanent Parliamentary Commission on Labor and Social Policy, July 30, 1999.

2. "Pyrvite pregovori mezhdu Bulgarskite profesionalni syjuzi i chlenove na pravitelstvoto" (First Negotiations between the Bulgarian Trade Unions and Members of the Government), *Trud*, December 29, 1989; "Bylgarskite profsyjuzi predlagat: Generalno sporazumenie s pravitelstvoto" (Bulgarian Trade Unions Propose General Agreement with the Government), *Trud*, January 5, 1990.

3. "Osnova za konstruktiven dialog: Nachalo na konsultatsiite mezhdu pravitelstvoto i sindikatite po zhisneno vazhni za trudovite hora problemi" (The Basis for a Constructive Dialogue: Start of Consultations between the Government and the Trade Unions on Problems of Vital Importance for the Working People), *Trud*, March 1, 1990.

4. "Prieti sa Obshti pravila: Zaraboti Natsionalnata komnisija za syglasuvane na interesite" (General Guidelines Were Adopted: The National Commission for Coordination of Interests Started Its Work), *Trud*, April 5, 1990.

5. Sporazumenie mezhdu pravitelstvoto na NR Bulgaria, Konfederatzijata na nezavisimite sindikati v Bulgaria, Konfederatzijata na truda Podkrepa i Natsionalnija syjuz na stopanskite rykovoditeli za reshavaneto na njakoi ostri sotzialni problemi, porodeni ot zadylbochavashtata se ikonomicheska krisa," (agreement among the government of Bulgaria, the Confederation of Independent Trade Unions in Bulgaria, Podkrepa Confederation of Labor, and the National Union of Economic Managers, on the resolution of some urgent problems arising from the deepening economic crisis), *Trud*, August 15, 1990.

6. Statut na Postojannata tristranna komisija za syglasuvane na interesite (Statute of the Standing Tripartite Commission for the Coordination of Interests), *Korespondentsko obuchenie*, March 1991. Sofia: CITUB.

7. Council of Ministers, Decree no. 8 of 29 January 1991, for the Liberalization of Prices and Social Protection of the Population.

8. There are no official statistical data on strikes in Bulgaria; the numbers used in this study are based on estimates of CITUB Organizational Department and Department, "Individual and Collective Labor Disputes."

9. Archive data: Minutes of sessions held by the National Standing Tripartite Commission for Coordination of Interests (January–September 1991).

10. The question of trade union property became a political issue, as in Hungary. The property of the CITUB was confiscated by the state in December 1991. This issue played a significant role in the development of interunion relations and tripartism. Starting from total confrontation between CITUB and Podkrepa on the one hand, and with the government on the other, the issue was resolved in 1993 through the redistribution of assets between the state, CITUB, and Podkrepa by a formula of 10:55:35. Because of protests from the other unions, CITUB decided to give up its share in favor of the creation of a fund for additional social security benefits.

11. "Sindikati i rabotodateli pak dadoha shans na pravitelstvoto: Prieti sa pravilata za rabota na Natsionalnata sistema za sotsialno partnerstvo" (Trade Unions and

Employers Gave a Chance to the Government, Once Again: The Guidelines for the Work of the National System for Tripartite Partnership Were Adopted), *Podkrepa*, May 30, 1992.

12. "Pravila za rabota na Natsionalnata sistema za sotsialno partnerstvo" (Regulations for the Work of the National System of Social Partnership), *Sindikalna praktika* 6 (1992): 7–11.

13. Bulgaria 2000. Government Program (Sofia: Council of Ministers, 1997).

14. By "hard" Europeanization I mean not only domestic efforts to implement the EU "hard" common law but also efforts to comply with the EU "soft" legislation, which is more characteristic for the social sphere.

15. Vladimir Kisjov, deputy minister of foreign affairs, and Ivan Neikov, minister of labor and social policy, interview by author, July–August 1999.

16. Interview data from the Ministry of Labor and Social Policy, Summer 1999.

17. Ivan Neikov, minister of labor and social policy, interview by author, March 12, 2000.

18. Interview data from the Ministry of Labor and Social Policy, Summer 1999.

REFERENCES

Agency for Economic Analyses and Prognoses. 1998. *Ikonomikata na Bulgaria pres 1998 godina: Godishen doklad* (The Bulgarian Economy in 1998: An Annual Report). Sofia: Agency for Economic Analyses and Prognoses.

Agh, Attila. 1999. "Processes of Democratization in the East Central European and Balkan States: Sovereignty-Related Conflicts in the Context of Europeanization." *Communist and Postcommunist Studies* 32: 263–79.

Balcerowicz, Leszek. 1999. "Europe Growing Together." In *The Enlargement of the European Union: Issues and Strategies,* edited by Victoria Curzon Price, Alice Landau, and Richard G. Whitman, 3–9. London: Routledge, 1999.

Borras, Susana, Nuria Font, and Neus Gomez. 1998. "The Europeanization of National Policies in Comparison: Spain as a Case Study." *South European Society and Politics*, Summer, 23–44.

Borras-Alomar, Susana. 1999. "The Europeanization of Politics in the Southern Members of the EU." In *Economic Integration in NAFTA and the EU: Deficient Institutionality*, edited by Kirsten Appendini and Sven Bislev. London: Macmillan.

Brabant, Jozef M. van, ed. 1999. *Remaking Europe: The European Union and the Transition Economies*. Lanham, Md.: Rowman & Littlefield.

Bulgarian Government. 1997. *Bulgaria 2001: Programa na pravitelstvoto na Republika Bulgaria, 1997–2001* (Program of the Government of the Republic of Bulgaria for the Period 1997–2001 "Bulgaria 2001"). Sofia: Bulgarian Government.

Bunce, Valerie. 1983. "The Political Economy of the Brezhnev Era: The Rise and Fall of Corporatism." *British Journal of Political Science* 13: 129–58.

Camdessus, Michel. 1998. "The Role of the IMF: Past, Present, and Future." Remarks at the annual meeting of the Bretton Woods Committee, Washington, D.C., February 13.

Center for the Study of Democracy. 1998. *Bulgaria and the European Union: Toward an Institutional Infrastructure*. Sofia: Center for the Study of Democracy.

Chirot, Daniel. 1980. "The Corporatist Model and Socialism." *Theory and Society*, March, 363–81.

Commission of the European Communities. 1997. *The PHARE Program: An Interim Evaluation*. Brussels: Commission of the European Communities.

Commission of the European Communities. 1999. "Applicant Countries and the Community *Acquis*." Brussels: Commission of the European Communities.

Council of Europe. 1998. *Revised European Social Charter*. Council of Europe, November.

Curzon Price, Victoria, Alice Landau, and Richard G. Whitman, eds. 1999. *The Enlargement of the European Union: Issues and Strategies*. London: Routledge.

Daskalova, Nadezhda. 1999. "Ikonomicheskijat i sotzialen syvet—otvarjane na sotzialnija dialog kym grazhdanskoto obshtestvo" (The Economic and Social Council: Expansion of Social Dialogue toward Civil Society). *Trud: Information Newsletter of the CITUB*, May–June, 4–5.

Done, Kevin. 1998. "Currency Board Is a Boost to Stability." *Financial Times*, March 8.

Economic and Social Committee of the European Communities. 1998a. "Opinion of the Economic and Social Committee on the 'Enlargement of the European Union.'" *Official Journal of the European Communities*, January 21, 1998.

Economic and Social Committee of the European Communities. 1998b. *Opinion on Reinforcing the Pre-accession Strategy (Own-Initiative Opinion)*. Brussels: Economic and Social Committee of the European Communities.

Elster, Jon, Claus Offe, and Ulrich K. Preuss. 1998. *Institutional Design in Postcommunist Societies: Rebuilding the Ship at Sea*. Cambridge: Cambridge University Press.

Falkner, Gerda. 1998. *EU Social Policy in the 1990s: Toward a Corporatist Policy Community*. London: Routledge.

Featherstone, Kevin. 1998. "'Europeanization' and the Centre Periphery: The Case of Greece in the 1990s." *South European Society and Politics*, Summer, 23–39.

Gorges, Michael J. 1996. *Euro-Corporatism? Interest Intermediation in the European Community*. Lanham, Md.: University Press of America.

Grabbe, Heather, and Kirsty Hughes. 1998. *Enlarging the EU Eastwards*. London: Royal Institute of International Affairs.

Grande, Edgar. 1996. "The State and Interest Groups in a Framework of Multi-Level Decision-Making: The Case of the European Union." *Journal of European Public Policy*, September, 318–38.

Hethy, Lajos. 1994. "Tripartism in Eastern Europe." In *New Frontiers in European Industrial Relations*, edited by Richard Hyman and Anthony Ferner, 312–36. Oxford: Blackwell.

Iankova, Elena A. 1998. "The Transformative Corporatism of Eastern Europe." *Eastern European Politics and Society*, Spring, 222–64.

Iankova, Elena A. 2000. "Multi-Level Bargaining in Bulgaria's Return to Capitalism." *Industrial and Labor Relations Review*, October, 115–37.

ISA Consult/NJM and PHARE Management Team at the Bulgarian Ministry of Labor and Social Welfare. 1994. *Interim Report on the Social Dialogue in Bulgaria*. Sofia: Ministry of Labor and Social Welfare, 2 October.

Jacoby, Wade. 1998."Tutors and Pupils: International Organizations, Central European Elites, and Western Models." Paper presented at the annual meeting of the American Political Science Association, Boston, September 1–3.

Ladrech, Robert. 1994. "Europeanization of Domestic Politics and Institutions: The Case of France." *Journal of Common Market Studies*, March, 69–88.

Lijphart, Arend, and Carlos H. Waisman, eds. 1996. *Institutional Design in New Democracies: Eastern Europe and Latin America*. Boulder, Colo.: Westview.

Mayhew, Alan. 1998. *Recreating Europe: The European Union's Policy toward Central and Eastern Europe.* Cambridge: Cambridge University Press.

Ministry of Labor and Social Policy. 1997. *Harta za sotzialno sytrudnichestvo* (Charter for Social Cooperation). Sofia: Ministry of Labor and Social Policy.

Ministry of Labor and Social Policy. 1998a. "Social Dialogue Reality in Bulgaria." *From Guidelines to Action: Bulgarian Ministry of Labor and Social Policy Bulletin* 2 (November).

Ministry of Labor and Social Policy. 1998b. *Pravila za dejnosta i organizatsijata na Syveta za ratifikatsija na Evropejskata sotsialna harta* (Regulations for the Work and Organization of the Council for the Ratification of the European Social Charter). Sofia: Ministry of Labor and Social Policy.

Mommen, Andre. 1993. "Toward Peripheral Capitalism: Neo-Liberalism and the Economic Transformation of Eastern Europe." *International Journal of Political Economy,* Spring, 35–63.

Neikov, Ivan. 1999. Statement of Ivan Neikov, minister of labor and social policy of the Republic of Bulgaria at the informal meeting of EU and applicant countries' ministers of labor and social affairs, Brussels, Belgium, March 9.

Ost, David. 1989. "Toward a Corporatist Solution in Eastern Europe: The Case of Poland." *East European Politics and Societies* 3: 152–74.

Petkov, Krustyo. 1996. "Shadow Partner." Mimeo. Brussels, June.

Rhodes, Martin, and Bastiaan van Apeldoorn. 1997. *The Transformation of West European Capitalism?* European University Institute Working Papers, RSC no. 97/60.

Rose, R. 1991. "What Is Lesson Drawing?" *Journal of Public Policy* 11: 3–30.

Schmitter, Philippe C. 1974. "Still the Century of Corporatism?" *Review of Politics,* January, 85–96.

Schmitter, Philippe C., and Jurgen R. Grote. 1997. *The Corporatist Sisyphus: Past, Present, and Future.* European University Institute Working Paper no. 97/4. Badia Fiesolana, Florence: European University Institute.

Thirkell, J. E. M., and Elena Atanassova Tseneva. 1992. "Bulgarian Labour Relations in Transition: Tripartism and Collective Bargaining." *International Labour Review* 131, no. 3: 355–66.

Tseneva, Elena. 1991. *Kolektivnoto trudovo dogovarjane: Sindikalna strategija i taktika* (Collective Bargaining: Trade Union Strategy and Tactic). Sofia: Kak Zhiveem.

Wyzan, Michael. 1999. "Bulgaria's Economy Anemic under Currency Board." *RFE/RL Newsline,* August 30.

9

European Integration and Minority Rights: The Case of Hungary and Its Neighbors

Margit Bessenyey Williams

> For a very long time, Trianon determined the parameters of Hungary's foreign policy. Our task in the new millennium is to break out of this logic of Trianon.
>
> István Szent-Iványi, Member of Parliament[1]

> The Union has no intention of importing instability, through unresolved disputes or tensions between future members. Rather, through enlargement, it seeks to export, or rather to extend, the zone of stability which it has created over almost half a century, a zone in which war has been banished and the inevitable differences which arise in politics can be resolved within a framework of law.
>
> Hans van den Broek, EU Commissioner[2]

> If we want to join Europe, then we have to behave like Europeans, and it is precisely for this reason that it is very important that we handle the minority problem within and outside our borders in an understandable and respectable way.
>
> Tamás Katona, Ministry of Foreign Affairs Official[3]

The initial establishment of democracy in Hungary in May 1990 following the collapse of the Berlin Wall opened up the possibility for the Hungarian government to reorient its foreign policy decisively toward the West. József Antall, the first postcommunist prime minister, declared that integration into all the major Western international organizations would be the new government's primary foreign policy goal.[4] The Hungarian political elite, however, has viewed the European Union (EU) as the most important Western organization to join.[5]

To nonmember countries, the European Union represents a community of democratic and wealthy states able to cooperate after centuries of conflict and war. Successive postcommunist Hungarian governments have emphasized the vital importance of accession into the European Union for the country's future.[6]

The European Union, like many other international organizations, lays down numerous conditions that the postcommunist governments have to meet prior to being accepted as members. While conditionality is not new, the Central and Eastern European (CEE) postcommunist governments must comply with two new requirements not explicitly demanded of previous accession candidates.[7] These "preaccession criteria" were first outlined in the presidency conclusions closing the summit of heads of state and government of the EU members in Lisbon (June 1992) and later restated in the concluding document following the June 1993 Copenhagen meeting.[8] Recognizing the importance of a functioning and rule-governed bureaucracy, the EU has made administrative reform an explicit criterion.

The other new condition relates to a country's regional relations. European Union officials and Western leaders perceive that the greatest potential threat to security and a cause of conflict in Europe relates to the lingering historical problems of ethnic minorities and unresolved state boundaries.[9] The EU, therefore, has explicitly required that prospective members demonstrate that they can cooperate with their neighbors and "normalize relations." Evidence of cooperation includes the signing of bilateral treaties, referred to as basic treaties, and participation in regional multilateral organizations.[10]

The position of the EU was made clear already in 1989. As the then president of the European Parliament, Enrique Baron Crespo, stated:

> The countries of central and Eastern Europe . . . have to improve relations with one another so as to be able to improve cooperation with us. . . . This process will certainly take a certain time, and until it is completed, I think it is premature to think about fuller integration of those countries with the West.[11]

The European Union's growing concern with human and minority rights in the wake of the first war in the former Yugoslavia was reflected in the association agreements negotiated after May 1992.[12] While the Hungarian, Czechoslovak, and Polish Europe Agreements (the original three that were signed in December 1991) made no specific mention of human rights, all subsequent agreements have contained such a clause.[13] The European Union's insistence on regional cooperation was also clearly specified in the presidency conclusions following the Essen European Council summit (December 1994).

> Being aware of the role of regional cooperation within the Union, the Heads of State and Government emphasize the importance of similar cooperation between the associated countries for the promotion of economic development

and good neighborly relations. . . . The Union and the associated countries have a common interest in preventing conflicts related to issues such as borders and frontiers, and should consult frequently on foreign and security policy issues of mutual concern.[14]

Minority problems have been singled out by the EU, for "if unresolved, could affect democratic stability or lead to disputes with neighboring countries. It is therefore in the interest of the Union and of the applicant countries that satisfactory progress in integrating minority populations be achieved before the accession process is completed."[15]

Using the Hungarian case, this chapter examines whether and how international organizations encourage the diffusion of norms fostering cooperation and Western understandings of minority rights. Hungary has a long history of tense relations with several neighboring states over the status and rights of the Hungarian minority population in those countries. The largest Hungarian minority populations reside in Slovakia, Romania, and the Vojvodina province of what remains of Yugoslavia, although Hungarians are also found in Croatia, Slovenia, Ukraine, and Austria.[16] Relations with several of these states have been conflicted at times.

This problem of the Hungarian minority has deep historical roots and has been referred to in Hungary as the "Trianon syndrome" and Hungary's "Achilles heel."[17] The loss of more than two-thirds of Hungary's prewar territory and close to three-fifths of its population as a result of the World War I Treaty of Trianon (1920) remains a major part of Hungary's collective historical memories.[18] These historical legacies still frame many people's views on relations with neighboring states.[19]

The issue of minority rights could not be addressed openly under communism, but it has since occupied a prominent position in the hierarchy of Hungarian foreign policy goals, given the significant numbers of Hungarians living in neighboring countries.[20] All Hungarian governments, regardless of political leanings, have felt morally and politically obligated to defend the rights of Hungarians abroad. Furthermore, it is a constitutional obligation (chap. 1, art. 6, para. 3) of the Hungarian government to take responsibility for the Hungarians living beyond the country's border.

At the same time, the EU has required that Hungary normalize relations with its neighbors. Improving bilateral relations has proved difficult, since it depends not only on the policies and actions of the Hungarian government but also on central governments and political leaders in the neighboring states, as well as representatives of the Hungarian ethnic minority at the transnational level.[21] Compounding the resolution of these issues is the existence of divisions within central governments and the Hungarian minority in the different countries.[22]

This chapter begins by examining the postcommunist Hungarian political elite's views regarding regional security and cooperation, the problems relating to the Hungarian minority living in neighboring countries, and the relationship between these issues and accession into the European Union. There was a significant gap initially between Hungarian and European understandings regarding how to protect minority rights, and the Hungarian political elite was also divided over this issue. The second section discusses the most important basic treaties Hungary signed with neighboring countries. The EU considers them to be the primary demonstration of cooperation between the CEE states. Furthermore, the plenary debates on ratification of these treaties in the Hungarian parliament illustrate particularly well the evolution in views among the Hungarian elite and the progressive acceptance of European norms. In the concluding section, I examine briefly what effect the basic treaties have had on relations between Hungary and its neighbors and whether the European Union has been able to influence the policies of other states.

This chapter will show that the European Union both directly and indirectly contributed to improvement in relations between Hungary and its neighbors. As the relationship between regional cooperation and European integration became clearer, Hungarian domestic perspectives on bilateral cooperation and minority rights evolved to prevailing EU positions to improve Hungary's chances for early accession. Indirectly, therefore, the attraction of EU membership propelled successive postcommunist Hungarian governments to comply with the preaccession criteria of the EU, including those relating to minority rights and bilateral relations, the areas where there was the greatest distance initially between EU and Hungarian positions. At other times, EU officials and Western political leaders directly intervened at strategic moments to pressure the Hungarian (and other) governments to reach agreement on and ratify the basic treaties or to indicate disapproval of specific actions or statements.

HUNGARIAN VIEWS REGARDING MINORITY RIGHTS

In his opening speech to the parliament in 1990, Prime Minister Antall noted two important foreign policy goals: Hungary's desire to become a member of Western organizations and a focus on the rights of the Hungarian minorities abroad.[23] In what is by now considered a classic political statement, the newly appointed prime minister stated that in spirit he was the prime minister of 15 million Hungarians.[24]

The position of the Hungarian political elite on all sides of the political spectrum was that security and stability could ultimately only be achieved if minority rights were adequately protected and democracy consolidated in the region.[25] "The stability of the region rests on everybody accepting both the principles and the practice of democracy. Consequently, today the precondition of any working security system is the rule of law and respect for human rights, particularly the rights of political, religious and ethnic minorities," argued Foreign Minister Jeszenszky.[26] The European Union and other Western organizations were viewed as playing a critical role in externally reinforcing nascent and often weak domestic norms relating to democracy and human rights.[27] Rapid integration into the Western community and the EU would prevent backsliding on political reforms and ensure the "irreversibility of [political] changes."[28]

Beyond the indirect EU influence in reinforcing political norms domestically, the first postcommunist government also believed that the EU should directly intervene in the affairs of other countries when governments violated the rights of the minority.

> I would like to emphasize here that the minority question is not only a Hungarian affair. In fact, it is an issue of common interest to the region and even to all of the states of Europe. . . . Promoting the rights of minorities should not be the exclusive purview of the Hungarian state because the minority issue is not only a domestic issue.[29]

The Antall government sought to "internationalize" the issue of the Hungarian minority.[30] Becoming a member of the European community of states and of European organizations would offer Hungarian delegates a new forum in which to publicize transgressions of minority rights as well as enact multilateral sanctions against countries in violation.[31]

> It has been a deliberate aim of Hungarian foreign policy to contribute to the enforcement of European norms in its immediate vicinity. . . . The objectives are to promote stability and the strengthening of the democratic system of institutions and also to advance genuine rapprochement. . . . Another major aim of Hungarian foreign policy has been to further the most comprehensive enforcement of human rights. In this effort, special emphasis is being placed on defining the rights of national minorities.[32]

Members of the conservative parties in the Hungarian parliament viewed it as "not only the right, but also everyone's obligation to monitor compliance with universally recognized norms and standards. . . . Violations of universally recognized human rights cannot be considered as internal affairs."[33] Furthermore, "we are convinced that if necessary, international organizations must take tough action or even impose sanctions if the defense of some minorities so require."[34]

While there was broad agreement among all the parties in the Hungarian parliament regarding the importance of European integration for the country and protection of Hungarian minority rights abroad, the parties nevertheless disagreed over how to achieve these goals. The primary division was over whether first to ensure the protection of minority rights or to normalize bilateral relations to meet EU conditionality.[35] As Gyula Horn, then an opposition member of parliament, put it:

> We are all struggling against a sort of double bind we find ourselves in, in that we have to do everything possible for the interests of the Hungarians living beyond our borders and at the same time we must maintain good relations with our neighbors. No one has yet been able to solve this dilemma.[36]

István Hegedûs, member of the Committee on Foreign Affairs, early on summarized this key foreign policy dilemma: "In our everyday politics, should we emphasize as our first priority regional cooperation or the minority rights issue?"[37]

It was the position of the first postcommunist government under Antall that minority rights should be improved first, with normalization in other areas, such as economic and trade relations or cultural exchanges, contingent upon the resolution of the former. György Csóti, vice chairman of the Committee on Foreign Affairs and an important foreign policy spokesman for the Hungarian Democratic Forum (MDF) party, made this sequence quite clear: "Hungary's relations with its neighbors are fundamentally determined by how they represent the interests of the Hungarian minorities in these countries, how they handle questions concerning the Hungarian minorities."[38] Even President Árpád Göncz, member of the opposition Alliance of Free Democrats (SzDSz) party, intimated that improvement in the rights of the Hungarian minority abroad had to precede other forms of interstate cooperation.

> What we want is the right for Hungarians and any other ethnic group to retain their identity, study in and use their mother tongue, foster relations with their brethren across the border and consequently make the borders permeable to allow for the free flow of ideas and movement of people, in a word, to bring what is part of Europe up to European standards. The more cooperation we get from a neighboring country in this matter, the closer we can work on other issues too.[39]

The opposition parties at the time, however, emphasized the necessity of normalizing bilateral relations as the way to encourage improvement in minority rights. The Antall government was criticized for "not mentioning the necessity of regional cooperation" and for elevating the rights of the Hungarian minority above all other foreign policy goals.[40] For the opposition, normalizing relations was one step in a long-term process of building trust and a cooperative relationship that would eventually benefit the Hungarian minority.[41] The basic treaties were seen as a means of improving Hungarian minority rights but not the capstone to improvement in this area.[42]

There were also strong differences of opinion between the opposition and the first postcommunist government regarding the impact of the government's statements and actions relating to the Hungarian minority abroad on the country's prospects for integration into the EU. The inflammatory remarks and actions of the government and members of the governing parties regarding minority issues, according to critics, were jeopardizing Hungary's goal of EU accession.[43] The problem was that "Hungary was unable to portray to its Western partners a credible, respected and positive picture of its policies relating to its neighbors. It was unable to convince others that Hungary wanted to participate in the promotion of regional stability."[44] As an SzDSz member of the Committee on European Integration Affairs argued, "the Hungarian situation from this perspective [international prestige] has really worsened in the last period. . . . Western observers, Western politicians really worry about whether Hungary's stable internal political situation and its relations with neighbors are being undermined."[45] The danger was that any negative views of Hungary held by Western leaders and officials would provide EU officials with an easy excuse to place Hungary in the same category as Romania and Slovakia with regard to accession.[46]

Following the 1994 national parliamentary elections, a new coalition government led by Gyula Horn, leader of the Hungarian Socialist Party (MSzP), came to power.[47] The government immediately made it clear that a less ideological and nationalist tone would be adopted with regard to the Hungarian minority issue.[48] In a pointed reference to the previous prime minister's famous statement about 15 million Hungarians, the new prime minister said that

> by constitutional law I am prime minister of ten and a half million people. . . .
> At the same time, I deeply feel my personal, and the government's constitutional, responsibility with regard to the fate of the Hungarians living beyond our borders. Furthermore, I am convinced that the realization of an improvement in the Hungarians' situation cannot be accomplished through loud declarations but will be manifested in concrete steps taken side by side with them.[49]

The new government proposed "new tools, methods, and a different style to distinguish this government's foreign policy from that of the past."[50]

In contrast to the Antall government's hierarchy of foreign policy goals, elevating Hungarian minority rights above cooperation, the new government would actively encourage the normalization of relations with its neighbors.

> I would like to state with regard to Hungary and its relations with its neighbors that (1) it is indispensable for Hungary's and the region's stability and security. (2) It is necessary so that we can meet our economic goals as well. Trade flows between Hungary and its neighbors are unjustifiably small, as are our economic relations in general. (3) Without this normalization of relations there is no possibility of improving the Hungarian minority situation. (4) We also need to normalize these relations because without this we will not receive Western support for our integration ambitions. There is nothing that makes the West more nervous than to accept quarreling Central or East European countries into multilateral structures. If we cannot settle these relations all our chances for integration are reduced.[51]

The normalization of relations, as exemplified in the signing of basic treaties, was crucial to advancing Hungary's goal of European integration.

> We can only count on NATO membership and broader integration if we achieve normalized relations with our neighbors. To my mind this is the most important conclusion. Beginning with the signing of basic treaties all the way to the maintenance of internal stability we have to do everything in the interest of integration. . . . The West will really only support us if we normalize these relations, if we can confirm that we are doing everything to achieve this.[52]

A treaty, furthermore, would be seen by neighboring governments as a gesture of friendship that would lead to other forms of cooperation, ultimately redounding to the benefit of the Hungarian minority population.[53] Prime Minister Horn criticized the prior Antall government for "neglecting the establishment of concrete steps with neighboring countries: joint banks, joint companies, treaties, agreements, etc."[54] The new government's "starting point [was] that it is only with the help of dialogue, with the building of confidence that these relations [with Slovakia or Romania] could be repaired and mutual cooperation built, could trust be strengthened.[55] Thus the signing of basic treaties could, and should, precede improvement in the situation of the Hungarian minority.[56]

HUNGARIAN BILATERAL RELATIONS AND THE BASIC TREATIES

Even without EU insistence on normalization of relations, the Antall government realized that Hungary's relations with its neighbors would have to be placed on some sort of new footing in the postcommunist period, that relations would have to be "rearrange[d] from the ground up and for the long term."[57] Hungary, alone among the CEE countries, shared a border with all three of the disintegrating federations in the region.[58] As a result, five of Hungary's immediate neighbors were newly formed states.[59]

The first bilateral treaty that Hungary concluded was with Ukraine on December 6, 1991. Agreement on this treaty was easier to achieve than with other states. Politicians in this state could not easily promote the idea of an ethnically homogeneous state, given the significant Russian minority population. Also, there was not a significant number of Hungarians living in Ukraine (about 160,000–200,000 out of a total Ukrainian population of approximately 48 million).

The Hungarian-Ukrainian treaty consists of nine bilateral agreements covering political, economic, and cultural issues, plus a joint declaration on minority rights containing language that refers to individual as well as collective rights.[60] The Ukrainian government was willing to provide guarantees for the administrative and cultural autonomy of the Hungarian minority in exchange for Hungary's renouncing any claims to future changes in Ukrainian territorial boundaries (article 2). A joint commission consisting of Hungarian and Ukrainian representatives would be established to monitor minority rights within each country.[61] Ukraine was Hungary's first neighbor to recognize formally the concept of collective rights, as outlined in the joint declaration.[62]

Even with language in the agreement that favored the preferred positions of the Hungarian government, ratification of this treaty was delayed and preceded by a very contentious debate in the Hungarian parliament.[63] The reference to Hungary's commitment to renounce any changes in territorial borders was the single most controversial issue during the Hungarian plenary parliamentary debate on the treaty.[64] The prime minister was forced to state defensively during the plenary debate that

> we are not setting a precedent in which this type of clause [regarding the peaceful renunciation of border changes] can be automatically requested by other neighboring countries that want to sign a basic treaty with us. . . . It is precisely for this reason . . . that this cannot be regarded as a precedent. . . . It is not binding, and it does not bind us to follow this type of formula with any other country.[65]

The Antall government's justification for including this phrase about border revisions was that Ukraine had never been a signatory to the Helsinki Final Act or other international documents that make reference to border changes.

The final vote ratifying the Hungarian-Ukrainian basic treaty did not follow party lines. Ironically, it was members of the opposition, the liberal Alliance of Free Democrats (SzDSz), and the Socialists (MSzP) that supported the Antall government's bid for ratification. The more conservative members within the government's parties as well as radical nationalists aligned around István Csurka opposed ratification of the treaty.[66]

Under Prime Minister Antall, basic treaties were also signed with Croatia, Slovenia, and Poland (as well as with Italy and Austria, with whom relations were unproblematic and where the Hungarian minority population is insignificant). Agreement on a basic treaty, however, was never reached with Romania and Slovakia in the first parliamentary cycle (1990–1994), the two states with the largest percentage of Hungarians.[67] The lack of agreements with Romania and Slovakia reflected in part the ideological bent of Antall's governing coalition, made up of parties unwilling to normalize relations until they had received adequate assurances that minority rights would be protected.

The second Hungarian postcommunist government under Prime Minister Horn felt that the inability to conclude treaties with Slovakia and Romania was the biggest foreign policy failure of the previous government.[68] It, therefore, set about to reach agreement on a treaty with these two countries as

quickly as possible. Agreement was reached first with the Slovak government, with Prime Ministers Meciar and Horn signing a basic treaty in March
1995 at the close of the inaugural ceremonies marking the Pact on Stability
in Europe.[69]

Both the indirect effects of EU conditionality as well as direct pressure on
the Slovak and Hungarian governments contributed to concluding this
treaty. Certain Western leaders in early 1995 had suggested that only Poland
and the Czech Republic should be considered priority integration candidates, with Hungary and Slovakia to be admitted together at a later date
given the two governments' continuing inability to resolve outstanding disputes.[70] In concluding a treaty, the Hungarian government demonstrated to
Western leaders and to EU officials that the country could abide by European
norms.[71] István Szent-Iványi, state secretary at the Ministry of Foreign Affairs,
opened the plenary debate on the treaty by stating that such cooperation
hopefully would accelerate Hungary's integration into Western organizations.

> It was not to please anyone else that we signed the treaty, but rather because
> we wanted to move Hungarian-Slovak relations from the impasse that they
> were in and to improve the framework of Slovak minority rights. Neverthe-
> less, it is significant and not without importance to us that from Washington
> to Paris and Bonn through London, from everywhere, we have received very
> favorable responses Everyone has uniformly understood that the signing of
> this treaty binds these two countries to the norms of Europe. . . . It has be-
> come clear today that Hungary is a country willing and able to cooperate and
> compromise.[72]

Many Hungarian foreign policy analysts have also clearly stated that direct
Western pressure led to the treaty.[73] The Europeans wanted to be able to
close the ceremonies launching the Pact on Stability in Europe with a bilateral treaty between countries having a significant history of conflict.

The Hungarian-Slovak treaty contains language that makes it accord with
the norms relating to minorities that are codified in the Charter of the United
Nations, the OSCE, and the Council of Europe. However, the treaty goes beyond the standard language in these international treaties by referring and
legally obliging the parties to commit to the Council of Europe's 1993 Parliamentary Assembly Recommendation 1201, which addresses collective rights
(article 15, paragraph 4 of the Hungarian-Slovak treaty). The most controversial passage of Recommendation 1201 (chapter 6, article 11) indirectly
raises the possibility that a national minority can have its own autonomous
administrative system and status when this group lives in a community in
which they are the majority.[74]

The plenary debate on the Hungarian-Slovak basic treaty in the Hungarian parliament was very divisive, and the reference in the treaty to Recom-

mendation 1201 was vigorously debated even within the international community.[75] Certain members of the Hungarian parliament referred to this treaty as "Hungary's third Trianon."[76] Despite some harsh and extremist language, the plenary debate in Hungary to ratify the treaty reveals an evolving discourse on the minority issue from a polarized, ideological stance toward a more pragmatic discussion of how concretely to protect and improve the rights of the Hungarian minority. In contrast to the earlier plenary debate on the Hungarian-Ukrainian treaty, the issues of renouncing territorial claims and border changes were not even raised during this debate, even though the two treaties contain similar language relating to territorial integrity and borders.[77] The primary issue during the plenary session on the Hungarian-Slovak treaty centered on whether the treaty would actually lead to concrete improvements for the Hungarian minority.

Critics argued that the Horn government should have waited for evidence of positive changes and only afterward sign a treaty giving international recognition to the Slovak government's efforts and actions. Many Hungarian members of parliament were not optimistic about what the treaty would achieve. As a Christian Democratic People's Party (KDNP) representative suggested, "We are naive in believing that this treaty can solve the conflicts of this region. It does not address the fact that here in the region of the Carpathian basin there have been so many misunderstandings and so many wounds created over the centuries that a single basic treaty can never solve."[78] The Horn government was accused of sacrificing everything to meet the goal of European integration and being "willing to endanger the country's and the nation's fundamental interests so that it could earn 'brownie points' with Western leaders."[79]

Adding fuel to the fire of the treaty's critics was the revelation that minutes before its signing Prime Minister Meciar had tried to attach an addendum to the treaty that outlined the Slovak government's understanding of how the collective status referred to in Recommendation 1201 should be interpreted. Not surprisingly, this Slovak interpretation was more restrictive than that of the Hungarian government.[80]

The Horn government, however, argued that attempts to improve bilateral relations with Slovakia and to establish a minimal trust between the two governments had to start somewhere.

> There is only one alternative to a compromise basic treaty and that alternative is not the perfect treaty but no treaty at all. The only alternative to a compromise solution is that we won't reach any solution, which I don't think would serve the interests of the Hungarians beyond our borders in any way. This try is a first step that is not insignificant. . . . The realization of this [treaty], I feel, will seriously help to settle the minority question, and over the long term creates the possibility that the whole region can successfully become integrated into the Euro-Atlantic organization.[81]

The prime minister began the second day of the plenary debate on the treaty by saying, "I have no illusions about what a single treaty can accomplish. It is just the first step, a foundation upon which we can build. In any case, we have started in the direction of finally normalizing our relations."[82] It would be but the first step in a long-term process of establishing cooperative ventures on a number of levels and across a range of issues, a relationship that would not focus exclusively on the Hungarian minority. The government's position was that the signing of the treaty left the Hungarian minority in no worse a situation than before, and perhaps slightly better to the extent that Slovakia had signed a treaty backed by internationally recognized norms under the pressure and supervision of Western leaders.[83]

The Hungarian-Slovak treaty was ratified by the Hungarian parliament after lengthy debate on June 13, 1995, with 244 votes in favor, 49 against, and 53 abstaining.[84] It took more than a year for the Slovak parliament to ratify the treaty. At the time of the ratification, the Slovak parliament attached to the treaty its interpretation of the disputed Council of Europe Recommendation 1201. International observers and Hungarian politicians quickly disavowed this as not being customary with regard to the ratification of legally binding international treaties.[85] This, as well as other actions taken by the Meciar government, alienated Slovakia from the West and led EU officials to downgrade Slovakia's chances at early accession.[86]

Prime Minister Horn also wanted to sign a treaty rapidly with the Romanian government to demonstrate Hungary's continued commitment to regional stability. In the spirit of cooperation, he called for a "historic reconciliation" with Romania.[87] However, as with other neighboring states, Hungarian-Romanian relations have foundered over the issues of the treatment of the Hungarian minority and territorial borders.[88] Harsh polemics have flowed on both sides. Ethnic clashes in Transylvania, the mistreatment of Hungarians by Romanians, and an ongoing conflict over the opening of the Hungarian consulate and the Bolyai University in Cluj (a city in Romania with a substantial Hungarian population) led to strong criticisms by the Hungarian government. In the face of worsening tensions between the Hungarian minority population and Romanians, the party of the Hungarian minority, the Hungarian Democratic Federation of Romania (UDMR), called for territorial autonomy.[89] The Romanian government, however, rejected these Hungarian demands for greater cultural or territorial autonomy. It feared that autonomy would be but the first step toward secession and possible reunification with Hungary, despite the repeated claims of the Hungarian government that it had no territorial claims against Romania.[90]

Hungarian-Romanian relations were made worse by a number of actions taken by the first postcommunist Hungarian government. The Antall government had initially rejected Romania's request to join the Central European Free Trade Area (CEFTA), a regional economic organization created after the collapse of communism. The Hungarian leadership feared that Romania's participation would delay Hungary's and the other CEFTA members' accession into the EU. Statements made by leading Hungarian foreign policy experts from the governing parties that Romania was not a democracy and should not be allowed to join Western organizations further aggravated relations.[91] Unlike the case of Slovakia, however, the Hungarian representative to the Council of Europe did not veto Romania's application for membership into that organization. The Hungarians had learned from their previous experience with Slovakia not to press Western delegates to deny membership to another CEE country, even if its record on minority rights was not exemplary. It elected to abstain rather than vote in favor of the Romanian application.[92]

The primary stumbling blocks in negotiating the basic treaty with Romania were the issue of collective rights and recognition of the inviolability of territorial borders. Hungarian officials insisted that some recognition of Recommendation 1201 be made, as in the Hungarian-Slovak treaty, arguing that the language on individual rights in existing international treaties did not sufficiently protect Hungarian identities.[93] The Romanian government's position, on the other hand, was that it abided by the relevant international treaties and that no further codification was needed.[94] The Romanian side was willing to make reference to the Council of Europe's Framework Convention for the Protection of National Minorities concluded in 1994. It was unwilling, however, to mention Recommendation 1201, which is more generous regarding the rights of minorities. For its part, the Romanian government insisted that the Hungarian government include a clause in the treaty renouncing once and for all changes to the Hungarian-Romanian border, citing the precedent in the Hungarian-Ukrainian treaty. Hungary argued that it already abided by existing international treaties, precluding that possibility.[95]

Relations between the two governments worsened after the Hungarian government (and specifically the Ministry of Foreign Affairs) helped draft, and officially endorsed, a declaration concluding the 1996 summit meeting of representatives of the Hungarian minorities from around the world held in Budapest. This declaration called for "the establishment of local governments and autonomy" for Hungarian minorities. It committed the Hungarian government to support the aspirations of the Hungarian minority by allocating a percentage of the Hungarian national budget to their cause. The declaration, furthermore, stated that self-rule was vital to preserving the identity of ethnic Hungarians.[96]

Western and American leaders sharply criticized the Horn government for supporting this declaration, and the public outcry within neighboring states reached new levels. The far right Slovak National Party, part of Prime Minister Meciar's coalition government, went so far as to suggest that the Slovak-Hungarian treaty be revoked.[97] On the Hungarian domestic political front, too, the Horn government was harshly criticized. Although it tried to displace the criticism by pointing out that this was not a legally binding document and should be considered more a political statement or rallying cry, the negative comments and repercussions continued.[98]

As was true with the Hungarian-Slovak basic treaty, it was primarily direct Western pressure that eventually led to the signing of a basic treaty between Hungary and Romania in September 1996. The immediate negative response from American and Western political leaders and EU and NATO officials regarding the Horn government's support for the controversial minority declaration directly contributed to a Hungarian about-face on inclusion of Recommendation 1201 and acceptance of a Romanian-proposed compromise.[99] The "two countries' quests to join NATO and the European Union brought about a compromise on issues that appeared to be insurmountably divisive."[100] Contingencies, like the timing of national elections, also contributed to reaching agreement on a treaty. Romania was set to hold presidential elections in a few months, and it was uncertain whether the compromise proposed by the Romanian government would remain "on the table" after the election.[101]

Most analysts and foreign policy experts, and even Horn government officials, acknowledge that the Hungarian-Romanian basic treaty is a weaker treaty than the one signed the prior year with Slovakia.[102] The primary weakness of the treaty related to the compromise that the Horn government accepted with regard to Recommendation 1201. Unlike the treaty with Slovakia, in which 1201 is specifically mentioned in the treaty (article 15), only the framework convention is referred to in the section on minority rights in the Hungarian-Romanian treaty. Other minority documents, including Recommendation 1201, are simply noted as being listed in the annex to the treaty.[103] More importantly, a footnote in the agreement set out the Romanian interpretation of this recommendation, which rejected group rights and territorial autonomy along ethnic lines.[104]

It is this footnote that lay at the heart of the opposition to the treaty.[105] While the Slovaks also rejected the Hungarian position on collective rights, applying a more restrictive definition, the Slovak interpretation took the form of an addendum to the treaty that was not signed by the Hungarians. By contrast, the Romanian interpretation is contained in a footnote that is part of the body of the agreement signed by both governments. According to critics, this gave the Romanian interpretation greater legitimacy[106] and would make it easier for the Romanian government to reject Hungarian minority proposals.[107]

In August 1996 the Horn government presented to the parliament a draft of the treaty in anticipation of its signing in the near future. Upon previewing the treaty, a conservative member of parliament, Tamás Isépy (KDNP), collected enough signatures to submit a motion (H/2834) calling for the Hungarian parliament to hold an extraordinary plenary session to debate the draft treaty, which it did on September 3. The motion, furthermore, called on the government to take into account the views of the Hungarian minority organizations in Romania in additional negotiations and to sign the treaty only after the government had received parliament's prior approval.[108] After a marathon thirteen-hour debate, the motion was defeated in parliament by a margin of 71 in favor and 235 against with no abstentions.[109] The urgency surrounding this unusual plenary session can be attributed in part to uncertainty about the upcoming Romanian presidential elections and the future political context within which ratification of the treaty would take place. Critics of the Hungarian-Romanian treaty could also point to the Slovak example, arguing that the position of the Hungarian minority in Slovakia had only worsened since that treaty had been ratified.[110]

The Horn government was subject to renewed criticism when opponents of the treaty found out that the signing of the treaty would take place in Timişoara, a city with an important Hungarian population. Timişoara is also an important symbolic site for Hungarians. There the communist regime of Ceausescu attempted to remove a Hungarian priest, László Tökés, from his parish in 1989.[111] Despite this last-minute controversy, Prime Minister Horn and President Iliescu signed the Hungarian-Romanian treaty on September 16, 1996. The Romanian parliament ratified the treaty in October prior to holding the presidential elections. The Hungarian parliament ratified the treaty later that year on December 10, with 249 in favor, 53 against, and 12 abstentions.[112]

CONCLUSION

Over the last decade, norms have become an important avenue of research within the field of international relations.[113] Norms, defined as collectively held expectations of behavior by actors, can be regulative, constraining behavior and specifying standards of proper behavior, and/or constitutive, creating new interests and identities and also new standards.[114] Norms shaping policy can operate at both international and domestic levels.[115]

The European Union has declared that there are certain standards of behavior in the areas of cooperation and minority rights that Hungary and the other CEE states are required to abide by prior to accession.[116] To use Checkel's terminology, the European Union and other international organizations have been the "norm makers" and Hungary has been the "norm taker."[117] This chapter has examined the extent to which there has been a diffusion of European understandings relating to cooperation and minority rights to Hungary, and what mechanisms the European Union used to educate and socialize the Hungarian political elite into these practices.

The views of Hungarian leaders and EU officials initially diverged greatly over minority rights. Hungarian officials and leaders believed that membership in international organizations would offer new international arenas through which to publicize violations of minority rights and to impose collective sanctions. Western leaders, however, made it clear that publicly criticizing the governments of neighboring states, as the Antall government did, was not an acceptable "European" way of enforcing rights and that Hungarian officials would not be supported in these actions. Furthermore, Hungarian representatives would have to use more subtle means than blocking other countries' accession into European organizations to signal its concern over rights violations. Minority rights, in other words, would remain primarily a matter to be settled bilaterally and was not the preserve of international society.

The most important way that the EU facilitated the emergence of cooperation in the CEE region has been through the consistent advocacy of cooperative interstate relations and respect for minority rights as preconditions to membership. The EU has applied constant pressure on the governments of these countries to demonstrate that they can cooperate bilaterally and multilaterally. There have been real economic and political costs to pursuing noncooperative relations with neighboring states, including the withholding of financial assistance, exclusion from EU initiatives, and, most importantly, the postponement of membership. Explicit EU pressure and the linking of respect for minority rights to Slovakia's EU associate membership, for example, led Prime Minister Meciar to allow an OSCE panel of independent experts to examine the problems of the Hungarian minority in Slovakia.[118] In the case of Romania, the EU delayed for almost a year the entry into force of the trade and cooperation agreement because of human rights violations.[119]

The EU, in other words, has established a stable pattern of rewards and incentives that has produced a long-term set of indirect pressures to encourage adoption of certain EU norms.[120] Conditionality, both through the "carrot" of membership and the "stick" of lost financial aid and participation in EU programs, has been an effective means through which to spread international norms and institutionalize them in new domestic contexts.

In addition to this constant indirect pressure for greater cooperation, EU and NATO officials and Western leaders directly intervened several times in specific situations to break a deadlock or force a compromise. These direct interventions facilitated agreement on contentious issues and led to the signing of basic treaties with Slovakia and Romania. In the case of the Hungarian-Slovak treaty, it was direct Western pressure that led the Hungarian and Slovak governments to sign the agreement at the conference for the Pact on Stability in Europe. In the case of Hungary and Romania, the West's clear and rapidly communicated disapproval of the Hungarian minority summit declaration led the Hungarian government to reevaluate its position, paving the way for a treaty. The ultimate incentive for the governments to reconsider preexisting positions in both cases was that it promised a step forward in the integration process.

Beyond the regulative effects of these European norms, the Hungarian political elite believed that adoption and institutionalization of these norms have important constitutive effects, reshaping how Hungary is and will be identified. The European Union embodies certain cultural values and practices that foster peace and stability. Being categorized as a European, and by extension a democratic, country serves as an identification marker that provides a guide to a state's expected behavior and actions.[121] European states try to resolve conflicts through compromise and negotiations rather than violence. As new states become members of the EU, a broader zone of peace will be created and the benefits of a pluralistic economic and security community will extend also to parts of the CEE region.[122]

Direct and indirect external pressure and interventions, however, do not always lead to the desired or cooperative outcome. Slovakia under Prime Minister Meciar illustrates that not all CEE leaders were inclined to accept the incentives proffered by the EU and adopt conciliatory relations with neighboring states. Given its size, economic performance, location, and initial participation in the Visegrad group, Slovakia could have been included in the first tier of EU candidates with Hungary, Poland, and the Czech Republic. Yet Prime Minister Meciar's political actions did not accord with European norms and the expectations of the international community. As a result, Slovakia was singled out for Western opprobrium and treated as a "rogue state," and it slipped into the second tier of EU accession candidates. The European Union's displeasure with that country is clearly evident in its *Agenda 2000* document in which Slovakia was singled out for not adequately meeting the political criteria relating to the rule of law and democracy.[123]

Quality of leadership and the domestic political environment within which political leaders operate, therefore, are key factors in understanding when and under what circumstances international influences have an effect.[124] Politics was important to the extent that the Horn government had a parliamentary majority to push through ratification of the Hungarian-Romanian treaty. The emergence of more cordial relations between Hungary and Romania and with Slovakia in the post-Meciar period were also the result of electoral fortunes and the appeal or rejection of the political programs offered by particular leaders in those countries.[125] While the external pressures have been the same, the timing and specific ways that different governments react to and act on these pressures have varied depending on the circumstances and institutions of each country.

The attraction of EU membership continues to shape domestic policy in other countries. Upon assuming power, Prime Minister Dzurinda pledged a radical departure in tone and policies from those of the previous government in the hope that Slovakia would be reinstated to the first group of countries negotiating accession into the European Union: "1999 is a historic year for Slovakia. We are turning back toward Europe, turning back to the European and Atlantic integration process."[126] The new government enacted several measures relating to minority rights that brought Slovakia more into line with European norms. As examples of the changes in policies and style, the Dzurinda government drafted a new minority language law that was approved by the Slovak parliament on July 11, 1999, overturning Meciar's unconstitutional 1996 minority language law, which had also violated the Hungarian-Slovak basic treaty. In the spirit of further cooperation, Slovakia and Hungary agreed to rebuild a bridge over the Danube in Esztergom that had been damaged during World War II and never repaired.[127] Clearly indicating Slovakia's more favorable status, the country has also been welcomed back into the Visegrad group.[128]

The Romanian government has also realized that accession into Western organizations requires concrete changes in policy and the institutionalization of European practices. The Romanian parliament had been slow to enact several of the measures initiated by President Constantinescu. It was not until after NATO announced that Romania would not be among the first group of countries to join NATO, while Hungary was named a new member, that concrete steps were taken to implement those measures.[129] The political elite in both Slovakia and Romania recognized that accession would only take place if their governments accepted the conditions of the EU and adhered to European and international norms, including those relating to minority rights. The attraction of membership, in short, continues to shape the calculations of political leaders in the region, although not necessarily at the same time and in exactly the same way.

While Hungary's accession into the EU seems assured, the question of how to draw some of the other states in the region into European networks remains a major unresolved issue.[130] To the extent that the societies and governments of Slovakia, Romania, or countries further east remain isolated from the EU and feel there is no possibility of membership, the danger of more authoritarian or nationalist policies increases and there are fewer incentives to institutionalize EU norms.[131] Critical to further diffusing European norms and drawing other countries closer to the core of Europe is the belief that there will be another enlargement round in the future. The European Union must offer a credible hope of future accession to those countries currently not invited to join and a strategy to achieve this goal so that the danger of a new "Wall" in Europe is reduced.

NOTES

1. Tibor Fényi, "Ki kell szabadulni a trianon szabta logikából," *Kritika,* August 1994, 38–42.

2. European Commission, *Agenda 2000: For a Stronger and Wider Union* (Luxembourg: European Communities, 1997).

3. *OGY* 5/23/90, 263. OGY refers to *Országgyülés* (parliament) of Hungary.

4. *OGY* 5/22/90, 193–94. These organizations are the Council of Europe, the European Union (EU), and the North Atlantic Treaty Organization (NATO).

5. I will refer in this chapter to the European Union rather than to the European Community (EC). The EU did not exist until the Treaty on European Union (TEU), also known as the Maastricht treaty, was ratified by the national parliaments of the member states. It formally came into being in November 1993.

The EU and the EC are still distinct legal and organizational entities. The European Community represents the supranational component of this international organization. The European Union incorporates two additional intergovernmental "pillars," one devoted to common foreign and security policy (CFSP) and the other to justice and home affairs (JHA).

6. While NATO was another important Western organization that Hungary desired to join, the EU was seen as offering a broader vision of security. Unlike NATO, the EU was seen as providing economic security, notwithstanding the effects of globalization and increased competition, in addition to more traditional geopolitical and military security.

7. All aspirants to membership since the 1960s have had to meet certain criteria, including broadly the consolidation of democratic practices and the establishment of a functioning and competitive market economy. Some of these requirements are explicitly described in various EU documents and pronouncements, while others are passed on to the governments of candidate countries more informally during meetings between the national political elite from the candidate countries and EU officials or Western political leaders.

8. European Commission, *The European Councils: Conclusions of the Presidency 1992–1994* (Luxembourg: Commission of the European Communities, 1995).

9. The EU is not the only international organization concerned with ethnic and minority conflicts in the post–Cold War period. In 1992 the United Nations (UN) General Assembly passed a resolution relating to the fair treatment of minorities and indigenous peoples, while that same year the Organization for Security and Cooperation in Europe (OSCE) established the new position of high commissioner for national minorities. Similarly, when NATO published its membership criteria in 1995, minority rights and the resolution of outstanding tensions were clearly specified as being "a factor in determining whether to invite a state to join the Alliance" <www.nato.int.docu/basictxt/enl-9501.htm> (March 4, 1998).

10. Providing a clear indication of where EU officials' priorities lay, the basic treaties are viewed as an "essential element" of stability, with "complementary arrangements" to cover other multilateral cooperative structures. European Commission, *The European Councils,* 118.

11. *Zagreb Vjesnik,* November 10, 1989, 4; JPRS-EER-90-015, February 5, 1990, 2.

12. The association agreement forms the legal basis governing political and economic relations between the EU and individual CEE countries. These agreements signed with the CEE states have gone beyond other arrangements made previously between the EU and third countries in terms of the extent of political dialogue. They are most often referred to as Europe Agreements, to distinguish them from other association agreements. An association agreement is not a prerequisite for EU accession. In the cases of Spain and Portugal, free trade agreements preceded accession.

13. This includes the separately renegotiated Czech and Slovak association agreements, which the two governments felt was particularly discriminative. Barbara Lippert, "Relations with Central and Eastern European Countries: The Anchor Role of the European Union," in *Prospective Europeans: New Members for the European Union*, ed. John Redmond (New York: Harvester Wheatsheaf, 1994), 197–217.

14. European Commission, *The European Councils,* 159.

15. European Commission, *Agenda 2000,* 42.

16. About 2 million ethnic Hungarians live in Romania (7–8 percent of Romania's total population and residing mostly in Transylvania) while more than 600,000 Hungarians reside in Slovakia, representing about 10 percent of the Slovak population. The balance is found in the sub-Carpathian region of Ukraine (150,000–200,000), the Vojvodina region of Yugoslavia (400,000), Croatia (27,000), and Slovenia (10,000). Estimates made by non-Hungarians put the total number of Hungarians in the Carpathian basin at approximately 2.7 million compared with the official Hungarian figure of 3.5 million. Fedor Mediansky, "National Minorities and Security in Central Europe: The Hungarian Experience," in *Nationalism and Post-Communism*, ed. Alexander Pavkovic, Halyna Koscharsky, and Adam Csornata (Aldershot, U.K.: Dartmouth), 101–20. Hungary and its neighbors argue over these numbers.

17. Fényi, "Ki kell szabadulni"; Misha Glenny, *The Rebirth of History: Eastern Europe in the Age of Democracy* (London: Penguin, 1990).

18. Jörg K. Hoensch, *A History of Modern Hungary, 1867–1986* (London: Longman, 1998), 102. Hungary subsequently regained much of this territory by allying itself with Hitler's Germany, only to lose it again after it was defeated during World War II.

19. Joseph Rothschild, *Return to Diversity: A Political History of East Central Europe since World War II* (New York: Oxford University Press, 1989); Péter Kende, "The Trianon Syndrome: Hungarians and Their Neighbors," in *Lawful Revolution in Hungary, 1989–1994*, ed. Béla Király (New York: Columbia University Press, 1995), 475–92.

20. Tamás Fricz, *A magyarországi pártrendszer 1987–1995: Kialakulástörténet és jellemzôk politológiai elemzés* (Budapest: Cserépfalvi Kiadó), 1996.

21. Brubaker uses the following terminology to distinguish among the three relevant groups. There is the "national minority" or minorities residing in a state. There is the "newly nationalizing state," not necessarily new de jure but one that might have reconfigured its borders recently (Yugoslavia, for example). Last, there is the "external national homeland" to which the minorities belong, or can be constructed as belonging, via ethno-cultural affinity but not legal citizenship. Roger Brubaker, *Nationalism Reframed: Nationhood and the National Question in the New Europe* (Cambridge: Cambridge University Press, 1996).

22. George Schöpflin, "Inter-Ethnic Relations in Transylvania," *Transylvania English Language Supplement,* March 1997, 2–4; Géza Jeszenszky, "Hungary's Bilateral Treaties with the Neighbors and the Issue of Minorities" (paper presented at the conference on bilateral treaties between the ex-Warsaw Pact states, Sarasota, Florida, April 1997).

23. *OGY* 5/22/90, 208; *OGY* 10/15/91, 10761, 10763.

24. He was not only referring to Hungary's population of approximately 10.5 million but also to the 5 million Hungarians living abroad. As one scholar put it, this 15 million was a "strongly rounded up number [that] includes not only the addition of the three million ethnic Hungarians living in neighboring countries . . . with some exaggeration—but in addition a totally mythical one and a half million spread out around the world. (The figure is fictitious because it includes everyone who ever migrated to the West. Most of these people of Hungarian descent do not identify themselves politically as Hungarian, not to mention that among the second and third generations of this diaspora most of them have already culturally assimilated into the host country.)." Kende, "Trianon Syndrome," 479.

Antall first referred to the 15 million Hungarians at MDF party headquarters on April 8, 1990, the second at the plenary session of parliament in June. Only in the second, "improved" statement did Antall include the phrase "in spirit." Ferenc A. Szabó, "Diplomácia, óh: A független magyar külpolitika elsô négy évérôl," *Társadalmi szemle,* January 1995, 57–62.

25. *Current Policy* no. 29/1991, 3.

26. *Current Policy* no. 40/1991, 7–8.

27. "The point is that it is above all out of political necessity that we need the EC [EU]. . . . The political future of the country is still open and a positive political coercion is . . . necessary for us. . . . Europe is a protection against proponents of parochialism. . . . the democratic transition can only be finished if political and economic consolidation can take place inside the EC." Mette Skak, *From Empire to Anarchy: Post-Communist Foreign Policy and International Relations* (New York: St. Martin's, 1996), 43.

28. *OGY* 11/16/92, 21410; András Fischer and Péter Gärtner, eds., *Back to Europe* (Budapest: Pergamon, 1991), 14.

29. *OGY* 10/15/91, 10761.

30. László Kiss, "Hungary," in *Political and Economic Transformation in East Central Europe,* ed. Hanspeter Neuhold, Péter Havlik, and Arnold Suppan (Boulder, Colo.: Westview, 1994), 244.

31. *OGY KB* 10/30/91, 42–43.

32. *Current Policy* no. 38/1991, 2.

33. *Current Policy* no. 8/1991, 2.

34. *Current Policy* no. 12/1992, 4.

35. András Balogh, "A külpolitika prioritása: Nyelvhelyisségi vagy politikai vita?" *Külpolitika,* Spring 1996, 3–11; Pál Dunay, "Regionális együttmûködés kelet–közép–európában: Befektetés eredmény nélkül?" *Külpolitika,* Summer 1997, 10–41; Andrew Felkay, *Out of Russian Orbit: Hungary Gravitates to the West* (Westport, Conn.: Greenwood, 1997); Dávid Meiszter and Pál Dunay, "Sikerek és kudarcok között: Magyar külpolitika 1990–1994," *Társadalmi szemle,* August–September 1994, 35–52; Alfred Reisch, "Hungarian Foreign Policy and the Magyar Minorities: New Foreign Policy Priorities," *Nationalities Papers,* Autumn 1996, 447–65.

36. *OGY* 9/16/92, 19305.

37. *OGY KB* 10/21/91, 72–73.

38. *OGY* 10/15/91, 10762.

39. *Current Policy* no. 43/1991, 4.

40. *OGY* 5/23/90, 238. Because of the prime minister's personal involvement in directing Hungary's foreign policy, the elevation of minority rights above all other foreign policy goals has sometimes been referred to as the "Antall doctrine." Meiszter and Dunay, "Sikerek és kudarcok," 36; László Poti, "A cseh köztársaság és magyarország külpolitikai irányváltásai," *Külpolitika*, Spring 1996, 75–82.

41. *OGY* 2/22/95, 5444.

42. *OGY KB* 10/12/94, 11, 13, 26; László Lengyel, "Kovács: Az alapszerzôdés eszköz a kezünkben," *Népszabadság*, March 28, 1996, 3.

43. Meiszter and Dunay, "Sikerek és kudarcok," 38, 39; Balogh, "A külpolitika prioritása," 6; László Lengyel, "Külpolitika vagy nemzetpolitika," in *Kormány a mérlegen 1990–1994*, ed. Csaba Gombár, Elemér Hankiss, Laszló Lengyel, and György Várnai (Budapest: Korridor, 1994), 346–68.

44. Meiszter and Dunay, "Sikerek és kudarcok," 38.

45. *OGY EIUB* 3/31/93, 68.

46. Gustav Molnár, "Magyarország és szomszédai," *Magyar szemle*, February 1994, 115–25.

47. Although Horn's party won a parliamentary absolute majority, the Socialists invited the Alliance of Free Democrats (SzDSz) to join them in forming a coalition government. This successor party to the Hungarian communist party wanted to demonstrate that it could work with other parties and reassure the international community that it was a different party than it was under communism. István Deák, "Post-Post Communist Hungary," *New York Review of Books*, August 1994, 33–38.

48. *OGY KB* 7/13/94, 41.

49. *OGY* 7/14/94, 152.

50. *OGY* 2/22/95, 5442.

51. Statement by Foreign Minister László Kovács, *OGY KB* 7/13/94, 32–33; italics added.

52. László Kasza, *Metamorphosis Hungarie 1989–1994* (Budapest: Századvég, 1994), 131, 139.

53. *OGY KB* 10/12/94, 26.

54. Kasza, *Metamorphosis*, 138–39.

55. *OGY* 2/22/95, 5443.

56. *OGY KB* 10/12/94, 26.

57 Kende, "Trianon Syndrome," 480.

58. Póti, "A cseh köztársaság és magyarország," 78.

59. These are the Serbia-Montenegrin federation, Croatia, Slovenia, Ukraine, and Slovakia after 1992.

60. At the time these agreements were signed Ukraine was not yet an independent state. Then chairman of the Ukrainian Supreme Soviet, Leonid Kravchuk, concluded these agreements, hoping that they would demonstrate that Ukraine could comply with European norms on minority rights and to give more weight to Ukraine's declarations of sovereignty made in the fall of 1990. Edith Oltay, "Minorities as Stumbling Block in Relations with Neighbors," *RFE/RL Research Report*, July 1992, 31–32.

61. Oltay, "Minorities as Stumbling Blocks," 31.

62. Reisch, "Hungarian Foreign Policy," 456. Ironically, given the future direction of the country, the Croatian government agreed to accept the same joint declaration on minority rights as the one signed with the Ukraine, but Hungarian-Croat relations were undermined by the war in the former Yugoslavia.

63. Ratification of the treaty was not even submitted to the parliament until May 1993, even though the Ukrainian parliament had already ratified it on July 1, 1992, because of concerns that it would not receive the necessary votes.

64. Meiszter and Dunay, "Sikerek és kudarcok"; *OGY* 5/11/93.

65. *OGY* 5/11/93, 26686.

66. *OGY* 5/11/93, 26689-90; Meiszter and Dunay, "Sikerek és kudarcok."

67. The Hungarian minority is concentrated in the southern part of Slovakia along nearly the entire length of the Hungarian-Slovak border in a region that the Hungarians call the Felvidék. In Romania the Hungarian minority is more dispersed. Many live in Transylvania, an area referred to in Hungarian as Erdély, and one not entirely contiguous with the Hungarian border.

Both the Slovak and Romanian governments have accused Hungary of wanting to reclaim historical territories in which the Hungarian minority resides. The dispersion of Hungarians in Romania, however, makes it virtually impossible for the Hungarian government to be able to achieve that goal even if it so desired. Accusations relating to Hungarian attempts to reclaim territory have usually been made by Slovak and Romanian nationalist politicians for domestic political purposes. Reisch, "Hungarian Foreign Policy."

68. Reisch, "Hungarian Foreign Policy," 44.

69. The Stability Pact originated in the eponymous Balladur Plan after the then French foreign minister proposed the idea at the Brussels European Council meeting in October 1993. Its purpose was "to resolve the problem of minorities and to strengthen the inviolability of frontiers. . . . The objective is to contribute to stability by preventing tension and potential conflicts in Europe; it is intended to promote good neighborly relations and to encourage countries to consolidate their borders and to resolve the problems of national minorities that arise; to this end it is an exercise in preventive diplomacy in which the European Union will have an active role to play as catalyst. . . . The objective of the project would be to facilitate rapprochement between those States and the Union and their cooperation with it by helping them to fulfill the conditions listed by the European Council in Copenhagen." European Commission, *The European Councils*, 117. The EU, one of the signatories to this pact, held an inaugural conference in 1995 to address the escalating tensions in the CEE region.

70. László Póti and Pál Dunay, "Relations with the Former Socialist Countries, 1989–1995," in *Lawful Revolution in Hungary, 1989–1994*, ed. Béla Király (New York: Columbia University Press, 1995), 444.

71. Lajos Pietsch, "Az atlanticizmus mindenekellőtt értékkategória: Martonyi János az új kezdeménezésről és integrációs esélyeinkről," *Magyar nemzet*, May 16, 1996, 19.

72. "A magyar-szlovák alapszerződés parlamenti vitájának jegyzőkönyve," *Külpolitika*, Spring 1995, 96.

73. Póti and Dunay, "Relations," 442; Balogh, "A külpolitika prioritása," 839; Géza Jeszenszky, "Viták a magyar-román szerződés körül," in *Magyarország politikai évkönyve 1996-ről*, ed. Sándor Kurtán, Péter Sándor, and László Vass (Budapest:

Demokrácia Kutatások Magyar Központ Alapítvány, 1997), 220; Pál Dunay, "Fogyatékos fordulat: Magyarország nemzetközi kapcsolatai 1994–1995," *Társadalmi szemle*, November 1995, 26–27; Sharon Fisher, "Domestic Policies Cause Conflict with the West," *Transitions*, June 1996, 57; Rudolf Chmel, "Miért lehetetlen a szlovák-magyar megbékélés?" *Magyar hírlap*, April 27, 1996, 17–18.

74. Article 11 reads as follows: "In the regions where they are in a majority, the persons belonging to a national minority shall have the right to have at their disposal appropriate local or autonomous authorities or to have a special status matching the specific historical and territorial situation and in accordance with the domestic legislation of the state." Zsófia Szilágyi, "Hungarian Minority Summit Causes Uproar in the Region," *Transitions*, June 1996, 47. As some have noted, while this recommendation recognizes the legitimacy of certain forms of collective rights, the nature of these collective rights is not self-evident and can be subject to conflicting interpretations. See András Balogh, "Az európai stabilitási egyezményről," *Magyar tudomány*, Winter 1995, 105.

75. Balogh, Az európai stabilitási," 840; Fisher, "Domestic Policies," 57.

76. "Leszák: Harmadik Trianon," *Magyar nemzet*, May 31, 1996, 5. As a conservative nationalist declared during the plenary debate: "We are afraid of the treaties signed in France, and in this century we have signed three of them: a first one following World War I in Trianon, a second one in Paris after World War II, and now once again one in Paris. Of the first two, we can say that we were losers in the two wars. But, respected delegates, we have lost nothing now." "A magyar-szlovák alapszerződés," 102.

77. Dunay, "Fogyatékos fordulat," 18–31.

78. "A magyar-szlovák alapszerződés," 107.

79. "A magyar-szlovák alapszerződés," 107.

80. Member of parliament György Csóti, interview by author, August 5, 1997; Balogh, "Az európai stabilitási," 839; Póti and Dunay, "Relations," 443.

81. *OGY* 2/22/95, 5452.

82. "A magyar-szlovák alapszerződés," 115.

83. "A magyar-szlovák alapszerződés," 114.

84. Dunay, "Fogyatékos fordulat," 28.

85. József György Farkas, "A kiegészítés nem része a szerződésnek," *Népszabadság*, April 4, 1996, 3.

86. Changes to referenda ballots, repeated violations of the Slovak constitution as well as of the Hungarian-Slovak basic treaty, the politicization of the civil service, a concentration of power in the hands of the prime minister, and government control of the media were among the most flagrant examples of how Prime Minister Meciar rejected European norms of political conduct while in power. Greg Nieuwsma, "Lessons in Democracy: Slovakia, Its Minorities, and the European Union," *Central Europe Review*, November 8, 1999, 1–2; Martin Bútora and Zora Bútoróva, "Slovakia's Democratic Awakening," *Journal of Democracy*, January 1999, 80–95.

87. This phrase had actually been used first by President Ion Iliescu in August 1995 and was later picked up by the Horn government. Michael Shafir, "A Possible Light at the End of the Tunnel," *Transition*, July 1996, 29–32.

88. Daniel N. Nelson, "Hungary and Its Neighbors: Security and Ethnic Minorities," *Nationalities Papers* 26, no. 2 (1998): 313–30; Reisch, "Hungarian Foreign Policy."

89. Ronald H. Linden, "Putting on Their Sunday Best: Romania, Hungary, and the Puzzle of Peace," *International Studies Quarterly*, March 2000, 129.

90. Reisch, "Hungarian Foreign Policy," 445; Oltay, "Minorities," 28, 30; Adrian Hyde-Price, *The International Politics of East Central Europe* (Manchester, U.K.: Manchester University Press, 1996), 118; Dan Ionescu and Alfred A. Reisch, "Still No Breakthrough in Romanian-Hungarian Relations," *REF/RL Research Report*, October 1993, 29. Romanian President Iliescu's fear of a strengthening relationship between Hungary and Transylvania also explain that country's reluctance to join multilateral regional organizations such as the Carpathian Euro-region. Hyde-Price, *International Politics*, 118; Reisch, "Hungarian Foreign Policy," 451; Vasil Hudák, ed., *Building a New Europe: Transfrontier Cooperation in Central Europe* (Prague: Institute for East-West Studies, 1996), 4–5.

91. Meiszter and Dunay, "Sikerek és kudarcok," 44.

92. Certain Hungarian analysts felt that this was also shortsighted of the Antall government. Meiszter and Dunay, "Sikerek és kudarcok," 45. "The goal of Hungarian policy cannot be to isolate Romania from Europe. . . . It would have been wiser for us to vote yes instead of a euphemistic no. This way Romania would have felt that it received support, even if in a backhanded way, and Europe would have seen this issue as a minor squabble. Observer status would have made Romanian policies more transparent, and would have facilitated accounting for those criteria that would later have been the basis for proceeding with full membership." Lengyel, "Külpolitika," 353.

93. Oltay, "Minorities," 31; Shafir, "Possible Light."

94. Shafir, "Possible Light"; Póti and Dunay, "Relations."

95. Oltay, Minorities," 28.

96. Szilágyi, "Hungarian Minority Summit," 49.

97. Szilágyi, "Hungarian Minority Summit," 47; Nelson, "Hungary," 319.

98. More recently, Hungarian political analysts have suggested that the Horn government made a shrewd domestic political calculation. Supporting a nonbinding political declaration allowed the government to "cover itself" with domestic political groups and repair its record on minorities before pushing through ratification of a nearly finalized Hungarian-Romanian basic treaty in the Hungarian parliament. Nelson, "Hungary," 325, 330.

99. Nelson, "Hungary"; Shafir, "Possible Light."

100. Shafir, "Possible Light," 30.

101. Romanian delegates intimated that the compromise proposal might be withdrawn after the elections. Shafir, "Possible Light," 30; Jeszenszky, "Viták," 223.

102. Compared with the Slovak treaty, the Romanian one is less able to guarantee the use of minority languages and to provide access to historic monuments and archival materials. This agreement contains no provision for the restitution of Hungarian church properties confiscated during the communist period. Shafir, "Possible Light"; Jeszenszky, "Viták."

103. This represents a compromise on the Romanian side as well, for the government's initial position was that Recommendation 1201 would not be mentioned anywhere in the treaty. The document can be found at <www.htmh.hu/bilat-frame.htm>.

104. The footnote states that "the Parties to the Treaty understand that Recommendation no. 1201 does not apply to collective rights, nor does it oblige the Parties to the Treaty to grant those persons the right to a special territorial autonomy or status based on ethnicity." Jeszenszky, "Viták," 221.

105. Jeszenszky, "Hungary's Bilateral Treaties"; Jeszenszky, "Viták"; Member of Parliament György Csóti, interview by author, August 5, 1997.

106. György Csóti, interview by author.

107. Jeszenszky, "Hungary's Bilateral Treaties."

108. Jeszenszky, "Viták," 222.

109. Jeszenszky, "Viták," 225.

110. The Meciar government passed a highly restrictive language law and an administrative redistricting law that went into effect at the beginning of 1996 in clear violation of the Hungarian-Slovak basic treaty and in defiance of the Slovak constitutional court's ruling that supported the Hungarian position. Nieusma, "Lessons."

111. The demonstrations and riots against Tökés's harassment by Hungarians and Romanians alike in Timişoara spread across the country and led to the collapse of the Ceauseşcu dictatorship.

112. The governing parties (MSzP and SzDSz) voted in favor of the treaty, whereas four opposition parties (KDNP, MDF, Independent Smallholders Party [Független Kisgazdapárt, FKgP], and the Alliance of Young Democrats [Fiatal Demokrátak Szövetsége, Fidesz] party) voted against. Members of the Hungarian Democratic People's Party (Magyar Demokrata Héppárt, MDNP) composed almost all the abstentions.

The following year on May 27, 1997, the parliament voted on the treaty's announcement in official parliamentary documents. At that time there were only seven members of parliament that voted outright against the treaty, with most that had previously opposed simply abstaining from the vote on this occasion. In the interim, a new government and president had been elected in Romania. Those previously opposed to the treaty wanted to somehow signal their support for the recent political changes in the neighboring country. The MDNP, previously abstaining, voted in favor of the treaty this time.

113. To cite only some of the most important works: Robert O. Keohane, *International Institutions and State Power: Essays in International Relations Theory* (Boulder, Colo.: Westview, 1989); Robert O. Keohane, Joseph S. Nye, and Stanley Hoffmann, eds., *After the Cold War: International Institutions and State Strategies, 1989–1991* (Cambridge, Mass.: Harvard University Press, 1993); Jeffrey T. Checkel, "The Constructivist Turn in International Relations Theory," *World Politics*, January 1998, 324–48; Jeffrey T. Checkel, "Norms, Institutions, and National Identity in Contemporary Europe," *International Studies Quarterly*, March 1999, 83–114; Andrew P. Cortrell and James P. Davis, "How Do International Institutions Matter? The Domestic Impact of International Rules and Norms," *International Studies Quarterly*, December 1996, 451–78; Andrew P. Cortrell and James W. Davis Jr., "Understanding the Domestic Impact of International Norms: A Research Agenda," *International Studies Review*, Spring 2000, 65–87; Martha Finnemore, *National Interests in International Society* (Ithaca, N.Y.: Cornell University Press, 1996); Martha Finnemore and Kathryn Sikkink, "International Norm Dynamics and Political Change," *International Organization*, Autumn 1998, 887–917; Alexander Wendt, *Social Theory of International Politics* (Cambridge: Cambridge University Press, 1999); and Peter J. Katzenstein, ed., *The Culture of National Security: Norms and Identity in World Politics* (New York: Columbia University Press, 1996).

114. Finnemore, "International Norm Dynamics," 891; Katzenstein, *Culture*, 5; Checkel, "Norms."

115. Cortrell and Davis, "Understanding the Domestic Impact."

116. While I recognize that there is some disagreement on specifically how minority rights are to be defined and what constitutes a minority, there is nevertheless a European consensus, based primarily on the various Council of Europe documents, relating to the rights of national minorities.

117. Checkel, "Norms," 84.

118. Reisch, "Hungarian Foreign Policy," 459.

119. Lippert, "Relations."

120. Juan J. Linz and Alfred Stepan, *Problems of Democratic Transition and Consolidation: Southern Europe, South America, and Post-Communist Europe* (Baltimore: Johns Hopkins University Press, 1996); Laurence Whitehead, "International Aspects of Democratization," in *Transitions from Authoritarian Rule: Comparative Perspectives*, ed. Guillermo O'Donnell, Philippe Schmitter, and Laurence Whitehead (Baltimore: Johns Hopkins University Press, 1986), 3–46.

121. Ted Hopf, "The Promise of Constructivism in International Relations Theory," *International Security*, Summer 1998, 171–200; Katzenstein, *Culture*, 2, 5.

122. Emmanuel Adler and Michael Barnett, eds., *Security Communities* (New York: Cambridge University Press, 1998).

123. European Commission, *Agenda 2000*, 40–41.

124. Linz and Stepan, *Transitions*, 35; Tim Snyder and Milada Vachudová, "Are Transitions Transitory? Two Types of Political Change in Eastern Europe since 1989," *East European Politics and Societies*, Winter 1997, 5.

125. New elections were held in Slovakia in September 1998 in which Meciar and the parties affiliated with his government were defeated by a highly significant 84 percent electoral turnout. A new coalition government led by Mikulás Dzurinda was formed that includes a party representing the Hungarian minority.

Similarly, the Romanian presidential elections held in November 1996 led to President Iliescu's defeat, with Emil Constantinescu becoming the new president. A coalition government was formed that also included a Hungarian ethnic party, the Democratic Alliance of Hungarians in Romania (Romániai Magyar Demokrata Szövetséy, RMDSz).

126. Marian Lesko, "De-Meciarization Is Feasible," *Transitions,* 1998 <www.ijt.cz/transitions/dec98/opindeme.html> (February 16, 1999). Even prior to the European Council meeting in Helsinki, Finland (December 1999), in which the Commission agreed to open accession negotiations with all remaining CEE countries, Commission officials had indicated a willingness to reconsider Slovakia's status in light of the recent political changes.

127. Donald G. McNeil, "Trying to Heal Old Hatred in Ruins on Danube, "*New York Times*, November 6, 1999, A1, A5.

128. Ron Synovitz, "Central Europe: Leaders Re-launch Visegrád Initiative," *RFE/RL* 1999 <euro.rferl.org/nca/features/1999/05/F.RU.990517140909.html> (May 31, 1999).

129. Béla Markó, "Romania's Hungarians Face a Catch-22 Situation," *Transitions* 1998 <www.ijt.cz/transitions/dec98/opinroma.html> (February 16, 1999).

130. While Hungary's accession seems certain, the timing of membership is highly questionable. EU officials have been unwilling to specify a date for accession despite increasing pressure by the CEE governments. Thus the date when

Hungary might join the EU ranges from 2003 (cited by the present Hungarian government) to a pessimistic 2010, when Poland will also be able to join as a first-round contender and the EU has completed its own internal reforms to accommodate many more members. The most recent consensus date seems to be 2004 so that the newest members will be able to participate in the European Parliament elections.

131. Snyder and Vachudová, "Are Transitions Transitory?" 5.

BIBLIOGRAPHY

Adler, Emanuel, and Michael Barnett, eds. *Security Communities.* New York: Cambridge University Press, 1998.

Agh, Attila. "Európa messzire van." *Magyar hírlap,* March 21, 1996, 7.

Balogh, András. "Az európai stabilitási egyezményrôl." *Magyar tudomány,* Winter 1995, 834–41.

———. "A külpolitika prioritásai: Nyelvhelyességi vagy politikai vita?" *Külpolitika,* Spring 1996, 3–11.

———. "A nemzeti kisebbségekkel összefüggô konfliktusok: Mítosza–közep-európai tanulságok." *Külpolitika,* Summer 1997, 3–9.

Brubaker, Roger. *Nationalism Reframed: Nationhood and the National Question in Europe.* Cambridge: Cambridge University Press, 1996.

Bútora, Martin, and Zora Bútorová. "Slovakia's Democratic Awakening." *Journal of Democracy,* January 1999, 80–95.

Checkel, Jeffrey T. "The Constructivist Turn in International Relations Theory." *World Politics,* January 1998, 324–48.

———. "Norms, Institutions, and National Identity in Contemporary Europe." *International Studies Quarterly,* March 1999, 83–114.

Chmel, Rudolf. "Miért lehetetlen a szlovák-magyar megbékélés?" *Magyar hírlap,* April 27, 1996, 17–18.

Cortell, Andrew P., and James P. Davis Jr. "How Do International Institutions Matter? The Domestic Impact of International Rules and Norms." *International Studies Quarterly,* December 1996, 451–78.

Cortell, Andrew P., and James W. Davis Jr. "Understanding the Domestic Impact of International Norms: A Research Agenda." *International Studies Review,* Spring 2000, 65–87.

Deák, István. "Post-Post-Communist Hungary." *New York Review of Books,* August 11, 1994, 33–38.

Dunay, Pál. "Fogyatékos fordulat: Magyarország nemzetközi kapcsolatai 1994–1995." *Társadalmi szemle,* November 1995, 18–31.

———. "New Friends Instead of Foes: Hungary's Relations with the West, 1989–1995." In *Lawful Revolution in Hungary,* 1989–1994, edited by Béla Király, 453–74. New York: Columbia University Press, 1995.

———. "Regionális együttmüködés kelet-közép-európában: Befektetés eredmény nélkül?" *Külpolitika,* Summer 1997, 10–41.

Engelberg, Stephen, and Judith Ingram. "Now Hungary Adds Its Voice to the Ethnic Tumult." *New York Times,* January 25, 1993, A3.

European Commission. *Agenda 2000: For a Stronger and Wider Union.* Luxembourg: European Communities, 1997.

———. *The European Councils: Conclusions of the Presidency 1992–1994.* Luxembourg: Commission of the European Communities, 1995.

Farkas, József György. "A kiegészítés nem része a szerzôdésnek." *Népszabadság,* April 4, 1996, 3.

Felkay, Andrew. *Out of Russian Orbit: Hungary Gravitates to the West.* Westport, Conn.: Greenwood, 1997.

Fényi, Tibor. "Ki kell szabadulni a trianon szabta logikából." *Kritika,* August 1994, 38–42.

Finnemore, Martha. "International Organizations as Teachers of Norms: The United Nations Educational, Scientific, and Cultural Organization and Science Policy." *International Organization,* Autumn 1993, 565–98.

———. *National Interests in International Society.* Ithaca, N.Y.: Cornell University Press, 1996.

Finnemore, Martha, and Kathryn Sikkink. "International Norm Dynamics and Political Change." *International Organization,* Autumn 1998, 887–917.

Fischer, András, and Péter Gärtner, eds. *Back to Europe.* Budapest: Pergamon, 1991.

Fisher, Sharon. "Domestic Policies Cause Conflict with the West." *Transition,* July 1996, 56–61.

Fricz, Tamás. *A magyarorszagi pártrendszer 1987–1995: Kialakulástörténet és jellemzôk politológiai elemzés.* Budapest: Cserépfalvi Kiadó, 1996.

Glenny, Misha. *The Rebirth of History: Eastern Europe in the Age of Democracy.* London: Penguin, 1990.

Hankiss, Elemér. "Imponderábiliák: A társadalmi tudat alakulása és a kormány." In *Kormány a mérlegen 1990–1994,* edited by Csaba Gombár, Elemér Hankiss, László Lengyel, and György Várnai, 31–53. Budapest: Korridor, 1994.

Hoensch, Jörg K. *A History of Modern Hungary: 1867–1986.* Translated by Kim Traynor. London: Longman, 1988.

Hopf, Ted. "The Promise of Constructivism in International Relations Theory." *International Security,* Summer 1998, 171–200.

Hudák, Vasil. Introduction to *Building a New Europe: Transfrontier Cooperation in Central Europe,* edited by Vasil Hudák, 1–10. Prague: Institute for East-West Studies, 1996.

Hyde-Price, Adrian. *The International Politics of East Central Europe.* Manchester, U.K.: Manchester University Press, 1996.

Ionescu, Dan, and Alfred A. Reisch. "Still No Breakthrough in Romanian-Hungarian Relations." *RFE/RFL Research Report,* October 1993, 26–32.

Jeszenszky, Géza. "Hungary's Bilateral Treaties with the Neighbors and the Issue of Minorities." Paper presented at the Bilateral Treaties between the Ex-Warsaw Pact States, Sarasota, Florida, April 3, 1997.

———. "Viták a magyar-román szerzôdés körül." In *Magyarország politikai évkönyve 1996-ról,* edited by Sándor Kurtán, Péter Sándor, and László Vass, 220–27. Budapest: Demokrácia Kutatások Magyar Központja Alapítvány, 1997.

Kasza, László. *Metamorphosis hungariae 1989–1994: Kasza László interjúi*. Budapest: Századvég, 1994.

Katzenstein, Peter J. "Introduction: Alternative Perspectives on National Security." In *The Culture of National Security: Norms and Identity in World Politics*, edited by Peter J. Katzenstein, 33–75. New York: Columbia University Press, 1996.

Katzenstein, Peter J., ed. *The Culture of National Security: Norms and Identity in World Politics*. New York: Columbia University Press, 1996.

Kende, Péter. "The Trianon Syndrome: Hungarians and Their Neighbors." In *Lawful Revolution in Hungary, 1989–1994*, edited by Béla Király, 475–92. New York: Columbia University Press, 1995.

Keohane, Robert O. *International Institutions and State Power: Essays in International Relations Theory*. Boulder, Colo.: Westview, 1989.

Keohane, Robert O., Joseph S. Nye, and Stanley Hoffmann, eds. *After the Cold War: International Institutions and State Strategies, 1989–1991*. Cambridge, Mass.: Harvard University Press, 1993.

Kiss, László J. "Hungary." In *Political and Economic Transformation in East Central Europe*, edited by From Hanspeter Neuhold, Peter Havlik, and Arnold Suppan, 229–54. Boulder, Colo.: Westview, 1994.

Kocsis, Károly, and Eszter Kocsis-Hodosi. *Hungarian Minorities in the Carpathian Basin: A Study in Ethnic Geography*. Toronto: Matthias Corvinus, 1995.

Krasner, Stephen D. *Sovereignty: Organized Hypocrisy*. Princeton: Princeton University Press, 1999.

———. "Westphalia and All That." In *Ideas and Foreign Policy: Beliefs, Institutions, and Political Change*, edited by Judith Goldstein and Robert O. Keohane, 235–64. Ithaca, N.Y.: Cornell University Press, 1993.

Lengyel, László. "Kovács: Az alapszerződés eszköz a kezünkben." *Népszabadság*, March 28, 1996, 3.

———. "Külpolitika vagy nemzetpolitika." In *Kormány a mérlegen 1990–1994*, edited by Csaba Gombár, Elemér Hankiss, László Lengyel, and György Várnai, 346–68. Budapest: Korridor, 1994.

Lesko, Marian. "'De-Meciarization' Is Feasible." *Transitions* 1998. <www.ijt.cz/transitions/dec98/opindeme.html> (February 16, 1999).

"Leszák: Harmadik Trianon." *Magyar nemzet*, May 31, 1996, 5.

Linden, Ronald H. "Putting on Their Sunday Best: Romania, Hungary, and the Puzzle of Peace." *International Studies Quarterly*, March 2000, 121–45.

Linz, Juan J., and Alfred Stepan. *Problems of Democratic Transition and Consolidation: Southern Europe, South America, and Post-Communist Europe*. Baltimore: Johns Hopkins University Press, 1996.

Lippert, Barbara. "Relations with Central and Eastern European Countries: The Anchor Role of the European Union." In *Prospective Europeans: New Members for the European Union*, edited by John Redmond, 197–217. New York: Harvester Wheatsheaf, 1994.

"A magyar-szlovak alapszerződés parlamenti vitájának jegyzőkönyve." *Külpolitika*, Spring 1995, 95–126.

Markó, Béla. "Romania's Hungarians Face a Catch-22 Situation." *Transitions*. 1998. <www.ijt.cz/transitions/dec98/opinroma.html> (February 16, 1999).

McCormick, John. *Understanding the European Union*. The European Union Series. New York: St. Martin's, 1999.

McNeil, Donald G. "Trying to Heal Old Hatred in Ruins on Danube." *New York Times,* November 6, 1999, A1, A5.

Mediansky, Fedor. "National Minorities and Security in Central Europe: The Hungarian Experience." In *Nationalism and Post-Communism,* edited by Aleksandar Pavkovic, Halyna Koscharsky, and Adam Csornota, 101–20. Aldershot, U.K.: Dartmouth, 1995.

Meiszter, Dávid, and Pál Dunay. "Sikerek és kudarcok között: Magyar külpolitika 1990–1994." *Társadalmi szemle,* August–September 1994, 35–52.

Molnár, Gustav. "Magyarország és szomszédai." *Magyar szemle,* Summer 1994, 115–25.

Nelson, Daniel N. "Hungary and Its Neighbors: Security and Ethnic Minorities." *Nationalities Papers,* Summer 1998, 313–30.

Nieuwsma, Greg. "Lessons in Democracy: Slovakia, Its Minorities and the European Union." *Central Europe Review,* November 8, 1999, 1–2.

Oltay, Edith. "Minorities as Stumbling Block in Relations with Neighbors." *RFE/RL Research Report,* July 1992, 26–33.

Pietsch, Lajos. "Az atlanticizmus mindenekelôtt értékkategória: Martonyi János az új kezdeményezésrôl és integrációs esélyeinkrôl." *Magyar nemzet,* May 16, 1996, 9.

Póti, László. "A cseh köztársaság és magyarország külpolitikai irányváltásai." *Külpolitika,* Spring 1996, 75–82.

Póti, László, and Pál Dunay. "Relations with the Former Socialist Countries, 1989–1995." In *Lawful Revolution in Hungary, 1989–1994,* edited by Béla Király, 413–51. New York: Columbia University Press, 1995.

Reisch, Alfred A. "Hungarian Foreign Policy and the Magyar Minorities: New Foreign Policy Priorities." *Nationalities Papers,* Autumn 1996, 447–65.

———. "Consensus on Hungary's Foreign Policy Frayed by Elections." *RFE/RL Research Report,* June 1994, 42–48.

Romsics, Ignác. "Nemzeti traumánk: Trianon." *Magyar tudomány,* Autumn 1996, 272–81.

Rothschild, Joseph. *Return to Diversity: A Political History of East Central Europe since World War II.* New York: Oxford University Press, 1989.

Schöpflin, George. "Inter-Ethnic Relations in Transylvania." *Transylvania English Language Supplement* 38, no. 3 (1997): 2–4.

Schwartz, Herman. "Defending the Defenders of Democracy." *Transitions,* January 1997, 80–85.

Shafir, Michael. "A Possible Light at the End of the Tunnel." *Transitions,* July 1996, 29–32.

Snyder, Tim, and Milada Vachudová. "Are Transitions Transitory? Two Types of Political Change in Eastern Europe since 1989." *East European Politics and Societies,* Winter 1997, 1–35.

Synovitz, Ron. "Central Europe: Leaders Re-launch Visegrad Initiative." *RFE/RL.* 1999. <euro.rferl.org/nca/features/1999/05/F.RU.990517140909.html> (May 31, 1999).

Szabó, Ferenc A. "Diplomácia, óh!: A független magyar külpolitika elsô négy évérôl." *Társadalmi szemle,* January 1995, 57–62.

Szilágyi, Zsofia. "Hungarian Minority Summit Causes Uproar in the Region." *Transitions,* July 1996, 45–49.

Szoltész, István, ed. *Országgyûlési Kézikönyv.* Budapest: Center for Parliamentary Management, 1992.

Szomolányi, Sona. "Why Slovakia's Transition Trajectory Has Been So Difficult." *Budapest Papers on Democratic Transition* 257 (1999): 1–18.

Van den Broek, Hans. *On the Road to Enlargement.* Brussels: Commission of the European Communities, 1997.

Wendt, Alexander. "Collective Identity Formation and the International State." *American Political Science Review,* June 1994, 384–96.

———. "Identity and Structural Change in International Politics." In *The Return of Culture and Identity in IR Theory,* edited by Yosef Lapid and Friedrich Kratochwil, 47–64. Boulder, Colo.: Lynn Rienner, 1996.

———. *Social Theory of International Politics.* Cambridge: Cambridge University Press, 1999.

Whitehead, Laurence. "International Aspects of Democratization." In *Transitions from Authoritarian Rule: Comparative Perspectives,* edited by Guillermo O'Donnell, Philippe C. Schmitter, and Laurence Whitehead, 3–46. Baltimore: Johns Hopkins University Press, 1986.

10

Harmonizing Laws with the European Union: The Case of Intellectual Property Rights in the Czech Republic

Melanie H. Ram

Although the Czech nation "has only recently regained its full national sovereignty," it has nonetheless "arrived at the conclusion that within the context of modern European developments the exchange of a part of its national sovereignty for a shared supranational sovereignty and co-responsibility is an inevitable step to be taken for the benefit of its own country and the whole of Europe."[1] So states the memorandum that the Czech Republic submitted with its application for accession to the European Union (EU) in 1996. Despite the costs and tremendous administrative tasks involved, EU membership has been the main foreign policy objective of all Czech governments since 1989. A unique confluence of domestic and foreign policies has thereby developed in the Czech Republic and the other EU associated states in Central and Eastern Europe (CEE) and the former Soviet Union (FSU).[2] As Czech prime minister Miloš Zeman (then parliament chairman) stated, "We shall not conceive our entry to the EU only as a foreign policy matter, but also as a domestic affair, because the impact of European norms on the Czech law is basically a matter of domestic policy."[3] This chapter suggests that the norms on which post-1989 governments and societies were built and shaped in the Czech Republic and other associated countries came primarily from the membership requirements of the European Union, especially the harmonization of laws requirement. While it is sometimes difficult to determine if these countries might have developed similar policies without a direct external influence or incentive, I argue that the EU has been the main source, guide, catalyst, and support for the particular reforms that have been chosen. This analysis supports the growing literature demonstrating how international organizations are "principals" rather than mere "agents" in international politics.[4]

Joining the EU requires not only the fulfillment of numerous tough economic criteria but also the approximation or harmonization of domestic legislation with EU law. In order to join the internal market alone, candidate
states must transform over forty thousand administrative acts into national
law in a wide variety of fields, including competition, social policies, product standards, agriculture, telecommunications, energy, the environment,
civil law, company law, consumer protection, and intellectual property.[5]
Prior to accession, a candidate state must also adopt the entire *acquis communautaire,* which currently constitutes over eighty thousand pages of primary and secondary binding legislation. All of the associated candidate states
in CEE and the FSU accepted this requirement, linking their domestic policies and policy-making processes to the EU long before they had any say in
the establishment of EU legislation or even an assurance of gaining EU membership. The accession process in essence requires the wholesale adoption
of Western norms of political and economic behavior and even commits candidate states to adhere to future EU law, whatever it may be. This chapter
considers if and how norms transmitted by international organizations, particularly the EU, have influenced domestic laws, views, and practices in the
Czech Republic.[6] While most scholars consider legal reform to be a domestic issue, Anne-Marie Burley and others have shown how supranational EU
law and EU legal institutions have influenced or determined the national
laws of member states.[7] There has been little research, however, on how the
EU has influenced the domestic policies and fundamental legislation of potential future members in CEE.

In the harmonization of laws process, intellectual property protection is
cited in the Europe Agreements as an area of "particular concern" to the EU
and is included in the White Paper of essential legislation for the candidate
states.[8] Associated countries must have a similar level of intellectual property protection (covering mainly copyrights, patents, and trademarks) prior
to gaining membership. Thus, using intellectual property rights as a case
study, I will assess the factors involved in the choice, speed of adoption,
and implementation of laws and institutions in the Czech Republic after
1989. Given the Czech Republic's comparatively advanced starting position
among the CEE countries and its selection as one of the first countries to
start EU accession negotiations, a detailed examination of the process of European integration and legislative harmonization from the first expression
of interest in EU membership to the start of negotiations in 1998 is possible
in this case. In addition, one can begin to evaluate the EU's long-term effects on society, if any. As the Czech Republic has had some history of intellectual property protection, it is also possible to see the impact of both
past and current factors.

Most Czechs view joining Euro-Atlantic institutions, and especially the European Union, as restoring the country to its rightful place in a democratic,

prosperous Europe, a position it might have retained had it not been for the West's "betrayal" in 1938 at Munich and the subsequent communist takeover in 1948. As the draft policy statement of the 1996 coalition government explained, "We are taking as a point of departure the conviction that the Czech Republic belongs to the Euro-Atlantic civilization space, historically, politically, culturally, and economically, and that it is connected with this space by the common values that we want not only to share but to develop, protect, and defend."[9] Accepting the "Western" norms underlying market democracies was therefore a given, but adopting and implementing the necessary legislation was more problematic.

Not surprisingly, the Czech government and population were not eager to cede considerable control over domestic policy making to a supranational institution of which the country was not yet a member. While Prime Minister Václav Klaus considered joining the EU to be necessary, he noted in parliament in 1996 that "it will be a curtailment of sovereignty. . . . Every citizen will gain something and lose something by the country's admission into the EU."[10] Others have expressed a similarly mixed view of EU membership. As one Czech professor indicated, for example, "membership in the EU is not ideal for us, for economic reasons, so we shouldn't join the EU for a long time. But we must be members . . . there is no other solution. We must join either the East or the West, and the West is better, though not ideal."[11]

Although most of the Czech population does not oppose EU membership, only 43 percent of people polled in 1996 were sure they would vote in favor of joining the EU, 23 percent were undecided, and 11 percent against.[12] Moreover, the number of people holding positive image of the EU among the Czech public has decreased since the revolution. While in 1990, 49 percent of the public viewed the aims and activities of the EU as positive, since 1993 most views have been neutral; a 1995 poll taken just months before the Czech Republic submitted its official application for EU membership indicated that only 26 percent of Czech citizens held a positive image of the EU.[13] In 1997, after the European Commission recommended the Czech Republic as one of the five candidate CEE/FSU countries with which to start negotiations, 34 percent of respondents to an EU poll expressed a positive image of the EU, 38 percent a neutral image, and 7 percent a negative one.[14]

Despite a largely ambivalent population, almost all Czech politicians and political parties have been committed to the goal of EU membership since the revolution. When decision-makers and opinion-formers in the Czech Republic were polled about their views on the EU at the end of 1997, a full 73 percent of them expressed a positive image of the EU, 19 percent were neutral, and only 1 percent negative.[15] As Jiří Payne, a member of the Czech parliament's Foreign Affairs Committee, noted, "it would be good if we were a member already and if we already had an impact on various decisions so we could steer the train and not just run after it."[16] Once membership is attained, Czech officials hope their country will play an important role in developing EU policies; until then, they realize they must accept the EU as it is when they join, even if this requires making considerable and sometimes unpopular changes in domestic policy and giving up some sovereignty. As Czech Civic Democratic Party (ODS) deputy Michal Frankl explained, "we must enter first, and then try to push it this way or that way after—that's the only option for us."[17]

Negotiations began on an association or Europe Agreement between the Czech and Slovak Federal Republic (CSFR) and the European Union in December 1990, only one year after the revolution. The Europe Agreement was ultimately signed the following December along with an interim agreement that entered into force on March 1, 1992. Due to the dissolution of the CSFR at the end of 1992, two agreements similar to the original were renegotiated separately with the Czech Republic and Slovakia, and the new Europe Agreement with the Czech Republic was signed on October 4, 1993. It was quickly ratified by the European Parliament the same month and by the Czech parliament in December of that year, entering into force on February 1, 1995.

The importance of harmonizing Czech legislation with EU law was emphasized in the Europe Agreement:

> The Contracting parties recognize that the major precondition for the Czech Republic's economic integration into the Community is the approximation of the Czech Republic's existing and future legislation to that of the Community. The Czech Republic shall endeavour to ensure that its legislation will be gradually made compatible with that of the Community.[18]

Little more than a year after the first free CSFR parliamentary elections in June 1990, and following the start of negotiations on the Association Agreement with the European Community, the Czech government adopted Resolution 396/91, "Ensurance of the Compatibility of Czechoslovak Legislation with the Laws of the European Community."[19] This was meant to ensure that all future Czech legislation (and all old laws under review) would be compatible with European Union law. With the adoption of this resolution, all Czech laws were required to contain a "compatibility clause," citing the relevant EU legislation and the degree of compatibility with EU law. If a new law is not completely compatible, the clause must explain why not, what is being done to make it compatible, and by what date full compatibility would be achieved. When the opposition Social Democrats (ČSSD) were elected to power in 1998, one of their top five priorities was "to quicken the adaptation of the Czech legislation to EU norms."[20]

The harmonization of laws process and the EU membership incentive has had a broad impact on the domestic reform process in the Czech Republic.

As Czech foreign minister Jan Kavan suggested, it has "indirectly" promoted democratization:

> When thinking about legislation, legislators have to bear in mind that they have to conform to the EU. . . . Their behavior, not just the law, is affected by the need to be perceived as a democratic country. If you want to be perceived as a democratic country, both by the EU and by NATO, then in a way it forces you to behave in a democratic manner, at least outwardly.[21]

Members of parliament and political parties also use EU requirements to support their political positions in parliament debates. Although some prominent Czech politicians have argued that the solution to problems in CEE countries "cannot be imported from outside,"[22] many of them believe that the EU has helped guarantee democracy in the Czech Republic, set the agenda for the issues to be addressed, accelerated the transition process, influenced decision-making processes in parliament, and closely guided legislative reform.[23]

HARMONIZATION OF INTELLECTUAL PROPERTY RIGHTS

An integral element of both a market economy and a democracy, intellectual property protection encourages innovation, creativity, freedom of speech, knowledge sharing, and investment in research and development. As the European Commission's White Paper guiding the legislative reform of associated CEE countries emphasizes, "it is vital to the construction of a modern society and to the emergence of innovative and high-quality goods and services."[24] Copyrights provide authors with rights to their original literary, dramatic, musical, and artistic works, including books, movies, compact discs, and computer software. A patent grants exclusive property rights to an inventor for an invention or process, thereby preventing others from making and selling the product or method. A trademark, which consists of a word, phrase, symbol, or design identifying the source of goods and distinguishing them from other goods, protects the value inherent in the name of a company or its products and prevents its use by potential competitors.

Intellectual property laws were integral to the economic development of the West. As Douglass North has shown, the major inventions in Europe came only after a patent system was developed to protect inventors' intellectual property.[25] Even the framers of the U.S. Constitution gave Congress the power "to promote the Progress of Science and useful Arts, by securing for limited Times to Authors and Inventors the exclusive Right to their respective Writings and Discoveries" (article 1, section 8). Thus the protection of intellectual property is essential to developing and transition economies as well as highly industrialized countries. Improving intellectual property rights would not only encourage greater foreign investment but also drive domestic innovation, foster artistic and creative efforts, and increase the availability of new goods, services, and technologies.

Yet some developing countries see piracy or lax protection of foreign intellectual property as "a legitimate means of transferring wealth and learning from the industrialized world, creating jobs and lowering the cost of developing technology."[26] Copyright, trademark, and patent infringement abroad has meant billions of dollars of lost income to holders of these rights in the United States alone. The Motion Picture Association of America, for example, claims American motion picture companies lose $2.5 billion a year in revenue due to video piracy (illegal copying and sale or distribution) worldwide.[27] According to a new report, U.S. industries lose $12.4 billion a year due to such copyright violations.[28] The research-based pharmaceutical industry similarly depends on patent protection for its work. As the International Federation of Pharmaceutical Manufacturers Associations notes, "Quite simply, without patent protection, the industry would not exist." The development and approval of a single new medicine may cost from $360 to $500 million; if these technologies can be easily copied and then sold more cheaply by others, there would be no incentive for research and development of such products.[29] Trademarks are equally valuable. In an ongoing trademark dispute, for example, the American brewer Anheuser-Busch and the Czech brewery Budejovicky Budvar have been negotiating for over a decade for exclusive rights to use the "Budweiser" name on their products around the world.[30]

External pressure on developing countries to reform their intellectual property laws to provide the necessary protection has been found to be largely ineffective. According to Susan Sell, this is due to a lack of change in value orientation and the absence of a politically influential domestic constituency that supports such laws. In many developing countries, domestic legislation has been revised in response to outside pressure, but views and practices remain unchanged.[31] As a patent consultant in China explains, "The main problem is . . . people don't think of intellectual property as property like other property."[32] Intellectual property protection in CEE requires changes in thinking as well as in law. Under the communist regimes in CEE, all inventions were considered state property and intellectual property had little significance to individuals. In the transition from closed to market economies, the adoption and implementation of EU-compatible intellectual property laws would increase the cost of goods for government, industry, and individuals. In addition, intellectual property protection would require judges and police to utilize scarce time and resources to prosecute nonviolent crimes with which they have had little if any experience. Thus, while protecting intellectual property would have some benefits, it would be an unlikely priority of reform efforts in transition countries. Reviewing the restoration of intellectual property rights to the Czech Republic after 1989 will indicate whether the EU has been successful (through its membership requirements and the incentive of membership) in transmitting its norms to candidate states.

An analysis of intellectual property rights allows for the examination of EU influence on laws outside the strictly economic sphere, yet with economic consequences. Moreover, the protection of intellectual property is measurable and the EU established short deadlines in this field for the fulfillment of specific requirements. Assessing the protection of intellectual property rights (in law and practice) has a number of advantages for evaluating the reform processes overall. First, it provides evidence of improvement in individual rights, as it transfers what had previously been state or collective rights to individuals. Second, such protection demonstrates improvement in fair economic competition, as domestic industries are no longer allowed to profit from the unfair use of "borrowed" intellectual property. Similarly, it may indicate the development of domestic industry as industries begin to profit from exploitation of their own new intellectual property rights. Third, because of the difficulty of enforcement, improvement in the knowledge and implementation of EU-oriented intellectual property laws (on the part of the public, lawyers, judges, police, and others) demonstrates a deeper effect of EU norms on reform beyond changes in the law and beyond the government elite. Finally, since it is an issue of comparatively low priority for both judges and police, the prosecution of intellectual property violations is a strong indication of progress and development of the judicial and law enforcement systems. Given the similar requirements for all Europe Agreement countries, conclusions may be broadly applicable to other CEEs undergoing transition.

The main EU requirements for CEE countries in the field of intellectual property were listed in the 1995 White Paper on preparation of the associated countries of Central and Eastern Europe for integration into the internal market of the Union. The stage 1 (priority) measures concern the alignment of CEE laws with certain established community rules and are described as especially important because they may affect the free movement of goods. For copyright and related rights, these are Directive 91/250/EEC (1991) on the legal protection of computer software; Directive 92/100/EC (1992) on rental and lending rights regarding copyrights; and Directive 93/98/EEC (1993) harmonizing the term of protection of copyright and certain neighboring rights. In the industrial property field (which includes patents, utility models, industrial designs, topographies of semiconductor products, trademarks, and appellations of origin of products), stage 1 measures required by the EU are Directive 89/104/EEC (1988) approximating trademark laws of member states, with the objective of "the protection of trade marks, the free movement of branded articles, and the protection of consumers who acquire branded articles" and Directive 87/54/EEC (1986) on the legal protection of topographies of semiconductor products, in order to protect information technology.[33]

Stage 2 measures include directives and regulations extending previously adopted Community measures or responding to new legal and economic developments affecting intellectual property. The stage 2 copyright directives are Directive 93/83/EEC on the coordination of certain rules on copyright and related rights applicable to satellite broadcasting and cable retransmission and a proposal for a directive on the legal protection of databases.[34] There is also a "particularly important" Council Regulation (EC) no. 3295/94 (1994) laying down measures to combat piracy and the circulation of counterfeit goods. Stage 2 measures concerning industrial property are Council Regulation (EEC) no. 1768/92 (1992) on the creation of a supplementary protection certificate for medicinal products; a proposal for a Parliament and Council regulation regarding creation of a supplementary protection certificate for plant protection products (COM(94)579); and a proposal for a Parliament and Council directive on the legal protection of designs (COM(93)344).[35]

All of the Europe Agreement countries are members of the World Trade Organization (WTO) and signed the recently negotiated Agreement on Trade-Related Aspects of Intellectual Property Rights (TRIPS). The TRIPS agreement was intended to bring intellectual property rights in all member states under common rules and to enable trade disputes regarding intellectual property rights to be resolved through the WTO dispute resolution system. Czechoslovakia was a founding member of GATT, and the Czech Republic joined the WTO when it was founded (superseding GATT) in January 1995. Yet, as the White Paper notes, "the single market often calls for closer and more structured harmonization of national legislation than do the international conventions." Although adherence to multilateral agreements may be necessary for EU membership, it is not sufficient.[36]

The Europe Agreement with the Czech Republic required equivalent protection of intellectual property as a condition of accession to the EU and establishes a deadline of five years after entry into force of the agreement:

> The Czech Republic shall continue to improve the protection of intellectual, industrial and commercial property rights in order to provide, by the end of the fifth year after the entry into force of this Agreement, a level of protection similar to that existing in the Community, including comparable means of enforcing such rights.[37]

The Europe Agreement further required the Czech Republic to apply for membership in the European Patent Convention on the granting of European patents (Munich Convention of 1973) by the end of 1996.[38] It also stated that the Czech Republic must join the other multilateral conventions on intellectual, industrial, and commercial property rights to which EU member states are parties.[39]

CZECH COPYRIGHT LAW

Copyright protection in the Czech Republic today benefits from its roots in the country's early history. When Czechoslovakia became an independent state in 1918, the Czech lands preserved the Austrian legal system, including its 1895 authorship law, which obligated the protection of authors' rights. As stipulated by the 1919 Peace Treaty of Saint Germain, Czechoslovakia joined the Berne Convention in 1921.[40] Even at this time, however, copyright protection was not easily enforced and for most of the country's history authors' rights have been severely limited.

Czechoslovakia's first independent copyright protection society, the Society for the Protection of Authors (OSA), was founded in 1919 to protect authors' rights for musical and theatrical performances (so-called small music rights). But the concept of such intellectual property was still new and café operators and other entertainment venues thought it ridiculous to pay composers and writers for use of their music. Not only were OSA efforts to collect royalties futile, but suits were also filed against OSA representatives for attempting to carry out their work. Until 1922, the government even forbade its officials from giving OSA any information on musical performances. By 1925, however, the government's stance changed and OSA participated in drafting the nation's first copyright law (Act no. 218 of 1926). The following year, OSA became a founding member of CISAC (Confédération Internationale des Sociétés d'Auteurs et Compositeurs [International Confederation of Societies of Authors, and Composers]), the international confederation of societies protecting creative rights.[41] While this copyright protection society survived in some form through almost the whole existence of Czechoslovakia and the Czech Republic, in practice it was only free to carry out its work until 1939 and then briefly from 1945 to 1948 following World War II and the German occupation. From 1948 to 1989, the organization's work was subject to the interests of the communist regime and from 1962 until 1992 it was directly under the control of the Ministry of Culture.[42] Thus independent copyright protection did not exist for most of Czech history.

Despite limits imposed on copyright protection in the communist years, history gives the Czech Republic some advantage in implementing copyright legislation. Whereas countries such as Ukraine, Romania, Albania, Estonia, and Latvia had to start from scratch in designing their copyright law, at least in the Czech Republic (as in Slovakia, Poland, and Hungary), copyright previously existed, functioned reasonably well for a decade or so, and had a partial formal existence under communism. Businesspeople subject to copyright fees know what a copyright is and realize they are supposed to pay for it. "We have the advantage of history, because we know it was here—we are only delayed," explained Josef Slanina, CEO and president of OSA.[43] Yet such historical experience is in some ways a liability in legal reform. Until 2000, the amended 1965 Copyright Act of Czechoslovakia remained in force in the Czech Republic. While other CEE countries (including Poland, Slovenia, Romania, Bulgaria, and some of the Baltic states) prepared completely new and modern copyright laws based on Western models, the Czech government chose instead to adopt incremental modifications to its existing legislation.[44] New amendments were adopted almost annually—in 1990, 1991, 1993, 1995, and 1996.

International Influence on Legislative Reform

The Czech government modified and eventually replaced the country's copyright law for several reasons. Some requirements stemmed from membership in the WTO and the TRIPS agreement. In addition, the Czech Republic had to adhere to certain agreements administered by the World Intellectual Property Organization (WIPO) that define international standards of copyright protection. These agreements, which the Czech Republic became a party to in January 1993, are the Berne Convention for the Protection of Literary and Artistic Works and the Rome Convention for the Protection of Performers, Producers of Phonograms, and Broadcasting Organizations. Signing these conventions was required under the Czech Republic's Europe Agreement. A 1990 agreement with the United States on mutual protection of investment created further legal obligations in this field. Moreover, as the chief of the Czech government's audiovisual and copyright department stated, changes had to be made to copyright legislation in establishing a market economy.[45] Despite various international sources and requirements for copyright protection, individuals in both the public and private sector suggest that the EU was the driving force behind reforms in Czech copyright law. As in other fields, the EU served as a guide to specific legislative changes, an essential source of information and funding, a catalyst and an incentive for undertaking reforms, and a tool to elicit adoption of and compliance with the law.

The EU first of all played a critical role in the reform of Czech law by providing the legislation required for membership and closely advising Czech officials on the compatibility of Czech law. EC directives and the EU 1995 White Paper were the primary models for the reform of Czech legislation and guided priorities in this field.[46] The Czech Ministry of Culture prepared the 1996 amendment with a commission of lawyers, academics, and copyright protection societies in response to two EC directives that were listed in the White Paper as priority requirements.[47] In addition, the government consulted the copyright legislation of EU member states (mainly France and Germany) and some other countries as models. The Slovenian copyright law, for example, was reviewed because of a recommendation by representatives of the EU PHARE program.[48] Czech government officials involved in revising the legislation in 1996 indicated that the main purpose of the amendment was to "put the law of the Czech Republic in harmony with the legal prescriptions of the European Community" as promised under the Europe Agreement.[49]

Officials also worked closely with representatives from the EU and CISAC, the international intellectual property organization responsible for implementing the PHARE copyright program. Moreover, the Czech government submitted its copyright legislation to EU advisers for evaluation. Following the adoption of the 1996 amendment, for example, the government asked the Czech Consortium for the Approximation of Legislation (which is funded by the EU PHARE program) to evaluate the Copyright Act. The international lawyers reviewing the legislation produced a detailed report assessing the compatibility of Czech law with EU copyright directives article by article and criticizing various provisions in the law for being either too general or too unclear. A discussion of this review was on the agenda of the Czech-EU Association Committee meeting in September 1996.

The EU also played an important role in accelerating copyright protection in the Czech Republic by providing access to essential information, organizing conferences, and providing economic and technical assistance, primarily through the PHARE program. The copyright society OSA, for example, received useful books and magazines on copyright issues and had access to conferences and advice through PHARE, which were all very helpful to carrying out its work. While some of this support would have been more useful earlier on (most was not available before 1993), it was nonetheless invaluable. Moreover, Czech copyright societies are in constant contact with PHARE and the copyright societies of EU member states for information on how new copyright concerns that arise in the Czech Republic have been resolved in Western Europe. OSA president Josef Slanina explained that his organization contacts PHARE and four or five copyright societies in EU member states for advice and model contracts for every new concern. The contracts he receives also serve as a primary information source for negotiating copyright fees.[50] An intellectual property program established by the EU (covering copyright and related rights) has also kept CEE government officials continually apprised of pending Community legislation and proposals on copyright issues.[51]

The EU was further influential as a justification for adopting new legislation in Parliament and as a tool for enforcing it. According to the Ministry of Culture, there was some opposition to the adoption of certain amendments to the Copyright Act (mainly by cable television operators and video and

CD renters). But the government was able to argue in parliament that "we have some obligation to the EU" to accept the proposed changes.[52] For example, in presenting the 1995 bill to amend the Copyright Act, the minister of culture explained that the amendment "is necessary on the one hand for technological development . . . and on the other hand for the endeavor of harmonization with the legal statutes of the European Union." He went on to explain that under the Association Agreement, the Czech Republic is obliged to harmonize its legal regulations with the laws of the EU. He noted that the amendment was also an obligation of a 1990 bilateral treaty with the United States.[53]

Finally, the EU appears to have influenced in some way the Czech Republic's approach to legislative reform. Both because there has been an incentive to show the EU that the country is moving ahead in the reform process and because of continual additions to required EU legislation, the Czech Republic has adopted a piecemeal approach to reform. Retaining its communist-era copyright law, the Czech government has prepared new amendments every year or so on the most pressing issues. This approach is not unique to the reform of copyright laws in the Czech Republic; it has occurred in many other fields as well.[54] While each amendment to the Czech law brought it closer to EU law, until 2000 the law remained only partly harmonized. As the government explains, small amendments were considered preferable to full replacement of the 1965 law, which would have slowed reform. A final version of the law would also depend on the outcome of discussions on copyright issues within the EU and WIPO.[55] Thus the government planned to begin recodifying the Czech law after the diplomatic conference of December 1996 in Geneva (where important treaties on copyright were expected to be concluded) and expected to adopt a new law fully replacing the 1965 Copyright Act by the year 2000.[56]

The Czech government also chose a piecemeal approach because recodification required a considerable amount of time and specialized personnel, neither of which were readily available.[57] Moreover, the government was hesitant to adopt certain principles prior to EU membership that might put the country at a disadvantage. For example, until 2000 Czech copyright protection lasted fifty years after the death of the author, twenty years short of the EU standard. While this provision clearly needed to be changed to conform to EU law, the government voiced the concern that doing so would cause works already in free use to regain protection.

The European Commission's 1997 *Opinion* on the Czech Republic's application for membership noted that for copyright and related rights in the Czech Republic "important gaps have to be filled (for computer programmes, rental and distribution rights and duration of protection of copyrights)."[58] Yet assessments of Czech copyright legislation have improved since this *Opinion* and have overall been positive. Most of the stage 1 and stage 2 EU requirements were met by 1996, except for the duration of copyright protection and some smaller issues.[59] Despite the inefficient approach to reform and the occasional attempt by the Czech government to ignore Western laws and try something that has never been done elsewhere (to purportedly make the Czech law the best of its kind), there is a general consensus that the law has gradually improved with each new amendment, that reforms have been made to increasingly approximate EU law, and that the law would likely be fully compatible around the year 2000.[60] Indeed, in April 2000 the Czech Senate narrowly passed the new Copyright Act, the most significant provision of which was an extension of the copyright protection term to seventy years. According to the minister of culture, who introduced the bill, the new law was one of the most important steps for harmonizing Czech law with EU law.[61] The European Commission's *2000 Regular Report* on the Czech Republic's progress toward accession acknowledges that "the new Copyright Act has been adopted in line with the *acquis*. Also the protection of the rights of performing artists, producers of phonograms and broadcasters have been strengthened. The rights of the audio-visual producers will be newly protected."[62]

Implementation and Impact of the Law

In general, Czech observers of the legal reform process are confident that if a particular stipulation is a requirement for EU membership it will eventually be incorporated into Czech law and at a faster pace than without this outside pressure. While government officials contend that improved copyright protection was necessary in any case for their new market economy, they also suggest that changes would probably have occurred more slowly without EU involvement and the incentive of membership.[63] Besides providing an incentive for reform, the EU has been influential by providing model laws, advising Czech officials on required changes, providing economic and technical assistance, and serving as a catalyst and tool in the legislative reform process. Legislative reform, however, does not necessarily indicate better protection in practice.

Improvements in enforcement of the new copyright legislation have been more gradual than changes in the law, largely because of a severe shortage of staff and resources, low remuneration for most government employees, and insufficient knowledge of EU law and foreign languages among judges and police. The copyright section of the Ministry of Culture, for example, has only three expert staff members managing all of its tasks.[64] Several PHARE programs have attempted to address these issues and the Czech government has continually strengthened its efforts. While it is difficult to demonstrate direct effects of the EU on enforcement of copyright law, there is evidence of improvement in copyright protection, and EU assessments, criticism, technical assistance, and the reform of legislation have certainly facilitated this.

In order to improve enforcement, the government amended the Penal Code in 1994, increasing the maximum penalties for copyright infringements. In addition, amendments to the copyright law in 1996 gave customs officials authority to seize products infringing copyrights, and in 1999 further amendments increased the authority of customs officials. In February 2000, a special Interministerial Commission was established under the Ministry of Industry and Trade to coordinate efforts to reduce copyright violations.[65]

Reform of the judiciary has been slow, especially because there is a considerable backlog of cases, a significant number of vacant posts, a lack of modern equipment, inadequate support staff, a lack of specialized knowledge of EU law on the part of judges (due especially to minimal foreign language skills), and insufficient knowledge of economic crime, corruption, and money laundering issues. While training in international and EU law is mandatory "in principle" for lawyers, the bilateral and multilateral projects that have provided this training have so far only reached approximately 4 percent of judges and 10 percent of state prosecutors. The European Commission states that "the situation should improve as a result of several Phare initiatives during 1999 and 2000."[66]

Copyright societies have noted some improvements over time in the judicial system. The reluctance of users to pay for copyrighted material had required OSA to bring two hundred to four hundred cases to the courts each year regarding payment of copyright fees and other issues. In 1990 and 1991, such cases were not even reviewed, since the courts had many more important cases to tackle. Subsequently the situation slowly improved and by 1996 many court decisions were received. The first execution of a court decision came in 1996, and this positive trend was expected to continue.[67] By the beginning of 2000, there had also been a number of criminal court decisions, although not in the "large" criminal cases.[68] Once citizens start seeing the courts enforce their decisions, the threat of domestic sanctions will provide a deterrent and it will become less necessary to take cases to court.

Piracy has also fallen considerably in the Czech Republic. According to the 1996 *MBI* [Music Business International] *World Report*, "the Czech authorities have continued to fight the pirates, with the effect that the piracy rate is now [in 1994] down to less than 7 percent in volume terms, while the value of pirate output is just US$2.5m." This is a decline of 45 percent from the previous year, and the lowest piracy rates in CEE.[69] As an internal report indicates, the Czech government has continued to pay attention to the piracy problem and is investigating "practical means of achieving more intense and better coordination in the use of existing means to combat the production, import and distribution of pirate recordings."[70] While the Czech Republic is currently on the USTR Special 301 watch list for copyright piracy, it joins fifty-eight other U.S. trading partners on Special 301 lists, including EU member states Italy and Greece, which are on the priority watch list. Although copyright piracy levels in the Czech Republic in 1999 may seem high at 30 percent for video piracy, 8 percent for records and music, and 42 percent for business application software, they pale in comparison to former Soviet countries such as Ukraine, with piracy rates estimated at 99 percent for video, 90 percent for records and music, and 91 percent for business application software. Developing countries on the USTR list tend to be worse than the CEE states (e.g., 35 percent, 95 percent, and 58 percent, respectively, for Brazil; 90 percent, 20 percent, and 85 percent for Indonesia; and 100 percent, 100 percent, and 98 percent for Vietnam). Italy's piracy rates (25 percent, 25 percent, and 44 percent, respectively) may be considered worse than those of the Czech Republic.[71]

Another indication of improvement in the Czech legal environment in the copyright field is the significant increase in the number of licenses and payments for use of copyrighted material, as well as a steady increase in income from abroad from copyright fees.[72] Foreign investment dependent on copyright protection has also increased, especially in film production, and many Czech films have been produced as a result of reforms in the copyright law and with the help of the European foundation Eurimage.[73]

Finally, there is evidence that the mere anticipation of future EU membership has affected Czech business practices regarding copyrights, irrespective of the enforcement of legislation. As the president of OSA attests, future EU membership for the Czech Republic provides him with an argument he uses "every day, several times at least" to convince broadcasters, music producers, organizers of public performances, discotheques, and others to pay copyright fees, and to gradually increase these payments to prepare for the eventual date of EU entry. The argument is very effective, he says, because by the time the Czech Republic becomes a member of the EU, these businesses must be competitive with their European counterparts to avoid bankruptcy. Moreover, broadcasters recall how easy it was for West Germany to close down East German radio stations upon reunification because the East German broadcasters did not respect copyright laws (protection being seven times lower in East Germany than in the West).[74] Thus, when requesting certain fees from broadcasters, Slanina arms himself with data on the percentages that West European broadcasters pay. The prospect of future EU membership has forced Czech businesses to accept the necessity of copyright protection.

Thus, while the Czech judicial system hinders full enforcement of copyright laws in the Czech Republic, the situation has been improving every year. All parties recognize that the EU will require implementation of harmonized laws before membership is possible. As Slanina expressed it, the EU will be certain to determine that it is not just "a beautiful law without practice," as under communism, but that there is a high level of protection as well.[75] The piecemeal approach to legislative reform suggests that the government intends to implement the new changes it adopts, and statistics indicate protection has improved.

CZECH PATENT AND TRADEMARK LAWS

A patent office was established in Czechoslovakia as early as 1919. The oldest trademark on Czech lands—that of Pilsner Beer—was registered in 1859 in accordance with the 1859 Austrian Trade Marks Act.[76] Since 1909, the territory was bound by the Madrid Agreement on the International Registration of Marks, and after independence Czechoslovakia became a member of the Madrid Union in 1919.[77] Czechoslovakia's industrial property protection system developed after World War I but was interrupted by World War II and subsequently by the communist regime since 1948. Only in 1989, says Eva Tesarová of the Czech Industrial Property Office, the "possibility [arose] to rebuild the system of industrial property protection" in the Czech lands.[78] As Czech patent lawyer Zdenka Pradna points out, Czechoslovakia's communist-era industrial property legislation was among the most "sovietized," and therefore "the task of restoring the usual rules similar to those which are valid in the west was quite enormous."[79]

The Czech Industrial Property Office is thus rooted in Czech history, but it has completely new challenges to meet. It is involved primarily with the registration and granting of patents and trademarks, as well as registering and protecting other forms of intellectual property with industrial applications, including utility models and industrial designs, topographies of semiconductor products, and appellations of origin of products. It also develops and protects industrial property rights and the Czech Republic's membership in international industrial property treaties.[80]

International Influence on Legislative Reform

The process of approximating Czech industrial property law with European Union legislation began as early as 1990. According to Svetlana Kopecká of the legal and legislative department of the Czech Industrial Property Office, "We started the process of restoration of the whole system of industrial property protection in 1990 to be compatible or to be in harmony with the law of the European Community."[81] The EU provided a clear incentive to make the legal changes because "it was stated in the Europe Agreement that we must reach the same level of industrial property protection [as EU member states]," Kopecká indicates. The Industrial Property Office notes that protection of industrial property is also an "integral part of trade and business in the Czech Republic" and thus a necessary part of the country's economic reform.[82] While Community law is fairly undeveloped in some areas of industrial property protection, there are a number of international treaties covering various aspects of industrial property rights. In addition to following existing EU directives, the Europe Agreement required candidate states to join many of these treaties. Thus, although the EU incentive served as a catalyst to reform and a certain level of protection was required prior to membership, international treaties and the laws of EU member states were also important as a source or guide for the Czech Republic's new legislation.

The Czech Republic now belongs to most international conventions on intellectual and industrial property rights. In 1991, the country acceded to the Patent Cooperation Treaty, which made it possible to acquire protection of an invention or utility model in several member countries by filing one international application with the Czech Industrial Property Office. For trademarks, the Czech Industrial Property Office can offer protection abroad under the Madrid Agreement and (as of September 25, 1996) the Madrid Protocol of 1989 on the International Registration of Marks. This agreement similarly enables protection in any or all countries party to it through one application that is filed with the International Bureau in Geneva through the country of origin's industrial property office. In addition, the Czech Republic is a member of the Paris Convention for the Protection of Industrial Property, the Nice Agreement Concerning the International Classification of Goods and Services for the Purposes of the Registration of Marks, and the Budapest Treaty on the International Recognition of the Deposit of Microorganisms for the Purpose of Patent Procedure. Being a party to all of the above agreements was an explicit obligation of the Czech Republic's Europe Agreement (article 67, annex 17).

Patent Law

With the Czech Republic's economic transition, a new patent law was immediately necessary, according to Eva Tesarová and Svetlana Kopecká of the Czech Industrial Property Office, because the 1972 patent law was incompatible with the requirements of a market economy.[83] The new law adopted in 1990 gives the patent owner an exclusive right for twenty years to use the invention, to authorize others to use it (through a license agreement), or to assign the patent to others. It also notes that "the provisions of international treaties by which the Czech and Slovak Federal Republic is bound shall not be affected by this Law," thus placing international law above national law (article 76). Industrial designs, which cover the appearance of a new product may also be filed and protected under the patent law.

The Czech Republic's obligations under international treaties were fully respected in the formulation of this law, according to the Industrial Property

Office, as were WIPO conclusions on the harmonization of patent laws. The law also respects the stipulations of the Paris Convention for Protection of Property Rights regarding the international right of priority of the inventor filing an application (articles 27, 48).[84] While there is no EU directive on patent protection, the reform of the Czech legislation was influenced by the European Patent Convention (EPC), which was established by an initiative of the former European Economic Community and is the basis of European patent law.[85] Working toward common goals, the EU continues to influence the EPC, and the European Patent Organization (EPO) has been in charge of implementing the EU Regional Industrial Property Program (RIPP) for the CEE countries since 1993.[86] As the Czech Industrial Property Office explains, "The entire patent law of the Czech Republic is very close[ly] related to [the] European patent system," including the conditions of patentability, the solutions excluded from patentability, the exceptions to patentability, and the time allowance for substantive examination of a patent application.[87]

The head of the legal and legislative department of the Czech Industrial Property Office indicated in 1996 that the Czech patent law was fully harmonized with the EPC.[88] As stipulated by the Europe Agreement, the Czech Republic applied for accession to the EPC in May of that year. In January 1999, the EPO officially invited the Czech Republic to accede to the EPC on July 1, 2000. The Czech patent law was further amended in 2000 to take account of EPC provisions regarding relations between the EU and national patent systems, thus assuring "a smooth accession" to the EPC.[89]

In part due to the stricter conditions of patentability of the new patent law, utility models were a new option offered under Czech law in 1992. Like patents, these "technical solutions" must be beyond skill in the art and susceptible of industrial application, but they require "a lower level of inventiveness" and provide a shorter term of protection of only four years from the filing date. Since the protection is based on registration without a substantive examination, the application process is also cheaper and quicker than for attaining a patent.[90] As there was no EC directive on utility models at the time, the legislation was based on German law.[91] The EU later adopted a Green Paper regarding the protection of utility models in the single market in July 1995, which is based on the same principles as the Czech law.[92]

Trademark Law

The Czech Republic's 1995 trademark law was based on EC Directive 89/104, a White Paper stage 1 measure, which was intended to approximate member state laws on trademarks.[93] In formulating the legislation, the Czech government also considered the Council regulation regarding the European Community trademark and requirements of the TRIPS agreement, the Paris Convention, the 1994 Trademark Law Treaty, and the Madrid Protocol.[94] A trademark is valid in the Czech Republic for ten years but can be continually extended upon application for renewal (article 23). The Czech trademark law explicitly states that a sign must be rejected for trademark registration if its use "would be contrary to the obligations of the Czech Republic under international treaties."[95]

The main reasons the Czech Republic drafted a new trademark law were international, and with the adoption of the 1995 law, the Czech Industrial Property Office considered the country's industrial property laws "fully harmonized" with EU law. The European Commission's *Opinion* on the Czech Republic of July 1997 concluded that "good progress" had been made in the adaptation of industrial property legislation.[96] Changes would be necessary in the future, however, as the EU adopts new regulations and directives with which the Czech Republic must again harmonize its own legislation. For example, the Czech Republic planned to introduce the SPC (supplementary protection certificate) for pharmaceutical products, as well as a law on the new EU regulation concerning the protection of products for plant production.[97] Both were listed in the 1995 White Paper as suggested stage 2 measures but were only at the proposal stage in the EU at that time. These measures were included in new industrial property legislation adopted by the Czech Republic in 2000.

For protecting information technology, the Czech Republic was also required by a bilateral trade agreement with the United States and an EU directive noted in the White Paper to protect topographies of semiconductor products (pertaining to the location and interconnection of circuit elements in an integrated circuit). Legislative specialists at the Industrial Property Office note the EU influence on the creation and content of the 1991 Czech law, including its definition of terms, authorized individuals, content of exclusive rights, and term of protection. They considered the 1991 legislation fully compliant with the 1986 EU directive.[98] Finally, two new Czech laws on industrial design and biotechnological inventions are aligned with EU law and entered into force in October 2000.[99]

In addition to establishing legal obligations and offering models for the reform of some Czech industrial property laws, the EU has provided various types of assistance through the PHARE program that facilitated changes in both law and practice. The Regional Industrial Property Programme (RIPP) was initiated by the EU in 1992 and later implemented by the European Patent Organization, with financing by the EU under the PHARE program. The program provides the CEE countries with legal advice on harmonization of industrial property legislation; training courses and seminars on various industrial property issues for government officials and others who work in this field; language courses in English, German, and French; computer software to facilitate various tasks of the Industrial Property Office; financing for an online connection to commercial industrial property databases; CD-ROM

publications on patents and trademarks granted in the region; exchange programs and international symposia; technical assistance by experts from EPO
and its member states; and publications for use by patent agents as well as
the general public.[100]

The RIPP keeps CEE representatives continually informed of proposals for
Community measures in the field of industrial property. In addition, the patent
library database of the Czech Republic's Industrial Property Office is now
linked to the information centers of the European Patent Office in Vienna and
The Hague, as well as other sources. This provides information on the most recent legal and technical developments in the field of industrial property.[101]
While there was no opposition to the adoption of the new industrial property
laws in the Czech Republic, according to the Czech Industrial Property Office,
EU technical assistance accelerated the process of reform. Training and language courses for employees and the exchange of information were invaluable for learning about the laws in force in the EU.[102]

Implementation and Impact of the Law

The European Commission's 1997 *Opinion* acknowledged that "considerable efforts have been made to ensure an appropriate enforcement for industrial property."[103] The *2000 Regular Report* takes note of a cooperation
agreement among the Czech Trade Inspection, police, Ministry of Finance
(customs and Industrial Property Office), and Ministry of Culture to fight
against patent and trademark infringement and other violations. It also notes
that the staff of 266 in the Industrial Property Office appears to be sufficient
to carry out its tasks.[104]

Foreigners have benefited most from the changes in the Czech Republic's
patent law. Since 1990, when the new patent law was adopted, domestic
patent applications dramatically decreased in the Czech Republic, down
from 4,874 to only 627 applications in 1995. On the other hand, the number
of applications filed by foreigners during this period increased by 32 percent,
greatly surpassing the domestic number in 1995 to a total of 2,892.[105] In addition, 18,104 Patent Cooperation Treaty designations were accepted, up
from only 1,618 in 1991, the first year the treaty was in force.[106] Foreign
patent applications increased by 37 percent from 1989 to 1990 alone, and the
differences are even more dramatic in light of the number of applications
from Western countries, especially those recognized as leading patent applicants worldwide. For example, the number of applications from the United
States and Japan more than doubled from 1989 to 1990, and those from Western Germany almost tripled, up from 178 in 1989 to 471 in 1990, constituting
almost one-quarter of all foreign applications in that year. Czechs fared
slightly better on the number of industrial design applications, up 16 percent
from 1989 to 1990, while foreign applications increased 105 percent at the

same time. From 1990 to 1995, domestic industrial design applications fell 89 percent and foreign applications rose 137 percent.[107]

Domestic patent applications have probably decreased because of the much stricter requirements than in the previous law, and because of the new option of attaining a utility model registration instead of a patent, which is quicker, cheaper, and easier.[108] Czech citizens have increasingly registered inventions at the office through this method. In 1995, there were 1,474 utility model applications in the Czech Republic, most of which (92 percent) were filed by Czechs.[109] The increase in foreign patent and design applications has nonetheless benefited the Czech Republic through larger fees collected by the Industrial Property Office, an increased chance of helpful technology transfer, and the greater likelihood of more domestic and foreign investment with the assurance of secure patent protection.

The trademark law has clearly encouraged domestic as well as foreign applications. The number of trademark applications filed in the Czech Republic has risen steadily since 1989, from only 662 applications in that year, to over 8,000 by 1992. Benefiting especially from the growth of the market economy and increased privatization, in 1995 there were 8,116 trademark applications from Czech citizens, 2,360 from foreigners, and an additional 7,078 through the Madrid Convention. The Czech number in this case rose 489 percent from 1990, while the domestic applications from foreigners rose a more modest 52 percent.[110]

CONCLUSION

In summary, the European Union has been closely involved in the reform of Czech intellectual property rights. It has played an important role in the design of new legislation and the speed, process, and priorities of reform in this field; it has been an integral source of funding and information; and it has provided an incentive for reform of both law and business practices. While a full transition to a market economy would have eventually required changes to be made in these laws, the EU served as a guide to the best way of making such changes and accelerated the process.

Regarding the copyright law, several amendments were made at a steady pace, with the White Paper and EC directives as the main guide to the priorities and details of legislative reform. Government officials also used the EU obligation as an argument in Parliament for adopting the amendments. The chief of the Czech Republic's audiovisual and copyright department in the Ministry of Culture summarizes that "the European Union helped us to make changes and the directives of the European Union showed the best way to do it."[111] The EU helped promote the reform of the copyright law with economic and material assistance as well as information. Although there have been some other external influences on the legislative reform process, it is generally agreed that the EU has been the most important one. The law has moved closer to fulfilling all EU requirements with each new amendment and the new Copyright Act was adopted in 2000. Enforcement in the courts is still poor but has improved year by year, and piracy rates have been greatly reduced and remain a focus of government attention. Both the government and outside observers believe copyright protection in the Czech Republic has significantly improved since 1989. Foreign copyright payments have also increased significantly following changes in the law, indicating increased legal use of Czech copyrighted material abroad.

In the field of industrial property (patents and trademarks), the Czech Republic became (or already was) a member of all the industrial property agreements it was required to join as a condition of EU membership, including the Patent Cooperation Treaty and the Madrid Agreement on the International Registration of Marks. According to government officials involved in the process, reform of Czech industrial property law was undertaken in order to harmonize Czech law with EU law and White Paper legislation in the areas it existed, as required by the Europe Agreement. European models, European Patent Organization advice, and international treaty requirements were followed in areas without EC directives. As one Czech lawyer notes, the Czech Industrial Property Office and the people with whom it worked "were able to remove in a comparatively short time the sins of the past and prepare new Acts compatible with European standards."[112]

Several new modern industrial property laws have been adopted, the latest amendments being made in 2000, and the Czech government applied to join the EPC before the end of 1996 as stipulated by the Europe Agreement. The EU also acted as a catalyst to the adoption of the new laws by providing technical assistance, training, legal aid, language courses, and especially information on industrial property laws in EU countries. Changes in the law and new laws in the industrial property field had the effect of a large increase in foreign patent and industrial design applications, a much smaller increase in domestic industrial design applications, and a sharp rise in trademark applications (especially from domestic sources). In view of future needs, the Industrial Property Office established the Industrial Property Training Institute focused on education and publication in this field. The institute hopes to provide postgraduate and retraining education to provide the skills for employment in patent centers and patent attorney offices, as well as supplemental preparation for becoming a patent attorney.[113]

The European Commission issued its *Opinion* in July 1997 recommending the start of negotiations with the Czech Republic for accession to the European Union. The Luxembourg Council meeting in December 1997 expressed its agreement with this decision and negotiations have been ongoing since 1998, with membership now possible in 2004. The strong desire for EU membership and the high salience of intellectual property to the EU moved this issue to a higher priority on the domestic political agenda than would otherwise be expected. As the likelihood of membership has grown, the Czech government's attention has increasingly focused on the issues of greatest concern to the EU in its domestic reform process.

Overall, in the case of intellectual property, EU advice, guidelines, obligations, and assistance clearly played a central role in the process and content of legislative reform in the Czech Republic. While the harmonization of intellectual property rights began as formal and gradual transposition of EU and international laws, my analysis shows that the laws have also begun to be internalized, with an increase in domestic sanctions for noncompliance and some change in behavior that are likely to grow in time. Intellectual property rights are one example of the extensive EU role in domestic reform in the region, as all candidate countries must follow similarly explicit EU requirements on various other issues. This case demonstrates that the EU impact on CEE reforms through the harmonization of laws process is far-reaching and pervasive. Despite the infringement of sovereignty, it is evident that Czech law has been increasingly influenced by the EU since 1989, even before there was any guarantee of future membership.

NOTES

1. Government of the Czech Republic, Memorandum Submitted by Czech Republic with Its Application for Accession to the EU, 441.2 (71.1) European Report, no. 2103 (January 31, 1996), 10.

2. The associated countries are the ten postcommunist countries that signed association or Europe Agreements with the EU: Poland, Hungary, Czech Republic, Slovakia, Slovenia, Bulgaria, Romania, Estonia, Latvia, and Lithuania.

3. As cited in "Czech Parliament Full of Eurooptimists: Zeman to Haensch," CTK News Wire, July 9, 1996.

4. See especially Martha Finnemore, "International Organizations as Teachers of Norms: The United Nations Educational, Scientific, and Cultural Organization and Science Policy," *International Organization* 47, no. 4 (1993): 565–97.

5. European Commission, "White Paper: Preparation of the Associated Countries of Central and Eastern Europe for Integration into the Internal Market of the Union," Brussels, May 3, 1995, COM (95) 163 final.

6. I use Stephen Krasner's definition of norms as "standards of behavior defined in terms of rights and obligations." As Finlayson and Zacher add, these obligations and rights "guide states' behavior in designing decision-making procedures and in formulating and implementing rules." Stephen D. Krasner, "Structural Causes and Regime Consequences: Regimes as Intervening Variables," in *International Regimes,* ed. Stephen D. Krasner (Ithaca, N.Y.: Cornell University Press, 1983), 2; Jock A. Finlayson and Mark W. Zacher, "The GATT and the Regulation of Trade Barriers: Regime Dynamics and Functions," in Krasner, *International Regimes,* 276.

7. See, for example, Anne-Marie Burley and Walter Mattli, "Europe before the Court: A Political Theory of Legal Integration," *International Organization* 47, no. 1 (1993): 41–76. See also Alex Easson, "Integration through Law: The Court of Justice and the Achievement of the Single Market and the European Union," in *European Integration: Theories and Approaches,* ed. Hans J. Michelmann and Panayotis Soldatos (Lanham, Md.: University Press of America, 1994), 77–97.

8. "Europe Agreement establishing an association between the European Communities and their Member States, of the one part, and the Czech Republic, of the other part," October 4, 1993, OJ, no. L 360, 31 Dec. 1994, chap. 3, art. 70; European Commission, "White Paper (Annex)," COM (95) 163 final/2, 352.

9. Government of the Czech Republic, "Draft Policy Statement" (July 10, 1996) *Denni Telegraf* (Prague), July 13, 1996, 5–6, translated in "Czech Republic: Government Issues Draft Policy Statement," FBIS-EEU-96-142, July 23, 1996.

10. "Czech Republic: Klaus Not Expecting EU Admission 'Soon,'" *Hospodarske Noviny* (Prague), December 13, 1996, 3, as cited in FBIS-EEU-96-242, December 13, 1996. President Havel, on the other hand, was fully supportive of European integration.

11. Charles University professor, Department of Social Work, Philosophical Faculty, interview by author, December 5, 1996, Prague, Czech Republic.

12. European Commission, Central and Eastern Eurobarometer, March 1997, text fig. 9 (poll conducted in the Czech Republic November 8–17, 1996).

13. European Commission, Central and Eastern Eurobarometer, March 1996, figs. 22, 45.

14. In comparison, in Romania, rejected by the European Commission for the start of accession negotiations just months before, a much higher number, 56 percent, held a positive image, with 25 percent neutral and 5 percent negative. European Commission, Central and Eastern Eurobarometer, March 1998, annex figs. 9, 15.

15. Data based on a sample from a special European Commission database of "decision-makers/opinion-formers having an impact on European integration" who receive the Commission's *European Dialogue* magazine. European Commission, Central and Eastern Eurobarometer, March 1998, annex fig. 7.

16. Jiří Payne, "Czech Republic: Deputy on EU Entry, Czech-German Declaration," *Denni Telegraf* (Prague), interview by Nikola Nikolova, August 20, 1996, 3, as cited in FBIS-EEU-96-163.

17. Michal Frankl, member of parliament, ODS, member of Foreign Affairs Committee, interview by author, December 3, 1996, Prague, Czech Republic.

18. "Europe Agreement—Czech Republic," chap. 3, art. 69.

19. Government of the Czech Republic, "Usnesení Vlády České Republiky ze dne 9. rijna 1991 c. 396, k usneseni vlády ČSFR c. 533/1991 o zabezpečení slučitelnosti československého právniho rádu s právem Evropských společenství," 9 October 1991.

20. "Zeman Government Priorities in First Version of Program Statement," *Carolina,* no. 298, July 31, 1998.

21. Jan Kavan, former member of parliament, ČSSD (Czech Social Democratic Party) and ČSSD foreign affairs spokesperson (at time of interview), interview by author, November 14, 1996, Center for Democracy, Prague.

22. Václav Klaus, "Klaus on Europe: So Far, So Good," *The Economist,* September 10, 1994, 34.

23. For further evidence of this, see Melanie H. Ram, "Transformation through European Integration: A Comparative Study of the Czech Republic and Romania" (Ph.D. diss., George Washington University, 1999).

24. European Commission, "White Paper (Annex)," 352.

25. As noted by Hernando de Soto, *The Other Path: The Invisible Revolution in the Third World* (New York: Harper & Row, 1989), 177.

26. John Burgess, "Global Product Piracy May Be Costing Firms Billions," *Washington Post,* February 27, 1988, B2.

27. Motion Picture Association of America, "Anti-Piracy" <www.mpaa.org/anti-piracy> (13 December 2000).

28. Joseph Kahn and Judith Miller, "Getting Tough on Gangsters, High-Tech and Global," *New York Times,* December 15, 2000.

29. International Federation of Pharmaceutical Manufacturers Associations (IFPMA), "Intellectual Property: Patents and Pharmaceuticals," IFPMA Issue Paper, February 1997 <www.ifpma.org/ifpma8a.html>.

30. Both the Czech and the American company took the name from the Czech town "Budweis" (in German), where the Czech brewery is located. Jim Salter, "Fight over Beer Name Heading to Court," *Daily Record* (Baltimore), September 24, 1996, 4.

31. Susan K. Sell, "Intellectual Property Protection and Antitrust in the Developing World: Crisis, Coercion, and Choice," *International Organization,* Spring 1995, 317.

32. Steven Mufson, "In Fight for Intellectual Property Rights in China, Pirates Still Winning," *Washington Post,* February 18, 1996, A29.

33. "White Paper (Annex)," 355–56.

34. This proposal became Directive 96/9/EC of the European Parliament and of the Council (1996) on the legal protection of databases.

35. "White Paper (Annex)," 357–58.

36. "White Paper (Annex)," 352.

37. "Europe Agreement—Czech Republic," art. 67, para. 1. A joint EC-Czech declaration attached to the Europe Agreement explains that "intellectual, industrial, and commercial property" in article 67 of the Europe Agreement "is to be given a similar meaning as in article 36 of the EEC Treaty and includes protection of copyright and neighbouring rights, patents, industrial designs, trademarks, etc."

38. "Europe Agreement—Czech Republic," art. 67; Government of the Czech Republic, Industrial Property Office, Ročenka/Annual Report (1995), 11. The date is five years from entry into force of the interim agreement.

39. "Europe Agreement—Czech Republic," art. 67. The multilateral conventions are listed in annex 17, para. 1.

40. OSA, *Ročenka 1995* (Annual Report), 39.

41. OSA, *Ročenka 1995,* 39.

42. Josef Slanina, CEO/President, OSA (Ochranny Svaz Autorsky/Society for the Protection of Authors), interview by author, December 19, 1996, Prague, Czech Republic.

43. Slanina, interview by author.

44. Slanina, interview by author.

45. JuDr. Hana Masopustová, chief of the department, Audiovisual and Copyright Department, Ministry of Culture of the Czech Republic, interview by author, November 21, 1996, Prague, Czech Republic.

46. Masopustová, interview by author.

47. Hana Masopustová and Anna Kokosková (Czech Republic Ministry of Culture), "Reflections on the Amendment to the Copyright Law," *IPAC/IVHS* 1 (1996): 2–4; Masopustová, interview by author.

48. Masopustová, interview by author.

49. Masopustová and Kokosková, "Amendment to the Copyright Law."

50. Usually information is sought from Germany, France, Belgium, and Portugal or Greece. The latter two are good models because they are the poorer EU member states, have less complex copyright laws, and have a similar size population to the Czech Republic. Slanina, interview by author.

51. "White Paper (Annex)," 357.

52. Masopustová, interview by author.

53. PS PČR I. Vol. obd. 1995, VII.vol.obd. ČNR Těsno. zprávy (Record of Parliamentary Debates), no. 37, December 13, 1995, 702, my translation.

54. As of 1996, there were eighteen amendments to the law concerning the press, twenty-nine to the civil law, and nineteen to the labor law; the bankruptcy law had two amendments even before the day it entered into force. Slanina, interview by author.

55. Masopustová and Kokosková, "Amendment to the Copyright Law," 10. Much EU law in this field is relatively new and still undergoing reforms. Even the required stage 1 and stage 2 measures listed in the 1995 White Paper were enacted by the EU only between 1991 and 1994.

56. Masopustová, interview by author.

57. Masopustová, interview by author.

58. European Commission, "Agenda 2000: Commission Opinion on the Czech Republic's Application for Membership of the European Union," *Bulletin of the European Union,* supplement 14/97 (Luxembourg: Office for Official Publications of the European Communities, 1997), 34.

59. Masopustová, interview by author.

60. Slanina, interview by author.

61. "Senate Passes Law to Extend Validity of Copyrights," Prague CTK, April 7, 2000, FBIS-EEU-2000-0407.

62. European Commission, *2000 Regular Report from the Commission on the Czech Republic's Progress toward Accession,* European Commission, November 8, 2000, 50.

63. Masopustová, interview by author.

64. *2000 Regular Report—Czech Republic,* 50.

65. *2000 Regular Report—Czech Republic,* 50.

66. *2000 Regular Report—Czech Republic,* 19–21.

67. Slanina, interview by author, December 19, 1996.

68. International Intellectual Property Alliance, "2000 Special 301 Report: Czech Republic," February 18, 2000, 79 <www.iipa.com/html/rbc_czech_republic.html>.

69. Music Business International (MBI), *MBI World Report 1996,* 178, 180–81; Slanina, interview by author.

70. Czech Republic, "Preliminary Report on Approximation of Internal Market Legislation in CR and the EU," (1996) ref. no. 1767/96-240, p. 6.

71. International Intellectual Property Alliance (IIPA), "USTR 2000 'Special 301' Decisions and IIPA 1998-1999 Estimated Trade Losses Due to Copyright Piracy and

1998–1999 Estimated Levels of Copyright Piracy," July 28, 2000 <www.iipa. com/html/piracy_losses.html>.
72. Josef Slanina, OSA company reports, 1995, unpublished.
73. Masopustová, interview by author.
74. Slanina, interview by author.
75. Slanina, interview by author.
76. Jan Hak, "Trade Marks in the Czech Republic," *Managing Intellectual Property* (London), *1995 Trade Mark Yearbook,* 23.
77. Government of the Czech Republic, Industrial Property Office, *Industrial Property Office, Czech Republic* (Prague: Industrial Property Office, 1994), 1, 12.
78. Eva Tesarová, head of the International Trademark Department, Industrial Property Office of the Czech Republic, "Contemporary State of the Industrial Property Protection in the Czech Republic" (Conference on Industrial Property in the European Integration, Krakow, Poland, September 15–17, 1996), 2.
79. Zdenka Pradna, "IP Developments in the Czech Republic," *Managing Intellectual Property* (London), December 1993, 49.
80. Government of the Czech Republic, *Industrial Property Office, Czech Republic,* 1.
81. Svetlana Kopecká, Legal and Legislative Department, Industrial Property Office, interview by author, December 3, 1996, Prague, Czech Republic.
82. Kopecká, interview by author; Tesarová, "Industrial Property Protection," 2.
83. Tesarová, "Industrial Property Protection," 3; Kopecká, interview by author.
84. Tesarová, "Industrial Property Protection."
85. Ulrich Schatz, "The European Patent Organisation and the CEECs" (Conference on Industrial Property in the European Integration, Krakow, Poland, 15–17 September 1996), 8. Schatz is the principal director, International Affairs, European Patent Office.
86. Schatz, "European Patent Organisation," 2, 8.
87. *Industrial Property Office, Czech Republic,* 3; Tesarová, "Industrial Property Protection," 2.
88. Kopecká, interview by author.
89. *2000 Regular Report—Czech Republic,* 50.
90. Tesarová, "Industrial Property Protection," 4.
91. Kopecká, interview by author.
92. Tesarová, "Industrial Property Protection," 4.
93. Tesarová, "Industrial Property Protection," 4.
94. Czech Republic, Ministry of Foreign Affairs, "Preliminary Report on Approximation of Internal Market Legislation in ČR and the EU," no. 1767/96-240 (unpublished paper reviewing results achieved from July 1995 to July 1996), 6; *Industrial Property Office, Czech Republic,* 13.
95. *Industrial Property Office, Czech Republic,* 5.
96. European Commission, "Agenda 2000: Commission Opinion on the Czech Republic," 34.
97. Kopecká, interview by author.
98. Kopecká, interview by author; Tesarová, "Industrial Property Protection," 4.
99. *2000 Regular Report—Czech Republic,* 50.
100. Schatz, "European Patent Organisation," 2–4.

101. *Industrial Property Office, Czech Republic,* 20.

102. Kopecká, interview by author.

103. European Commission, "Opinion on the Czech Republic," 34.

104. *2000 Regular Report—Czech Republic,* 50.

105. The numbers include applications for author certificates, which are no longer an option under the current law. Tesarová, "Industrial Property Protection," 3; CSFR, *Annual Report of the Federal Office for Inventions 1990/1991,* tab. 1; Industrial Property Office, Ročenka/Annual Report (1995).

106. Tesarová, "Industrial Property Protection in the Czech Republic," 3; Industrial Property Office, "Patent, Utility Model, Industrial Design, and Trademark Applications in the Czech Republic, 1989–1995"; Industrial Property Office, *1993 Annual Report,* tab. 1.

107. CSFR, *Annual Report of the Federal Office for Inventions 1990/1991,* tab. 1, 3; Industrial Property Office, Ročenka/Annual Report (1995), 3.

108. Kopecká, interview by author.

109. Tesarová, "Industrial Property Protection," 4.

110. *Industrial Property Office, Czech Republic,* 12; Tesarová, "Industrial Property Protection in the Czech Republic," 7; *Annual Report of the Federal Office for Inventions 1991/1992,* tab. 9.

111. Masopustova, interview by author.

112. Hak, "Trade Marks in the Czech Republic," 23.

113. *Industrial Property Office, Czech Republic,* 22.

11

The Diffusion of EU Social and Employment Legislation in Poland and Hungary

Beate Sissenich

International norm projection takes place in a variety of contexts, but the enlargement of existing international organizations is likely to facilitate such a transfer of norms.[1] Prospective members must legitimize their entry by fulfilling a list of criteria set by the organization. For several reasons, eastward enlargement of the European Union constitutes a particularly plausible setting for the diffusion of norms and/or institutions. (1) The degree of institutional density of the EU is unparalleled by any other intergovernmental body. The EU fulfills multiple functions, covers a vast and increasing array of policy areas (many of which have traditionally been considered the sole prerogative of the nation-state), is the source of supranational legislation and of jurisprudence superseding national law, and includes a variety of mechanisms for economic redistribution among its member states. (2) The next wave of enlargement will consist of former state-socialist countries that have been undergoing political and economic transformation. Thus preparations for EU accession coincide with a period of internal fluidity that is likely, all else being equal, to make these countries unusually receptive to outside attempts at norm projection. (3) The gap between accession candidates and the EU has never been as wide as it is in the current wave of enlargement, both because of the level of socioeconomic and institutional development in Central and Eastern Europe and because of the maturation of the integration project. The Community with which Greece, Spain, and Portugal had to catch up in the 1980s was a far less elaborate structure than the European Union is now. At the same time, the latest entrants to the EU (Sweden, Finland, and Austria) began the accession process from a level of comparable or superior socioeconomic development to the EU average, and they did so after decades of functioning as democracies and market economies. (4) The

EU has never before set up such an extensive apparatus to deal with the accession of multiple (in this case no fewer than ten) countries in a standardized and synchronized fashion. While the negotiations are still conducted with each country individually, the criteria and procedures, as well as financial instruments, are the same for all current accession candidates in Central and Eastern Europe.[2] Hence EU enlargement offers us the opportunity to study a deliberate, large-scale effort at institutional diffusion across multiple countries.

This chapter addresses the question of transnational institutional diffusion by looking at whether and how EU social policy is approximated and implemented in Poland and Hungary. Diffusion denotes a process of communication and interaction between source and target that may or may not lead to, and is therefore distinct from, adoption of an innovation—in this case, of European social legislation by candidate countries in Central and Eastern Europe.[3] Such communication can take several forms, such as coercion, dissemination, learning, and imitation. The institutions at issue in this chapter are primarily of a regulative nature—explicit (and often written and enforceable) rules as found in the social legislation of the EU. At the same time, disaggregation of EU social policy reveals certain normative elements as well. These are values and norms held by prominent actors that create social obligations and expectations concerning appropriate behavior but lack legal sanctions.[4] In the case of EU enlargement, the relationship between the source and the target of diffusion is rather hierarchical, as it is the EU that is setting the criteria on the basis of which countries may join the organization. We can therefore expect the diffusion process to take on a predominantly coercive character—although, as we will see, certain elements of EU social policy lack precise legal formulations and exist primarily as values arising from similar practices among the member states. Exactly how the EU approaches social policy diffusion and how accession countries deal with pressures for adoption represent a unique and fascinating example of institutional and norm diffusion under complex circumstances.

EU social policy comprises hard legislation with relatively straightforward performance criteria and clear obligations for member states, elements of policy coordination between member states, and procedures for consultation and decision making among peak-level European labor and employer organizations. The obligations of member states vary across European social policies, as does the power of the Commission to enforce them. The politics and consequences of European social policy are likely to become more salient as socioeconomic variance in the EU increases with the entry of new member states. In the context of international norm projection and institutional diffusion, EU social policy is interesting for several reasons. First, it constitutes an instance of reregulation of social standards and practices at the supranational level that partly counteracts the predominant project of market building in Europe. Second, EU social policy explicitly delineates a role for nonstate actors in the policy-making process at the European level, which makes it unique among EU policy fields. Third, EU social policy is differentiated in itself (combining hard and soft legislation, procedural rules and outcome-driven law) and may therefore give rise to various types of diffusion pressures, such as coercion, coordination, and imitation of best practice.[5]

Both Poland and Hungary are widely considered among the frontrunners in fulfilling the criteria of accession; therefore, they constitute prima facie cases in which institutional diffusion appears to be most likely.[6] Trade with the EU may constitute one indicator of the pressures on both countries to adopt EU standards: Hungary's exports to the EU amounted to 73 percent of its total exports in 1998 and Poland's amounted to 68 percent.[7] At the same time, Poland and Hungary vary along a number of domestic dimensions: size, government stability, legacies of collective action under state socialism, and economic structure. The population of Hungary is roughly one–fourth that of Poland.[8] Foreign direct investment since 1989 has been higher in Hungary than in any other country in Central and Eastern Europe. Between 1994 and 1997, foreign direct investment (FDI) averaged 5.56 percent of GDP annually in Hungary, compared with 2.78 percent of GDP in Poland.[9] Poland has experienced frequent changes in government since 1989 and faces highly unstable coalitions, whereas Hungary has been led by three consecutive governments since the end of state socialism, all of which came to power in regularly scheduled elections.[10] Finally, the two countries diverge in their legacies of collective action. Polish labor's confrontational approach both under state socialism and in the postsocialist period contrasts sharply with political accommodation and the retreat into the second economy in Hungary prior to 1989, as well as with a consensual style of bargaining after the change of regime.[11] At present, bifurcation and politicization of labor unions in Poland and extreme organizational fragmentation among Hungarian labor and employer organizations indicate that structures of interest representation remain weak in both countries. This weakness may work to the detriment of the *quality* of legislation, as policy is thus made without the benefit of sector-specific knowledge of the actors concerned. Poorly written legislation, in turn, tends to generate problems at the implementation stage. Whereas certain nonstate actors in Poland, notably farmers, have mobilized against burdensome EU policies,[12] in Hungary strategies of evasion or compliance with EU policies appear to be more likely.[13] Perhaps surprisingly, in both countries, nonstate actors have been involved only marginally in efforts at adopting EU social legislation. Despite extensive ties to European umbrella organizations, employers and labor in these countries have not demonstrated any significant leverage over EU accession preparations in a policy area that is presumably of concern to them.

This chapter analyzes the pressures for social policy diffusion at the source (in the EU itself), assesses the accession preparations in social policy in Poland and Hungary, and examines the social dialogue and its effects on accession countries.

EUROPEAN UNION SOCIAL POLICY
AND TOOLS OF ENFORCEMENT

European social policy is primarily situated in the first pillar of the EU and is thus governed by the treaty establishing the European Community.[14] But a social purpose of integration is laid down even in the overall framework of the Treaty on European Union (TEU).[15] Article 2 of the TEU calls for the Union to promote "economic and social progress," "balanced and sustainable development," and the "strengthening of economic and social cohesion." More specifically, article 2 of the EC treaty lists among the goals of the Community a "high level of employment and social protection, equality between men and women, . . . raising the standard of living and the quality of life, and economic and social cohesion and solidarity among the Member States."[16] Primary (i.e., treaty-based) law relevant to employment and social affairs concerns the free movement of workers,[17] employment policy,[18] social policy,[19] the promotion of economic and social cohesion,[20] and the protection of health.[21] Treaty law serves as the basis for secondary EU legislation, three types of which are legally binding. *Regulations* are directly binding in all member states and supersede national law, *directives* require transposition into national law and implementation by the member states, and *decisions* are directed at specific natural or legal persons and can be invoked before the courts. In addition, case law issuing from the European Court of Justice (ECJ) is binding and supersedes national law. The totality of EU law is often referred to as *acquis communautaire* and the laws that relate to social and employment matters as the social *acquis*.

There are at present fifty-seven directives in the field of social policy, covering labor law (ten directives), equal opportunities for men and women in the workplace (eight), occupational health and safety (thirty-three, including amendments), public health (three, including amendments), and free movement of workers (three). In addition to these directives, the social *acquis* contains important "soft" elements that require coordination rather than harmonization of member state policies and for which the Commission does not have the same level of enforcement capacity as it does for directives. EC employment guidelines, for example, are a relatively new policy tool[22] that requires the coordination of member state employment policies around annual guidelines set by the Council.

Member states thus face extended tasks of official data collection, development of monitoring capacities for labor market supply and demand, and coordination of human resource development.

Responsibilities of member states are much less clear in the case of social dialogue—a procedure for peak-level consultations between Europe-wide employer and labor organizations with the possibility of concluding agreements that will lead to Community legislation. Such legislation may then be implemented by labor and employer organizations in the member states or via transposition through member state legislatures.[23] Although the social dialogue is a Community-level procedure, it requires functioning structures of economic interest representation in the member states. However, there is no one single model of social partnership and industrial relations in the member states of the EU; rather, structures of interest representation remain nationally specific and diverse.[24] Nor are there reliable criteria for what governments, labor unions, and employers often refer to as the "European social model," which is presumed to be worth preserving and exporting. The absence of explicit responsibilities of member states (and hence applicant countries) creates a conundrum for the Commission. While its *Regular Report*s on enlargement preparations clearly indicate an interest in preparing the accession candidates for their participation in the social dialogue, it has little enforcement capacity in this area and must therefore limit itself to expressions of approval or disapproval. Such expressions may exert normative pressure but are a far cry from the coercive potential of EU directives.

Not incorporated in the social *acquis* of the EU, but included in the many accession requirements for the Central and Eastern European countries, are the systems of health, social protection, and education. Traditionally, the organization and financing of these policy areas were entirely under member state control. However, from the Copenhagen criteria for accession the EU has derived the requirement of macroeconomic and budget stabilization in the accession countries, which in turn serves as justification for demanding that these states revamp their health, social security, and education systems. In the absence of any explicit and detailed EU criteria for reform, however, the accession countries have had to rely on other international institutions, notably the World Bank, for technical assistance. Since 1997, the EU has been coordinating its efforts in the accession countries with the World Bank, but the role played by the Bank and other international financial institutions in social sector reform has varied across countries.[25] The requirement of in-depth reform in areas that are not formally subject to EU authority illustrates a problematic aspect of the current accession process: the EU can impose more stringent obligations on prospective than on current member states. Furthermore, enforcement mechanisms vis-à-vis member states are differentiated and specific, whereas accession candidates face one enormous categorical threat: indefinite delay of entry. Not only can a country's sluggish performance in one policy area result in the postponement of its admission to the Union, but lagging accession preparations in one country may affect the speed of accession of other countries as well.

SIGNIFICANCE OF EU SOCIAL POLICY IN THE
ENLARGEMENT PROCESS

In assessments of the potential for the diffusion of EU social policy in Central and Eastern Europe, one important question is what, if any, pressures for diffusion exist at the *source*, both at the level of the EU as a whole and in its member states. In the literature on European integration, the question of whether Community social policy represents a significant step toward the harmonization of living and working conditions among member states is highly contested.[26] Some argue that social policy has always been marginal to the integration project, which has instead focused on market building.[27] Others, by contrast, point to the pioneering role of equal opportunity legislation and case law in introducing the issue to member states' agendas.[28] Recent treaty revisions have seen a strengthening of the social dimension of integration, but skeptics remain vocal, especially concerning the actual implementation of EU social law. Our discussion assesses the significance of Europe's social dimension for the enlargement process along several criteria. First, what types of arguments are made about the increased socioeconomic variance that will result from enlargement and the effects it will have on current member states? If European social policy is intended to level the playing field between citizens in different member states, then greater socioeconomic diversity in the Union should increase the salience of joint social policy and its application in the current and future member states. We should therefore expect the European Commission as well as government leaders from current member states to insist on full implementation of Community social legislation in the candidate countries.[29] In other words, increased socioeconomic variance in the enlarged Union should generate coercive pressure from the Commission and member states for the diffusion of social law. Second, what do public opinion data reveal about citizen perceptions of enlargement and other areas of EU activities? Specifically, how prominent are socioeconomic concerns among citizens of the current member states? To what extent are they linked to attitudes about enlargement? Third, how has the implementation of social legislation fared compared to other policy areas? Based on the experience of current member states, what is the likelihood that diffusion of social legislation will encounter obstacles in the candidate countries?

Arguments about the Effects of Increased Socioeconomic Variance in the EU

Evaluations of the socioeconomic gap between the ten CEE candidate countries and the EU disagree on the size of the gap but not on the fundamental fact that the difference in socioeconomic standards between the EU and prospective members is greater than in any previous enlargement.[30] Consequently, some fear that the accession of Central and Eastern European countries will generate a race to the bottom in the enlarged Union. Such a risk of declining social standards could presumably take several forms: Workers in Germany and Austria may not be able to compete with cross-border commuters from Central and Eastern Europe who, while sharing similar skill levels, are able to work at reduced wages thanks to lower costs of living.[31] Another fear that looms large among political publics, notably in Germany and Austria, is massive westward migration—regardless of expert assessments according to which levels of migration will remain low.[32] A third way in which enlargement is said to potentially contribute to a watering down of social standards is by eastward migration of manufacturing and services. Again, it remains doubtful whether accession per se will raise the risk of capital exit to levels higher than at present, but certainly this risk is cited as a strong argument in favor of full adoption of all EU social legislation prior to accession. Full adoption of the *acquis*, including social legislation, would thus contribute to leveling the playing field between old and new member states.

Public Opinion in EU Member States

It is difficult to assess the importance attributed to EU social policy by EU citizens with respect to enlargement from available data. Recent public opinion data (table 11.1) indicate a decided lack of enthusiasm for enlargement among citizens of EU member states and reveal that respondents consider the fight against unemployment and poverty, the maintenance of peace and security in Europe, and environmental protection to be greater priorities for EU action. Whereas 90 percent of respondents from all member states (who were interviewed in the fall of 1999) said that the fight against unemployment was a priority for EU action, only 28 percent of respondents said that "welcoming new member countries" should be a priority for the EU; 59 percent of respondents said enlargement was *not* a priority. Interestingly, while "maintaining peace and security in Europe" was seen as a priority by 89 percent of respondents, the majority of respondents do not appear to draw a link between the maintenance of political stability in Europe and EU enlargement. Similarly, the fight against poverty and social exclusion, which 87 percent of respondents viewed as priority for EU action, does not reveal any interest in economic growth and prosperity in CEE. Of twelve areas of EU action about which respondents were asked, enlargement was least likely to be named as a priority area. This suggests that EU citizens tend to view the fight

Table 11.1.   EU Actions: Priority or Not? (EU 15)

EU Actions	Should Be a Priority %	Should Not Be a Priority %
Fighting unemployment	90	6
Maintaining peace and security in Europe	89	6
Fighting organized crime and drug trafficking	88	8
Fighting poverty and social exclusion	87	8
Protecting the environment	83	12
Guaranteeing the rights of the individual and respect for the principles of democracy in Europe	80	12
Protecting consumers and guaranteeing the quality of products	80	14
Getting closer to European citizens, for example, by giving them more information about the EU	70	20
Successfully implementing the single European currency, the euro	60	31
Reforming the institutions and bodies of the EU and the way they work	51	33
Asserting the political and diplomatic importance of the EU around the world	50	37
Welcoming new member countries	28	59

Source: Standard Eurobarometer Report no. 52, April 2000. Percentage "don't know" not shown.
Note: The question posed to respondents reads as follows: "I am going to read out a list of actions that the European Union could undertake. For each one, please tell me if, in your opinion, it should be a priority or not."

against unemployment, poverty, and social exclusion as a goal that renders enlargement minimally relevant.[33]

The average level of support for enlargement across all member states was 43 percent in the fall of 1999 (cf. table 11.2).[34] However, support varies considerably across member states, with Sweden (62 percent in favor), Denmark, and Greece in the lead. Trailing behind in support for enlargement were Germany, Austria, and France (34 percent in favor). It is striking that support for enlargement does not appear to be correlated with a given member state's level of economic prosperity. Nor does the future decline in EU structural funding for current beneficiaries (notably Greece and Spain) appear to create resistance to enlargement among their citizens.

Interestingly, when asked specifically about the enlargement criteria they considered important, respondents were less likely to focus on economic criteria. Instead, respect for human rights and democracy, fighting against organized crime and drug trafficking, and protection of the environment were listed as important accession criteria by 95 percent, 93 percent, and 91 percent of respondents, respectively (table 11.3).[35] The vast majority of respondents also considered the full implementation of EU law an important criterion for enlargement. Somewhat paradoxically, then, EU citizens consider the fight against unemployment, poverty, and social exclusion as far

Table 11.2.   Average Percentage Support for the Fifteen New Countries (Including Norway and Switzerland) in Spring and Autumn of 1999 (EU 15)

Country	Spring '99	Fall '99
Sweden	56	62
Denmark	62	60
Greece	58	57
Netherlands	55	55
Spain	51	48
Finland	51	49
Italy	45	47
Ireland	45	47
EU 15	42	43
Belgium	39	42
Luxembourg	45	41
United Kingdom	40	41
Portugal	38	40
Germany	38	38
Austria	29	35
France	33	34

Source: Standard Eurobarometer 52.
Note: Question: "For each of the following countries, would you be in favor of or against it becoming part of the European Union?" Listed in this question are the ten CEECs, Turkey, Malta, Cyprus, Norway, and Switzerland. This table reports average levels of support for enlargement in each member state as calculated by *Eurobarometer 52* (sec. 3.8)

more important than enlargement, but when asked about enlargement criteria, they give precedence to political criteria, internal security, and environmental protection over economic criteria. Although there are no data available to back up this claim, one might at least wonder whether EU citizens are not implicitly referring to a minimum level of social standards when they insist on "respect for human rights and democracy" as a membership criterion.

Clearly these public opinion data do not contain any information about the extent to which EU citizens consider existing EU social policy as relevant for dealing with socioeconomic concerns either in the present Union or in its enlarged version. Thus we cannot draw any direct conclusions about the salience of EU social policy for the enlargement process. What the data do reveal, however, is the prominence of socioeconomic concerns. First, EU citizens are far more likely to consider the fight against unemployment and social exclusion a priority for EU action than EU enlargement. Second, over three out of four EU citizens are concerned about the economic and financial implications of EU enlargement. Third, more than four out of five EU citizens state that a new member state has to implement the entire *acquis*. This suggests that political leaders in the member states will be sensitized to the socioeconomic costs of enlargement and that the social partners in the member states will, at a minimum, have an interest in seeing the

Table 11.3.   Importance of Enlargement Criteria (EU 15)

Enlargement Criteria	Important %	Not Important %
The country has to respect human rights and the principles of democracy	95	2
It has to fight organized crime and drug trafficking	93	3
It has to protect the environment	91	5
It has to be able to pay its share of the budget	83	8
It has to accept whatever has already been decided and put in place throughout the process of building Europe	81	10
Its joining should not be costly for existing member countries	79	13
Its level of economic development should be close to that of other member states	75	17
It has to be prepared to put the interest of the EU above its own	70	18

Source: Standard Eurobarometer 52, April 2000. Percentage "don't know" not shown.
Note: Question: "For each of the following criteria, please tell me if it seems important to you or not in deciding whether a particular country should join the European Union, or not."

social *acquis* applied in Central and Eastern Europe. At the same time, the data show an overwhelming sense of reluctance among EU citizens that runs somewhat counter to the repeated public proclamations by member state governments in support of speedy enlargement. In conclusion, just as the main impetus within the EU for accepting new members comes from governments and political elites, so any pressure for diffusion of EU social policy in the candidate countries will come from the Commission and member state governments and not primarily from member state electorates.

Transposition of EU Social Legislation in the Current Member States

If the salience of EU social policy among the citizens of member states can be gauged only indirectly, it is not much easier to determine the likelihood that the EU social *acquis* will be implemented in the accession countries in comparison with other policy areas. One indicator of possible resistance to implementation of different parts of the *acquis* is the number of infringement proceedings initiated against current member states. As already mentioned, directives require transposition by member states into national law and follow-up through implementing measures. Upon transposition of a directive, each country is required to notify the European Commission. Failure to transpose adequately will result in infringement proceedings by the Commission, which may culminate in a ruling by the ECJ against the member state and in the subsequent imposition of fines. Note that infringement proceedings look only at transposition and not at the implementation of Community law. Consequently, they reveal little about the ability or likelihood of member states to engage in strategies of avoidance and are likely to overestimate the degree of compliance with EU law. Nevertheless, infringement data give a first approximation of what areas of EU law are most amenable to adoption in the member states. In 1998 social affairs accounted for 4 percent of all EU directives but 6.8 percent of cases in which infringement proceedings had been opened.[36] Similarly, whereas the share of environmental law among EU directives was close to 10 percent, it constituted 18.6 percent of all infringement proceedings. By contrast, although internal market legislation accounted for nearly 46.7 percent of all directives, its share of infringement proceedings was significantly lower at 24 percent. Agriculture accounted for 27 percent of all directives but only for 14.5 percent of infringement proceedings.[37] By this measure, we can say that the potential for obstacles to transposition is relatively greater in social affairs than in internal market or agricultural legislation. From the member states' implementation gap in social policy, the candidate countries might draw two conclusions: (1) EU social legislation is inherently difficult to implement (for instance because of the burdens it places on small and medium enterprises or because it conflicts with prevailing practices in gender relations). (2) More likely, they may assume that social legislation is a relatively low priority among EU policies and therefore not subject to the same levels of scrutiny as internal market legislation. Consequently we might expect to find reluctance, though perhaps not outright resistance, among the candidate countries in transposing and implementing EU social policy.

In sum, the evidence about EU pressure for diffusion of the social *acquis* in CEE is ambiguous. The majority of EU citizens are preoccupied with socioeconomic concerns and do not consider enlargement a priority. As for possible enlargement criteria, more than three out of four EU citizens point to the importance of economic and financial measures and more than four out of five EU citizens call for full adoption of the *acquis* in the new member states. Nevertheless, it is not clear from the evidence available that respondents consider implementation of the *social acquis* in CEE as crucial in deciding whether or not to support enlargement. At the same time, the transposition of EU social directives in the member states has encountered a disproportionate degree of noncompliance compared with other policy areas. This implementation gap suggests that EU social legislation may generate resistance among interested parties in CEE as well. Although evidence about sluggish member state compliance is useful, the fact is that more stringent criteria apply to prospective entrants than to long-time members.[38] Whereas the Commission has few instruments for enforcing the actual implementation of EU law in member states, its reports about the state of legal approximation and implementation in the candidate countries are influential in determining the speed of accession. A delay in enlargement because of implementation lags in specific policy areas may be a crude enforcement mechanism, but it is a far more powerful instrument than anything the Commission can wield against member states. It is therefore in the Commission's own interest, as the executive branch of the EU, to push for thorough transposition and implementation of Community legislation while it has the means to do so. Even in the face of bad faith among the member states in addressing the readiness of the candidate countries, we can expect the Commission to scrutinize transposition and implementation very carefully in the accession countries, especially in areas where implementation has previously proven to be problematic.

ASSESSING THE DIFFUSION OF EU SOCIAL AND EMPLOYMENT POLICY IN POLAND AND HUNGARY

Having found the pressures for full implementation of the social *acquis* in CEE to be rather mixed at the *source* of EU law, I will now focus on the *targets* of diffusion, in particular Poland and Hungary. Negotiations on social and employment policy with both countries were opened in September 1999 and provisionally closed in the fall of 2000. Both countries have stated their full endorsement of the social *acquis* and have requested transition arrangements only in special areas. Poland has asked for a transition period until 2006 for two directives on the use of protective equipment in the workplace and has also reserved the right to ask for another transition period concerning the EU directive on work with biological agents.[39] The transition request is supported by an argument about the likely economic hardship faced by small and medium enterprises that are forced to rapidly introduce expensive new equipment. Hungary has asked for a transition period until 2006 for the directive on tar yields in cigarettes, also using economic hardship as a justification—in this case the cost of new plant varieties and processing technology imposed on tobacco growers, who are regionally concentrated in the impoverished east of the country.[40] Both countries thus take the position that fulfilling the social *acquis* is largely uncontroversial.[41]

The Commission, for its part, appears to reject the view according to which the social chapter of the negotiations is unproblematic.[42] It responded to the negotiating positions of both countries by requesting further information on a variety of areas covered by the social chapter, such as social protection, labor law, equal treatment of men and women, discrimination, employment, social dialogue, health and safety, and public health. Reactions by the candidate states take several forms: (1) pointing to transition periods granted to member states for complying with the same directives; (2) calculating the costs to the economy generally, and small and medium enterprises in particular, that arise from complying with certain directives; (3) listing and explaining the legislative acts in planning through which EU law is to be transposed, complete with timetables; (4) elaborating implementing measures both for the "hard" *acquis* and for employment and antidiscrimination policy; (5) describing and justifying the status quo (e.g., concerning health care and the social dialogue at various levels).[43] The 1999 *Regular Report* on Poland, a tool by which the Commission communicates its assessment of the state of accession preparations to the public at large, criticized the "limited tangible progress" on transposition and the lack of enforcement capacity, particularly concerning equal opportunity legislation. It also emphasized the need to prioritize employment policy and called for strengthening structures of social dialogue. Interestingly, the *Regular Report* also acknowledged political obstacles to far-reaching reforms, specifically the mobilization of medical personnel against health care reform.[44] In its 2000 *Regular Report* on Poland, the Commission reinforced its concerns about the lack of progress in social policy transposition and implementation, listing health and safety at work, equal treatment for women and men, labor inspection, and technical modernization of the social insurance fund as the main problem areas. The report manifests the increasing attention paid by the Commission to the need for improved administrative capacity at all levels of government. Without efforts at state capacity building, the Commission noted, enforcement of EU law will remain weak.[45]

In the case of Hungary, the 1999 *Regular Report* noted advanced standing concerning transposition but "limited progress" more recently, especially concerning occupational health and safety and labor law. It criticized the diminished competencies of Hungarian tripartite institutions resulting from the reorganization of government consultation with socioeconomic interests in 1999 but also pointed to organizational fragmentation as an obstacle to effective interest representation.[46] In its 2000 *Regular Report* on Hungary, the Commission stated that "transposition has advanced well" but noted that implementation and enforcement measures were lagging.[47]

Much of the legal harmonization takes place through ministerial regulations rather than parliamentary legislation, a fact that may increase the speed of harmonization but certainly weakens the status of parliaments vis-à-vis the executive.[48] Transposition can take two basic forms: literal integration of a directive's text in national law, which leaves questions of implementation entirely unaddressed; or substantive transposition, which renders a given law vulnerable to charges of misspecified interpretation of EU directives. In the early preaccession phase, the EU specified no precise criteria of what constitutes satisfactory transposition and generally seemed to accept formulations that sought to capture the content of EU law. More recently, according to ministerial officials, the Commission has begun to insist on *literal* transposition of EU law into national law, leaving implementation to be addressed in subsequent measures.[49]

Since 1998 the Commission has placed increasing emphasis on the *imple-mentation* of EU social policy in the accession countries. Although legal har-monization remains a daunting task,[50] modernizing administrative structures to enable them to apply the *acquis* effectively has become a major concern of accession preparations. The most obvious threat arising from insufficient administrative capacity, and one that is widely discussed and highly politi-cized in the accession countries, is delay in the accession timetable. Another is a country's loss of financial assistance, as happened when Poland lost 16 percent of allocated PHARE funding in 1998 because of inadequate project proposals.[51] Recognizing the importance of state capacity for taking on the responsibilities of membership, the EU decided in 1998 to allocate one-third of PHARE funding to "institution-building" measures. Of course, beyond monitoring legal transposition, the Commission has never had much control over whether and how member states go about implementing EU legisla-tion. Hence, there are no common standards for effective public manage-ment, nor any explicit rules about administrative-institutional requirements arising from membership. Instead, the primary tool for "institution building" has been to match member state administrative experts ("preaccession ad-visers") with the EU integration departments in each ministry in the appli-cant countries in a twinning program. The program is demand-based; ac-cession countries formulate their needs and choose among proposals of different member states, whose motivation to participate is threefold: the net contributors, especially, want to see EU funds used effectively in the acces-sion countries and view enhanced administrative capacity as prerequisite for this. Furthermore, by building horizontal ties with the public administrations of accession countries, member states hope to create long-term strategic al-liances that will strengthen their own bargaining position in the European Council. Finally, at least for the larger member states, participation in twin-ning also carries some prestige and the hope to propagate distinct ap-proaches to administering EU law at the national and subnational level. In contrast to legal harmonization, the diffusion of administrative practices is a more horizontal process that allows accession countries a modicum of choice. At the same time, the presence of foreign civil servants (most of whom do not speak the language of the country to which they are as-signed) in the midst of the everyday activities of ministerial departments runs the risk of being perceived as intrusive. While the twinning program makes avoidance (by transposing Community law without implementing it) more difficult for accession countries, preaccession advisers have little lever-age over noncooperative ministerial departments that choose to withhold information or delay the circulation of policy documents.[52]

Improving administrative capacity in the accession countries implies a va-riety of changes: improvements in the legal framework of the civil service (including mechanisms to establish transparency and accountability); decentralized decision making and strengthened regional and local government; cross-sectoral coordination both within and between ministries; development of consultation networks with technical, governmental, and non-governmental agencies; and detailed impact assessment of EU policy for each sector, as well as of interaction effects between sectors.[53] In social policy, institution-building tasks involve improvement of monitoring and statistical documentation facilities, integration of hitherto separate departments, and the establishment of new agencies and/or departments to fulfill new functions arising from membership in the EU. For instance, three separate Hungarian agencies (National Labor Inspectorate, Occupational Health Inspectorate, and National Public Health Inspectorate) currently deal with tasks of occupational and public health and safety. Organizational restructuring will take the form of enhanced cooperation and joint data collection, but it will stop short of consolidation into one entity. Poland's National Labor Office dissolved its regional offices and reallocated their functions to the level of local government in order to implement employment policy more effectively, an important goal in light of Poland's persistent high unemployment levels and strong regional disparities. Hungary's *National Program for the Adoption of the Acquis*, commended by the Commission for its precise timetables for legal harmonization and its thorough assessment of budgetary, staffing, and technical needs, projects a need for ten thousand additional staff in public administration offices dealing with adoption of the *acquis*.[54] The program's projected distribution of additional staff across policy areas reveals justice and home affairs (30 percent) and employment and social affairs (23 percent) as priority areas.[55] Of particular importance is public health, which is the target of 64 percent of planned expenditure for adoption of the *acquis* in employment and social affairs. Other areas of the social *acquis* appear comparatively marginal as targets of institution building: employment accounts for 9 percent and equal treatment of men and women for 7 percent of planned expenditure for adoption of the *acquis* in the social field.[56] No comparable data are available for Poland, whose *National Program for the Preparation of Membership in the EU* has been criticized by the Commission for its lack of precision concerning the timing of reforms, financial requirements, and institutional prerequisites.[57]

In sum, adoption of EU social law in Hungary and Poland appears to be driven by Commission pressure, whose scrutiny contradicts the view that the social *acquis* is straightforward and easy to transpose and implement. When the two countries have asked for transition periods concerning the social chapter, it has been on the basis of cost considerations, particularly with respect to small and medium enterprises and farmers. Poland can be seen as lagging behind Hungary in the transposition of EU social legislation, but both countries have to make significant efforts to create the administrative structures necessary for effective implementation of such laws. In this context, the

Commission's emphasis on institution building at the national and subnational level is remarkable and largely unprecedented in the history of European integration. In contrast to legal transposition, the EU lacks reliable criteria of institutional capacity and therefore has resorted to pairing member state experience with the needs of accession countries. While the accession countries perceive this exercise as intrusive and burdensome, it has the interesting side effect of building horizontal networks among administrators in current and future member states that may serve as the basis for coalition building in EU decision making. Despite this large-scale effort to strengthen institutional capacity in the candidate countries, a considerable gap remains between legislative commitments and actual implementation of Community law.

SOCIAL DIALOGUE ON ACCESSION TO THE EU

So far, this assessment of Poland's and Hungary's adoption of EU social policy has focused on hard law and the administrative structures necessary to implement it. An additional key element of EU social policy is the social dialogue, the EU-wide procedure that presupposes functioning structures of socioeconomic interest representation at the national level. As already noted, the social dialogue does not impose any immediate obligations on member states, nor are there binding criteria for functioning structures of social partnership.[58] One Commission official described the weak role of the Commission concerning tripartism and social dialogue as follows: "We use the hard *acquis* for leverage in the accession countries. But with respect to soft law, interference is highly politically sensitive. All we can do is watch and listen carefully. Given the diversity of arrangements in the member states, our capacity for interfering with tripartite institutions in the accession countries is indeed quite small."[59] Nevertheless, improvement of social dialogue (in particular, bilateral negotiations between employers and labor) should constitute one of the objectives of accession preparations, according to a Commission proposal concerning the accession partnerships.[60] In its *Regular Reports* for 2000, the Commission voiced explicit criticism of the actual functioning of social dialogue in both Hungary and Poland. The work of the Polish Tripartite Commission was "hampered" by the absence of the All-Poland Alliance of Trade Unions (OPZZ), the report stated, and bipartite consultations had failed to concretize, as did autonomous sectoral negotiations. Aside from calling for "considerable further effort" to develop Poland's social dialogue, the Commission drew an interesting link between administrative capacity and consultation with the social partners. Thus it saw social dialogue as necessary for effective implementation of EU law at the local level, while administrative capacity building constitutes a prerequisite for stronger social dialogue. Most remarkably, perhaps, the report explicitly called on the Polish government to take the initiative to develop social dialogue.[61] Similarly explicit criticism was voiced against Hungary, where, according to the 2000 *Regular Report,* certain consultative bodies are primarily used as tools for the dissemination of government information. As in Poland, the report called on the Hungarian government to undertake "active promotion of sound developments in social dialogue."[62] Disagreement between Hungary and the Commission on the functioning of social dialogue led to a delay in the provisional closing of the negotiations on social policy and employment in the fall of 2000. Hungary remains subject to Commission review of social dialogue every six months.[63]

The Commission is not alone in noting the weakness of actual consultative mechanisms in Central and Eastern Europe. Various authors have commented on the overall powerlessness of organized labor in Central and Eastern Europe, based on such criteria as organizational fragmentation, rapid loss of membership since 1989, ideological weakness, prevalence of enterprise-level collective bargaining, and poor enforcement capacity of trade unions vis-à-vis their rank and file.[64] Others attribute the even greater organizational weakness of employers to the absence of well-articulated workers' interests.[65] By formal criteria of institutional arrangements, tripartism may be well established in Central and Eastern Europe.[66] But when effective outcomes of tripartism for workers are at issue, assessments tend to be more skeptical. Instead of material gains for workers, tripartite consultation appears to have primarily served the purpose of information and pacification.[67]

In both Hungary and Poland, consultation of social partners concerning matters of European integration has been perfunctory. To begin with, organizational fragmentation or polarization weakens the status of both employer organizations and labor in these two countries. In Hungary, six labor confederations organize approximately 40 percent of the workforce. In addition, there are roughly sixty unaffiliated unions that in some cases have cooperation agreements with sectoral affiliates of the larger confederations.[68] Despite attempts by outside actors such as the European Trade Union Confederation (ETUC) or the German Friedrich Ebert Foundation to encourage cooperation between confederations and consolidation of organizational structures, each of them defends its independence by pointing to similar fragmentation in EU member states such as France or Italy.[69] Five of the six confederations are affiliated with the ETUC.[70] Among Hungarian employer organizations, fragmentation and competition are even more pronounced, with cross-membership a common occurrence. Several among them do not distinguish clearly between the functions of employer organizations and those of business organizations, sometimes leading to direct competition with the economic chambers.[71] In the absence of reliable statistics, estimates suggest that the employer organizations at the national level together cover about 30 percent of all enterprises and 63 percent of all workers.[72] Due to the competition for membership in one of the two official European-level employers' confederations, eight of the nine Hungarian employers' organizations founded a confederation to represent Hungarian employers in international affairs (the Confederation of Hungarian Employer Organizations for International Cooperation—MMNSZ/CEHIC). The organization has no independent standing in the domestic context and is an actor only at the international level. This development suggests that pressure from European-level organizations can contribute to signs of organizational consolidation, but it remains to be seen whether the presence of this new actor will be able to change the organizational structure and identity of existing Hungarian employer organizations or their impact on social legislation.

In Poland, industrial relations and social dialogue are hindered by the polarization between the two main trade union confederations (Solidarity and the postcommunist OPZZ) and fragmentation on the employer side. Solidarity has roughly 1.3 million members, whereas OPZZ claims to have 2.7 million members among the active workforce, together accounting for approximately 23 percent of the active population.[73] Neither organization is sufficiently independent from the large political parties: Solidarity sees itself as a "political movement" and serves as rank-and-file organization for the currently governing Solidarity Electoral Action (AWS). OPZZ performs similar functions for the Democratic Left Alliance (SLD).[74] Solidarity is a member of the ETUC and has been able to block affiliation of OPZZ with the same confederation. On the employer side, organizational structures are still in great flux. The two largest confederations, Confederation of Polish Employers (KPP) and Polish Confederation of Private Employers (PKPP), claim to cover enterprises with a total of 2 million workers and 400,000 workers, respectively.[75] Organizational instability is likely to persist as long as privatization remains incomplete.

The Hungarian institutions of social dialogue function slightly better than those in Poland, despite recent modifications that have been criticized by both labor and employer organizations. The National Council for the Reconciliation of Interests was founded in 1988 and served as vehicle for consultation throughout much of the transformation period. The liberal-conservative coalition under Viktor Orbán, in office since 1998, revamped the institutions of social dialogue by disaggregating their functions and opening participation to other economic actors and the nonprofit sector.[76] Five new consultative bodies have been formed to deal with labor and wage policy, macroeconomic policy, social services, regional development, and European integration. Representatives from both labor and employer organizations have criticized the new institutions as merely serving the dissemination of government information, in particular concerning European integration.[77] The absence of horizontal links between the different consultative bodies presents an obstacle to an integrated approach to social and economic policy consultation.

At the same time, the restructuring constitutes an attempt to shift away from tripartism and toward interest group pluralism.

In Poland, tripartism has suffered from politicization and instrumentalization by each of the successive governments, which has been condemned by labor as well as employer organizations. The Tripartite Commission, founded in the early 1990s, lacks a legal basis that defines its composition and competencies.[78] OPZZ withdrew from the Tripartite Commission in April 1999 to protest the government's refusal to consult the social partners on the budget. Its complaint resulted in a reprimand by the ILO against the Polish government. OPZZ has pursued a strategy of mass demonstrations and public criticism. While the Polish government claims to consult societal interests on all legislation concerning European integration, the issue of EU membership has not yet appeared on the agenda of the Tripartite Commission. Although the European Commission, in its 1999 and 2000 *Regular Reports,* urgently called on the Polish government to improve the social dialogue, OPZZ and others seeking to broaden and regularize social dialogue have not exploited such outside criticism to demand more meaningful consultations.

While the social partners in both countries view tripartite consultative forums as ineffective for joint deliberation on matters pertaining to European integration, they have made minimal attempts at inserting themselves in the debate on accession preparations. Both labor and employer organizations have focused on pursuing affiliation with international and European-level confederations. Neither in Hungary nor in Poland has labor produced a strategy for dealing with specific issues of the social *acquis*; public statements have been limited to endorsements of accession in general and wage equalization in particular, despite the fact that wage policy is outside of EU competence.[79] Labor also emphasizes the importance of free movement of persons and rejects any transition period on this arguably fundamental element of the EU.[80] Consultation on details of legal harmonization by line ministries and interministerial working groups occasionally allows experts from labor and employer organizations to offer opinions on technical aspects of transposing the social *acquis*. In Hungary at least, such technical consultation tends to privilege employers over workers.[81] Internally, the different organizations focus on informing and educating their members on EU accession, a formidable task indeed and one for which resources are always inadequate. The complexity of European legislation, the lack of language skills and organizational resources, and the reluctance of government to include the social partners in the negotiation process all make political mobilization concerning European integration rather unlikely. Even their transnational networks of affiliation and resource exchange with Europewide organizations have not enhanced the social partners' leverage over the implementation of EU social policy in Poland and Hungary. In contrast to well-publicized and highly controversial policy areas such as agriculture, the social policy of the EU is not viewed as salient to the pressing problems facing employers and labor in both countries. Conversely, the social part-ners do not articulate a European dimension on pressing issues such as unemployment, the structure of social dialogue, wages, industrial restruc-turing, and social security.

In sum, both in Hungary and in Poland, government consultation with the social partners tends to be of varying quality, depending on the issue at hand. Concerning European integration, however, consultation has taken the form of a one-sided and belated flow of information about government activities, with few possibilities for intervention by the social partners. The latter, in turn, appear to lack both the resources and the motivation to artic-ulate detailed responses to elements of the social *acquis*. As neither govern-ment nor the social partners have undertaken any thorough impact studies of EU legislation on specific sectors and industries, potential costs and ben-efits of EU legislation for different social groups are not obvious. These find-ings concerning the noninvolvement of well-connected nonstate actors in the diffusion of EU social legislation in Poland and Hungary suggest that "transnational advocacy networks" by themselves will have a limited effect on domestic nonstate actors if the latter do not share a similar view of the salience of issues.[82] The Commission's increasingly urgent calls for improve-ments in domestic structures of social dialogue, an area that is not explicitly regulated by EU law, illustrates the paradoxical situation that the Commis-sion can hold the candidate countries to standards that have not been for-mulated for the member states.

CONCLUSION

The adoption of EU social policy in Poland and Hungary shows both the po-tential and the limits of institutional diffusion from international organiza-tions to states in Central and Eastern Europe. At the source of diffusion, the evidence is rather mixed: EU citizens are quite concerned about socio-economic issues but do not necessarily draw a link between them and their opinions on enlargement. Nor is there much indication that they consider ex-isting Community social legislation as crucial in the enlargement process. The somewhat sluggish compliance of member states with Community so-cial policy, meanwhile, suggests that obstacles are likely to be encountered in the accession countries as well, whether for technical reasons or due to the perception that social policy is a low priority. On the other hand, the Eu-ropean Commission applies increased scrutiny in assessing the adoption of social law in the candidate countries. The target countries for diffusion of EU policies in Central and Eastern Europe regard the social *acquis* as uncontro-versial, but Commission evaluations of their actual progress in this area indicate significant disagreement. Whereas the Commission has relatively clear standards for evaluation concerning the transposition of EU directives, its expectations regarding effective implementation are much less transparent. Ironically, in this case its enforcement power may be greater vis-à-vis prospective members than current member states, where Commission monitoring does not go beyond the transposition stage. A similar dynamic of instituting more exacting standards for future than for current members is also at work in areas such as health, social protection, and education reform, where the EU calls for extensive restructuring in the accession countries while having no legal apparatus for addressing similar issues in its member states. Consequently, the EU lacks detailed criteria for what constitutes adequate performance by the accession candidates and relies on other international agencies, notably the World Bank, for technical assistance with reforms in these areas. It remains to be seen whether the rather undifferentiated disciplinary device available to the EU for enforcing its demands—delayed membership in the Union—is effective beyond the superficial level of legal harmonization.

Efforts by the EU to improve the capacity of accession countries to implement EU social policy illustrate another ironic effect of enlargement and of European integration more generally: the functions of the nation-state are not at all shrinking as a result of delegating authority in some policy areas to the supranational level. Rather, prospective EU membership gives rise to new and highly complex tasks for which the accession countries are thus far insufficiently prepared. Substantial staffing needs are one obvious indicator for the need to enhance state capacity. Administrative decentralization, horizontal coordination between ministries, and the strengthening of regional and local government are long-term tasks, indicating that European integration does not simply imply the disappearance of state structures. On the contrary, both the absorption of EU funds for structural development and the implementation of Community law require highly effective structures of government at all levels. Even more ironically, the EU institution-building program for the candidate countries creates horizontal networks of communication and exchange among administrators in current and future member states that may nurture strategic alliances in Council decision making. There is no reason to assume that such alliances necessarily pursue the goal of ever closer integration. One can just as easily imagine Euroskeptical countries engaging in such horizontal alliance building, as appears to be the case between Great Britain and Poland.

Finally, the absence of nonstate actors from accession preparations in the one policy area in which their participation is laid down in the treaty base of the EU suggests that enlargement has so far been a top-down process that has strengthened the executive in the accession countries. Without any legal specifications of member state obligations concerning national-level consultations with the social partners, the EU has had to rely on normative rather than coercive pressures to convince governments in Poland and Hungary to integrate the social partners in accession preparations—with minimal success. In many ways, the noninvolvement of labor and employer organization is perhaps overdetermined: accession preparations have thus far focused on transposition rather than implementation; compared with other socioeconomic issues, the EU social *acquis* has been of limited salience in the accession countries; costs and benefits arising from EU social legislation for specific sectors have not been assessed; organizational fragmentation and limited resources make the articulation of interests in a complex and still distant policy area both difficult and unlikely; and the symbolic value of membership in the EU for citizens and elites in Central and Eastern Europe limits the discursive space in which costs and benefits of membership can be discussed critically. The relative silence of labor and employer organizations, despite explicit calls for their involvement by the European Commission, suggests that transnational organizational networks do not necessarily enhance the leverage of social actors in their domestic environment. At the same time, noninvolvement of nonstate actors indicates that the diffusion of Community social legislation has thus far been a top-down and intergovernmental process. The absence of organized interests from Poland's and Hungary's accession preparations means that both countries are likely to encounter difficulties in the implementation stage.

NOTES

I gratefully acknowledge the support provided by the following institutions for the dissertation research on which this chapter is based: Peace Studies Program at Cornell University, European Trade Union Institute (Brussels), Central European University (Budapest and Warsaw), Max Planck Institute for the Study of Societies (Cologne), and the International Dissertation Field Research Fellowship Program of the Social Science Research Council. Ronald Linden and Valerie Bunce offered helpful comments.

1. For general discussions of norms in politics and international relations, see Peter Katzenstein, ed., *The Culture of National Security: Norms and Identity in World Politics* (New York: Columbia University Press, 1996); Friedrich Kratochwil, *Rules, Norms, and Decisions* (New York: Cambridge University Press, 1988); James G. March and Johan P. Olsen, *Rediscovering Institutions: The Organizational Basis of Politics* (New York: Free Press, 1989); Nicholas Onuf, *World of Our Making: Rules and Rule in Social Theory and International Relations* (Columbia: University of South Carolina Press, 1989); Thomas Risse-Kappen, *Cooperation among Democracies: The European Influence on US Foreign Policy* (Princeton, N.J.: Princeton University Press, 1995).

2. Heather Grabbe and Kirsty Hughes, *Enlarging the EU Eastwards* (London: Pinter, 1998); Alan Mayhew, *Recreating Europe: The European Union's Policy towards*

Central and Eastern Europe (Cambridge: Cambridge University Press, 1998); Christopher Preston, *Enlargement and Integration in the European Union* (New York: Routledge, 1997).

3. See David Strang and Sarah Soule, "Diffusion in Organizations and Social Movements: From Hybrid Corn to Poison Pills," *Annual Review of Sociology* 24 (1989): 265–90.

4. See the threefold typology of regulative, normative, and cognitive institutions in W. Richard Scott, *Institutions and Organizations* (Thousand Oaks, Calif.: Sage, 1995), 35.

5. For a discussion of different types of isomorphism (coercive, normative, and mimetic), see Paul DiMaggio and Walter Powell, "The Iron Cage Revisited: Institutional Isomorphism and Collective Rationality in Organizational Fields," *American Sociological Review* 48 (1983): 147–60.

6. The so-called Copenhagen criteria specified by the European Council in 1993 are as follows: (1) stability of institutions guaranteeing democracy, rule of law, human rights, and protection of minorities; (2) existence of a functioning market economy; (3) capacity to cope with the competitive pressures and market forces within the EU; (4) ability to take on the obligations of membership, including adherence to the aims of political, economic, and monetary union.

7. Economist Intelligence Unit, *Country Report Poland* (first quarter 2000), 31; and *Country Report Hungary* (first quarter 2000), 43.

8. Poland: 38.7 million (1999); Hungary: 10.06 million (1999). Economist Intelligence Unit, *Country Report Poland*, 5; and *Country Report Hungary*, 5.

9. World Bank, *Hungary on the Road to the European Union* (Washington, D.C.: World Bank, 1999), 66.

10. On recent coalition instability in Poland and the weakness of party structures, see George Blazyca and Marek Kolkiewicz, "Poland and the EU: Internal Disputes, Domestic Politics, and Accession," *Journal of Communist Studies and Transition Politics* 15, no. 4 (1999): 131–43.

11. Anna Seleny, "Old Political Rationalities and New Democracies," *World Politics*, July 1999, 484-519, describes marked differences in political styles between Poland and Hungary that she summarizes as "mobilization versus bargaining" (488). For data on collective action in Poland, see Grzegorz Ekiert and Jan Kubik, *Collective Protest and Democratic Consolidation in Poland, 1989-1993*, Pew Papers on Central Eastern European Reform and Regionalism, no. 3 (Princeton, N.J.: Center of International Studies, Princeton University, 1997).

12. Note in particular the anti-EU discourse and activism of the radical farmers' union Samoobrona ("Self-Defense") under the leadership of Andrzej Lepper. On farmers' contentious politics in Poland, see Krzysztof Gorlach, "Freedom for Credit: Polish Peasant Protests in the Era of Communism and Post-Communism," *Polish Sociological Review* 1, no. 129 (2000): 57–85.

13. See Christine Oliver, "Strategic Responses to Institutional Processes," *Academy of Management Review* 16 (1991): 145–79.

14. Intergovernmental Conference on the Common Market and EURATOM, *Treaty Establishing the European Economic Community and Connected Documents* (Brussels: Secretariat of the Interim Committee for the Common Market and EURATOM, 1957), in force since January 1, 1958 (OJ L1/1, amended by Amsterdam Treaty OJ

1997 L179/12). For the consolidated version incorporating the changes made by the Treaty of Amsterdam, see OJ C 340 (10.11.1997), 173–308.

15. Conference of the Representatives of the Governments of the Member States, *Treaty on European Union* (Luxembourg: Office for Official Publications of the European Communities, 1992), signed on February 7, 1992. For the consolidated version incorporating the changes made by the Treaty of Amsterdam, see OJ C 340 (10.11.1997): 145–72.

16. Treaty on European Union, OJ C 340 (10.11.1997), 145–72, art. 2.

17. Articles 39–42, EC Treaty. See also Roger Blanpain, *European Labour Law*, 6th rev. ed. (The Hague: Kluwer Law, 1999), 44.

18. Articles 125–130, EC Treaty.

19. Articles 136–150, EC Treaty.

20. Articles 158–162, EC Treaty.

21. Article 152, EC Treaty.

22. Established by Title VIII in the Treaty of Amsterdam and the extraordinary European Council in Luxembourg in November 1997 *(Presidency Conclusions on the Extraordinary European Council Meeting on Employment, Luxembourg, 20 and 21 November 1997).*

23. The social dialogue was first established through the Agreement on Social Policy of 1992 and included in the Treaty on European Union via the Amsterdam treaty (art. 139, TEU).

24. See Wolfgang Streeck, "The Internationalization of Industrial Relations: Prospects and Problems," *MPIfG Discussion Paper* 98/2 (Cologne: Max-Planck-Institut für Gesellschaftsforschung, 1998), for an argument about the persisting importance of national-level industrial relations in the EU; see also Elena Iankova's chapter in this volume.

25. "Memorandum of Understanding between the European Commission, the European Bank of Reconstruction and Development, and the International Bank for Reconstruction and Development on Cooperation for Pre-accession Preparation of Central and East European Countries," March 1998. The guiding principles of World Bank assistance to the accession countries are contained in its "country assistance strategies," and specific recommendations for the accession process are made available through "country economic memoranda." On the (often competing and contradictory) influence of different international agencies on social sector reform in Eastern Europe, see Bob Deacon with Michelle Hulse and Paul Stubbs, *Global Social Policy: International Organizations and the Future of Welfare* (London: Sage, 1997).

26. For a thorough review of the literature on European social policy and recent changes in the treaty base, see Gerda Falkner, "EG-Sozialpolitik nach Verflechtungsfalle und Entscheidungslücke: Bewertungsmaßstäbe und Entwicklungstrends," *Politische Vierteljahresschrift*, June 2000, 279–301; G. Falkner, *Social Europe in the 1990s: Towards a Corporatist Policy Community* (London: Routledge, 1998).

27. Wolfgang Streeck, "From Market Making to State Building? Reflections on the Political Economy of European Social Policy," in *European Social Policy*, ed. S. Leibfried and P. Pierson (Washington, D.C.: Brookings Institution, 1995), 389-431; Corinne Gobin, *L'Europe syndicale* (Brussels: Éditions Labor, 1997).

28. George Ross, "Assessing the Delors Era and Social Policy," in Liebfried and Pierson, *European Social Policy*, 357–88; Catherine Hoskyns, "Women, European

Law, and International Politics," *International Journal of the Sociology of Law,* November 1987, 299–316; Éliane Vogel-Polsky and Jean Vogel, *L'Europe Sociale 1993: Illusion, alibi ou réalité?* (Brussels: Éditions de Université Libre de Bruxelles, 1991).

29. Among the member states, those with higher domestic social standards are likely to be more concerned about seeing the social law of the EU applied in Central and Eastern Europe.

30. Compare the following two aggregate measurements: average per capita GDP in the EU in 1997 was US$21,640, whereas in the ten CEE accession countries it was US$3,643 (or 16.8 percent of the EU average). By contrast, average per capita GDP based on purchasing power parity in 1995 was ECU 17,260 in the EU and ECU 5,775 (or 33.5 percent of the EU average) in the CEE accession countries. See European University Institute, Robert Schuman Centre, "Socioeconomic Discrepancies in the Enlarged EU," *Policy Papers,* RSC no. 99/2 (Florence: EUI, 1999): 4–5 (my calculations). For projections on how long income convergence between CEE and the current member states of the EU will take, see World Bank, *Hungary on the Road to the European Union,* 27–31.

31. Ewald Walterskirchen, Raimund Dietz, *Auswirkungen der EU-Osterweiterung auf den österreichischen Arbeitsmarkt* (Vienna: Bundeskammer für Arbeiter und Angestellte, 1998).

32. European Commission, "The Impact of Eastern Enlargement on Employment and Wages in the EU Member States," May 2000 <europa.eu.int/comm/employment_social/empl&esf/docs/boeri2.pdf> (July 16, 2001); a summary of this report can be found in "Social Impact of EU Enlargement," *European Industrial Relations Review,* July 2000, 32–34; an assessment of costs and benefits with emphasis on Austria is provided in Christian Keuschnigg and Wilhelm Kohler, "Eastern Enlargement to the EU: Economic Costs and Benefits for the EU Present Member States?" final report, Study XIX/B1/9801 <europa.eu.int/comm/budget/pdf/elargisb1/def_austria1.pdf> (December 15, 2000), which concludes that the benefits of enlargement accruing to current member states that share borders with applicant countries will override the costs.

33. *Standard Eurobarometer Report* no. 52, April 2000, section 3.7 ("Support for the Union's Priorities") <europa.eu.int/comm/dg10/epo/eb/eb52/eb52_en.pdf> (December 15, 2000).

34. Data from fall 1999. *Standard Eurobarometer* no. 52, sec. 3.8 ("Support for Enlargement"). Note that the question referred not only to the thirteen applicant countries, but also included Norway and Switzerland. The latter two, while not currently seeking to join the EU, enjoy much greater support among EU citizens than do the actual candidate countries, a fact that potentially biases the responses concerning aggregate support for enlargement (in an upward direction).

35. *Eurobarometer* no. 52, sec. 3.8.

36. Commission of the European Communities, *Sixteenth Annual Report on Monitoring the Application of Community Law (1998),* COM (1999) 301 final (July 9, 1999): 139, 209–10 (my calculations). Note that the sector categories in the two tables are not entirely congruent: I have drawn the data on number of directives on "customs and taxation" from the following subsectors of internal market directives (209): "customs union," "direct taxation," "VAT," and "other indirect taxes."

37. The ratio of the share of infringement proceedings to the share of directives in a given policy area allows us to condense these two measures into one indicator that

can be compared across policy areas. A ratio higher than 1 indicates a disproportionate number of infringement proceedings in a given policy area. Thus, for social
and employment directives, we obtain a ratio of 1.71 and for environmental legislation a ratio of 1.88; by contrast, the ratio concerning internal market directives was
.52 and for agriculture .54.

38. The candidate countries are fully aware of this. A statement I heard repeatedly
in interviews with Polish and Hungarian government officials (Budapest, February–April 2000, and Warsaw, October–November 2000) was that "everybody knows
that Greece would not be able to join the EU today if it were held to the same standards as we are!"

39. Republic of Poland, "Poland's Negotiating Position in the Area of Employment
and Social Policy," submitted May 31, 1999 <www.ukie.gov.pl/cona/snen/13en.pdf>
(July 16, 2001). The directives in question are 89/655/EEC, 89/656/EEC (in both
cases, transition requests concern equipment in operation before December 31,
2002) and 90/679/EEC (protection of workers from risks related to exposure to
biological agents at work). See the update on the negotiations at <www.euractiv.
com/cgi-bin/eurb/cgint.exe/11435?714&1015=&3&1014=enforce4> (September 13,
2000).

40. Republic of Hungary, "Negotiating Position of the Republic of Hungary on
Chapter 13: Social Policy and Employment," CONF-H25/99 <www.mfa.gov.hu/eu-
anyag/SZI/Allaspont/positionpapers.htm> (July 16, 2001). The directive in question
is Dir. 90/239/EEC.

41. What *is* controversial, but not part of the social *acquis* proper, is the freedom
of movement for persons, which several member states would like to see introduced
in the Central and Eastern European countries only after an extensive transition period.

42. In its 1999 composite report on accession preparations in all candidate countries, the Commission notes that progress in social and health policy is "rather slow."
Commission of the European Communities, *Composite Paper: Reports on Progress
toward Accession by Each of the Candidate Countries,* COM (1999) 500 final (Brussels, October 13, 1999), 24.

43. Republic of Poland, "Response to the Common Position of the European
Union: Chapter 13: Social Policy and Employment," Conference on Accession of the
European Union—Poland, CONF-PL47/99 (Brussels, November 5, 1999).

44. Commission of the European Communities, *1999 Regular Report from the
Commission on Poland's Progress towards Accession,* October 13, 1999, COM (1999)
509 final: 47–48.

45. Commission of the European Communities, *2000 Regular Report from the
Commission on Poland's Progress towards Accession,* November 8, 2000
<europa.eu.int/comm/enlargement/dwn/report_11_00/pdf/en/pl_en.pdf> (July 16,
2001).

46. Commission of the European Communities, *1999 Regular Report from the
Commission on Hungary's Progress towards Accession,* October 13, 1999, COM
(1999) 505 final: 44–46.

47. Commission of the European Communities, *2000 Regular Report from the Commission on Hungary's Progress towards Accession,* November 8, 2000 <europa.eu.int/
comm/enlargement/dwn/report_11_00/pdf/en/hu_en.pdf> (July 16, 2001).

48. Nevertheless, as of March 2000, Poland had a legislative agenda of two hundred bills to be passed in order to approximate Polish law to the EU *acquis* (Jan Maksymiuk, "Poland Wants EU Membership by 2003," *RFE-RL Newsline,* March 16, 2000). This kind of workload makes meaningful deliberation rather improbable.

49. Officials at the Hungarian Ministry of Social and Family Affairs, interview by author, March 2000.

50. There are approximately seventy thousand pages of *acquis communautaire* in need of transposition and/or implementation. See Commission of the European Communities, *2000 Regular Report from the Commission on Hungary's Progress towards Accession,* November 8, 2000 <europa.eu.int/comm/enlargement/dwn/report_11_00/pdf/en/hu_en.pdf> (July 16, 2001).

51. Jan de Weydenthal, "Poland: Loss of EU Aid Shows Need for Institutional Streamlining," *RFE-RL,* May 27, 1998. See also Jacek Kucharczyk, "European Integration in Polish Political Debates 1997-1998" (manuscript, Institute of Public Affairs [Instytut Spraw Publicznych], Warsaw, 1999).

52. Preaccession advisers, interview by author, April 27, 2000 (Budapest), and June 20, 2000 (Warsaw).

53. World Bank, *Ready for Europe: Public Administration Reform and European Union Accession in Central and Eastern Europe* (Washington, D.C.: World Bank, 2000).

54. Hungarian Ministry of Foreign Affairs, State Secretariat for Integration, *National Programme for the Adoption of the Acquis—Hungary,* revised version 1999, July 1999, 15838-3/1999, v. 1: 3. For the Commission's approving comments, see the *1999 Regular Report from the Commission on Hungary's Progress towards Accession,* October 13, 1999, COM (1999) 505 final: 83–84. What percentage of this increase is to be filled through internal restructuring rather than new recruitment remains to be determined, especially given the simultaneous need for further budget consolidation.

55. Hungarian Ministry of Foreign Affairs, State Secretariat for Integration, *National Programme for the Adoption of the Acquis—Hungary,* 10. "Justice and home affairs" refers to border control, asylum and migration policy, combating organized crime, and Europol cooperation.

56. Hungarian Ministry of Foreign Affairs, State Secretariat for Integration, *National Programme for the Adoption of the Acquis—Hungary,* revised version 1999 (July 1999), 15838-3/1999, v. 2: 68–126.

57. Commission of the European Communities, *1999 Regular Report from the Commission on Poland's Progress towards Accession,* October 13, 1999, COM (1999) 509 final: 82. See also UKIE Poland, *National Programme of Preparation for Membership in the European Union,* accepted by the Council of Ministers May 1999, updated in 2000 <www.cie.gov.pl/tem/dokumenty.html> (July 16, 2001).

58. But note an earlier Commission criticism concerning weaknesses in social dialogue structures in the accession countries: European Commission, *Commission Opinion on Hungary's Application for Membership in the European Union,* COM (97) 2001 fin, Brussels, July 15, 1997, 76 (calling for organizational consolidation both among labor and among employers).

59. Interview by author, Budapest, April 18, 2000.

60. Commission for the European Communities, "Proposal for a Council Decision on the Principles, Priorities, Intermediate Objectives, and Conditions Contained in

the Accession Partnership with the Republic of Hungary," COM (1999) 525 final, October 13, 1999, and "Proposal for a Council Decision on the principles, priorities, intermediate objectives and conditions contained in the accession partnership with the Republic of Poland, COM(1999) 529 final, 13 October 1999.

61. Commission of the European Communities, *2000 Regular Report from the Commission on Poland's Progress towards Accession,* November 8, 2000, chap. 13 <europa.eu.int/comm/enlargement/dwn/report_11_00/pdf/en/pl_en.pdf> (July 16, 2001).

62. Commission of the European Communities, *2000 Regular Report from the Commission on Hungary's Progress towards Accession,* November 8, 2000, chap. 13 <europa.eu.int/comm/enlargement/dwn/report_11_00/pdf/en/hu_en.pdf> (July 16, 2001).

63. Interviews by author, Brussels, March 11, 2001, and Budapest, April 23, 2001.

64. Paul Kubicek, "Organized Labor in Postcommunist States: Will the Western Sun Set on It, Too?" *Comparative Politics,* October 1999, 83–102; David Ost, "Illusory Corporatism in Eastern Europe: Neoliberal Tripartism and Postcommunist Class Identities," *Politics and Society,* December 2000; David Ost and Marc Weinstein, "Unionists against Unions: Toward Hierarchical Management in Post-Communist Poland," *East European Politics and Societies* 13, no. 1 (1999): 33; András Tóth, "Development of the Hungarian Motor Vehicle Industry: The Case of the Audi Engine Plant" (unpublished manuscript, January 2000); László Neumann, "Decentralized Collective Bargaining in Hungary" (unpublished manuscript, 1999).

65. Franciszek Draus, *Les organizations patronales dans les pays de l'Europe centrale et orientale (Pologne, République tchèque, Hongrie),* report 64 (Brussels: European Trade Union Institute/Max-Planck-Institut für Gesellschaftsforschung, 2000).

66. L. Héthy, "Tripartism and Industrial Relations in Hungary," and Elżbieta Sobótka, "The Role and Functioning of Tripartite Institutions in Social Dialogue at the National Level in Poland," in *Social Dialogue in Central and Eastern Europe,* ed. G. Casale (Budapest: International Labour Office, Central and Eastern European Team, 1999), 180–201, 264–69. For a critique of using primarily institutional criteria for assessing institutions of social dialogue in Western Europe, see Frank L. Wilson, "Interest Groups and Politics in Western Europe: The Neo-Corporatist Approach," *Comparative Political Studies,* October 1983, 118–19; see also Elena Iankova's chapter in this volume.

67. See Werner Reutter, "Trade Unions and Politics in Eastern and Central Europe: Tripartism without Corporatism," in *The Lost Perspective? Trade Unions between Ideology and Social Action in the New Europe,* ed. P. Pasture, J. Verberckmoes, and Hans de Witte (Aldershot, U.K.: Avebury, 1996), 2: 137–57; Ost, "Illusory Corporatism."

68. See "Industrial Relations Background in Hungary," *European Industrial Relations Review,* February 2000, 16–23; Ildikó Krén, "Gewerkschaften in Ungarn— Pluralismus ohne Frauen?" (unpublished manuscript, January 2000).

69. Hungarian trade union representatives, interview by author, Budapest (2/9/2000, 2/11/2000, 2/24/2000, 3/3/2000, 4/12/2000, 5/3/2000).

70. All with the exception of ÉSZT, the Intellectual Workers' Trade Union Association.

71. L. Héthy, "Tripartism and Industrial Relations"; Draus, *Les organizations patronales.*

72. Draus, *Les organizations patronales*, 84.

73. "Industrial Relations Background: Poland," *European Industrial Relations Review*, August 1999, 22–27.

74. Trade union officials who win political office are required to resign from trade union functions in Solidarity, but not in OPZZ (Solidarity, interview by author, June 14, 2000; OPZZ, interview by author, June 20, 2000).

75. Draus, *Les organizations patronales*, 43, 49.

76. Csaba Öry and László Herczog, "The New System of Social Dialogue in Hungary" (unpublished manuscript, June 1999); G. Casale, "Tripartism and Industrial Relations in Central and Eastern European Countries," in Casale, *Social Dialogue*, 1–36.

77. Representatives of Hungarian trade unions and employer organizations, interview by author, January–May 2000.

78. Instead, it was founded by a pact between the government and a variety of trade unions (Pact on State Enterprises, February 1993). See "Industrial Relations Background: Poland," 25.

79. Aside from my own interviews, I am relying on D. Boda and L. Neumann, "The Hungarian Social Partners' View on the Labor Issues of European Accession" (unpublished manuscript, May 2000, National Labor Center, Research Unit, Budapest).

80. In light of the low rates of labor mobility *within* both countries, freedom of movement constitutes a symbolic rather than a real value for the vast majority of workers. Perhaps in recognition of this, Hungary was the first candidate to agree to the seven-year transition period for the free movement of workers requested by the EU (June 2001).

81. However, neither government nor the social partners appear to be willing to discuss the extent of such consultations in detail, as informal contacts tend to be regarded as illegitimate holdovers from the past.

82. See Margaret Keck and Kathryn Sikkink, *Activists beyond Borders* (Ithaca, N.Y.: Cornell University Press, 1998).

12

The Pivotal EU Role in the Creation of Czech Regional Policy

Wade Jacoby and Pavel Cernoch

Most European states have programs to build economic strength in traditionally poor regions. The EU constrains its member states in the kind of regional policy they can pursue, and it cofinances major projects that it approves. In this chapter, we show how the European Union (EU) propagates both regulative and constitutive norms to influence the regional policy of the Czech Republic.

Regulative norms provide order and constraints to state policies.[1] For example, EU regional policy aims to support economic innovation, job creation, environmental protection, and the development of efficient energy and transport networks. Socialist Czechoslovakia had no regional policy in that detailed sense, and even the democratic governments after the 1989 Velvet Revolution pursued a centralist regional policy, using it merely to redistribute state funds to alleviate regional unemployment.

Constitutive norms create new actors or new interests, and the EU also has pushed the Czech Republic to create new actors in this policy domain. Most important, the EU structural funds presuppose that independent municipal and regional actors will help set development priorities and implement and monitor programs. When the EU urged the creation of new regional actors, it provoked real reservations among many political elites. For a long time, the centralist attitude mentioned above delayed the establishment of self-governing "higher territorial regions" as they were foreseen by the 1992 Czech constitution.

In this chapter we argue that once the Czechs applied for EU membership, EU pressure grew for the introduction of a new understanding of regional policy. In subsequent years, EU Commission officials tried to introduce and nurture a set of fairly detailed regulative and constitutive norms for regional policy making in the Czech Republic. While a few Czech officials found wisdom in such norms, the norms were much more widely accepted and used because of EU prestige and power. We do not argue either that all of these norms were nonexistent in the Czech Republic before its intensive contact with the EU or that the norms in question are so widespread now as to be beyond challenge. On the contrary, throughout the chapter, we stress the fights around these norms and the vulnerabilities they still face today. In so doing, we will show how the EU strengthened some norms while building others more or less from scratch.

What do we mean by norms? First, we mean more than the sociological conception of informal practices, because we are also interested in the process by which those practices attain the status of law.[2] Second, we follow Finnemore and Sikkink in distinguishing between norms and institutions. Norms are "standards of appropriate behavior for actors with a given identity"; institutions are more comprehensive and often represent an aggregation of different norms.[3] Accordingly, in this chapter, we focus on three kinds of standards of appropriate behavior. The first set of standards include fundamental principles about how current EU member states handle regional policy procedures. Some specific principles to which we will call attention are regulative norms, such as multiannual budgeting, interregional competition, and a preference for using EU structural funds for investment rather than redistribution. The second encompass the adoption of specific pieces of the *acquis communautaire,* which the EU requires all prospective members to adopt.[4] Examples here are often constitutive norms, including the requirement of detailed coordination between regions and the central government or the formal separation of management and monitoring. We call them constitutive because these norms presuppose the existence of certain kinds of political actors, some of which did not exist in the Czech Republic. In many of these cases, legislatures legally codify these "standards of appropriate behavior." The third kind of standards of appropriate behavior comprises technical standards for, say, building a bridge using EU structural funds. By our account, all three categories are norms, but we will have more to say about the first two simply because they have been the most controversial politically.[5]

All norms are meaningful within particular contexts. Because the same norm can be powerful in one context and widely ignored in the next, we think it useful to note that the current EU enlargement is different from previous enlargements in three ways that matter for the transmission of norms: first and most obvious, the *acquis* is larger for this wave of countries than for previous waves. That means the density of norms to be adopted—especially after the treaty amendments of Maastricht, Amsterdam, and Nice—is higher than in previous cases.[6] Second, a larger number of prospective members wait at the EU door. The large numbers compel the EU to reorganize before accepting new members, and they simultaneously increase the importance of precedents set by early entrants for later entrants. Third, while new members have always had to adopt the *acquis* with, at most, temporary derogations, the EU now asks more in terms of preaccession preparation than it did in previous waves. Of course, Austria, Sweden, and Finland were relatively closer to prevailing EU practices at the time of their accession than are the CEE states. Yet the less prepared southern tier states of Greece, Portugal, and Spain were also allowed in with little advance preparation. Indeed, in the Greek case, the Commission was concerned enough about the extent of needed reforms that it issued a negative opinion—*avis*—which was then overridden by the Council.[7] All three contextual aspects complicate accession, so the run-up to membership has taxed each CEE state's ability to comply with a bewildering array of norms.[8] We demonstrate this claim through a case study of the development of regional policy instruments in the Czech Republic.

REGIONAL POLICY AS A CASE STUDY

In the context of this volume, we favor a focus on regional policy for several reasons. First, it is obviously a very important policy area; indeed, it is the second most expensive thing the EU does. Second, there are lots of norms to implement; because EU regional policy laws have "direct effects" on member states, there is little formal regional policy *acquis* for new members to adopt through their own legislatures. However, a significant number of strict norms regulate how the member states seek and use structural funds. Member states that break these norms expect to be penalized with the loss of some EU matching funds. Third, Czechoslovakia had very few regional policy instruments; thus it started nearly from scratch in 1990. Fourth, regional policy interest organizations have been weak or nonexistent. Hence the Czech government has not had to confront actors with strong identities, deep pockets, and formidable organizational skills that could be used to defend prerogatives inherited from the old order or new postcommunist gains that might be threatened by EU procedures.[9] Taken together (table 12.1), the case is interesting because there is relatively low potential for strict "path dependence": old institutions and established actors are few and weak, the financial rewards for conforming are high, norms are abundant, even if the amount of formal *acquis* that must be adopted is relatively low.

We do not claim that the regional policy dynamics we highlight hold true for all policy areas in which the EU has urged reforms. In fact, the impact of EU norms varies across policy areas. In this chapter, we focus on two potential dimensions of that variation: the density of the *acquis* and the density of policy domain actors prior to the onset of reform. We hypothesize that the likelihood that EU norms will be adopted follows from two questions. First, is the policy area one in which the EU has a large body of legislation that it expects the prospective new members to approximate? If it is, we expect that the job of taking on large numbers of new norms and institutions simultaneously might severely tax actors in that policy domain. Ceteris paribus, we would expect some confusion and the uneven incorporation of norms under these conditions. Second, is the policy area one in which well-established actors already are present? If so, we expect well-established actors to have their own norms and institutions against which they would measure the acceptability of EU norms. Without denying that the pressure to adopt the new norms may be significant, our expectation is that well-established actors may show more skepticism—openly or covertly—about the appropriateness of the new norms to their situation.[10]

These two hypotheses suggest four clusters of policy cases. First, if one can expect a relatively low influence of EU norms in areas where EU norms are few and domestic actors are well established, then Czech health policy would surely be an example, for the *acquis* is fairly light, and preexisting actors are quite dense. Second and third, we would expect a somewhat more effective infusion of norms *either* where preestablished actors are weak (e.g., consumer protection) *or* where the number of EU norms are quite high (e.g., agriculture, where the *acquis* is enormous but Czech interest organizations are well established). In each of these two cases, we suspect that one variable tends to promote the spread of norms while the other tends to suppress them. Finally, only where both variables point to the importance of EU norms (e.g., regional policy, where the EU norms are numerous and Czech interest associations quite weak) should we expect norms to play a dominant role.

THE MISMATCH BETWEEN MOTIVES AND MECHANISMS

There is one broader feature of EU enlargement to which our findings from regional policy can be generalized. We call this (with apologies for excessive alliteration) the mismatch between motives and mechanisms. Many times, CEE elites face a large gap between will and skill in a policy area between what they want to do and what they can do. Clearly, access to structural funds is a very high priority for all prospective members. The EU provides

Table 12.1. Stylized Expectations of Where EU Norms Might Be Strong and Weak

Density of EU Norms Available	Density of Actors Prior to Onset of Postcommunist Reforms	
	Low Density of Actors	*High Density of Actors*
Low density of norms	Consumer protection	Health policies
High density of norms	Regional policy	Agriculture

structural funds to member states for disbursement through the state's regional policy instruments. The EU will only approve projects for which the member is also spending its own money. But the Czech Republic has been slow to develop the political infrastructure appropriate to formulating and implementing regional policy. Mechanisms have followed motives only with a long lag time.

There are at least two important causes of delay, one domestic and one international. At one level, Czech parties have disagreed over how to implement provisions for decentralization that are contained (but poorly specified) in the 1992 Czech constitution. One result of this dispute has been a long delay in the building of the regional governments that will play a key role in any regional policy. The second dimension of this political struggle occurs between Prague and Brussels. We will describe some of the details of this struggle, but for now it is important merely to see that delays in implementing regional policy are important because structural funds are a "use 'em or lose 'em" proposition. Indeed, many member states have to forgo some potential funding every year because they are unable to meet all the strict guidelines set by the EU.[11]

THE EU AS NORM GENERATOR

CEE efforts to prepare for membership are affected by the policy that exists among EU member states. They must adopt the norms and institutional practices established by Council, Commission, and Parliament.[12] As is well known, the EU has had an increasing tendency toward common policy making since the ratification of the Maastricht treaty in 1993. The heads of the EU member states meet at regular summit meetings (the European Council) where common policy making is discussed.[13] Policy decisions that result from these Council meetings then set the agenda for the European Commission, which can then propose new legislation.[14] As stated earlier, the importance of EU norms extends beyond mere regulative norms, such as technical standards for individual policy areas. EU norms can also play a constitutive function by helping to organize actors and channel their political behavior. We demonstrate these dual functions of EU norms through a case study of regional policy.

THE STRUCTURAL AND COHESION POLICY OF THE EUROPEAN UNION

The two central priorities of EU regional policy are to reduce existing economic and social disparities among regions and to reduce unemployment in the weakest EU regions.[15] EU structural and cohesion funds contribute financially to the regional policies of the member states as they seek to create appropriate conditions for investment and job creation. While the member states retain the responsibility for defining their development priorities, the cofinancing role of the EU requires that individual projects take account of the European dimension of economic and social development. What is this "European dimension"? For the period 2000–2006, which covers the last stage of membership preparations of the first wave of new member states, the Commission set three priorities: regional competitiveness, social cohesion and employment, and the development of urban and rural areas.[16]

The Commission turns these priorities into norms, which apply to countries wishing to join the EU. While the Council of Ministers is responsible for laying down general provisions for the use of structural funds, the Commission sets the detailed guidelines for their use.[17]Authorities of the respective recipient countries use these guidelines to prepare their specific programs. For the purpose of our study, it is this specific role of the Commission that characterizes it as a supervising institution, or "nanny," for the respective recipient states. States that violate its norms may well lose funding.

It is hard to overestimate the importance of regional policy to EU activities. Spending from the structural fund is the second largest component of the EU budget, trailing only the Common Agricultural Policy (CAP).[18] Access to these funds is predicated on planning competence and administrative mastery of complex procedures. These controls are sufficiently strict that many subnational governments in longtime member states are unable to gain access to moneys to which their region is nominally entitled. That is, certain administrative competencies are a prerequisite for receiving structural funds. But because almost all EU regional policy legislation is directly applicable, prospective members do not need to "approximate" EU laws so much as create competent regional actors.[19] The absolute need for such regional planning and administrative competence amounts to a vital constitutive norm.

CZECH REGIONAL POLICY

Although we will provide a detailed chronology of changes (table 12.2) in Czech regional policy, the best place to start is neither the beginning nor the end, but the middle. In 1997 the EU Commission published an initial opinion on the 1996 Czech application for EU membership. Written around projections of future reforms, the opinion was generally positive about Czech

Table 12.2.   Chronology of Key Steps in the Development of Regional Policy (RP) in the Czech Republic

1990	Dismantling of central planning and widespread discredit of notion of RP.
1991	Regional Policy Act subsumes RP under economic policy. Key objective is the achievement of minimal living and working standards for all citizens.
1992	Government Resolution on Principles of Regional Economic Policy. Principal RP goal is to support the development of a market economy, especially through the promotion of small and medium-size enterprises (SMEs).
1994	EU cross-border programs started on Czech-Austrian and Czech-German borders.
1995	Ministry of Economics renamed Ministry for Regional Development and awarded the coordinating role in RP.
1998	Government position document (Res. 159) outlining RP negotiating position with EU.
1998	Government releases principle of regional policy (Res. 235) as stopgap measure until formal legislation can be prepared. Broadens aims of 1992 principles, especially in regard to building regional governance competencies.
1998	Regional coordination committees and regional development agencies established. Both bodies devoted to easing transition to eventual regional level of government.
1998	Eurostat and Czech Statistical Office agree to boundaries of eight NUTS II units. Each unit will have its own regional management and monitoring committees. (NUTS stands for Nomenclature des Unités Territoriales Statistiques, the EU defined regions for statistical and analytical purposes. For more, see pp. 325, 333 below.)
1999	Act on Regional Development Support. Outlines RP responsibilities of new Czech regions and establishes instruments and central coordination framework for RP.
1999	Government announces program for eighteen problem districts.
1999	Czechs ask EU to support three pilot regional operational programs and two sectoral operational programs.
2000	Constitutional Act on the Formation of the Regions (passed in 1997) takes effect on January 1 and creates fourteen regional governments in Czech Republic.
2000	Publication of the *National Strategy of Regional Development of the Czech Republic,* a document outlining the transfer of resources from EU structural funds through the regional development plan (written between February and December 1999).

prospects for meeting the terms of membership in the medium term. Yet the basic optimism could not mask the EU concern that, as the opinion notes, "Currently, the Czech Republic has no regional policy."[20]

In historical perspective, the Czech reluctance to develop instruments of regional policy is particularly striking. One of the primary motives for several new EU members in the past few decades has been the promise of access to structural funds that may help develop their weaker regions. In the Czech case, however, Prime Minister Václav Klaus's preference for centralized control long prevented even the formal establishment of the agents that would conduct a regional policy.[21] Such agents did not exist in a policy domain that is undeniably crucial to EU member states, which speaks strongly to Czech reservations about some EU norms and institutions. We will see that when the Klaus government finally agreed to allow regional bodies, it insisted on inflating their number and diminishing their size so that no one region could develop a large power base.[22]

Two background conditions apply to any discussion of Czech regional policy: first, much Czech thought about regional policy in the early 1990s came against the immediate backdrop of state socialist policies of Czechoslovakia, under which "regional policy" was reduced to the redistribution and reallocation of resources under socialist economic planning. Such planning allowed the state to guarantee both high employment and relative income equality. "Regional policy" meant the intervention of a centralist government into economic and social developments in different parts of the country. It implied little in the way of autonomous local capacity. After 1989, enthusiasm for market economies and uncertainty about the durability of the Czechoslovak state cast long shadows over all thinking about regional policy. By 1993 the country separated into independent Czech and Slovak Republics.

Against these two background conditions, a range of serious economic problems soon appeared, including the decline of state-owned heavy industry, the decline of the collectivized agricultural sector, the very low mobility of the workforce (due in part to lack of accessible housing), and pollution and environmental problems. In the hardest-hit regions, such as north Bohemia and northeast Moravia, some officials began to call for policies to address regional development, retraining, and restructuring. Job creation in regions with industrial decline became a priority, as rising unemployment figures revealed a growing cleavage among regions. Through the early 1990s overall Czech unemployment was remarkably low, but aggregate unemployment and regional disparities grew sharply throughout the second half of the 1990s. By the time the Czech government adopted the regional development strategy in July 2000, the unemployment rate had reached 9.0 percent. In the worst-affected areas of north Bohemia, unemployment had reached 20.7 percent by 2000 (Most district) and in North

Moravia, it reached 18.4 percent (Karviná district). In five other districts from both regions, the unemployment rate was higher than 15 percent (Chomutov, Louny, Ostrava, Teplice, and Bruntál).[23] Figure 12.1 shows these developments using Eurostat's measure of interregional differences in unemployment. The standard deviation is weighted by the size of the region according to EU statistical formulas. Starting in 1995, the data show a sharp jump in regional unemployment disparities, and this trend holds whether one talks about the larger (NUTS II), intermediate (NUTS III), or smaller (NUTS IV) Czech statistical regions.

In the early stages of unemployment growth, the government chose not to use regional policy to buck the trend. The government's response in the early 1990s was a mixture of the old logic of the socialist era—saying that regional problems have to be addressed by central government intervention—and a new market-oriented focus on the development of infrastructure and support for small and medium-sized enterprises. After the separation of Slovakia, the Klaus government focused on some selected industrial crisis points but neglected both interministerial coordination at the central level and coordination with actors at the regional and municipal levels. As such, Czech regional policy tended more toward "bailouts" than development.

Figure 12.1   Development of Interregional Unemployment Disparities in the Czech Regions

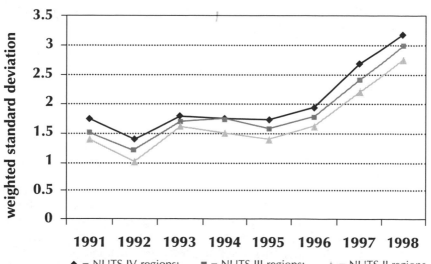

◆ = NUTS IV regions;   ■ = NUTS III regions;   ▲ = NUTS II regions

Source: J. Blažek and P. Severa, "Nky se otevírají," *Ekonom* 42, no. 35 (2000): 27.

The strong role of the central government was due not only to ideology but also to the fact that regional governments, which existed in communist Czechoslovakia merely as an extension of the central communist government, were abolished in 1990. The resulting lack of regional authority was apparent in comparison with many EU member states, even strongly unitary states. But Czech-EU differences in such matters hardly bothered Klaus, for the Euroskepticism articulated by his Civic Democratic Party (ODS) dominated the political debate about European integration in general and regional policy in particular. As Laure Neumayer pointed out, Klaus's "resistance against the political aspects of European integration became the foundation of officially sanctioned Euroskepticism. This two-sided approach consisted of intensive criticism of the EU as well as a perpetual presentation of the Czech Republic as the best prepared candidate for membership." Neumayer identifies four basic pillars of ODS policy toward the EU: (1) the defense of the nation-state as the only source of identity and the only possible framework to guarantee economic freedom in Europe; (2) defending European diversity against alleged Brussels-driven uniformity; (3) insistence on the maintenance of "freedom"; and (4) a standing condemnation of the EU democratic deficit.[24]

Neither Klaus's Euroskepticism nor his centralism went unchallenged by the opposition. The Social Democrats (ČSSD) saw growing unemployment in structurally weak regions as a potential source of votes, and they responded with a stronger emphasis on a pro-European regional policy approach. Pro-EU arguments began to appear in the party's election campaigns and found a prominent spot in the party program. In contrast to the ODS position, the opposition stressed its regional development priorities calling in their 1997 platform for a

> deepening of political and economic democracy, especially by developing local and regional self-governance. This does not concern only the mere existence of regions, districts and municipalities, but also the growth of their influence on the formulation of national policy by empowering them with competencies and own financial resources. . . . The battle against Euroskepticism should elaborate better ways for Czech participation in the process of European integration while maintaining the equality of all involved actors.[25]

An important lever for challenging central control lay latent in the Czech constitution of 1992, whose article 99 foresaw the creation of a layer of self-administered regional governments (also called higher territorial administrative units) between the existing central and municipal levels. According to the constitution, "The Czech Republic is composed of municipalities which are the basic territorial administrative units and regions which are higher territorial administrative units."[26] The authors of the constitution saw the creation of regional governments as a step toward diffusing political power. But some Czech politicians were wary of decentralization, whether out of concern for weakening political authority during the transition or out of fear that overly strong regional competencies might exacerbate Bohemian-Moravian tensions.[27] Consequently, the framers of the Czech constitution left vague the provisions for regional governance.

The Klaus government did not show much enthusiasm for giving up power to regional authorities, and for several years no significant legislative efforts were made to establish the regions or define their competencies. In the wake of the 1996 parliamentary elections, the reelected coalition, led by Klaus's ODS, abolished the Ministry of Economics in a cabinet reshuffle, and created the Ministry for Regional Development (MRD). Although this new ministry was charged with coordinating regional policy at the central level, it soon became apparent that it was weak and had significant competence only with regard to the difficult housing situation in the country, thus earning it the nickname of "housing ministry." The stalemate dragged on. Despite the constitution's call for regional governments and the EU Commission's not so subtle warnings that some form of regional planning competence was required of all members, the Czechs essentially stood pat. While the EU paid a Czech regional planning group for three separate studies of foreign systems of regional policy formation, ODS dominance continued to block the space for such a transfer.

This stalemate, based as it was on a domestic balance of power, did not come apart all at once. But when it did come apart, EU actions played an important role. In January 1996, the Czech Republic applied for EU membership, and, as noted above, the Commission prepared the required opinion on the readiness of the Czech Republic to join. As a consequence of the lack of interest in regional policy by the ODS-led government, the Commission's initial assessment in this area was blunt: "Currently, the Czech Republic has no regional policy. Indeed, regional development initiatives are implemented through sectoral policies at national level. Economically weak areas are selected annually on the basis of principally unemployment rates. In 1996, for example, the chosen area covered 18.4 percent of the population of the Czech Republic."[28] The Commission noted the recent creation of the MRD but remarked that due to the ministry's limited finances for regional investment, the cofinancing capacity necessary for projects financed from EU structural funds could not yet be established.

Though we are arguing that norms established by the EU for structural funds had an impact in this case, we must be careful to circumscribe the general claim: in respect to the creation and structure of regional governments in the Czech Republic, the EU was not in a position to comment. Such questions remain the sovereign decisions of each state. Had the Commission urged on Czech politicians a particular design for regional government, existing member states would likely have unleashed a vitriolic protest. In its opinion, the Commission was nevertheless able to point at the functional *necessity* of authorities able to formulate regional development priorities. They were further able to specify the need for some kind of partner on the Czech side able to develop and articulate such plans. On these points, the Commission noted that

> Czech authorities still have to introduce important reforms to comply with EC's structural policies. . . . Financial resources at the disposal of regional policy should be increased and efficient instruments need to be created. . . . Czech authorities have to determine the future legal basis of a Czech regional policy in order to provide the appropriate legal structure for the actions envisaged to counteract regional disparities and for financing structural policy expenditure.[29]

The Commission's opinion sparked a new discussion among Czech politicians about the need for a regional policy. The MRD saw itself as the responsible body for the preparation of structural funds, but it had a weak voice in the Klaus cabinet. In fact, some of the most interesting initiatives came from outside the cabinet. Actors who gained experience working with EU PHARE funds first seized the opportunity to erode the domestic stalemate.[30] Here, in turn, it becomes difficult to see where "external influences" end and "domestic politics" begins.[31] The Commission delegation in Prague, responsible for coordinating PHARE programs, was looking for appropriate partners in the Czech administration in order to implement PHARE projects aimed at preparing the ground for regional policy and public administration reform.[32]

In searching for partners, the delegation had two major actors from which to choose. First, the MRD had established the European integration and structural funds unit headed by its own ministry official, Eva Píšová, and had established a team of foreign and local experts all financed from the PHARE budget. The second alternative lay within the broad ambit of the Ministry of Labor and Social Affairs (MLSA). This ministry had created an independent foundation, the National Training Fund (NTF), tasked with running public management-related PHARE programs.[33] Miroslava Kopicová directed the NTF and benefited from being relatively independent from the inflexible ministry hierarchy. Because the Klaus government refused to deal seriously with the reform of regional policy, the delegation decided to cooperate with the more independent NTF on preparatory programs for public administration reform. On the basis of a good working relationship, these programs were later extended to preparatory training programs for structural funds. Thus a partnership forged for one set of policies became a channel for reform of another policy area.

The erosion of the regional policy stalemate had begun with the Commission opinion and the delegation's PHARE initiatives, but these developments could pose no more than an annoyance to the Klaus government as long as it remained firmly in the saddle. A major change occurred in late

1997, however, when the Klaus government resigned over corruption charges leaked by his own party. An interim caretaker government lead by the former governor of the Central Bank, Josef Tošovský, was appointed by President Václav Havel to rule until the general elections in April 1998. Although it governed for only six months, the Tošovský government unblocked the issues of public administration reform and regional policy and paved the way for future reforms. Most important, in late 1997 the Constitutional Act on the Formation of the Higher Territorial Administrative Units was passed by both chambers of the parliament. This represented the first major step toward fulfilling the provisions of article 99 of the constitution, though, as it would turn out, the political maneuvering was not yet finished.

A Social Democrat minority government, headed by Prime Minister Miloš Zeman, emerged from the April 1998 elections.[34] The government was willing to enter into a substantial dialogue with the Commission on the critical issues raised in the Commission's 1997 opinion. Its primary move to address the issue of regional policy and territorial reform was to appoint a new deputy minister of interior, Yvonne Strecková, with exclusive responsibility for public administration reform and the creation of higher self-governing territorial units. With regard to regional policy, the government adopted *The Principles of the Government Regional Policy*. This document reflected the principles of regional policy of the EU and identified two types of problem regions according to the classification of structural funds: economically weak regions (what the EU calls objective 5b regions) and structurally weak regions (objective 2). The new government hewed closely to EU norms on its definitions of these regions: The structurally weak regions were defined by a high concentration of traditional industry and a high level of urbanization and unemployment. Economically weak regions comprise mostly rural areas with lower levels of urbanization and economic development.[35]

In the Commission's eyes, these moves constituted real progress—the first they had seen in a while. Based on this progress, the delegation started a PHARE-financed pilot project for the afflicted region of north Bohemia. This project was run by the MRD, which now began to develop a regional policy according to the EU framework. The ministry's first regional operational program involved not just the central government but also actors from the regional and municipal levels. Before the creation of the higher territorial units in January 2000, these regional actors were mainly mayors and representatives of regional development agencies, some of which were set up with PHARE financial support. In 1999 the regional actors formed special Regional Coordination Committees (RCC), which also included representatives of the state administration. These committees assumed the de facto role of informal nonelected governments on the subnational level. With regional elections in fall 2000 leading to the establishment of the higher territorial units on January 1, 2001, the regions incorporated the RCC into their administrative structures.[36] Thus did Commission pressure, PHARE seed money, a latent constitutional provision, and a change of government produce new momentum for regional policy in the Czech case.

This case allows us to identify a number of relevant norms that the EU is bringing into the candidate countries. Five in particular stand out. First, the EU presumes that states have in place formal regional actors who have the authority to formulate regional policy objectives. As we have seen in the Czech case, when domestic politics blocks the creation of formal actors, Commission pressures seem to have resulted in a set of informal actors (the RCCs). Second, the EU promotes the coordination of regional policy between the central government and the regions concerned. Third, the EU pushes the expectation that the allocation of structural funds will be based on competitiveness among regions. Fourth, the EU insists that states separate management and monitoring of regional policy. And fifth, the EU understands regional policy as an instrument of job creation and investment incentives, instead of a mere redistribution mechanism.[37]

CHANNELS FOR EU NORMS

Once the opening for EU norms grew wider, how precisely did the EU exploit the chance to affect Czech practices? Once the Commission launched the negotiation process with the first group of candidate countries in March 1998, the *acquis* was divided into thirty-one chapters, and each became subject to a screening process. During this period, the Commission explained to the candidate countries the amount the *acquis* contained in the individual policy areas. The candidate countries responded by describing the extent to which they already complied with EU law and further specified time periods over which they could likely achieve full compliance.[38] At times, screening was exasperating. The Commission obliged the CEE states to screen their regional policy instruments in April 1999, even though new regulations for the 2000–2006 budget period were soon to come on line. Thus, a few months later, the Commission decided to screen the chapter again.[39] After completion of screening in 1999, substantial negotiations began on each chapter.[40]

Both exercises—screening and the negotiations—are distinguished by the transmission and explanation of norms to the prospective member states. This learning process has been instrumental for setting up a reform agenda, timetable, and prioritization in the candidate countries.[41] In its regular reports the Commission assesses the progress of each country in meeting the norms and the institutional requirements it has laid out. Besides explaining the *acquis* in this highly structured process, the EU made substantial funds available to support the development of necessary administrative structures for a successful implementation of EU policies and also to start concrete work by financing pilot projects.

In addition to screening laws and paying for reform initiatives, personnel training represents a third major tool of the transmission of norms. Here again, the EU has dealt with multiple partners. In the Czech case, the MRD was responsible for the original regional development agencies that coordinated regional policies on the so-called NUTS II level as well as for business support projects for SMEs, and the MLSA was responsible for regional labor offices, which, in turn, were responsible for regional employment policies. As before, the NTF acted independently through PHARE-funded projects in support of the MLSA activities. To these were added a fourth player, the Ministry of the Interior, which, as noted, had responsibility for public administration reform and territorial reform under the new government. In order to channel EU norms into the Czech Republic, projects had to be launched in cooperation with all three ministries. The formula was usually that provision of financial assistance was conditioned on ministries using the funds for projects that would implement regional policy objectives as they are being applied in the EU.

On the personnel front, the MRD launched a project entitled Training Program for the Implementation of Structural Funds and the Cohesion Fund, through which public officials were acquainted with EU priorities in regional development. The Commission required compliance with these priorities in order to receive money. The program aimed to develop standardized, widely available training for public employees. The first priority was to "train the trainers" who would carry the norms of EU regional policy into the farthest reaches of Czech public administration and into the new regional governments. The main instrument here is "module courses" that encapsulate the main regulative norms for consultation, priority setting, financial controls, and monitoring. Participants will also deploy EU SWOP programming, in which all planning documents must address the region's "strengths, weaknesses, opportunities, and problems." The initial target called for sixteen hundred participants to be trained in the period between October 2000 and May 2001. A central priority of the project is to develop a sustainable network of training institutions, which would be accessible to regional decision makers even after the project ends.[42]

While the Commission agreed to implement this project with the MRD, it chose to coordinate preparations for using the European Social Fund (ESF) through the MLSA.[43] In this case, the Commission suggested that, due to its competence, the NTF should be entrusted with the management of the special preparatory program for the ESF. In this way, the EU introduced a certain competitive factor between the MRD and the MLSA-NTF. As for the substance of the project, in accordance with established norms in the EU, the Czech government passed a declaration that established the required institutional framework for the future implementation of ESF projects by articulating three main priorities:[44]

- Establish programming units within all relevant ministries to plan projects.
- Establish administrative units within ministries to run individual projects.
- Appoint premonitoring steering committees to oversee projects.

This institutional structure was supplemented by a time scale that was laid down in a subsequent government resolution in January 1999.[45] It, too, had three main features, all of which were dominated by considerations of potential EU membership:

The regional development plan was synchronized with the 2000–2006 EU budget.

- Conditions were added to qualify for prestructural funds from the EU.
- Pilot operational programs were to be developed modeled on the guidelines for structural fund projects.

The Czech government also finalized a special preparatory program for structural policy (SPP). Besides the personnel training initiatives already mentioned, SPP opened three other routes for the diffusion of EU norms. First, the Commission's new "twinning program" selected a Scottish-French-Irish consortium to provide long- and short-term, on-site experts and produce manuals for writing a "national development strategy." Second, the Czechs began using the EU ISPA program (for environmental and transport projects) and SAPARD program (for rural development projects).[46] Each program is covered by EU directives that specify long lists of regulative norms to be followed. Both programs, because they are explicitly designed to build the Czech "legal and administrative framework," also contain constitutive norms. Third, the Czechs have begun three kinds of pilot programs that go beyond institution building to begin to tackle problems of unemployment, investment distortions, and human resources.[47]

In short, these examples demonstrate the far-reaching impact of EU norms in the candidate countries when their adoption is tied to the overall goal of EU membership. With these two recent government resolutions, the Czech Republic broke new ground in its regional policies, harmonized its regional policy objectives with those of the EU, and began to channel its own funds into related projects. As noted earlier, the Czech

Republic also took steps to separate the management and the monitoring of regional policies.[48]

To be sure, the Commission's regular progress report in late 2000 raised several cautionary notes—including a continued lag in some administrative capacities and the as yet unadopted norm of multiannual budgeting for regional policy projects.[49] Only after significant funds have flowed through the Czech system will we be able to truly judge the robustness of new norms of coordination, monitoring, and document preparation.[50] Initial funding for the largest pilot program (northwest Bohemia) will be only 10–20 percent of the target amount of €100 million per year in 2006.[51] Finally, while all Czech regions must *prepare* for EU programs, only a few will *receive* significant funding in the preaccession period. Although northwest Bohemia receives funding from five separate projects, other regions must do the norm-driven work but receive no immediate rewards.[52] The argument, then, cannot be that the Czechs have already done all that the EU has asked. Nor can we claim that the EU is well situated to reinforce all Czech actors' preparatory investments, for some regions are, at least temporarily, all dressed up with no place to go. But it is nevertheless clear that EU pressure played a significant role in shifting the structure of domestic governance and policy implementation.

CONTINUED POLITICAL OPPOSITION TO EUROPEAN NORMS

Given the evidence that EU pressure is significant, it should not be surprising that it is also controversial. While CEE adoption of EU policy objectives results directly from the logic of preparation for membership, EU pressure to adapt policies does not wash away all other political considerations. A good illustration is the size and shape of the new regional governments. As indicated earlier, while the EU sets guidelines on policy priorities for the use of structural funds (see appendix A on p. 364), it does not have a say in how member states organize their territorial governments. Given the demographics of the Czech case and prevailing EU accounting standards, creating only eight regional territorial units would have eased coordination of regional policies. This efficiency gain would have come if the official Czech regional governments had been coterminous with the so-called NUTS II regions—the key target areas for EU policies. But though larger regions would have avoided an extra layer of regional authority—NUTS III regions—Czech politicians could reach a political consensus only by strengthening the role of thirteen larger cities (plus Prague) as regional centers.

Even this larger number of (smaller) regions was no simple accomplishment. Old opponents of European regional policy, such as former prime minister Klaus, reacted very sharply to attempts by the Czech regions to take over more European normative behavior than strictly necessary, especially fiscal and budgetary competence. In opposition, Klaus's criticism of Europe has become even more strident, and the ODS vice chairman, Petr Nečas, warned that "the nation-state, national interests, and national identity should not be sacrificed for cheap pseudo-Europeanism." Klaus's vocabulary during 2000–2001 grew sharper, with references to "hurray-Europeanism" and criticism of the EU "protectorate mentality." Since ODS voters are generally among the strongest supporters of Czech membership in the EU, Euroskeptic ODS elites tend to complain, but without providing alternative proposals. Some speak as if EU membership is a fait accompli. When asked about the wisdom of EU membership, Jaroslav Zvěřina, the chairman of the Parliamentary Committee for European Integration, said, "What kind of question is this? We simply have to belong to Europe. I have no better wisdom for the moment."[53]

Against this ambivalence, a major conflict erupted over attempts of the new fourteen regional governments to create an "association of Czech regions," which presumably would give them a stronger voice in the Committee of Regions in Brussels. Klaus, using the royal "we," remarked after meeting the regional governors: "We follow with bewilderment the efforts to create an Association of Czech Regions. We tried to explain to the governors that the association of Czech regions *is* the Czech Republic."[54] With regard to the relationship of the regions toward the EU, Klaus argued, "The representation of the regions of the Czech Republic in Brussels is in reality the Ministry of Foreign Affairs and the Czech embassy. In no way is it the Association of Czech Regions."[55]

Klaus's remarks demonstrate very clearly the lines of controversy. The introduction of EU-style regional policy into the Czech Republic stimulates the devolution of significant government powers. The principle of subsidiarity follows once regional policies take effect and clashes directly with long-standing centralist habits. With accession preparations in full swing, those who promote the ideal of strong central government struggle to hold their ground. A more diverse and self-confident regional political layer of government is emerging in the Czech Republic—a development difficult to imagine without the influence of norms from the EU.

CEE residents talk often of the desire to "return to Europe," often invoking the metaphor of a "common European home." Pursuing this metaphor, we might think of EU common policies, including those in regional policy, as a kind of external scaffolding from which elites can renovate the national edifice. But scaffolding is normally used to modernize *existing* structures, in this case the traditional regional policies of individual member states. In the Czech case, given the paucity of such structures, the scaffolding has served not just as external platform but also as the framework of the new building.

New actors have coalesced around its structures. Its improvised platforms have been transformed into a foundation, and its poles have been turned into the spindly pillars of a new building. The whole thing is unmistakably improvised, but it is just as unmistakably there.

APPENDIX A
AREAS ELIGIBLE FOR FINANCIAL SUPPORT
FROM THE EU STRUCTURAL FUNDS

Regional Competitiveness

Improving transport networks
Efficient energy networks and support for renewable resources
Telecommunications and information society
Environmental protection
Modernization of productive industries through research and innovation

COMPETITIVE ENTERPRISES

Prioritizing small and medium-sized enterprises instead of large industries
Supporting business innovations
Strengthening the potential of tourism, culture, and the environment

JOB CREATION

Promoting employment through active labor market policies
Parts of the population disadvantaged by the opening of the labor market
Promoting employability through retraining and lifelong learning
Developing entrepreneurship
Ensuring equal employment opportunities for women

Territorial Development

Urban development integrated into regional policy
Rural development for modernization of the agricultural sector
Coastline and fishery development

NOTES

The authors would like to thank Jiří Blažek, Ronald Linden, and Don Norton for comments on an earlier draft of this chapter.

1. John Ruggie, "What Makes the World Hang Together? Neo-Utilitarianism and the Social Constructivist Challenge," *International Organization* 52, no. 4 (1998): 855–85.

2. Important works in this tradition are Ann Swidler, "Culture in Action: Symbols and Strategies," *American Sociological Review*, April 1986, 273–86; Jeffrey Checkel, "The Constructivist Turn in International Relations Theory," *World Politics* 50, no. 2 (1998): 324–48.

3. Martha Finnemore and Kathryn Sikkink, "International Norm Dynamics and Political Change," *International Organization* 52, no. 4 (1998): 887–917; quote from page 891.

4. The *acquis communautaire* is the body of law developed since 1957 out of the legislation, legal rulings, and political decisions of the EEC, EC, and now the EU.

5. We could imagine political conflict around the third area as well, for states with severe budget constraints may view some EU-mandated building standards as unnecessarily expensive "gold plating." As of now, we have seen no evidence of this in the Czech Republic.

6. Michel Baun, *A Wider Europe: The Process and Politics of European Union Enlargement* (Lanham, Md.: Rowman & Littlefield, 2000), 4–8.

7. John Pinder, *European Community: The Building of a Union,* 2d ed. (New York: Oxford University Press, 1995), 62–65.

8. In one important way, however, we think this enlargement is likely to be quite similar to previous waves: the hardest work begins once membership is achieved. See Panos Kazakos and P. C. Iokamidis, eds., *Greece and EC Membership Evaluated* (New York: St. Martin's, 1994).

9. Aydin Hayri and Gerald McDermott, "The Network Properties of Corporate Governance and Industrial Restructuring: A Post-Socialist Lesson," *Industrial and Corporate Change* 7, no. 1 (1998): 153–93.

10. This claim is a hypothesis that is explored more fully below. We can imagine situations in which the opposite hypothesis—that preexisting actors could help promote more norm adoption—might also hold. Thomas Risse's work on "argumentative communicative action" is very suggestive in this regard. Risse, "Let's Argue! Communicative Action in World Politics," *International Organization* 54, no. 1 (2000): 1–39. One of the authors has also argued that a well-established "civil society" is a propitious condition for the transfer of institutions from one country to another. Wade Jacoby, *Imitation and Politics: Redesigning Modern Germany* (Ithaca, N.Y.: Cornell University Press, 2000).

11. Tanja Börzel, "Toward Convergence in Europe? Institutional Adaptation to Europeanization in Germany and Spain," *Journal of Common Market Studies* 37, no. 4 (1999): 573–96.

12. In actuality, current member states vary in their compliance rates. See Jonas Tallberg, *Making States Comply: The European Commission, the European Court of Justice, and the Enforcement of the Internal Market* (Lund, Sweden: Lund University, 1999); Francesco Duina, *Harmonizing Europe: Nation-States within the Common Market* (Albany: State University of New York Press, 1999).

13. Although the European Council was not foreseen in the founding treaties, the heads of state have been meeting regularly at least three times a year since 1974.

14. A comprehensive review of policy making in the EU is Simon Hix, *The Political System of the European Union* (New York: St. Martin's, 1999).

15. On EU structural funds, see Lisbet Hooghe, ed., *Cohesion Policy and European Integration: Building Multi-Level Governance* (New York: Oxford University Press, 1996).

16. European Commission, *The Structural Funds and Their Coordination with the Cohesion Fund: Guidelines for Programmes in the Period 2000-2006* (Luxembourg: European Commission, 1999).

17. The relevant provisions on the structural funds for the budget period 2000-2006 are laid down in article 10 of the Council Regulation (EC) 1260/99.

18. Depending on the pace of enlargement, by 2006 up to 30 percent of total EU structural fund spending could flow to CEE countries. European Commission, *Agenda 2000*, 63.

19. In other words, regional policy is a domain dominated by "direct effects" rather than one in which EU directives must be "transposed" into national law. For this distinction, see Hix, *Political System*, 117–27.

20. European Commission, *Opinion on the Czech Republic* (Brussels: European Commission, 1997), 83.

21. For details of the Czechoslovak communists' extreme regional redistribution policies, see Jiří Blažek, "The Czech Republic on Its Way toward West European Structures," *European Spatial Research and Policy* 4, no. 1 (1997): 57–58.

22. Jaroslav Dupal and Miloš Červený, TERPLAN, interview by author (Jacoby), Prague, July 21, 1998, and July 1999. See also Martin Hampl et al., *Geography of Societal Transformation in the Czech Republic* (Prague: Department of Social Geography and Regional Development of Charles University, 1999).

23. *Regional Development Strategy of the Czech Republic*, Government Document 682/2000, Prague, July 2000, 8.

24. Laure Neumayer, "Political Parties and European Integration in Central Europe: Poland, Hungary, Czech Republic," *Integrace,* February 2000, 21. (Author's translation of Laure Neumayerová, "Politické strany a evropská integrace ve střední Evropý: Polsko, Maďarsko, Česká republika.")

25. ČSSD, *An Alternative for Our Country*, ČSSD party program, approved by the 28th Party Congress on March 15, 1997, chapter I.2 <www.socdem.cz> (March 13, 2001) (author translation of ČSSD, Návrh střednědobého programu, ALTERNATIVA PRO NAŠI ZEMI Program schválený XXVIII. sjezdem ČSSD dne 15.3.1997).

26. Constitution of the Czech Republic (Prague, 1992).

27. Jiří Blažek and Sjaak Boekhout, "Regional Policy in the Czech Republic and the EU Accession," in *Transition, Cohesion, and Regional Policy in Central and Eastern Europe,* ed. John Bachtler, Ruth Downes, and Grzegorz Gorzelak (Aldershot, U.K.: Ashgate, 2000), 309–10.

28. European Commission, *Opinion on the Czech Republic*, 83.

29. European Commission, *Opinion on the Czech Republic*, 84.

30. PHARE is the primary EU vehicle for delivering aid to candidate countries.

31. This point is developed for regional policy in Germany in Thomas Conzelmann, "'Europeanization' of Regional Development Policies? Linking the Multi-Level

Governance Approach with Theories of Policy Learning and Policy Change," *European Integration Online Papers* 2, no. 4 (1998). See also Wade Jacoby, "Exemplars, Analogies, and Menus: East Europe in Cross-Regional Comparison," *Governance* 12, no. 4 (1999): 454–78.

32. Responsibility for public administration reform lay with the Ministry of Interior.

33. As in regional policy, the Czechs have been very reluctant to initiate a thoroughgoing reform of public management. A fuller treatment is outside the scope of this chapter, but, as in regional policy, important reasons for resistance lie in a combination of ideological antipathy toward the public sector and the pragmatic calculation that power vested in other actors could be used to counter the centralizing tendencies of the Klaus government. The latter justification, it turns out, is only slightly less attractive to the Social Democrats than it was to the ODS.

34. The Social Democrats have a toleration agreement with the ODS—the largest opposition party—in which the ODS received some important parliamentary posts in exchange for a promise not to vote against the government during any future no-confidence votes.

35. Blažek and Boeckhout, "Regional Policy," 302–3.

36. These RCCs were established in the fourteen regions corresponding to the lower Eurostat classification of NUTS III regions. On the more important NUTS II level, the previous regional management and monitoring committees were transformed into regional councils. In accordance with the EU constitutive norm of separating management and monitoring, these councils will appoint regional development committees to monitor regional operational programs.

37. See EU Commission, *The Czech Republic's Progress toward Accession,* Regular Progress Report, November 8, 2000, 60–62.

38. Wade Jacoby, "Priest and Penitent: The EU as a Force in the Domestic Politics of Eastern Europe," *East European Constitutional Review* 8, no. 1–2 (1999): 62–67.

39. Jiří Blažek, "(In)consistency and (In)efficiency of the Czech Regional Policy in the 1990s," *Acta Universitatis Comenianae—Geographica-Supplementum* 2, no. 2 (1999): 179.

40. These membership negotiations are not negotiations in the narrow sense of the word. Rather, they are meetings of ministry and Commission officials who assess and document progress in individual areas and countries. The eventual result will be an accession treaty that takes account of exceptions and possible transition periods a country may need in order to achieve full compliance with the *acquis.*

41. For a discussion of screening, see Baun, *A Wider Europe,* 105–10.

42. Ministry of Regional Development (MRD), *Preparation of the Czech Republic for the Implementation of EU Cohesion Policy from the Year 2000,* Structural Funds Series, vol. 5 (Prague: MRD, 1999), 23.

43. The Commission is clearly concerned that a change in ministers within the MRD in June 2000 might lead to the elevation of what it calls "political criteria" over "questions of policy." EU Commission, *The Czech Republic's Progress toward Accession,* Regular Progress Report, November 8, 2000, 82.

44. Government Declaration no. 417, June 17, 1998 (Prague: Office of the Czech Government, 1998).

45. Government Declaration no. 40, January 11, 1999 (Prague: Office of the Czech Government, 1999).

46. ISPA = Instrument for Structural Policies for Pre-accession; SAPARD = Special Accession Programme for Pre-accession Aid for Agriculture and Rural Development

47. MRD, *Preparation*, 18–53.

48. Thirty-two different governmental and nongovernmental organizations are represented in both the Czech National Programming Committee and the Monitoring Committee. MRD, *Preparation*, 69–73.

49. EU Commission, *The Czech Republic's Progress toward Accession*, Regular Progress Report, November 8, 2000, 60–62.

50. Blažek, "(In)consistency," 179–82.

51. MRD, *Preparation*, 59.

52. Blažek, "(In)consistency," 183; MRD, *Preparation*, 54–61.

53. All three quotes from *Respect* 29/2000, accessed on the Euroskop Web site: <www.euroskop.cz/euroskop/site/oko/tisk/respekt1/32.html> (March 10, 2001) (author's translation).

54. ČTK, February 16, 2001, <www.ceskenoviny.cz>.

55. ČTK, February 16, 2001, <www.ceskenoviny.cz>.

13

Political Business Cycles in EU Accession Countries

Mark Hallerberg, Lúcio Vinhas de Souza, and William Roberts Clark

The ten Eastern European countries currently engaged in accession negotiations with the European Union all experienced rapid transition from communist to democratic systems. Included in this process was a rapid change in the role of the state in the economy and in the use of monetary policy. Previously, state planning played a dominant role. Governments set artificial exchange rates that provided opportunities for arbitrage on the black market. Much international trade operated in practice as barter.

Given these initial conditions, the move to a market-based economy was a shock in monetary policy terms in all countries because they were missing basic monetary institutions to regulate their economies. Most countries needed to establish central banks from scratch. This included not only technical decisions about how to regulate commercial banks, the money supply, and the like but also political decisions about whether or not the bank should be politically independent. The new democracies of Eastern Europe also had to consider what to do with their exchange rates with other countries, particularly whether they should let their currencies float on world markets or fix them and, if so, to which international currency (or basket of currencies) as an anchor.

This chapter considers the origins of monetary institutions in Eastern Europe. We first consider the accession process to date as well as the exchange rate regimes accession states have used. We indicate the critical role played by international organizations, especially the International Monetary Fund, in establishing macroeconomic institutions like central banks and currency boards in countries that had little or no experience with such institutions.

We also discuss the practical implications of monetary institutional choice on the presence or absence of political business cycles in Eastern European accession countries. Based on the model we develop in Clark and Hallerberg for OECD countries and in Hallerberg, Vinhas de Souza, and Clark for Eastern European countries, we examine whether these states manipulated the macroeconomy in election years.[1] There are two possible dimensions on which manipulation can occur. First, states can have looser monetary policy that lowers interest rates and spurs economic growth. Second, on the fiscal side a state can spend more money with the same tax base and/or cut taxes. While one might expect that simple monetary institutions like the exchange rate should not affect fiscal cycles, our model, based on a simple Mundell-Fleming framework,[2] indicates that there should be fiscal cycles when the exchange rate is fixed and monetary cycles when the exchange rate is flexible *and* when central bank independence is low.

Despite the theoretical model, our initial expectations would be that such cycles should be absent in Eastern European countries. Unlike in OECD countries, where the connection between the state of the economy and support for incumbents is well established, microlevel survey research from Eastern European countries seems to suggest that voters do not similarly reward incumbents.[3] The presence of such cycles in Eastern Europe would lead to a set of questions. If the microfoundations for such cycles appear absent, why do governments engage in them? How has the prospect of future EU membership affected the severity of such cycles? What implications would such cycles have for the introduction of the euro in accession countries' economies?

Our misgivings about applying the theoretical model to Eastern Europe were misplaced. As this chapter demonstrates, we find strong evidence in support of the theoretical model based on Clark and Hallerberg[4]—countries with flexible exchange rates have looser monetary policies in election years than in nonelection years in countries with dependent central banks. If a country has a fixed exchange rate regime, it manipulates its economy in election years through running larger budget deficits instead of looser monetary policy. One finding that differs from Clark and Hallerberg[5] is that, in countries with independent central banks, there is a monetary *contraction* in election years. This suggests that newly created independent central banks may use electoral years to send signals to markets that they are truly independent.

THE ACCESSION PROCESS AND ACCESSION COUNTRY MONETARY AND EXCHANGE RATE ARRANGEMENTS

The European Commission, according to the provision of article O of the Treaty of European Union (TEU), launched, on March 31, 1998, official accession processes with Bulgaria, Cyprus, the Czech Republic, Estonia, Hungary, Latvia, Lithuania, Malta, Poland, Romania, Slovakia, and Slovenia.[6]

Substantive negotiations for accession were opened on November 10, 1998, with Cyprus,[7] the Czech Republic, Estonia, Hungary, Poland, and Slovenia, the so-called first wave countries. This set of countries was selected on the basis of their level of fulfillment of the economic and political criteria set out by the European Council held in Copenhagen in July 1993[8] as benchmarks for future member countries. These six entrants would add over 63 million inhabitants to the current EU population (almost two-thirds of them in Poland alone) and over €240 billion to its GDP (again, over half of this figure in Poland). That will mean, respectively, a 17 percent increase in the Union population, but a mere 3 percent increase in its GDP. The so-called second wave entrants (Bulgaria, Latvia, Lithuania, Malta, Romania, and Slovakia) would add to these figures another 57 million people and €97 billion (or a 15 percent increase in the population of the Union, but an even more marginal increase of 1.2 percent to its GDP). This reflects the lower level of development of the two biggest countries in this group, Bulgaria and Romania.

This division was, in practical terms, ended by a series of new EU Commission recommendations published on October 13, 1999.[9] In a wide-ranging modification of the EU accession procedures *and* foreign policy that was approved by a European Council meeting held in Finland in December 1999, substantial negotiations for accession were opened with *all* application countries in 2000. Turkey was also added to the application country list, but without any date for the opening of negotiations. The official opening of substantive negotiations for accession with all the new accession countries occurred on February 15, 2000, in Brussels, during the last Portuguese presidency of the Union.

This will be the biggest wave of expansion of the Union since its birth in 1957 (in number of countries, but not in share of GDP or even share of population to the existing Union), surpassing the North Sea accession of 1973 (the Kingdom of Denmark, the Republic of Ireland, and the United Kingdom), the Mediterranean accession of 1982 (the Greek Republic), the Iberian accession of 1986 (the Kingdom of Spain and the Portuguese Republic), and the Nordic-Central European accession of 1995 (the Republic of Austria, the Republic of Finland, and the Kingdom of Sweden). The complexity and duration of the related negotiation process could perhaps equal—and even surpass—the almost ten-year-long negotiations of the Iberian accessions,[10] at least for some of the countries. Such a prolonged preaccession period is even more likely when one remembers that the comprehensiveness and extension of European legislation, and realms of integration that are included in the current negotiations, surpass by far the ones covered on all previous expansion waves.

In this negotiation process, there is one major institutional difference, among the many from the previous expansion waves, that concerns us here: the new entrants cannot benefit from the use of opt-out clauses, which were used by the United Kingdom and the Kingdom of Denmark for EMU (Economic and Monetary Union), and also by the United Kingdom for the social chapter. Therefore, the *acquis communautaire* is expected to be, in time, *taken in full* by all future new entrants, including, of course, EMU participation and all the requisite "criteria."[11] All future entrants are supposed to become, eventually but not immediately, members of the common currency area, which became a reality with the introduction of the euro in eleven of the fifteen European Union (EU) member states in January 1999.[12] Already the "Copenhagen criteria" of 1993 include a provision that future accession countries shall have "the ability to take on the obligations of membership, including adherence to the aims of political, economic and monetary union."[13] This is also implicitly stated in the Amsterdam treaty, which declares that all future member countries "shall adhere to the goals of EMU."

The European Commission has discussed in some detail how it envisions eventual accession country participation in EMU. In its 1998 "composite paper," which presents an integrated analysis of the assessment performed in the applicant countries, the European Commission's phasing of EMU integration for future members envisage a three-phased process.[14] The first is a preaccession phase, during which the accession states fulfill general EU membership criteria. The second is the accession stage per se, in which the states already in the EU but outside the euro area—according to the terms of the Treaty of the European Union (TEU)—treat the "exchange policy as a matter of common interest" and eventually coordinate policy through a structure similar to the exchange rate mechanism (ERM). The third and final phase is the actual euro phase. This timing would *explicitly* exclude a simultaneous accession to the European Union and to the common currency framework, which is also implicit in the so-called Maastricht criteria. This clarifies the statements in the European Commission's *Agenda 2000,*[15] which, in principle, do not seem to exclude a twophased process, in which entry in both the EU and the EMU could be simultaneous; no exchange rate coordination framework was actually specified. These statements were confirmed by the 1999 version of the composite paper, which did not introduce any substantial modifications concerning EMU.[16]

The common goal of eventual EMU membership is expected to impose a common set of norms concerning macroeconomic performance on future members of the European Union. Governments will be expected to make low inflation and low budget deficits primary goals. They will also have to make their central banks independent (if they have not done so already). This requirement is already having an effect on the institutional independence of central banks even before accession. In early 2001 national parliaments both in the Czech Republic and in Hungary attempted to restrict the autonomy of their monetary authorities. Both were ultimately blocked by the large shadow of EU enlargement.

Membership in EMU will entail further restrictions on government behavior. According to the Stability and Growth Pact (SGP), member states that have budget deficits above 3 percent of GDP can be subject to fines. The Preaccession Economic Program (PEP) framework, which was designed as a precursor to the notification procedures established at the SGP for the EU member countries for the accession countries, started in 2001. The European Commission requires each accession country to prepare a PEP once a year. The PEP consists of a discussion of recent macroeconomic developments, a forecasted medium-term framework, and detailed descriptions of five-year fiscal projections and policy options. On the basis of it, the Commission will form a judgment of the adequacy for the accession country proposed policy options and submit recommendations.[17]

Given this background, we discuss the evolution of exchange rate regimes, and we also consider the institutional structure of their domestic institutions, particularly whether or not the countries have independent monetary authorities.

Monetary Authorities in Central Eastern Europe

As a general rule, most transition economies adopted, at some point early in their transition process, macroeconomic stabilization programs[18] with some form of exchange rate anchor. Most of these initial peg strategies were later abandoned or softened in the face of growing external imbalances. Such changes happened relatively swiftly, as in Poland, or spectacularly in the midst of a speculative attack, as was the case in the Czech Republic.[19]

The learning curve of these countries had to be very steep: hardly ten years ago, the current universal two-tier bank structure was not only absent but irrelevant. The central bank, for all practical purposes, was a department of the Ministry of Finance, and its only real function was to produce the means of exchange to allow the trading of plan-determined quantities among individual consumers.[20] Several of these countries—Estonia, Latvia, Lithuania, Slovakia, and Slovenia—were newly independent and had to build national institutions virtually from scratch, including their monetary authorities. The concept of a central bank, let alone one that was independent from the control of an (eventually) elected government, was generally unknown at the beginning of the transition process. Western advice played a critical role in establishing central banks.

The development of institutions able to carry out monetary policy actions, as well as the instruments to carry it through, took time. Initially, more blunt direct monetary control instruments were used (interest rate and credit caps, high reserve requirements, "moral persuasion," etc.) for three reasons: (1) the monetary authorities themselves had not learned how to use modern monetary policy tools,[21] (2) the transmission channels for the proper use of those tools—working financial markets—were absent in these economies (and still are today, but to a lesser degree), and (3) the lack of stable relationships among the central bank's target variables and its instruments. Only more recently have market-based indirect monetary policy instruments—repos, Lombard facilities, government securities auctions—been introduced.[22]

Price stability is often a primary goal of the central bank. This can be accomplished through direct or indirect strategies. To try to meet an inflation target indirectly assumes some sort of stable links between the final target and an aggregate(s), which the central bank attempts to influence. These aggregates are the so-called intermediate targets, but inflation is the final target. There are two possible types of indirect strategies: one based on a stable rate of exchange between the domestic currency and the currency of a low inflation country, and the other based on controlling the growth rate of a domestic money supply aggregate. The use of any type of pegging regime is therefore equivalent to the use of indirect inflation targeting. No single exchange rate regime is optimal for all nations at every time; nevertheless, only a free float is usually considered sustainable on a long-term perspective,[23] since other strategies are vulnerable to exogenous shocks and ultimately collapse.[24]

The extreme case of the peg strategy is the currency board arrangement (CBA), which requires the official foreign exchange reserves to be—at least—equal to the amount of domestic currency issued (at a given *fixed* exchange rate): under a strict CBA there is no actual domestic monetary policy, since both the monetary base and the level of interest rates are endogenously determined. Modified CBAs, though, may perform limited monetary policy actions, through the use of some types of CB-like instruments, such as lender of last resort (LLR) facilities or limited open-market operations. Once again, both the impetus to use a currency board, as well as the technical prowess to develop one, came in all cases from external counsel. As the following narrative shows, the International Monetary Fund was the most important external actor to assist accession countries,[25] at least in the early stages, given that EU institutions (including European Central Bank [ECB] technical assistance missions) progressively took center stage.[26] European Union–sponsored research projects on economic conditions in Eastern Europe as well as more informal contacts with Western economists also played a role, even at the beginning.[27]

Usually, the justification for choosing a CBA is linked to the need to give credibility to a stabilization policy, or, in the case of Eastern Europe, to sheer inexperience in the conduct of monetary policy by the monetary authorities of these countries. Among its stated advantages, a CBA entails automatic balance of payment adjustments, essentially in the same way that a gold standard exchange system would operate: in case of a deficit in the capital and current accounts, money supply is reduced, causing, ceteris paribus, the interest rate to rise, which leads to (1) reduced domestic activity and reduced imports and (2) an increase in foreign capital inflows. It should also result in reduced inflation expectations (depending on the anchor currency chosen).

Among its drawbacks, a CBA means not only the loss of monetary policy as a countercyclical tool, but it can actually be *procyclical* (reinforcing economic booms and troughs). The lack of LLR features by the monetary authority increases both the short-run probability and effects of financial sector crisis (regardless of the beneficial long-run effects caused by the reduction of moral hazard). The need to perform active policy actions is heightened in periods of market instability, as was clearly the case in Eastern Europe during the series of Baltic banking crisis of 1993–1995. A CBA also discourages the development of domestic money and capital markets.[28] Nevertheless, the most fundamental problem[29] of a CBA lies in the question of its exit strategy. There is no clear optimal path from virtually the absence of monetary policy under a CBA regime toward a full-fledged and even independent central bank.

We present below a description of the recent monetary and exchange rate history of the individual accession countries.

Bulgaria

Bulgaria uses a currency board regime that linked its lev to the deutsche mark (DM) up to the end of 1999. It was introduced as part of a one-year standby IMF program in the spring of 1997, which aimed to bring macroeconomic stabilization to the country (almost immediately reducing hyperinflation from over 1,000 percent a year to around 5 percent). Starting from January 1999, the anchor currency of the arrangement became the euro.

Bulgaria went through a conventional transition stabilization program in the early 1990s, which proved to be unsuccessful: neither disinflation nor external balance was reached. As a result, by November 1996 the IMF started to press the Bulgarian authorities to introduce a CBA, against the initial opposition of a skeptical Bulgarian National Bank. With the worsening of the crisis by the spring of 1997 and the election of a new government, this plan was finally accepted, as a part of a comprehensive package of stabilization reforms (including fiscal consolidation and wage and price reforms), and implemented by mid-1997. The CBA was installed on the modified structure of the BNB (Bŭlgarska Narodna Banka or Bulgarian National Bank), which phased out all its monetary operations, retaining only the minimum reserve requirement tool. The CBA "entry" rate of the lev was 1.000 to DM 1.

Broadly speaking, the short-lived CBA experience in Bulgaria is so far successful: inflation has been substantially reduced, external balance has been achieved, and the economic contraction seems to have bottomed out.

Czech Republic

The Czech Republic's koruna (CZK) followed a peg to a DM/US$ basket until May 1997, which it was then forced to abandon after a speculative attack on its currency. The CNB (Ceska Narodni Banka or Czech National Bank) follows today a float regime, coupled with inflation targeting (DIT).[30]

Among the Eastern European countries endowed with a CB, the Czech Republic can be singled out for its ability to hold on to a fixed exchange rate regime for a record period of time. The CZK held its basket peg in a very narrow +/– 0.5 band from December 1990 until February 1996 (when the bands were extended to +/– 7.5 percent). The system survived the Czechoslovakia partition of early 1993 without disturbances.

The monetary policy intermediate target evolved from the domestic credit volume target (1990) to a net domestic asset in the banking system target (1991–1992) to, finally, a M2 (money and quasi-money) "corridor." The initial phase of blunt direct policy instruments (rate and credit ceilings) lasted for only two years, essentially ending by October 1992.

The initial choice of a "nominal anchor" foreign exchange regime was actually defined by the stabilization program jointly designed with the IMF in 1990, with the peg being set after a substantial cumulative "entry" devaluation of 95 percent. This actually explains the longevity of the peg: devaluation *deliberately,* substantially undershoots the "equilibrium" entry level, creating a "cushion" that permits a persistent real appreciation of the koruna to be absorbed without changing the parity. The negative effects of that were (1) a very high initial adjustment contraction of the GDP—a 16 percent fall in 1991—and (2) the undervaluation "cushion" reduced incentives to real adjustment (i.e., the "nominal anchor" was not binding), with the mounting pressures spectacularly exposed by the currency crisis of 1997.

Classically, the violation of the uncovered interest rate parity condition led to the increase in short-term foreign capital inflows between 1993 and 1995 (when they reached an amazing 17.4 percent of the Czech GDP), leading to equally classical and costly sterilization interventions by the CNB (the costs were estimated to equal 0.5 percent of GDP in 1995 alone) and the subsequent fall of the inflows in 1996–1997, when the situation was perceived to be increasingly unsustainable, finally leading to the breakdown of the system.

Estonia

Estonia has a currency board system administered by the Eesti Pank (Bank of Estonia, BoE) which linked the Estonian kroon (EEK) to the deutsche mark by a rate of EEK 8 to DM 1. Starting in January 1, 1999, the Estonian kroon was fixed against the euro, at the same conversion rate of the DM in the common currency.

When adopting a CBA in mid-1992, as a component of a stabilization and reform package, Estonia's main aims were stability and credibility. The ruble was replaced by the kroon. The new, two-tier banking system was centered, from the very beginning, around a currency board–type of monetary authority. Its main function is the acquisition of hard currency in the interbank forex market. Nevertheless, it also has some monetary policy tools: central bank bills (issued since 1993, but in very small amounts), (low) reserve requirements and (unused) standing deposit facilities. No LLR instruments are available, and the result of the 1992–1994 banking crisis was that the number of banks operating in the country was reduced to a third of its original figure. Capital movements were fully liberalized already by late 1993.

Due to increasing capital inflows (parallel to an increasing trade deficit), the real exchange rate has experienced that familiar peg phenomenon, a substantial real appreciation. The lack of a more sophisticated set of macroeconomic policy tools, which could enable the monetary authority to cool down the economy and achieve a sustainable external balance, may cast doubts on the long-term prospects of the CBA.

Hungary

The Hungarian forint was, since 1995, in a crawling peg with a variable preannounced devaluation rate (of 0.4 percent a month) toward a DM/US$ basket (with weights of, respectively, 70 percent and 30 percent), within a +/– 2.25 percent intervention band. This basket was converted, since January 1, 1999, into a euro/US$ one, with the same relative shares. The MNB (Magyar Nemzeti Bank or National Bank of Hungary [NBH]) switched to a full (100 percent) euro crawling peg by January 1, 2000, with a preannounced monthly devaluation rate of 0.3 percent.

The two-tier banking system was established in 1987 (Hungary was an early reformer), but the current legal framework for the NBH was introduced in 1991 (with several additions since). It defined NBH aims as safeguarding the internal and external purchasing power of the Hungarian currency. This implied the problem (between 1991 and 1994, the first phase of the transition) of too many final goals for monetary policy, which included both inflation control or external balance. In practical terms, policy emphasis shifted from one to the other. This problem was compounded by a postponement of fiscal adjustment. When the fiscal deficit reached 9 percent of GDP in 1995, the situation became unsustainable, resulting in the adjustment program of March of that year. This also caused the clear selection of price stability as the ultimate goal of monetary policy, with the nominal exchange rate being used as an intermediate target: the forint was devalued by 9 percent and the current preannounced crawling band system introduced, as a replacement of the previous adjustable peg to a DM/US$ basket (with a 50 percent/50 percent composition).

The preannounced devaluation aims to undershoot forward-looking inflation expectations, taking into consideration productivity improvements and underpinning disinflation. The sustainability of such a regime, of course, depends on the maintenance of fiscal balance and a sensible wage policy.

The fluctuation band was extended to ±15 (the same range in the ERM-2) on May 3, 2001, in a move widely seen as a preparation for a full-fledged float later that year and accompanied by substantial changes among top MNB officers.

Latvia

Latvia uses a peg regime, through which the lats, the currency that replaced the temporary Latvian ruble or "rublis" (which was the country's first step of monetary independence from the "ruble zone" and lasted from May 1992 to October 1993), is linked to the IMF fiduciary account unit, the special drawing rights (SDR, which is actually a basket of currencies of IMF member countries). The SDR weights roughly reflect Latvia's external trade composition (only a third of its foreign trade is with the euro area). Another reason for this choice is that the creation of the Latvian currency was one of the results of the IMF-backed stabilization program of 1992.[31] There are no immediate plans to change this arrangement.[32]

The Bank of Latvia (Latvijas Banka) uses the exchange rate peg to the SDR as an intermediate target and net domestic assets as an operational target. As a full-fledged central bank, it has the standard set of indirect monetary policy tools: repurchase agreements (repos), a Treasury bill market, reserve requirements (uniformly held at the 8 percent introduced in July 1993), and LLR facilities, which it chose not to use during the 1994–1995 banking crisis, arguably the most severe in the wave of Baltic financial sector crises in the first half of the 1990s. The four major banks among the seventeen that collapsed accounted for 46 percent of all private deposits—in an environment without deposit insurance. The Bank of Latvia decided to use the opportunity to introduce sweeping regulatory and prudential reforms to consolidate the financial sector.

The Latvijas Banka, in spite of deviating superficially from its Baltic neighbors on the use of a CBA strategy, has consistently emulated at least one feature of it: it aims to keep nearly 100 percent of its domestic liabilities covered by foreign reserves (the lower point was reached during the banking crisis period, when they reached 60–70 percent).[33]

Lithuania

Lithuania uses a modified currency board arrangement, introduced in 1994, which pegs the Lithuanian litas to the U.S. dollar. Its monetary authority, the BoLi (Lietuvos Bankas, Bank of Lithuania) has available to it certain types of market based instruments.

Lithuania, like its two Baltic neighbors, reappeared as an independent state in the early 1990s (in modern times, it had experienced only a brief period of autonomy from 1919 to 1940), with the collapse of the Soviet Union, to which it had been annexed after the military invasion of 1940.

The ruble was initially replaced, as in Latvia, by an interim coupon currency issued by the newly created BoLi, from May to October 1992 and then by the talonas, which was, in its turn, replaced by the litas in June 1993. The talonas, initially in a float regime, lost over 50 percent of its value between its introduction and April 1993. Some exchange rate stability was regained with the introduction of the litas. Nevertheless, the government, with the support of the IMF, decided to press for the constitution of an Estonian-type CBA in October 1993, against the will and the advice of the BoLi.

The CBA was finally introduced in April 1994—*on the unchanged administrative structure* of the BoLi.[34] Its CBA, therefore, since the very beginning has to be characterized as a modified CBA, since some central bank instruments (e.g., reserve requirements and short-term credit facilities, including for LLR operations; all those tools were necessary and duly used during the great 1995–1996 banking crisis) were preserved.

The Lithuanian strategy, presented at the Monetary Policy Program for 1997–1999, was to move toward a full-fledged CB. It had three phases. During the first one, the aim was to introduce and develop open market operations and a Lombard facility with the currency board still in existence (1997–1999); during the second phase (1999–2000), the law on the credibility of the litas was amended; the third and final phase (2000 on) would aim to link the litas to the euro or, temporarily, to a basket that would include it. At that moment, the BoLi plans to be prepared to meet the requirements of ERM-2 membership.

The BoLi has partially modified the timetable described above.[35] It has resolved:

- not to carry the planned repeg of the litas to the euro in 2000
- to repeg the Litas directly to the euro somewhere in the second half of 2001, skipping an intermediate peg to a U.S. dollar/euro currency basket

(which also means that the unique experiment to switch from a CBA to a CB was left for the moment of actual euro area participation)

The pegging of the litas directly to the Euro is defended on the basis that "no principal decisions concerning the litas exchange rate will be taken in 1999–2000; therefore, in the future, this plan will have to be carried out faster." Additionally, such a peg would be more transparent and easily understood by the agents, and, at the same time, would send a clear signal to them to increase the use of the euro in their international settlements in trade with the European Union.

Poland

The Polish zloty (PLZ) was in crawling peg against a basket of currencies, which was modified in early 1999 into a euro/U.S. dollar basket (the former basket included the deutsche mark, the U.S. dollar, the pound sterling [GBP], the French and Swiss francs [FRF and CHF]), weighted with, respectively, 65 percent and 35 percent. A float of the currency, coupled with DIT, was finally introduced in April 2000.

The choice of a peg exchange rate regime in Poland was linked to the need to fight hyperinflation in the country in 1989–1990 (i.e., the monetary/exchange rate policy was a part of a short-term stabilization program), at the moment that the two-tier banking system was introduced into the country. Additionally, the limited nature of instruments available at that time to the NBP (Narodowy Bank Polski or National Bank of Poland)—ceilings, reserve requirements, "moral suasion"—conditioned the choice for this policy option.

A very high liquidity in the banking system—caused by an unexpectedly positive situations in the balance of payments and the government budget—led to the imposition of very heavy reserve requirements of 30 percent in 1990 (the registered trade surplus was also a result of the substantial undershooting of the "entry level" exchange rate chosen for the initial peg with the U.S. dollar in 1990). Nevertheless, the sharp economic downturn characteristic of the initial stage of transition experienced by Poland in 1991 led to another devaluation in May of that year and to the introduction of a crawling peg of the PLZ to a currency basket (US$, DM, GBP, FRF, CHF) by October.

The 1992–1995 period was one of slow disinflation with a parallel development of monetary instruments: money market operations and refinancing facilities became the most important policy tools. Capital flows were already highly liberalized by 1992. Additionally, the initial fall in GDP turned into sustainable export-led growth by 1993, albeit with high unemployment. The classical problem of foreign capital inflows and monetary expansion that developed was initially dealt with by the combined reduction of the crawl rate and sterilization operations, and in May 1995 by the introduction of a crawling band regime with +/− 7 percent intervention bands, increasing the ability of the NBP to perform active monetary policy while retaining the anchor features of the regime.

Romania

Romania has used a dirty float regime since 1992, with the National Bank of Romania (NBR)—the Romanian Central Bank—intervening in the market to support the leu in a discretionary fashion.

The country has been plagued by systematic macro instability since the beginning of the transition process. Even now, high and persistent inflation (making it the sole exception among all the accession countries), incomplete privatization, and internal and external imbalances are all observed. This seems to be related to the particularly brutal way in which the formal authoritarian regime was overthrown there and its effects, even today, on the construction of a working political consensus among agents.

In institutional terms, several problems remain. For instance, even after the new 1998 central banking law, which established that the NBR's "key objective is to ensure the stability of domestic currency with a view to maintaining price stability" and also granted the bank a larger degree of autonomy, the financing of the government is still permitted.

Slovakia

Slovakia used a peg regime with intervention bands, through which the National Bank of Slovakia (Národná Banka Slovenska, NBS) pegged its koruna to a basket made of the deutsche mark and the U.S. dollar (with weights of, respectively, 60 percent and 40 percent). The intervention bands had to be progressively widened since the introduction of the regime in 1996, from +/− 1.5 percent to +/− 7.0 percent. After a series of speculative attacks, the NBS was forced to abandon the peg and float the koruna in October 1998.

The Slovakian central bank was created in 1992 and entered into operation in 1993, after the breakup of the Federal Republic of Czechoslovakia. Its main objective is the stability of the Slovakian crown (koruna, SKK). The exchange rate regime was initially a fixed peg to a basket (US$, DM, ATS, CHF, and FRF, with weights of 49.06 percent, 36.16 percent, 8.07 percent, 3.79 percent, and 3.79 percent, respectively) in the Czech model, accompanied by a domestic M2 growth target ("supporting economic growth" was added to its list of aims in 1995) as intermediate target. The currency basket of the peg was modified to US$/DM in July 14, 1994 (40 percent/60 percent).

The period 1993–1994 corresponds to the stabilization years for its new SKK, with a relatively small devaluation "entry" of 10 percent in 1993. The set of instruments initially used was more blunt than its Czech counterpart (credit limits, restrictions to the internal convertibility of the currency—which only became "article 8" compatible, that is, convertible according to IMF requirements on October 1, 1995—and reserve ratios), in spite of the availability of the discount and Lombard rates and repo and Treasury bill auction instruments since 1993. In 1996, to deal with the usual problem of capital inflows in peg regimes, reserve requirements were raised to a uniform level of 9 percent; the SKK bands were widened from 1.5 to +/– 3 percent and then to +/– 5 percent.

Slovenia

Slovenia uses a float system for its tolar (created in 1991), administered by the Bank of Slovenia (Banka Slovenije, BoS), with the BoS targeting a domestic money aggregate (M3: money, quasi-money, and time deposits), while informally shadowing the DM. This system has been very successful so far, delivering both disinflation and external balance, with only minor exchange rate adjustments: in 1996–1997, the tolar experienced a nominal depreciation of 6.9 percent to the deutsche mark.

The BoS is a full-fledged central bank, created as an independent entity after the separation of the country from the Federal Republic of Yugoslavia in the early 1990s.[36]

Tables 13.A1 and 13.A2 in appendix A at the end of this chapter summarize both the exchange rate arrangements described here and the relative independence of the central banks of these countries.

MACROECONOMIC CONSEQUENCES OF INSTITUTIONAL CHOICE

The political business cycle literature considers how incumbent governments attempt to manipulate the macroeconomy before elections. Exactly *how* governments boost the economy before elections is the subject of Clark and Hallerberg.[37] They consider the relevance of a standard Mundell-Fleming model for opportunistic political business cycles. The Mundell-Fleming model factors in the role of the level of capital mobility as well as the exchange rate in determining the relative effectiveness of monetary and fiscal policy in influencing the macroeconomy. When capital is not mobile, both monetary and fiscal policies affect economic growth. When capital is mobile, the exchange rate becomes an important variable. If the exchange rate is fixed, monetary policy becomes an ineffective policy instrument, and fiscal policy is the only way that the government can influence the macroeconomy. The opposite is the case when the exchange rate is flexible—monetary policy is effective but fiscal policy is not.

Clark and Hallerberg[38] apply this framework to discussions about the presence or absence of opportunistic political business cycles. They also consider the importance of domestic institutions in preventing opportunistic political business cycles. Independent central banks are expected to eliminate cycles even when capital is mobile and exchange rates are flexible. Independent central banks do not adjust policy according to the whims of the electoral calendar, while dependent central banks do. Clark and Reichert[39] find evidence that independent central banks *can* block *opportunistic* changes in macroeconomic variables, like economic growth and unemployment. Clark and Hallerberg[40] find similar results for the importance of independent central banks based on changes in policy *instruments* such as the money supply.

Based on Clark and Hallerberg,[41] we expect that the policy instruments governments use to manipulate the economy in election years depend on the exchange rate regime and on whether or not the central bank is independent. If the exchange rate is flexible, then fiscal policy is ineffective and monetary policy is the only tool that governments can potentially use. If central banks are politically independent from governments, then even this tool is not available. Conversely, if exchange rates are fixed, monetary policy is an ineffective policy tool and we anticipate that governments rely on fiscal policy instead. Table 13.1 summarizes the predictions of the model.

Table 13.1. Predictions about the Effects of Exchange Rate Regime and Central Bank Independence on Opportunistic Political Business Cycles

	No Central Bank Independence	Central Bank Independence
Capital mobility and fixed exchange rates	**Fiscal cycles,** **No monetary cycles**	**Fiscal cycles,** **No monetary cycles**
Capital mobility and flexible exchange rates	**Monetary cycles,** **No fiscal cycles**	**No fiscal or** **Monetary cycles**

Note: This table also appears as figure 2 in William Roberts Clark and Mark Hallerberg, "Strategic Interaction between Monetary and Fiscal Actors under Full Capital Mobility," *American Political Science Review*, June 2000, 323–46.

The regression model and a detailed analysis appears elsewhere.[42] We recapitulate their findings here to stress the importance of the institutional choices discussed in the previous section. If the type of institution affects the likelihood of political business cycles as well as the type of cycle a country experiences (fiscal or monetary), then decisions on whether to use a flexible or a fixed exchange rate, as well as whether to have a dependent or an independent central bank, impact the political life of a country.

Our study includes data for all ten Eastern European accession countries for the years 1990–1999. Table 13.2 considers our evidence for the presence of monetary political business cycles. The dependent variable is M1. To consider the effects of election, we create a dummy variable coded as "1" if a legislative election took place either in the current quarter or in the previous three quarters. As in Clark and Hallerberg,[43] central bank independence and the exchange rate regime are coded as dummy variables, with independence and a "fixed" regime, respectively, each coded as a "1." We include two con-

Table 13.2.   Monetary Political Business Cycles in Eastern Europe, 1990–1999

Variable	Coefficient and Standard Error
Variables of Interest	
Election	.15**
	(.06)
Central bank independent	.08
	(.08)
Fixed exchange rate	−.0001
	(.04)
Election*central bank independent	−.21***
	(.07)
Election*fixed exchange rate	−.17**
	(.07)
Central bank independence*fixed	−.006
	(.06)
Election* central bank independent* fixed exchange rate	.17*
	(.10)
Control Variables	
Change in M1$_{t-1}$	.64***
	(.05)
Prices$_{t-1}$	.007**
	(.002)
Constant	.03
	(.05)

N = 262, R-squared = 0.79   * p < .1 ** p < .05, *** P < .01
Regression with panel-corrected standard errors and country dummies (not reported). Alternative equations that include additional lags of the dependent variable and of prices yield virtually identical results.

Table 13.2a. Conditional Coefficients for Election under Different Configurations of Central Bank Independence and Exchange Rate Regime

	Exchange Rates	
Central bank independence	Flexible	Fixed
High	−.06*	−.06
	(.03)	(.05)
Low	.15**	−.01
	(.06)	(.03)

* $p < .1$ ** $p < .05$, *** $P < .01$

trol variables: a one period lag of the money supply and a one period lag of the inflation rate.

Tables 13.2 and 13.2a provide strong evidence that there have been regular monetary cycles in the Eastern European countries under discussion, but that these cycles depend on the level of central bank independence as well as the exchange rate regime in place. Table 13.2 illustrates the standard regression. Our variable of interest, "election," is significant and carries the expected sign, indicating that electorally induced monetary cycles occur *when central banks are dependent and when there are flexible exchange rates,* but it alone cannot tell us all we would like to learn about the effects of elections. We need to consider the conditional coefficients and conditional standard errors.

Table 13.2a therefore presents conditional coefficients under different assumptions about central bank independence and the exchange rate. It is clear that the exchange rate regime plays a critical role. Regardless of the level of central bank independence, governments do not try to manipulate the economy through monetary expansions in preelectoral periods when the exchange rate is fixed. The level of central bank independence, on the other hand, plays a role when the exchange rate is flexible, that is, under conditions where the Mundell-Fleming model tells us that monetary policy should be effective. When the bank is dependent on the government, there is a strong increase in the money supply in preelectoral periods. When the bank is independent, however, there is a tightening of the money supply. The second set of regressions examines whether or not there are fiscal cycles when exchange rates are fixed. The dependent variable is the yearly deficit level as a percentage of GDP. The coding of "election" follows the coding that Franzese[44] suggests for yearly data. Instead of coding a year in which there is a legislative election as "1" and a year in which there is not an election "0," we consider the proportion of an election year that falls before the election as well as the proportion in the previous year. To facilitate the computation of conditional coefficients, we code the exchange as "1" if there is a flexible exchange rate in place.

Table 13.3 presents evidence that governments with fixed exchange rates engage in fiscal expansions. The conditional coefficients indicate that budget

Table 13.3.   Fiscal Political Business Cycles in Eastern Europe, 1990–1999

Variables	Coefficient (Standard Error)
Variables of Interest	
Election	−1.5
	(.8)
Flexible	−.71
	(.61)
Election*Flexible	.76
	(1.39)
Conditional Coefficients	
Election | Flexible = 0	−1.5**
	(.8)
Election | Flexible = 1	−.78
	(1.1)
Control Variables	
Intercept	−.7
	(.5)
$\Delta \text{Deficit}_{t-1}$	.46***
	(.11)
Δ Gdp	.05
	(.03)

N = 87, r-squared .27, * p < .1 ** p < .05, *** P < .01

deficit worsens 1.5 percent in preelectoral periods in countries with fixed exchange rates. In countries with flexible exchange rates, there is a smaller move downward, but in this case the coefficient is statistically indistinguishable from zero.

WHY DO ACCESSION COUNTRIES ACT LIKE CURRENT EU MEMBER STATES? IMPLICATIONS FOR ACCESSION TO THE EUROPEAN UNION

This chapter confirms that the governments of accession countries act very much like their OECD and EU counterparts. They manipulate the economy before elections where possible, but the tools they use to do so depend on the exchange rate regime and the institutional framework. If the country has a flexible exchange rate, the government relies on monetary expansions, while if the country maintains a fixed exchange rate, the government engages in fiscal expansions. Independent monetary authorities can eliminate monetary cycles in countries with flexible exchange rates.

These results appear puzzling. At the beginning of the chapter we noted that there is survey evidence for accession countries that fails to support the contention that voters are most concerned with their economic well-being when making their decision whom to back in elections. Instead, more political explanations, such as a person's attitudes toward past communist regimes, are better predictors of voter attitudes and, by implication, voting behavior.[45]

Our narrative about the development of exchange rate regimes and central banks indicated that accession countries learned from Westerners, initially from the IMF and later from the EU, how to establish economic institutions such as central banks and currency boards. It is fair to ask whether accession governments also learned how to manipulate the economy. A direct connection is unlikely—we have difficulty imagining an IMF team openly advising its host government to increase the money supply shortly before an election so that the incumbents have a better chance of winning. Yet it does not seem to be a great stretch to believe that Western governments may have served as "models" to their Eastern European counterparts on how to manipulate the economy in the hope of winning elections.

A second question is whether the EU accession process has affected the likelihood of political business cycles across countries. Our expectation a priori is that the integration process should not have a *direct* influence. The reason is that, while countries must accept the *acquis* more or less whole, there is no expectation that they cease from political manipulations of the economy to join the European Union; indeed, as other research has indicated,[46] current European Union members have had significant political business cycles during their memberships in the Union. Despite our misgivings, it is plausible that states expecting to join the European Union sooner than others would act differently from states expecting to join the European Union at a later date. States that consider themselves further behind may want to exhibit "more responsible" behavior to demonstrate their economic fitness for EU membership. A possible test for such disparities is to compare regressions for countries the European Commission originally labeled as "first wave" and "second wave" countries. Unfortunately, subdividing the already small data set still further leads to unreliable regression estimates that yield no clear differences between the two waves.[47]

A more indirect way that the difference between "first wave" and "second wave" countries could be in evidence is in the development of their monetary institutions. States that the European Commission considered the most likely to be part of the first wave of entrants may have more developed institutions more generally. They may be more likely to have independent central banks than second wave countries, and also be more likely to fix their currencies to the euro. Table 13.4 subdivides the accession countries according to their original "wave" and compares both the level of independence of their central banks and our coding for whether their exchange rates were flexible or fixed. There are no obvious differences between the two groups. The first wave countries do

Table 13.4.   Differences in Central Bank Independence and Exchange Rate Regime According to "First Wave" and "Second Wave" Labeling by the European Commission

Country	Central Bank Independence	Exchange Rate Regime
"First Wave"		
Czech Republic	Independent	Fixed 1990–1997Q2, flexible 1997Q3–1999
Estonia	Independent	Flexible 1990–1992Q2, Fixed 1992Q3–1999
Hungary	Dependent	Flexible 1990–1995Q1, Fixed 1995Q2–1999
Poland	Dependent	Flexible 1990–1999
Slovenia	Independent	Flexible 1990–1999
"Second Wave"		
Bulgaria	Independent	Flexible 1990–1997Q2, Fixed 1997Q3–1999
Latvia	Independent	Flexible 1990–1993Q3, Fixed 1993Q4–1999
Lithuania	Dependent	Flexible 1990–1994Q3, Fixed 1994Q4–1999
Romania	Dependent	Flexible 1990–1999
Slovakia	Dependent	Flexible 1993–1999

have one more independent central bank than the second wave countries, but the continuation of not completely independent central banks (during the sample period) in both Hungary and Poland—two countries that have been on virtually everyone's list as likely to be included in any "first wave"—indicates that a norm of complete central bank independence had *not yet* spread to all countries. Similarly, dividing the countries according to wave does not reveal any clear pattern in the likelihood of adopting a given type of exchange rate.

The fact that Eastern European countries already exhibit macroeconomic behavior before elections that mirrors the behavior found in Western Europe should be instructive to European Union policy makers who are considering the impact of European Union enlargement on the European economy.[48] As long as states continue to have flexible exchange rates and dependent central banks, there will likely be a political cycle that the money supply, and by implication the inflation rate, will follow.

Over time, however, the ten Eastern European accession countries will presumably join the euro area. The road to EMU requires that the future member states implement truly independent central banks. As such institutions are put in place, monetary political business cycles should disappear even before states become members of the euro area. Once the Eastern European states become members, monetary policy will be set by the ECB and, for the purposes of this discussion, exchange rates will become irrevocably fixed. Like their Western European counterparts who are already part of the euro area, the accession countries will give up their ability to manipulate monetary policy. Therefore, political business cycles can continue under EMU, but only in the form of the use of fiscal policy. European policy makers then have two problems to deal with: (1) will fiscal political business cycles have any negative effects on the euro area as a whole, and, if so, (2) what measures can be taken to prevent such cycles?

The initial evidence presented here indicates that states do have budget balances that are worse in preelectoral periods than in electoral periods, but the scale of this cycle has been no worse than in the European Union member states before the Maastricht treaty. Clark and Hallerberg[49] estimate that the gross debt burden worsened anywhere between 1.5 and 3 percentage points of GDP in the EU fifteen that had fixed exchange rates during the time period 1981–1992; the estimates here are that the budget balance worsened 1.5 percent of GDP in the ten Eastern European states over a roughly comparable ten-year period.[50] Given that the original members of the euro area were able to proceed and to meet the Maastricht criteria despite the presence of such cycles, *there is no reason to believe that the cycles as they now exist in the accession countries should lead to any delays in EMU membership.* Similarly, there is no reason to believe that the established norm of budget discipline which states are expected to adopt to join EMU will prevent political manipulations of fiscal policy before elections.

Presuming that the size of the cycles remains roughly the same under EMU, whether the cycles themselves should be a concern once the accession countries join EMU is debatable. On the one hand, the overall size of the new economies as a proportion of total EU GDP will remain small long after enlargement (even assuming real convergence toward the EU average GDP levels, this would truly be a generation-long process),[51] and the theoretical impact of euro membership on any politically motivated fiscal expansion in any one accession country should be tiny. Yet markets could react negatively if a country's deficit crossed 3 percent of GDP and punish the whole euro area. The reaction of the markets to the Russian default in 1998 indicates that negative news from even relatively small economies can have a broader impact. The Russian Federation's economy is currently half of the size of the economy of the Federal Republic of Brazil, yet its default initially led investors to reassess their holdings across the globe. Furthermore, even something smaller than a full default could still theoretically impact the external value of the euro: outside observers may read any deviance from the 3 percent norm as an indication that all states have the ability to ignore the European Union's fiscal rules.

CONCLUSION

This chapter first reviewed the creation of exchange rate regimes and central banks in Eastern Europe. It also reviewed evidence presented in Hallerberg,

Vinhas de Souza, and Clark[52] establishing that Eastern European accession countries established monetary institutions, such as central banks and exchange rate regimes, only with the sometimes substantial help of Western international organizations, particularly the International Monetary Fund. This chapter also indicated that the Eastern Europeans may have learned about more than economic efficiency when it comes to directing their economic policies. The behavior of incumbents in these countries before elections looks very much like the behavior of their future colleagues in the European Union Council.

Any future membership in Economic and Monetary Union will embed EU entrants into a tighter web of EU-level regulations on macroeconomic policy. States will delegate control over their monetary policies to the European Central Bank in Frankfurt. They will also be expected to adopt the norm of budget discipline, which in practice means deficits that do not exceed 3 percent of GDP except during serious economic decline. Yet these norms will not prevent governments from running fiscal political business cycles in the form of larger budget deficits in preelectoral years.

APPENDIX A

Table 13.A1.   Exchange Rate Arrangements of the Accession Countries

Country	Currency	Exchange Rate Regime	Date of Introduction
Bulgaria	Lev	Currency board regime (anchor is the euro)	July 1997
Czech Republic	Koruna	Managed float	May 1997
Estonia	Kroon	Currency board regime (anchor on the euro)	June 1992
Hungary	Forint	Sliding peg: 0.3% monthly- with intervention bands (+/– 15%) toward the euro	May 2001
Latvia	Lats	Peg with IMF special drawing rights, with intervention bands (+/– 1%)	October 1993
Lithuania	Litas	Currency board regime (the anchor is the US$)	March 1994
Poland	Zloty	Managed float	April 2000
Romania	Leu	Managed float	August 1992
Slovakia	Koruna	Managed float	October 1998
Slovenia	Tolar	Managed float	October 1991

Sources: Lucio Vinhas de Souza, Holger van Eden, Elisabeth Ledrut, Albert de Groot, and Gerbert Romijn, "EMU and Enlargement: A Review of Policy Issues," Economic Affairs Series, Working Paper ECON 117 EN (Luxembourg: Directorate General for Research, European Parliament, 1999).

Table 13.A2. Central Bank Independence in the Accession Countries

Country	Monetary Authority Status	Independence Index
Bulgaria	CBA	0.875(a)
Czech Republic	Legally independent central bank*	0.875(a)
Estonia	CBA	1.000(a), 0.74(b)
Hungary	Legally independent central bank*	0.312(a)
Latvia	Legally independent central bank	0.85(b)
Lithuania	CBA	0.125(a), 0.82(b)
Poland	Legally independent central bank	0.50(a)
Romania	Legally independent central bank*	0.50(a)
Slovakia	Nonindependent central bank*	n.a (assume low)
Slovenia	Legally independent central bank*	n.a (assume high)

Sources: Lucio de Souza, Holger van Eden, Elisabeth Ledrut, Albert de Gerbert Romijn, "EMU and Enlargement: A Review of Policy Issues," Economic Affairs Series, Working Paper ECON 117 EN (Luxembourg: Directorate General for Research, European Parliament, 1999). Kuusta Äimä, "Central Bank Independence in the Baltic Countries," *Review of Economics in Transition,* No. 3 (Helsinki: Suomen Pankki, 1998). Prakash Lougani and Nathan Sheets, "Central Bank Independence, Inflation, and Growth in Transition Economies," *Journal of Money, Credit, and Banking* 29, no. 3 (1997): 381–99; Alex Cukierman, Steven B. Webb, and Bilin Neyapti, "Measuring the Independence of Central Banks and Its Effect on Policy Outcomes," *World Bank Economic Review* 6, no. 3 (1992): 353–98.
*Lending to government is still permitted
Note: Äimä's index is based on the so-called Cukierman's index, which can vary from 0 (no independence) to 1 (complete independence). Cukierman's is built as a linear combination of the following variables:
1. CEO
   a. Duration of term in office of CB's CEO
   b. Who appoints CB's CEO
   c. How CB's CEO can be dismissed
   d. Is CB's CEO allowed to hold other offices
2. PF
   a. Who formulates monetary policy
   b. Conflict resolution procedures with government
   c. CB's role in budget definition
3. OBJ
   a. CB statutory objectives
4. LM
   a. Limits on advances to government
   b. Limits on lending to government
   c. Who decides the terms of any lending
   d. Set of CB's potential borrowers
   e. Type of lending limits
   f. Maturity of loan
   g. Limits on interest rates
   h. Limits to primary market lending
Cukierman uses both (arbitrarily) weighted and simple averaged combinations of the variables above. Äimä uses a weighted combination of .20 for (1), .15 for (2), .15 for (3), and varied weights for items in (4). Due to questions of comparability among his set of countries, Äimä estimates an alternative index that completely leaves out (4), reweighting the remaining criteria. These are the values presented above. Lougani and Sheets use a similar procedure but put more weight on (1) and (2), which explains the sharply different results for Estonia and Lithuania.

NOTES

1. William Roberts Clark and Mark Hallerberg, "Strategic Interaction between Monetary and Fiscal Actors under Full Capital Mobility," *American Political Science Review* 94, no. 2 (2000): 323–46; and Mark Hallerberg, Lúcio Vinhas de Souza, and

William Roberts Clark, "Political Business Cycles in EU Accession Countries," *European Union Politics* 3, no. 2, June 2002, 231–50.

2. The classic articles are Robert A. Mundell, "Capital Mobility and Stabilization Policy under Fixed and Flexible Exchange Rates," *Canadian Journal of Economics and Political Science*, November 1963, 475–85; J. Marcus Fleming, "Domestic Financial Policies under Fixed and Floating Exchange Rates," *IMF Staff Papers* 9 (1962): 369–80. The framework contends that one must consider both the exchange rate regime and the level of capital mobility in order to understand when monetary and fiscal policy serve as effective policy instruments to manipulate the economy.

3. Richard Rose, William Mishler, and Christian Haerpfer, *Democracy and Its Alternatives: Understanding Post-Communist Societies* (Baltimore: Johns Hopkins University Press, 1998).

4. Clark and Hallerberg, "Strategic Interaction."

5. Clark and Hallerberg, "Strategic Interaction."

6. Malta was only added to this list in October 1998, when the Council accepted Malta's request to reactivate its candidature, which had been presented in 1990 but withdrawn following the change in government on the island after the general elections of 1996. A new government, elected in September 1998, reverted to this position.

7. It must be noted that the specific political situation in Cyprus, namely, its division between a Greek Cypriot south and a Turkish-occupied north, casts some doubts on the final outcome of the accession negotiations.

8. These criteria, known as "Copenhagen criteria," are that the new entrants should present: "i) stable institutions, guarantees the rule of law, human rights and the protection of minorities; ii) can be regarded as a functioning market economy able to cope with the competitive pressure and market forces within the Union in the medium term and iii) should be capable in the medium term of applying the *acquis* provided it continues its efforts on its transposition and intensifies its works on its implementations." See European Commission, *Composite Paper* (Brussels: European Commission, 1999.)

9. European Commission, *Composite Paper.*

10. Lúcio Vinhas de Souza, "The Portuguese Legal Framework for Foreign Direct Investment," in *Competitiveness in International Business,* ed. Denise Dimon, Irene Tomlinson, and Susan Nichols (College Station: Texas A&M University Press, 1996).

11. A number of numerical benchmarks were defined in the framework of the Maastricht treaty. These so-called EMU, or Maastricht convergence criteria, aim to ensure monetary and fiscal stability in the joint currency area. The criteria force countries desiring full EMU membership to converge in the monetary and fiscal sphere. Two of the criteria are monetary, one is linked to currency rate stability, and the final one is fiscal. *The inflation convergence criterion* is defined as an inflation rate that should not exceed by more than 1.5 percent the average inflation rate of the three best-performing countries. *The interest rate convergence criterion* means that the average long-term nominal interest rate should not be more than 2 percent above the average interest rate of three countries with the lowest inflation rate. *The ERM criterion* postulates that the currencies of future EMU members should have been in the ERM (exchange rate mechanism) without devaluation or revaluation for at least two years. *The excessive debt criterion* is composed of (1) a budget deficit component, which declares that a country's budget deficit should not exceed 3 percent of its GDP, and (2) a stock of debt component, which states that the stock of outstanding government

debt should not exceed 60 percent of that country's GDP (or otherwise be in a descending sustainable trajectory toward these benchmarks).

Additionally, an "operational" criterion was also set concerning the legal and institutional features of the national central bank (CB), namely, its independence from government interference, a mandate toward price stability, the prohibition of monetary financing of deficits, and the availability of a set of market-based instruments that enable the CB to conduct monetary policy actions.

12. The founding members of the euro area are Austria, Belgium, Finland, France, Germany, Ireland, Italy, Luxembourg, Netherlands, Portugal, and Spain. The currently nonparticipating member states are Denmark, Sweden, and the United Kingdom. Greece joined the euro area in January 2001. The European common currency itself entered into circulation in January 2002.

13. Heliodoro Temprano-Arroyo and Robert A. Feldman, "Selected Transition and Mediterranean Countries: An Institutional Primer on EMU and EU Accession," *Economics of Transition* 7, no. 3 (1999): 746.

14. European Commission, *Composite Paper* (Brussels: European Commission, 1998).

15. European Commission, *Agenda 2000* (Brussels: European Commission, 1997).

16. See European Commission, *Composite Paper,* 1999.

17. As an example, the PEP for Hungary, submitted in April 2001, can be found at <www.meh.hu/PM/Dokumentumok/program20010426_en.htm> (August 1, 2001).

18. These macro programs encompassed, of course, several different policy actions. On the monetary side, one of the main initial concerns was the elimination of the monetary overhang: centrally planned economies traditionally generated a surplus of legal tender, given the limited amount of goods and services available for consumption. A substantial part of this overhang was held by households outside of the former monobank financial system. The liberalization of prices and external trade, besides the macro balance and allocative microefficiency issues involved, aimed at eliminating part of this surplus.

19. For a stylized description of the general trajectory, see László Halpern and Charles C. Wyplosz, "Equilibrium Exchange Rates in Transition Economies," IMF Working Papers, WP/96/125, 1996.

20. Among the state enterprises and government departments, not even this means of exchange function of money was necessary: barter (interunit transfers of goods and services for settlement) was used instead.

21. Which, even in Western Europe, were only slowly and progressively introduced between the 1950s and the 1990s.

22. It is estimated that, on average, only three years separated these two distinct phases. It was a much faster process than its counterpart in Western Europe. See Olga Radzyner and Sandra Reisinger, *Central Bank Independence in Transition: Legislation and Reality in Central and Eastern Europe* (Österreichische Nationalbank, 1998).

23. A full fixing (like the euro) merges the national currency in a composite currency that floats itself: in these terms, a full fixing to the euro is actually a floating regime from the point of view of the aggregate.

24. The "shock-isolation" capabilities of a float regime can be intuitively demonstrated in a simple IS-LM analytical framework. Both foreign demand and foreign price shocks are cushioned by a floating exchange rate. Nevertheless, a foreign interest rate

shock is not cushioned by a float or a peg, but the shock works on opposite directions (in a float, a fall in the "world" interest rates causes a capital inflow and an appreciation of the exchange rate, leading the IS curve to shift to the left, and conversely in a peg regime), but, in the case of the float, an activist monetary policy can be used as an effective instrument by the domestic policy maker.

25. See also Aziz Ali Muhammed, "The Role of International Financial Institutions," in *East-Central European Economies in Transition*, ed. John P. Hardt and Richard F. Kaufman (Armonk, N.Y.: M. E. Sharpe, 1995), 191–204; Jozef van Brabant, *The Political Economy of Transition* (London: Routledge, 1998); see Temprano-Arroyo and Feldman, "Selected Transition," for further details on the role of international organizations in the reorganization of transition economies more generally.

26. As an example of this, Estonia, whose monetary authority was set up and funded by the IMF, decided in early 2001 not to renew the standby agreement it had with the Fund since its inception as a country.

27. For a comprehensive discussion of alternative exchange rate regimes, see Lúcio Vinhas de Souza, Holger van Eden, Elisabeth Ledrut, Albert de Groot, and Gerbert Romijn, "EMU and Enlargement: A Review of Policy Issues," Economic Affairs Series, Working Paper ECON 117 EN (Luxembourg: Directorate General for Research, European Parliament, 1999).

28. Some specific examples could be supplied that contradict this last statement, most famously, Hong Kong, a CBA "country" which, even today, is one of the most dynamic financial markets in Asia. Its importance was partially derived from its special role as an intermediary in most financial transactions with the communist People's Republic of China (PRC), which may have more than compensated for the disadvantages of the CBA system. The Hong Kong market's diminishing importance since being absorbed into the PRC can be seen as supporting this conclusion.

29. Other weaknesses of peg regimes are:

- It is very difficult to determine the equilibrium exchange rate of a national currency in a peg.
- The economy becomes vulnerable to shocks in the country to which the national currency is pegged.
- The destabilising effects of capital inflows, when a misaligned fixed exchange rate violates the uncovered interest rate parity condition (by creating exploitable "risk-free" interest rate differentials), force the CB to costly and ultimately ineffective sterilization operations.

30. The Czech Republic is a good example of the fragility of apparently positive macroeconomic developments in a transition economy that lacked adequate microfoundations. Those weaknesses were "for all too long hidden behind a curtain of macroeconomic success." See Claudia Maria Buch and Jörg Döpke, "Real and Financial Integration in Europe—Evidence for the Accession States and for the Pre-Ins," Kiel Working Papers, no. 917, 1999.

31. Marja Nissinen, *Latvia's Transition to a Market Economy* (New York: St. Martin's, 1999).

32. Einars Repse, "The Implications of EMU for the Policies of the Bank of Latvia" (speech by the governor of the Bank of Latvia, Vienna, 1998).

33. Kuusta Äimä, "Central Bank Independence in the Baltic Countries," *Review of Economies in Transition*, no. 3 (Suomen Pankki [Bank of Finland], 1998).

34. It must be noted that some authors, such as Kuusta Äimä, "Central Bank Independence," have a much more negative interpretation of the monetary policy developments in Lithuania and the very institutional design of the Lithuanian monetary authority, linking them to, in essence, a power struggle within the Lithuanian government. According to this interpretation, the institution of the CBA *increased*, in practical terms, the margin of maneuver of the government in terms of economic policy due to the elimination of a competing center of authority—the BoLi. The government is also strong vis-à-vis the BoLi because, almost uniquely among CBAs, the exchange rate of the litas can be changed by a mere *government* decision, albeit in consultation with the BoLi. This has led some authors to ask if the Lithuanian arrangement deserves to be called a CBA at all; see Äimä, "Central Bank." Such a situation is actually the opposite of the expected outcome of a CBA. Historically, the institution of the CBA was imposed on the BoLi by a government decision against the bank's advice, after it had achieved the stabilization of the litas and without any real modifications of its internal structure. The high turnover of BoLi's governors—*seven* since its founding in 1990, two of them temporary—grants it the lowest score in actual independence among the Baltic monetary authorities according to the Cukierman index. Some of them were dismissed due to direct conflicts with the Lithuanian government. In 1993, for example, the governor refused to allow the use of the BoLi profits to finance the government's budget, and the government promptly fired him. The following governor, after an interim administration and already under the CBA legislation, even allowed the use of the BoLi's reserves as collateral for loans provided by private banks to the government.

35. Bank of Lithuania, *Monetary Policy Programme for 1997–1999* (Vilnius, 1997).

36. Note that the central bank existed before independence, since the former Bank of Yugoslavia actually operated as a federation of regional central banks, uncannily similar to the European Central Bank.

37. Clark and Hallerberg, "Strategic Interaction."

38. Clark and Hallerberg, "Strategic Interaction."

39. William Roberts Clark and Usha Nair Reichert, "International and Domestic Constraints on Political Business Cycle Behavior," *International Organization* 52, no. 1 (Winter 1998): 87–120.

40. Clark and Hallerberg, "Strategic Interaction."

41. Clark and Hallerberg, "Strategic Interaction."

42. Hallerberg, Vinhas de Souza, and Clark, "Political Business Cycles."

43. Clark and Hallerberg, "Strategic Interaction."

44. Robert J. Franzese, "The Political Economy of Public Debt: An Empirical Examination of the OECD Postwar Experience" (paper presented at the annual meeting of the Midwest Political Science Association, Chicago, 1996).

45. Rose, Mishler, and Haerpfer, *Democracy*, 1998.

46. Clark and Hallerberg, "Strategic Interaction."

47. While we would be happy to provide the results on request, there are simply too few observations for us to have confidence that there is anything to learn from them one way or the other.

48. This discussion is developed further in Hallerberg, Vinhas de Souza, and Clark, "Political Business Cycles."

49. Clark and Hallerberg, "Strategic Interaction."

50. The figure for the coefficient in Clark and Hallerberg's "Strategic Interaction" is the coefficient when there were fixed exchange rates and no fiscal institution (i.e., strong finance minister or negotiated fiscal contracts) in place.

51. See Vinhas de Souza et al., "EMU and Enlargement."

52. Hallerberg, Vinhas de Souza, and Clark, "Political Business Cycles."

14

Conclusion: International Organizations and East Europe—Bringing Parallel Tracks Together

Ronald H. Linden

Since the extraordinary events of 1989, studies of change in post–Cold War Europe have proceeded along essentially parallel tracks. Students of European organizations, especially the EU and NATO, have explored the politics, institutions, and goals of those organizations and how these are changing in the face of new demands and a raft of new applicants.[1] Students of Eastern Europe have generated an enormous library of studies of the changing politics and economics in this region.[2] But, remarkably, there have been very few explorations of how these developments have been or might be affected by the region's attempts to "join Europe." Most of the studies of international organizations (IOs) have focused on the organizations themselves and what effect bringing in new members might have for their mission, budget, institutions, and practices.[3] Few empirical studies of the way things have changed in East Europe demonstrate the effect of international factors, including the influence of the West.[4]

This volume aims to bring those tracks together. The studies included all begin from the assumption that there is, or might be, an impact on the new democracies of Eastern Europe stemming from their association with their *objects desire*, international, and especially European, organizations. The authors have all asked the question, What difference does it make to these countries that they seek to join the EU or NATO or that they want to please the IMF or World Bank? Have they had to act certain ways, develop certain institutions, and implement certain laws? What did the international organizations want? What leverage did they have available to get what they wanted? Above all, what difference have the efforts to join made in these countries' political institutions or dynamics, economies, social welfare policies, foreign policies?

Such questions, while seemingly straightforward, do not necessarily lend themselves to straightforward answers. For one thing, the range of impact is potentially as broad as the forms of human social interaction in modern society. In theory the desire to join an organization that establishes a full set of constitutive and regulatory norms[5] could require a complete overhaul of an applicant's social, political, and economic relations. The IO could insist on changes in the way money is raised and spent, policies are adopted and implemented, minorities are treated, stores open and close, armies and navies go to war. The *acquis communautaire* of the EU, which constitutes the entire body of laws and obligations of EU membership, exceeds eighty thousand pages, specifies ten thousand pieces of legislation, and constitutes a virtual encyclopedia of the ways public human behavior can be regulated. Thus the first question a student of this intersection of international and national politics must address is what area or sector to investigate. The authors of this volume have covered several, including economic policy, public participation, law, regional policy, social welfare negotiations and policies, civil-military relations, and foreign policy.

Second, if this is a study of norms and their impact, what norms are in play? Have the EU, NATO, or other organizations spelled out what they expect applicant countries to do and if so, how explicitly? Here all of the authors note the role the EU has played in making clear what it expected in the way of democratic and economic institutions and practices, at least in general terms. These were set out by a European Council in Copenhagen in 1993 and more explicitly in the EU's *Agenda 2000* criteria in 1997.[6] After that, the EU began reviewing the behavior of each applicant country according to explicit criteria and began issuing annual reports.[7] This process generates enormous pressure on the applicant states to conform to what the EU expects of them in the realm of creating a democratic society and the ability to engage in international economic competition. In this volume the role of these general but powerful expectations is explored by Annette Freyberg-Inan for Romania and Zlatko Šabič for Slovenia. In some cases EU expectations were also embodied in charters and covenants for certain sectors. Elena Iankova, for example, looks at the use of the European Social Charter with regard to Bulgaria, and Beate Sissenich, the social *acquis*, for Poland and Hungary. Wade Jacoby and Pavel Cernoch examine regional policy and Melanie Ram investigates intellectual property rights in the Czech Republic.

The screening process for foreign policy norms and practices has not been as formal but is no less specific. NATO and the EU have made it clear that normalizing relations between neighbors, regardless of the merits or righteousness of past ethnic or territorial claims, is a sine qua non of membership. Hence, in my chapter on Bulgaria and Margit Williams's on Hungary, we see adaptation, including abandonment of past conflict-inciting behavior, as a product of these countries' desire to join. NATO had a domestic side to its expectations as well, focusing on what it saw as optimum civil-military relations, including unquestioned, traceable civilian control. As Andrew Michta shows, this was applied explicitly and directly in the Polish case.

But what if norms are not explicit, if particular expectations of political or economic behavior are not spelled out—can we still expect to see an impact? Shouldn't we be alert to this possibility, perhaps under the heading of unintended consequences, as Frank Schimmelfennig notes in the introduction. Our collection includes two cases that illustrate the power of the IOs on developments in Eastern Europe, even when explicit norms are nonexistent. Alex Grigorescu explores possible explanations for the spread of laws covering transparency. For East Europe he concludes that neither the logic of appropriateness (i.e., the adoption of norms due to a sense of group identity) nor the logic of consequences (the adoption of norms due to cost-benefit calculations) are sufficient to explain this development. In part, this is because the implementing organizations, the EU and NATO, are not themselves transparent, nor did they make it a condition of membership that applicant states become transparent. Mark Hallerberg, Lúcio Vinhas de Souza, and William Clark find that East European states' banking and fiscal cycles reflect an almost identical dynamic to those in the West, even though no EU incentives or sanctions encouraged them. In this instance the East European governments copied the West European examples, even though there is little evidence supporting the link between the public's perception of their immediate economic situation and their political support for the particular regime.[8] Nonetheless, they essentially followed a Western model. However, with regard to governing transparency, the East European states' behavior does not reflect the existing models; in many cases laws were adopted that provided for greater transparency than in the older democracies.

In situations in which there were norms and models, what were the mechanisms of transference? How did the "nannies" get the applicants to follow the norms? In virtually all cases the main incentive dangled before the new democracies was membership. All of the East European states have committed themselves to becoming members of both the EU and NATO. Eventually these two organizations acceded to the proposition that some of these states would join, sooner or later, if they "behaved." This was not true for the IMF or World Bank and generally not true for the Council of Europe, which as Frank Schimmelfennig points out, used an "intermediate strategy" of letting in members before they met the criteria and then encouraging them to do so.[9]

For the financial organizations, as well as for both the EU and to a lesser extent NATO, the promise of funds was a second, powerful mechanism. These were typically dispensed with "conditionality," that is, on the basis of behavior that met or promised to meet certain criteria. While for the IMF and World Bank these funds were loans, for the EU it was primarily PHARE assistance that provided the carrot. Originally designed to provide technical and financial support to the economies of Poland and Hungary, this program broadened in both substantive and geographic scope to become the main preaccession assistance vehicle of the EU.[10] NATO too has provided some funds, though the Partnership for Peace program, like the Europe Agreements, itself acts as a lever, a sort of halfway house on the road to full membership.[11] These forms of assistance were often precisely targeted to a specific goal, such as the technical assistance offered to states to help administer the newly crafted or "harmonized" laws (see Ram on intellectual property) and institutions (see Sissenich on "twinning").[12]

A third lever utilized by the IOs in Eastern Europe has been more political than economic and more rhetorical than financial. This involves the bargaining and negotiating that has gone on between the organizations and the Central and East European states. The power disparity between the lovers and the beloved is great, suggesting that the former have little leverage. Hence these negotiations might be better characterized as a form of the "arguing" Thomas Risse identifies in the adopting of human rights norms.[13] In our cases, several of the authors point to the importance of the EU judging which of the Central and East European states were ready to begin negotiations and which were not, first made explicit in 1997. Annual assessments followed of their political and economic behavior as well as negotiations over the implementation of the *acquis*. With the addition of five other East European states to the negotiating queue in 1999, virtually all of the East European states are now judged every year. The studies by Freyberg-Inan, Šabič, Iankova, Ram, Sissenich, and Jacoby and Cernoch ascribe substantial significance to these reports and opinions. The EU has made it clear that meeting these criteria before admission is the way to Brussels; hence, the East European states have shown a high degree of sensitivity to this form of assessment. As Jacoby and Cernoch put it, norms have "far-reaching impact . . . in the candidate countries when their adoption is tied to the overall goal of EU membership." While it would be too much to call it "shaming" (as Risse and Sikkink do in describing exchanges in the human rights area), it is certainly "judging" and, as with shaming, certainly serves to establish in-group and out-group identities.[14] As Slovakia learned in 1997, a poor report gets one sent to detention.[15]

NATO too makes its judgments clear, as Andrew Michta's exploration of the Polish case makes clear. NATO also had the opportunity to judge the behavior of some of its candidate members in 1999. During the buildup and subsequent military campaign against Slobodan Milošević and Yugoslavia, Bulgaria and Romania moved to cut ties with Yugoslavia, extended full troop transit and overflight rights to NATO, and refused overflight rights to Russia. In a remarkable approximation of membership, NATO extended protection to Serbia's neighbors in response to threats from Belgrade.[16] For some of these neighbors, their ability to pass this test entitles them to favorable consideration for NATO membership.[17]

To both the major IOs the East European states have been able to show how they would behave as members: by adopting and implementing legislation, by adjusting fiscal and monetary policies, by institutionalizing certain kinds of domestic relations (e.g., between management and labor, civilians and the military), and by acting as good alliance members internationally. While their net contributions may still be considered substandard—or even negative[18]—the overall behavior of the East European states has provided a huge payoff to these alliances: the creation of a more secure and stable environment in the East. Compare this with the conflict and challenge to resources represented by developments in the area of the former Yugoslavia. Without the desire to join or, more critically, the prospect of success for applicants, the European IOs would have precious little leverage. But how long will the respective publics, East and West, display patience or bear the costs of possible membership? As Geoffrey Harris notes in his chapter, "EU governments are under virtually no domestic pressure to enlarge the EU." On the East European side, the evidence is clear that public support for an endless queue is not to be taken for granted.[19]

ASSESSING THE IMPACT

More than a decade after the fall of communist regimes, state-dominated economic systems and the international hegemony of the Soviet Union, democracy has taken hold in the region, governments have been elected and unelected, the publics of Eastern Europe have become subjects as well as objects of policy, and, to varying degrees, the basic structures of market-based economic systems have been put in place. New international alliances have been forged, partly with existing alliances and partly in new forms, such as CEFTA.[20] While the region is only beginning to be institutionally integrated with Western Europe and there is reason to be frustrated over the slow, deliberate approach of both the EU and NATO, the process of democratization and, in most cases, a return to economic growth after virtual free fall, give reason to be optimistic.

But what has been the effect on such progress of these states' attempts to join the West? What have our authors found to be the contribution of norms, backed up by various forms of incentives? This can be assessed across several dimensions and a summary here cannot do justice to the complex texture of the individual studies. Still, we can draw some conclusions about the nature and form of such an impact before moving on to consider possible reasons for the differences in that impact.

Several of the authors point to significant legal or institutional changes. Grigorescu notes the adoption of far-reaching transparency laws in several East European states. Sissenich describes the impact of European Commission pressure on the adoption of social legislation in Poland and Hungary, and Iankova notes the impact on (mostly preexisting) labor-management-government negotiating bodies in Bulgaria. Several authors also note the emergence of ministries or interministerial bodies with specific responsibility for responding to EU directions. Examples of the institutional impact of international organizations include the stimuli to create regional bodies seen in the Czech Republic, described by Jacoby and Cernoch, and the movement to create strong central banks or even currency boards spurred by the IMF, noted by Hallerberg, Vinhas de Souza, and Clark. Armed forces reduction and reorientation were noted in Poland and Bulgaria by Michta and myself, respectively.

Does that mean that actual policies favored by the powerful IOs have been put into place? Here the answer is more mixed. In the military realm, for example, there seems to be more "talking the talk" than thoroughgoing implementation of the full range of NATO expectations.[21] EU pressure kept Hungary eager to pursue basic treaties and pursue workmanlike, if not always fulsome, relationships with its neighbors on the issue of treatment of minorities, as Williams shows.[22] Ram identifies several concrete and significant changes in Czech intellectual property law, and trade and patent law that interactions with the EU has produced. Clearly Romania, according to Freyberg-Inan, and Slovenia, according to Šabič, were trying to do what they thought key economic organizations, especially the EU and IMF, wanted them to do.

But Freyberg-Inan also makes clear, and the EU itself has noted, that Romanian compliance has been inconstant and ineffective.[23] Implementation of EU-type social policies and especially the creation of new institutions has been sluggish in Poland and Hungary, according to Sissenich. Grigorescu notes that actual practices of transparency across the region, including implementation of key legislation in the area of access to information, have been uneven, at best. We see a picture overall that is closer to that of institutional imitation than one of thorough policy transposition.[24] This should not be surprising, given the scope and density of the transformation expected.

But it is also a function of the recent history of this region and the peculiar nature of the "two-level" bargaining in which the new democratic governments must engage. For example, it has not escaped the notice of most of the observers in this volume that no sooner had these states regained their sovereignty from Soviet dominance than they had to begin making preparations to hand pieces of it over to Western IOs.[25] The new governments faced the contradictory desires of their populations for greater control over their own destinies, at last, but also a rapid "return to Europe." Under these circumstances, adjusting to multiple European IO mandates has not been easy. Nor should we expect it to be so, given the difficulties experienced, for example, by more experienced democracies in accommodating themselves to the demands of the European Monetary Union.

The problem for the East European states is that they are expected by their nannies to comply with the norms even *before* being allowed to join the organizations. The applicants can only belong to NATO and the EU when they prove themselves first—even if previous joiners did not have to. Earlier applicants to the European Community, for example, Spain and Greece, were granted long and varying "transition periods" to allow them to accommodate to Community economic practices.[26] The East European states have been offered no such option, as a two-speed Europe has been ruled out.

Moreover, the stakes involved in adaptation, the consequences of making or not making the required changes, are profound. They include not just the loss of specific concrete benefits (e.g., structural funds or security assurances) but of the applicant's sense of *drushtvo*, or community. Europe itself is in fact "two-speed"; France and Germany are part of the EMU but Great Britain is not. But for the East European states, being left out of East Europe means being left behind, cut off in a "new Yalta." The domestic political consequences of this for the region, not to mention the political parties that lead or hope to lead the governments in Central and Eastern Europe, are not salutary.

Hence political leaders are in something of a bind. The process of approaching and negotiating with European IOs is elite dominated. But the consequences are not. Elites whose political futures depend on making progress toward "joining Europe" stake a lot on trying to achieve the institutional and policy changes required—or at least giving that appearance—while not exacerbating the already difficult consequences of domestic upheaval. Several of the authors point to the fact that the process of trying to join the European organizations has put some distance between the governments and the governed, that the elites are essentially forcing through the costs of these accessions. While surveys show general support for joining the EU and NATO, they also show substantial variance across countries, across social groups, and over time.[27]

If elites want it and some of the public is wary, does democracy suffer? Harris's essay in this volume illustrates the central role of elites on both sides of the Continent, despite the intermediate role parliaments should play. Freyberg-Inan goes further, arguing that the accession process in Romania has hurt democratic development there; Sissenich makes a similar point for Central Europe. She is echoed by Williams in a study not in this volume, who considers that the EU is "exporting the democratic deficit."[28]

Several authors point to beneficial effects on democratic development of interactions with IOs. Grigorescu sees a clear effect on governments' willingness to disclose information to their own citizens, though he attributes this to the indirect effect of releasing information to IOs, not to IO insistence. The benefits of greater civilian control of the military, illustrated by Michta, and of having government closer to the regions governed, described by Jacoby and Cernoch, are a direct result of NATO and EU intervention, respectively. In some cases the effect of interaction with IOs appears to be "democracy-neutral," that is, it does not seem to invigorate the movement to greater democracy nor does it retard it. In the Bulgarian case, examined in different aspects by Iankova and myself, neither the institutional changes put in place by EU-style tripartism nor the foreign policy changes wrought by different governments played a significant role in increasing—or decreasing—public input into policy making.[29]

WHAT MADE THE DIFFERENCE? THE QUESTION OF WHEN NORMS MATTER

The literature on norms is rapidly producing schemes that aim to assess the conditions under which norms travel, either across national boundaries or from the international organizations or community into states, and when they make a difference in policy. Finnemore and Sikkink argue that "norm entrepreneurs" utilize international organizations and create a "norms cascade," in which norms held by powerful, successful states are adopted by other states that are eager to share in the group's success, reputation, and esteem.[30] Risse and Ropp describe a "spiral model" of norm transfer during which, in the early stages, states act out of instrumental rationality and make tactical concessions. But "talk is not cheap," and soon the norms become part of the state's institutions and modes of behavior.[31] Whether and when norms become practice depend, in their view, on several sets of factors, including the openness of the society in question, the "world time" of the norm cycle (i.e., is it dominant), and the presence or absence of key "blocking factors," especially elites. Cottrell and Davis as well as Checkel also stress elites, in particular their relationship to society, but Checkel also stresses the degree to which there is a "cultural match" between the externally generated norm and domestic society.[32] How does the evidence from our cases bear on these propositions?

Elite dynamics are clearly central. Virtually all of the studies in this volume point to the importance of how elites see the country in its relation to the IO, how they identify themselves, what their tasks are, and which policies must be implemented in order to please the IOs. The proof of this is shown in the cases where elite circulation made the difference in compliance: a change of government in the Czech Republic moved regional policy closer to EU norms (Jacoby and Cernoch); a change in Hungary brought in a government more willing to put Trianon behind it (Williams); different parties in Bulgaria envisioned their country's place in Europe and its role in nearby conflict differently (Linden). The public played a role in all these cases—after all, they elected the old and new governments—but it was the role of limiter rather than definer. Such a role is described by Checkel as "statist" (i.e., societal pressure was secondary).[33] In addition to typifying a top-down infusion of norms and derivative acts, the elites in Eastern Europe heightened the salience of the external norms by accepting them and attesting to their legitimacy, a point stressed by Cortell and Davis.[34]

But elites, like the ideas they proselytize, "do not float freely."[35] East European elites operate within the domestic political, economic, and cultural environment bequeathed to them by their predecessors. This makes the domestic situation more complex than a pure institutional analysis might suggest. One of the most surprising and intriguing results of the studies in this volume, a common thread that stands out as much as the importance of elites, is the importance of these states' predemocratic legacies. As Ken Jowitt has noted,[36] the East European states lurched into the post-1989 period not with a clean slate but with certain political, psychological, and cultural dynamics that affect the way the transition becomes a transformation. In the cases treated in this volume, these legacies played an important part in shaping the impact of the states' interaction with IOs. Alex Grigorescu notes the persistence of the "culture of secrecy" in the region and ascribes the unevenness of transparency practices noted above to that, in part. Andrew Michta stresses the high degree of politicization of the military in Poland under communism but also its long-standing commitment to serving and preserving the Polish nation. A strong desire to avoid duplicating the first historical pattern while maintaining the second facilitated the country's adjustment to NATO demands on civilian control. The complete absence of regional government and a strong tradition of centralism in Czechoslovakia left the Czech Republic initially without the regional authorities needed to utilize EU structural funds, a institutional gap it was obliged to remedy, as Jacoby and Cernoch point out.[37]

Social and political divisions—derived in part from the searing divisions produced by decades of communist rule—hurt implementation of social policy in Poland, as Sissenich notes, and framed the foreign policy debate between Socialists and the UDF in Bulgaria, as my chapter makes clear. Finally, in some cases the legacy of pre-1989 made importing norms and practices easier. According to Iankova, Bulgarian sensitivity to maintaining social peace gave it a head start on establishing and maintaining tripartite institutions, which the EU and IMF would later push for.

If elites and their relationship to society are critical and a country's legacy sets the terms of the elite manipulation, do the norms and the nannies matter at all? Wouldn't we be better off to ignore the IOs and focus instead on the importance of the domestic debate and existing political culture? That would beg the question and leave out the determination of what the elite debates were about and what norms were presented for emulation. It is the international organizations, in this case especially the EU and NATO, who are the norm "entrepreneurs," the critical agents who dominate the current "world time." They offer to the governments of the East European states concrete benefits in the currency of economic assistance, access to markets, or enhanced security.

But they offer the current governments of virtually all hues something even more significant: acceptance into a community of values, one that virtually all contenders for power and the public aspire to. In 1989 the Soviet-installed regimes of more than forty years' duration fell, in part because ultimately they could not create a sense of governing legitimacy. They provided economic growth for a time as well as security, but throughout the region each succeeding generation learned that these regimes were not *nash*— ours. The authors in this volume are right to highlight aspects of the communist legacy, but there is another aspect to that legacy: the desire to "return to Europe." What people mean by that varies, both among themselves and from the "regulatory" tasks that international institutions impose on them. Most broadly, this "return" aims at what Vaclav Havel labels the "third meaning" of Europe, that is, beyond its geography and organizations. "This Europe," he says, "represents a common destiny, a common, complex history, common values and a common culture and way of life. More than that, it is also, in a sense, a region characterized by particular forms of behavior, a particular quality of will, a particular understanding of responsibility."[38] While the current custodians of the "European soul" may be moving slowly and with excruciating deliberation, it is their institutions that represent Europe in all its meanings. As we have seen in this volume, the "constitutive" role of these organizations is critical and is not diluted by being codified in eighty thousand pages of an *acquis*. "International institutions do not merely create political efficiencies," Peter Katzenstein writes. "Their form reflects collective identities that embody substantive political purposes."[39] It is these purposes that the IOs seek to specify in their norms, and it is through their achievement that the states and peoples of Eastern Europe seek to retrieve an identity long denied.

NOTES

1. On the EU, see Alan Mayhew, *Recreating Europe* (Cambridge: Cambridge University Press, 1998); Heather Grabbe and Kirsty Hughes, *Enlarging the EU Eastwards* (London: Royal Institute of International Affairs, 1998); Karen Smith, *The Making of EU Foreign Policy: The Case of Eastern Europe* (New York: Macmillan, 1999); Jozef

van Brabant, *Remaking Europe: The European Union and the Transition Economies* (Lanham, Md.: Rowman & Littlefield, 1999). On NATO, see Ian Q. R. Thomas, *The Promise of Alliance* (Lanham, Md.: Rowman & Littlefield, 1997); Gerald B. Solomon, *The NATO Enlargement Debate, 1990–1997* (Westport, Conn.: Praeger, 1998); James W. Morrison, *NATO Expansion and Alternative Future Security Alignments* (Washington, D.C.: National Defense University, l995).

2. See, among others, Klaus von Beyme, *Transition to Democracy in Eastern Europe* (London: Macmillan, 1996); Minton F. Goldman, *Revolution and Change in Central and Eastern Europe* (Armonk, N.Y.: M. E. Sharpe, 1997); Fritz Plasser, Peter Ulram, and Harald Waldrauch, *Democratic Consolidation in East-Central Europe* (London: Macmillan, 1998); Stephen White, Judy Batt, and Paul G. Lewis., eds., *Developments in Central and East European Politics 2* (Durham, N.C.: Duke University Press, 1998).

3. On the EU, see, for example, Grabbe and Hughes, *Enlarging the EU,* chap. 7; Helene Sjursen, "Enlargement and the Common Foreign and Security Policy: Transforming the EU's External Identity," in *Back to Europe: Central and Eastern Europe and the European Union,* ed. Karen Henderson (London: UCL Press, 1999), 37–51; David Phinnemore, "The Challenge of EU Enlargement: EU and CEE Perspectives," in Henderson, *Back to Europe,* 71–88; and Brian Ardy, "Agricultural, Structural Policy, the Budget, and Eastern Enlargement of the European Union," in Henderson, *Back to Europe,* 107–28. On NATO, see Charles-Philippe David and Jacques Levesque, *The Future of NATO: Enlargement, Russia, and European Security* (Montreal: McGill-Queen's University Press, 1999).

4. For some who begin to look at this impact, see Geoffrey Pridham, Eric Herring, and George Sanford, *Building Democracy? The International Dimension of Democratization in Eastern Europe,* rev. ed. (London: Leicester University Press, 1997); Michael A. Rupp, "The Pre-accession Strategy and the Governmental Structures of the Visegrad Countries," in Henderson, *Back to Europe,* 89–105; Janice Bell and Tomasz Mickiewicz, "EU Accession and Labour Markets in the Visegrad Countries," in Henderson, *Back to Europe,* 129–50; Katarzyna Zawakinska, "From Transition to Accession: Agriculture in the Czech Republic, Hungary, and Poland and the Common Agricultural Policy," in *The Eastern Enlargement of the EU,* ed. Marek Dabrowski and Jacek Rostowski (Norwell, Mass.: Kluwer Academic, 2001), 169–202; Jan Zielonka and Alex Pravda, eds., *Democratic Consolidation in Eastern Europe,* vol. 2 (New York: Oxford University press, 2000).

5. Peter J. Katzenstein, *Cultural Norms and National Security* (Ithaca, N.Y.: Cornell University Press, 1996), 18–19. In his introduction to this volume, Frank Schimmelfennig refers to these as "community norms" and "specific norms," respectively.

6. *Conclusions of the Presidency, European Council of Copenhagen, June 21–22, 1993,* Europe Documents, 1844/45, June 24, 1993; *Agenda 2000: For a Stronger and Wider Union* (Strasbourg: European Union), July 15, 1997, Doc97/6. <www.eurunion.org/whatsnew/index.htm>.

7. These are accessible at <europa.eu.int/comm/enlargement/index.htm>.

8. Richard Rose, William Mishler, and Christian Haerpfer, *Democracy and Its Alternatives: Understanding Post-Communist Societies* (Baltimore: Johns Hopkins University Press, 1998), chap. 8; Hubert Tworzecki, "Welfare-State Attitudes and Electoral Outcomes in Poland and Hungary," *Problems of Post-Communism* 47, no. 6 (2000): 17–28.

9. See Jeffrey Checkel's discussion of the Council of Europe's "soft conditionality" in "Compliance and Conditionality," Working Paper no. 00/18 (Oslo: ARENA/Universitetet i Oslo, 2000).

10. The PHARE program is described in Mayhew, *Recreating Europe,* 138–50. On the shift in PHARE goals, see "Phare Focus Sharpens," *European Dialogue,* September–October 1998, <europe.eu.int/comm/dg10/eur_dial/98i5a2s0.html> (March 26, 2001). Between 1990 and 1996 PHARE commitments totaled Ecu 6.636 billion; see "Phare Impact Seen as Positive," *European Dialogue,* November–December 1997, <europe.eu.int/comm/dg10/eur_dial/97i6a3s0.html> (March 26, 2001).

11. In 1998 the Congressional Research Service estimated the NATO Common Funds program, designed to assist the new Central European members, at $1.7 billion; John P. Hardt and Milana I. Gorshkova, "NATO and the European Union: Economic Capacity of New Member Countries, and Opportunity Costs," *CRS Report for Congress,* April 23, 1998, 3.

12. On "twinning," see also Elena Iankova, "Institutional Twinning in Central and Eastern Europe's Return to Europe" (paper presented to the annual convention of the International Studies Association, Los Angeles, California, March 15–18, 2000).

13. Thomas Risse, "International Norms and Domestic Change: Arguing and Communicative Behavior in the Human Rights Area," *Politics and Society* 27, no. 4 (December 1999): 529–59.

14. Thomas Risse and Kathryn Sikkink, "The Socialization of International Human Rights Norms into Domestic Practices: Introduction," in *The Power of Human Rights: International Norms and Domestic Change,* ed. Thomas Risse, Stephen C. Ropp, and Kathryn Sikkink (Cambridge: Cambridge University Press, 1999), 15.

15. For the EU view, see *Agenda 2000,* vol. 1; for discussion, see Karen Henderson, "Slovakia and the Democratic Criteria for EU Accession," in Henderson, *Back to Europe,* chap. 13.

16. See transcript of press conferences by NATO Secretary-General Javier Solana on April 12, 1999, <www.nato.int/docu/speech/1999/s990412a.htm> (March 23, 2001) and April 28, 1999, <www.nato.int.docu/speech/1999/s990428a.htm> (March 23, 2001); see also an earlier report by ABC News, March 24, 1999, <www.abcnews. go.com/sections/world/DailyNews/kosovo990324_bombing2.html#sidebar>.

17. At a conference of nine applicant countries in Vilnius in May 2000, Romanian foreign minister Petre Roman said, "As recent developments in Kosovo have demonstrated, from the point of view of the Alliance, countries like Romania, which are placed in the geographic proximity of troubled areas that generate security risks, can play an important role in preventing crises from spreading. Romania as well as Bulgaria, demonstrated their capacity as reliable partners for the Alliance, whilst positively answering to all NATO political and military requests." See his speech at <www.urm.lt/nato/rom.htm> (February 9, 2001). As Bulgarian Defense Minister Boyko Noev put it, "Bulgaria's policy during the Kosovo crisis was undoubtedly a test." BTA *Radiotelevizionen Monitor* (Internet version), December 23, 1999 (Foreign Broadcast Information Service, December 23, 1999). This point was reiterated explicitly to me during numerous interviews in Romania and Bulgaria in December 2000.

18. See the discussion of new NATO members in Jeffrey Simon, "NATO's Membership Action Plan (MAP) and Prospects for the Next Round of Enlargement," *Oc-*

casional Papers, East European Studies Program (Washington, D.C.: Woodrow Wilson Center, 2000).

19. Heather Grabbe and Kirsty Hughes, "Central and East European Views on EU Enlargement: Political Debates and Public Opinion," in Henderson, *Back to Europe*, 185–202.

20. See Matthew Rhodes, "Post-Visegrad Cooperation in East Central Europe," *East European Quarterly*, March 1999, 51–67; Adrian Hyde-Price, *The International Politics of East Central Europe* (Manchester, U.K.: Manchester University Press, 1996), 108–39.

21. Anton A. Bebler, ed., *Civil-Military Relations in Post-Communist States* (Westport, Conn.: Praeger, 1997), sec. 3; Biljana Vankovska-Cvetkovska, "Between the Past and the Future: Civil-Military Relations in the Balkans," *Südosteuropa* 48, no. 1–2 (1999): 29–47; Daniel N. Nelson, "Civil Armies, Civil Societies, and NATO's Enlargement," *Armed Forces and Society* 25, no. 1 (1998). On "talking the talk," see Risse and Sikkink, "Socialization," 12ff.

22. On this, see also Ronald H. Linden, "Putting on Their Sunday Best: Romania, Hungary, and the Puzzle of Peace," *International Studies Quarterly* 44 (March 2000): 121–45.

23. See *2000 Regular Report from the Commission on Romania's Progress towards Accession,* November 8, 2000, <europa.eu.int/comm/enlargement/dwn/report_11_00/word/en/ro_en.doc>.

24. Wade Jacoby calls this responding to "ceremonial myths as a substitute for the kind of real implementation which their underdeveloped public administrations cannot deliver." See Wade Jacoby, "Priest and Penitent: The European Union as a Force in the Domestic Politics of Eastern Europe," *East European Constitutional Review* 8, no. 1–2 (1999): 62–67. On policy transfer, see Heather Grabbe, "The Transfer of Policy Models from the EU to Central and Eastern Europe: Europeanisation by Design" (paper prepared for the 1999 annual meeting of the American Political Science Association, Atlanta, Georgia, September 2–5, 1999).

25. On this aspect, see Attila Agh, "Processes of Democratization in the East Central European and Balkan States: Sovereignty-Related Conflicts in the Context of Europeanization," *Communist and Post-Communist Studies* 32 (1999): 263–79.

26. Michel Galy, Gonzalo Pastor, and Thierry Pujol, *Spain: Converging with the European Community* (Washington, D.C.: International Monetary Fund, 1993), 6–11; Iacovos S. Tsalicoglou, *Negotiating for Entry: The Accession of Greece to the European Community* (Aldershot, U.K.: Dartmouth, 1995), 41–42, 65–67, passim.

27. Central and Eastern Eurobarometer, May 1998, <europa.eu.int/comm/dg10/epo/ceeb8/ceeb08.pdf>; *NATO Review*, May–June 1997, 16–18; Marek Kucia, "Public Opinion in Central Europe on EU Accession: The Czech Republic and Poland," *Journal of Common Market Studies*, March 1999, 143–52; Rachel Cichowski concludes, for example, that "pensioners and farmers are clearly more skeptical about their future as 'Europeans.'" See "Western Dreams, Eastern Realities: Citizen Support for the European Union in Central and Eastern Europe" (paper prepared for the 1999 meeting of the American Political Science Association, Atlanta, Georgia, September 2–5, 1999); a 1996 Eurobarometer survey found that in the ten applicant countries 33 percent of the respondents felt that farmers would lose out as ties increased with the EU, 26 percent state enterprises, 25 percent manual workers, and 23 percent people on low incomes; *European Dialogue,* March–April 1996, 27.

28. Margit Bessenyey Williams, "Exporting the Democratic Deficit," *Problems of Post-Communism*, January–February 2001, 27–38. Cf. Nelson's comment that "NATO enlargement has, thus far, been the pursuit of elites—not a 'cause' for the peoples of east-central, southeastern or post-Soviet Europe" ("Civil Armies," 5).

29. It is possible to argue that foreign policy in Bulgaria was less democratic under the Kostov government because it acted contrary to the clear preferences of the public. But lack of popularity and lack of democracy are not the same thing. The Kostov government stimulated and took part in public debate on its NATO policy and submitted the granting of permission for NATO overflights to parliamentary approval, as it was obliged to do.

30. Martha Finnemore and Kathryn Sikkink, "International Norm Dynamics and Political Change," *International Organization* 52, no. 4 (Autumn 1998): 887–917.

31. Risse and Ropp, "International Human Rights Norms."

32. Andrew P. Cortell and James W. Davis Jr., "How Do International Institutions Matter? The Domestic Impact of International Rules and Norms," *International Studies Quarterly* 40 (1996): 451–78; Jeffrey T. Checkel, "Norms, Institutions, and National Identity in Contemporary Europe," *International Studies Quarterly* 43, no. 1 (March 1999): 83–114.

33. Checkel, "Norms, Institutions," 90.

34. Cortell and Davis, "How Do International Institutions Matter?" 456.

35. Cf. Thomas Risse-Kappen, "Ideas Do Not Float Freely: Transnational Coalitions, Domestic Structures, and the End of the Cold War," *International Organization* 48, no. 2 (Spring 1994): 185–214.

36. Ken Jowitt, *New World Disorder* (Berkeley: University of California Press, 1992), chap. 8.

37. This has also begun to happen in Slovakia; see Terry Moran, "Slicing Up Slovakia," *Business Central Europe,* March 2001, 40–41.

38. Vaclav Havel, "The Hope for Europe," *New York Review*, June 20, 1996, 38.

39. Katzenstein, *Cultural Norms*, 29.

Index

About the Contributors

Pavel Cernoch holds a Ph.D. from Charles University in Prague and teaches there at the Jean Monnet Centre for European Studies. He worked previously as a foreign aid coordinator at the diplomatic mission of the European Commission in Prague and has coauthored a handbook for Czech public officials, *A Guide to the EU* (2000). He is working on a forthcoming book on the enlargement of the European Union.

William Roberts Clark received his Ph.D. from Rutgers University in 1994 and is an assistant professor in the Department of Politics at New York University. His primary research interest is the comparative study of monetary institutions in an open economy setting. He has published papers in *International Studies Quarterly, International Organization, International Negotiation,* and the *American Political Science Review.* He is author of a forthcoming book entitled *Capitalism, Not Globalism: Capital Mobility, Central Bank Independence and the Political Control of the Economy.*

Annette Freyberg-Inan received her Ph.D. in political science from the University of Georgia in December 1998. She currently teaches for the Civic Education Project at the University of Bucharest and is a founding member of the Invisible College Bucharest. Her main areas of research are international relations theory, international political economy, political psychology, and Romanian politics. She is the coeditor of the *Romanian Journal of Society and Politics* and author of the forthcoming *What Moves Man: The Realist Theory of International Relations and Its Judgment of Human Nature.*

Alexandru Grigorescu received his Ph.D. in political science from the University of Pittsburgh in 2002 and is a visiting assistant professor in the Department of International Relations at Lehigh University.

Mark Hallerberg received his Ph.D. in political science from the University of California at Los Angeles in 1995 and is assistant professor in the Department of Political Science at the University of Pittsburgh. His research focuses on fiscal policy within the European Union, Economic and Monetary Union, and German politics. He has published articles in *Comparative Political Studies, World Politics, Politische Vierteljahresschrift, European Journal of Public Policy,* and the *American Political Science Review.*

Geoffrey Harris is head of the Division for Interparliamentary Relations—Europe (Enlargement) in the general secretariat of the European Parliament. From 1989 to 1992 he was principal adviser to the president of the European Parliament. His current responsibilities concern the enlargement process and cooperation between the EP and the parliaments of all European countries not in the EU. He is the author of *The Dark Side of Europe* (1993).

Elena A. Iankova received her Ph.D. from Cornell University in 1997 and is currently a visiting scholar at the Johnson School of Management, Cornell University. She is the author of two volumes forthcoming in 2002, *Between Extrication and Integration: Eastern European Capitalism in the Making;* and *Governed by Accession? Europeanization and Domestic Change in Central and Eastern Europe.*

Wade Jacoby is associate professor of political science at Brigham Young University. He received his Ph.D. in political science from MIT in 1996 and has published articles in *Comparative Political Studies, Politics and Society, Governance, German Politics and Society,* and *East European Constitutional Review.* He is also author of *Imitation and Politics: Redesigning Modern Germany* (2000).

Ronald H. Linden is professor of political science and former director of the Center for Russian and East European Studies at the University of Pittsburgh. A Princeton Ph.D. (1976), Dr. Linden is the author of numerous works on Eastern Europe and international relations, including "Putting on Their Sunday Best: Romania, Hungary, and the Puzzle of Peace," *International Studies Quarterly* (2000). From 1989 to 1991 he served as director of research for Radio Free Europe in Munich, Germany.

Andrew A. Michta is the Mertie Willigar Buckman Professor of International Studies at Rhodes College in Tennessee. A Ph.D. from Johns Hopkins

University School of Advanced International Studies (1987), he is the author of four books, including *The Soldier-Citizen: The Politics of the Polish Army after Communism* (1997) and *The Government and Politics of Postcommunist Europe* (1994), and the editor or coeditor of three others, including *America's New Allies: Poland, Hungary, and the Czech Republic in NATO* (1999) and *Polish Foreign Policy Reconsidered* (1995).

Melanie H. Ram is a research associate at the Institute for European, Russian, and Eurasian Studies at George Washington University and a program officer for the Japan International Cooperation Agency. She holds a Ph.D. from George Washington University (1999) and is the author most recently of "Minority Relations in Multiethnic Societies: Assessing the European Union Factor in Romania," *Romanian Journal of Society and Politics* (2001). Her research focuses on the EU influence on policies of candidate states, especially legal reforms, minority rights, and subregional cooperation.

Zlatko Šabič, assistant professor, is a member of the chair of international relations in the Department of Political Sciences at the University of Ljubljana, Slovenia, and director of research of the Central and East European International Studies Association. He is editor in chief of the *Journal of International Relations and Development*.

Frank Schimmelfennig received his Ph.D. in 1995 from the University of Tübingen (Germany). He is a postdoctoral research associate at the Institute of Political Science of Darmstadt University of Technology, where he is researching the enlargement of Western regional organizations. He is the author, most recently, of "The Community Trap: Liberal Norms, Rhetorical Action, and the Eastern Enlargement of the European Union," *International Organization* (2001) and "International Socialization in the New Europe: Rational Action in an Institutional Environment," *European Journal of International Relations* (2000).

Beate Sissenich is a Ph.D. candidate in the Department of Government, Cornell University, and a visiting fellow at the Institute for Social and Economic Research and Policy at Columbia University. She is writing a dissertation entitled "State Building by a Nonstate: European Union Enlargement and the Diffusion of EU Social Policy in Poland and Hungary."

Lúcio Vinhas de Souza is a researcher at the Tinbergen Institute, Erasmus University, Rotterdam, the Netherlands, and a Marie Curie Fellow at the European Center for Advanced Research in Economics and Statistics, Free University of Brussels, Belgium. Most of his research deals with macroeconomic issues of transition economics, mainly related to the monetary aspects of the accession of Eastern European countries to the European Union. He has worked as a consultant for the European Parliament, the World Bank–backed Global Development Network project, the Central Bank of Estonia, and several European Union PHARE projects. He has published articles in, among other journals, *CEPAL Review* and the *Journal of European Integration*. His most recent work is "Exchange Rate Strategies of New EU Entrants," in E. Pentecost and A. Van Poeck, eds., *European Monetary Integration: Past, Present, and Future* (2001).

Margit Bessenyey Williams received her Ph.D. from Indiana University in 1999 and presently teaches at the University of South Florida in the Department of Government and International Affairs. Her research interests include the influence of international organizations on domestic politics and policies, with particular emphasis on European regional organizations and the governance problems facing postcommunist governments. Her article "Exporting the Democratic Deficit? Hungary's Experience with European Integration" was published in *Problems of Post-Communism* (2001). She is presently working on a book that examines the influence of the European Union on the transitions in Spain and Hungary.